Marconi

FATHER OF WIRELESS,
GRANDFATHER OF RADIO,
GREAT-GRANDFATHER OF THE CELL PHONE,

The Story of the Race to Control Long-Distance Wireless

Contents

INTRODUCTION

Marconi was a giant in his time, akin to Bill Gates and Steve Jobs of today. As a technological inventor/entrepreneur/businessman, he foreshadowed the booming era of Silicon Valley one hundred years later, paving the way for the communications revolution of today's Wi-Fi, smart phones, and ultraportable computers. His creation, however, was such a breakthrough in long-distance communication, especially over water, that governments, particularly their navies, craved to control his invention. Rising from an obscure Italian farmland attic, he stitched together what no one else could until he was acclaimed throughout the industrial world with notoriety similar to today's most celebrated entertainment stars.

As I became more and more fascinated by this multitalented, complex man, half Italian, half Irish, but thought by many of his contemporaries to be English, I discovered that though he was the subject of many biographies, none fully appreciated the startling successes and setbacks of his scientific and business activities and their interconnection.

Nor have those who have written of his entrepreneurial accomplishments woven into their accounts adequate recognition that Marconi strode on a world stage, honored and decorated in Great Britain, France, Italy, Spain, and the United States. He was a friend and acquaintance of kings and queens, prime ministers and popes, and leading businessmen and social lions. He was himself also a sailor, a yachtsman, a naval cadet and army officer, an ardent patriot, a wartime diplomat and intrepid voyager in U-boat infested waters, even a senator in the Italian parliament and president of the Royal Academy of Italy.

Amazingly this steel-willed, driven, cold-blooded domineer possessed an extraordinary amorous sensitivity. He was deeply attached to both his wives, even after his divorce from his first wife. But he was unable, or perhaps unwilling, to resist his susceptibility to intense infatuations with the stream of desirable women attracted to his fame.

It is to capture the depths of this remarkable man as well as to set out clearly his contributions to our lives today that I have embarked on this tale set in a world careening from late-Victorian and Edwardian exuberance into the grim consequences of the Great War and the next approaching storm.

The London *Times* said upon Marconi's death in 1937 that it was difficult to imagine any diminution of the fame of Guglielmo Marconi, that he might even be regarded as the supremely significant character of the epoch, the name by which the age is called. Some who saw his funeral procession in Rome thought that they had never seen anything like it. The dense crowds stood for hours and hours in the heat, and the heart and soul of Rome and the whole nation seemed to go with him.

What the *Times* foresaw has not happened. In the years intervening since 1937, there have been many portentous events. Yet it is possible that the paper was just premature in its prediction. When we look about us at the ubiquitous cell phone implementing Marconi's concepts and what he envisioned, making a reality of point-to-point and person-to-person communication, through the air, at innumerable places around the globe, perhaps ours is the age that should be called the Marconi Era.

Anyone who is struggling in obscurity to become someone or has wondered what route a famous person might have taken to achieve a lofty stature will be engrossed watching Marconi twist and turn through events—some of his own making, some not, and some incredible—as his efforts in competition with governments, corporations, and other inventor-scientists became the early history of wireless, long-distance maritime and military communication, radio, radar, and ultimately, the cell phone.

Respectfully yours,

Calvin Durand Trowbridge, Jr.
October 15, 2009

Galesville, Maryland
Martinsburg, West Virginia

Woodmancote near Cirencester
Gloucestershire

CHAPTER 1

Whiskey & Wine

Annie Jameson of Wexford County, Ireland, had a lovely voice, lovely enough to win her an engagement in 1862 at the Royal Opera House at London's Covent Garden. Petite, vivacious, and only sixteen, she had with her parents' warm encouragement studied and practiced to develop her talent. Her success, however, gave them a problem. Many elements of London society, particularly the theater society, were promiscuous. No proper Victorian parents would place their daughter in a position where her reputation could be soiled by association. Annie's parents, the Andrew Jamesons of Daphne Castle in Wexford, straightlaced and self-respecting, were the epitome of the prosperity that had come to the United Kingdom's international merchants. Andrew's father, John Jameson, and two other Scotsmen, Arthur Haig and Daniel Dewar, had crossed the Irish Sea to Dublin to learn the art of making whiskey. Haig and Dewar returned to Scotland while John Jameson remained. He established a mill in Enniscorthy to grind wheat for his Jameson Irish Whiskey, which his son Andrew now distributed in Europe and parts of the British Empire. To assuage the disappointment of their high-spirited daughter, the Jamesons agreed that Annie could continue voice training in Italy, if properly chaperoned. They prevailed upon the family of Andrew's banker in Bologna, Antoni de Renoli, to invite Annie to live with them while she continued her study of singing and opera at Bologna's Conservatoire. Annie accepted and arrived at their home the next year, in 1863.

On most Sundays over the previous six years, their son-in-law, Giuseppe Marconi, and their seven-year-old grandson, Luigi, visited the

1

Marconi

De Renolis. Luigi was the only child of the marriage of Giuseppe to their daughter, Lucia, who died shortly after childbirth. The thirty-four-year-old Giuseppe had grown up in the Apennine Mountains near Bologna in the tiny village of Capugnano in Poretta Pass close by the village of Poretta. On high fields and slopes below the mountain peaks, generations of Marconis, roughened and made rigorous by harsh winters, had grown maize and oats and felled birches and firs. Not as wealthy or polished as English country squires, the Marconis nonetheless were landowners, proud of their family heritage. Nor did they live in a remote backwater. In good weather, Poretta Pass was a convenient route between Bologna and cities north of Florence like Pisa and the coastal city of Leghorn. Poretta had a well-known spa, which was particularly popular in the summer because of Poretta's high, cool altitude.

Giuseppe had always enjoyed working the rugged land and the hunting and fishing that it offered. But when his younger brother was murdered by mountain bandits, Giuseppe lost his enthusiasm for the area. He and his widowed father sold their land in Capugnano and moved thirty miles east down to the foothills of the Apennines. In the town of Pontecchio, eleven miles west of Bologna, Giuseppe acquired a working estate, Villa Grifone. The estate sat on a wooded hillside, overlooking a wide valley. The grounds included terraces bordered by lemon trees in tubs, a kitchen garden and a flower garden, meadows, orchards, vineyards, and valley hillsides, beautiful green country pleasing to the eye. Not far from the cypress tree–lined drive leading to the green-shuttered stone villa, a swollen fishing stream dashed down the hillside in the springtime. Even in summer months, it never ran dry.

Giuseppe met Annie while visiting his in-laws on a Sunday soon after her arrival and was smitten by her. Annie had porcelain skin and auburn hair. She wore a fashionable taffeta dress with a long, full skirt pinched in at her tiny waist, her shoulders covered by a light Irish woolen shawl. Annie entranced Giuseppe. After that first meeting, he found many occasions to visit the de Renoli villa and to listen to Annie's beautiful voice. She uncovered in the austere, somber, dark-haired man a latent fondness of music. Despite the difference in their ages, the couple fell in love.

After a year of courtship, Annie willingly accepted Giuseppe's marriage proposal. Forsaking the Conservatoire, she returned to Daphne Castle to tell her parents of her decision to marry Giuseppe. Not surprisingly, the Scotch-Irish, Protestant couple adamantly opposed the union. From their perspective, Giuseppe presented numerous disadvantages, being seventeen years older, a widower who already had a child, and a foreigner, all in addition to being a Roman Catholic. Annie could hardly have made a poorer choice. The Jamesons commanded her to remain at home in Ireland, and then they took pains to introduce her to suitable young men of Wexford.

To all appearances, Annie docilely obeyed, but secretly she and Giuseppe corresponded. Annie's sister, Elizabeth, and her British Army beau, Lieutenant Thomas Prescott, smuggled their amorous notes in and out of Daphne Castle. Annie attended all the local social functions and dances pressed upon her by her parents. Her heart, nonetheless, remained committed to Giuseppe. She played the role expected by her ever watch-ful mother only to avoid detection of her secret plan. In fact, Annie and Giuseppe anxiously looked forward to her majority of eighteen, when she could steal away from Daphne Castle. After a seemingly endless wait, one night Elizabeth helped her to slip away unnoticed to Dublin. From there, she crossed the Irish Sea to Holyhead in Wales. She traversed the width of Wales and England to the southeastern port of Dover, where a paddle steamer brought her across the English Channel. Meanwhile, Giuseppe crossed the Alps by horse-drawn carriage.

In the French seaside village of Boulogne-sur-Mer, Annie reunited with Giuseppe. On April 16, 1864, they married. The bride and groom returned to Bologna and happily split their time between their country estate at Villa Grifone and their new formidable city townhouse, Palazzo Marescalchi, which was located in the heart of Bologna. Within a year, Annie and Giuseppe's first son, Alfonso, was born.

Nine years later, on April 25, 1874, Giuseppe and Annie had their second and last child, Guglielmo Marconi.

Giuseppe was then forty-five and Annie was twenty-eight. Shortly af-ter Guglielmo's birth, the servants and peasants from Villa Grifone came to visit and crowded about the bed. One old man, a gardener, remarked on Marconi's large ears. According to family legend, Annie quickly and prophetically retorted that with such ears, Marconi would be able to hear the still, small voice of the air.(FN 1)

During the first five years of his life, Guglielmo accompanied his mother as she traveled back and forth from Villa Grifone to Bedford,

Marconi

England, where she would be closer to Alfonso, who was attending boarding school. Guglielmo's father never left Villa Grifone, preferring to be home to run the estate. Annie spent so much time in England that at the age of five Marconi enrolled in school there. After that year Alfonso finished boarding school, and Annie, Alfonso, and Guglielmo returned to Italy. Once back at Villa Grifone, Giuseppe hired a local grammarian and insisted that the boys study Italian. At this point, it could hardly have been said to be Marconi's native tongue. Annie insisted that the boys continue to learn English, even if she had to tutor them herself, which she did. A schoolroom was set up at Villa Grifone. The private instructor drilled his students summer, fall, and spring. Marconi did not take well to this, avoiding his tutor whenever he could, preferring to be outdoors or holed up in Giuseppe's library.

The library was well stocked. Marconi pored over Greek history and mythology and tales of Captain Cook's voyages. Annie's sister Elizabeth had married Lieutenant Thomas Prescott. By good fortune for Annie, he had been assigned overseas, first to Florence and then to Leghorn, an important Italian naval base only a hundred miles southwest of Bologna. Elizabeth and her four daughters often visited Annie at Villa Grifone. Daisy, the youngest daughter, was only slightly older than Marconi. When Daisy visited, she and Marconi would pull thick picture books off the shelves and spend the summer afternoons lying on the sofa in the cool, half-darkened room, passing the books back and forth or reading aloud to one another.

As Marconi grew, scientific writings on electricity replaced the stories of Achilles and the *Odyssey* as his favorite reading material. Benjamin Franklin's life and work fascinated Marconi. While not the earliest to think of it, Franklin was the first to prove that lightning was electricity. Franklin invented the lightning rod and received a medal from the Royal Society in London for the books he wrote on electricity. For young Marconi, struggling with his father, Franklin was an inspiring figure: a rich and famous scientist and statesman, an innovator and a man with a multitude of thoughts. Years later, Daisy recalled how Marconi used to say to her if only she knew what a lot of ideas he had in his own head. Frequently he shared these ideas with her. She made no pretence of understanding.

One day Daisy had been painting in the Villa Grifone schoolroom. Marconi bounced in and sat down to watch, not noticing until too late her palette of oils on the chair. His white flannels were completely soaked in an array of color. With an unhappy exclamation, he sprang up. Daisy had no sooner doused him with turpentine than the luncheon bell rang. Giuseppe ran the household like a martinet. Failure to appear promptly for a meal, hands scrubbed, was a major rudeness. It incurred his wrath, something Marconi frequently endured because he was daydreaming or deeply absorbed in a project or off on a ramble. Forgetting the paint, Daisy and Marconi scurried to wash and be seated. It wasn't two minutes before Marconi, who had been trying to contain his amusement at the secret accident, began to squirm as the turpentine ate through the flannel to his skin. Giuseppe angrily commanded him to sit straight and be still. His youngest son obeyed in agony. His seat was on fire. At last Annie rescued him. She allowed him to whisper his dilemma in her ear and sympathetically excused him from the table.

At meals, Giuseppe liked to educate the family by asking questions about politics and history. The subjects bored Marconi. To Giuseppe's ir-ritation, this impious, unmindful little scion drifted off or suddenly out of the blue interrupted the conversation with an irrelevant inquiry of his own. Even as a very young boy, if Daisy were there, Marconi would direct questions to her and then laugh merrily at her uncertain response until he felt the baleful chill of his father's penetrating gaze. But at other times, if Daisy heaped Marconi with praise, he modestly silenced her, saying that she should be quiet, that she thought too much of him.

After he turned ten, experiments began to preoccupy Marconi, and he talked to Daisy constantly about "my electricity." Giuseppe discour-aged his son's experiments. He preferred that his son focus on practi-cal matters like farming. Annie, however, always supported her younger child. As a result, he repeatedly dragged her out to the farthest corner of the garden, where he concealed his latest developments from Giuseppe. To construct mechanical toys and apparatus for his boyish experiments, Marconi rummaged about the villa and its outbuildings, uncovering bits and pieces of metals and materials. After successfully creating an electric battery-operated bell, his next effort quite upset Daisy. Dismantling her sewing machine, Marconi attached it to a hand-turned meat roasting jack with a leather strap. By working the sewing machine foot pedals, the roaster turned automatically. Daisy wept at the destruction of her indis-pensable machine. When Marconi was able to restore it to its original working order, she was so impressed that she forgave him. Not all of his efforts were mechanically or electrically focused. Instinctively inspired by Jameson family tradition, he devised a working still that he tucked away in the woods, a secret he divulged only to Daisy.

Another experiment, witnessed by friends, caused the family great embarrassment and Giuseppe great anger. During one vacation at Poretta, no one observed that Marconi had been unusually preoccupied. He had brought a biography of Franklin with him. From accounts of Franklin's experiments, he conceived the idea of hanging dinner plates across a stream near a public road in a particular arrangement. Lacking wire at Poretta, he substituted string. He attached it to batteries. When everything was ready, he closed the circuit, hoping the line would conduct the electricity. Instead it first smoked, and then it burned. The dinner plates crashed into pieces against the rocky brook bottom. Giuseppe was not amused. Giuseppe felt that his son's experiments were a waste of his time and a waste of materials. He opposed spending money on such excesses. The dinner plates, a harebrained public display, humiliated Giuseppe and increased his opposition to such pursuits. Henceforth, to punish similar idle occupation, Giuseppe destroyed any experiments he came across.

With age, Giuseppe grew meaner and tighter. He loved to tell the story of the visit by Bologna fund-raisers. They wanted to restore the city cathedral. Giuseppe's farming success and size of his Villa Grifone estate and Bologna townhouse rendered him an obvious target for funding good work. In his position, he was reluctant to refuse outright. Yet in no way would he donate. Ingeniously, from his point of view, the dry-humored Giuseppe magnanimously promised a glorious gift, a magnificent cross, to be delivered upon completion of the restoration. It would cost him nothing, he was sure, since he would be long dead, as he was, before the restoration was finished.(FN 2)

Despite his growing frugality, Giuseppe sometimes displayed a more generous, if contradictory, side. While discouraging his son's purposeless pursuits, he still seemed to recognize Marconi's interest and aptitude in science. Perhaps if only to keep Marconi more fruitfully focused, for four summers in a row Giuseppe hired a civil engineer, Armando Carli, a University of Bologna graduate, to tutor the soon-to-be-teenager in the principles of physics.

At age thirteen with a friend, Giulio Camperio, Marconi climbed to the Camperios' attic. Emulating another Franklin experiment, the boys mounted a zinc device on the rooftop, hoping to collect static electricity released by lightning. They prayed for a thunderstorm. When rain pelted them and tumultuous thunder crashed about in the sky, they were delighted. Each time they thought their apparatus had captured enough static, they released it to ring an electric bell wired to their apparatus. The ringing provided satisfying proof that, like Franklin, they had succeeded.

Marconi followed this success by developing at Villa Grifone an experiment that was quite puzzling to the Prescott cousins. They had forced their way into his workroom, which was filled with gadgets and apparatus. Gazing about uncomprehending at the white jars, pots filled with water, and curved pieces of wood wrapped in zinc, Daisy challenged Marconi, asserting that there was nothing much to see. What had he devised? Half-teasing her and half-serious, Marconi placed on one side of his laboratory a needle suspended from its holder so that it could swing freely and on the opposite side of the room a compass. He promised to make the freely swinging needle and the needle in the compass move simultaneously in synchronized movements with no wire between them. He seated himself before a mysterious, pear-shaped glass jar that emitted a flickering bluish light. He did not tell Daisy that the jar was filled with static electricity. He tapped the glass. The two needles spun about in identical movements. Daisy searched everywhere for hidden connections from the jar to the needles. Finding none, she was convinced that Marconi was a genius and could talk about nothing else at lunch.

If Marconi experienced identity problems in his formative years, it would not be surprising. Frequently he was separated from his father and his home at Villa Grifone. Annie had developed an increasing sensitivity to the cold winter winds rushing down on Villa Grifone and Bologna from the Apennines. She therefore preferred to spend as much of the winter as possible with Elizabeth in Florence and Leghorn, on the warmer, milder, Mediterranean side of the mountains. Further, Lieutenant Prescott, in a move calculated to benefit his rising military career, accepted a long-term assignment to India, leaving Elizabeth behind in Italy. Annie felt obliged to visit her husbandless sister during the winter. Of course, Annie could not ignore the very appealing social aspects of the English communities that were well established in Florence and even in Leghorn.

Marconi

A pattern developed where Annie and the boys would winter with Elizabeth in Florence or Leghorn. In the early summer Elizabeth and her children would gather with the Marconis, sometimes including Giuseppe, at Poretta. The women would enjoy the spa, and Giuseppe would visit old friends. Then the Prescotts would spend a long part of the summer with the Marconis at Villa Grifone. Marconi's winter separations from his father and home were on top of the early years when Marconi was in England.

In addition to these absences when Marconi lived under motherly, English-oriented conditions as compared to the strict, work-oriented ethic of Giuseppe's household, Marconi was subject to a number of other conflicting influences. Annie was a devout Anglican, and although the boys had been baptized Catholic, Giuseppe, despite his own Catholicism, did not prevent Annie from raising the boys as Protestants. Every evening she read aloud to her children two chapters from the King James Bible, which doubled nicely with their English lessons. On Sundays when Annie, Marconi, and Alfonso were in Florence or Leghorn, they attended Anglican services. The household language at Villa Grifone and Palazzo Marescalchi was the local Italian dialect. In Florence and Leghorn, it was English. In heritage, Marconi was half Italian, one-quarter Scotch, and one-quarter Irish. Marconi also had two parents who treated him quite differently. Annie doted on him, encouraged him, and smothered him with love. Giuseppe, old enough to be Marconi's grandfather, was a disciplinarian. He had little empathy for Marconi's interests and belittled him.

It was not until Marconi was fourteen that he was enrolled in a formal school. For the prior nine years, his education had been the instruction he received at home. He entered the Instituto Cavellero in Florence, where Annie was spending the winter with Elizabeth. He had a miserable year there, in great measure caused by his poor Italian and lack of experience with boys his own age. No event at Instituto Cavellero piqued Marconi's pride more than the requirement to stand and recite poetry. In front of the other boys, his teacher and sometimes the school principal would hold him up as a bad example for the class, ridiculing his Bolognese dialect as hopelessly provincial.

His classmates would howl with laughter, slapping their thighs, and make fun of his accent.(FN 3) At this time most Italians spoke their local dialects and nothing else. Only in Rome and parts of Tuscany—where the language recognized as "Italian" was created from the Florentine dialect— did the man on the street speak "Italian." The king himself spoke Piedmontese, even to his cabinet. Bologna did not regard itself as backwater to Tuscany, but here came Marconi, tutored by a country teacher from Pontecchio, to Florence, the seat of the country's formal language. Giuseppe and Annie may have been insensitive to the problem. Annie spoke English in Florence and Leghorn with her English friends, and the diameter of Giuseppe's life was the distance from Poretta to Palazzo Marescalchi.

Annie did little to help Marconi in another respect. She stood out as foreign as she waited for him outside school every day. Her daring hats, no doubt highly fashionable in her Florentine English circles, did nothing to endear Marconi to the pack of boys eager for an easy victim. Even Marconi's best and perhaps only Florence school friend, Luigi Solari, admitted he was unsure whether he first noticed Marconi or his mother. So different from the gayness Marconi had exhibited as a child, Solari recalled Marconi as habitually wearing a stern expression. Withdrawn, shy, perhaps worried, certainly not gregarious like his mother, Marconi's reserve was misread by his schoolmates as arising from a sense of superiority, of being stuck up. He was thought of as being foreign, different. His teachers found him to be backward in his responses to their questions and in his interactions with the other students. Nonetheless, the older Luigi liked Marconi and became a lifelong friend, over the years Marconi's best friend.

Marconi attended the Instituto Cavellero in Florence for only one year. Fortunately for Marconi, Elizabeth moved from Florence to Leghorn. Annie, of course, followed her there. It was clear that Marconi's formal education must continue. At the age of fifteen, he was enrolled in the Technical Institute at Leghorn. Giuseppe rented an apartment at Viale Regina Margherita for Annie and Marconi. As it turned out, Elizabeth remained in Leghorn for many years, and Marconi attended the Institute for four years until his graduation. Leghorn, on Italy's upper west coast, had always been a reprieve for Marconi. For a teenage, inland boy, it was an exciting town, to be on the sea, to sail in the inner harbor, with boats everywhere to be seen. Home of the Regia Marina, the Italian Naval Academy, and an important base for the Italian navy, the streets were filled with sailors looking important and smart in their well-tailored uniforms. One of Marconi's enduring delights was sailing, which he learned at age nine in the harbor at Leghorn on one of his earlier visits with Annie.

Marconi

Their rented apartment was a few doors from the Camperios, who had three children—Marconi's friend, Giulio; a daughter, Sita; and Filippo, whom Marconi hero-worshipped because he was a cadet at the Italian Naval Academy. Like other technical schools, the Technical Institute at Leghorn focused primarily on teaching mathematics, science, Italian, and French, and a degree would lead to specialist qualifications in commerce or agronomy or to possible admittance to a university. The universities were not well attended. The University of Bologna, one of Europe's oldest, had less than six hundred students. While at the Technical Institute, Marconi took language classes, but he concentrated on physics and chemistry. He took chemistry from Professor Bizzairini. He was particularly excited by Professor Giotti's lectures on theoretical physics. After attending the Institute for two years, Marconi had surpassed the school's ability to teach him additional physics and electricity. The school arranged that he study for the next two years with Professor Vincenzo Rosa, a physics professor in Leghorn. Rosa gave Marconi special courses in electrical training and electrophysics.

In Leghorn, Marconi was introduced to Nello Marchetti, a charming older man who was going blind. Marconi offered to read aloud to him. Marchetti was a veteran of the wars that freed Italy of foreign control. He had served at the front lines as a telegraph operator. Discovering Marconi's interest in electricity, Marchetti instructed Marconi in Morse code on a telegraph key set on a sunny windowsill between geraniums. Samuel Morse, a portrait painter, had devised the code on a ship returning home to the United States from Europe. He subsequently was instrumental in persuading Congress to fund the first long-distance telegraph line. Until the completion of the first transcontinental telegraph line, the fastest coast-to-coast communication in the United States required seven days, part of which relied on the Pony Express.

For Marconi, the years in Leghorn were happy ones, especially after his Florentine experience. No longer did he have to be rousted out of bed and chased to school in the morning; instead, he went off eagerly. For the first time there were lots of congenial girls and boys about him. Here on the cobblestoned streets, he discovered horseplay, girls, and flirting. Looking back, he boasted to one of his daughters that during hide-and-seek he always hid closest to the prettiest girl. But he was too shy to reveal his crush on Sita Camperio, his friend's older sister.

To everyone's surprise, Giuseppe gave Marconi a small sailboat. It exhilarated Marconi to race across the bow of the Naval Academy's launch, its shrill whistle blowing in warning and its cadet officers with looks of superiority lolling on the stern deck. The gift of the sailboat was a rare display of generosity by Giuseppe. Perhaps Giuseppe hoped it would stimulate Marconi to work harder to qualify for the Naval Academy, one of the only goals father and son shared in common.

There were other good moments as well. Marconi learned to play the piano and to accompany his mother. She taught him to share her love of opera.

Marconi's last year at the Technical Institute did not end well. Because of his lack of education in liberal arts, he fell short on the matriculation exam for entrance to the University of Bologna. Nor did he satisfy the requirements to enter the Naval Academy. One exam he did pass deferred his military service and elevated his rank. Instead of serving as an enlisted man for two years as Italians were required to do, he could defer service for several years and then enroll as an officer for only eighteen months. This exasperated Giuseppe. The boy wasn't smart enough to qualify for officers' school now, but he could become an officer later.

With rejections from both the university and the Naval Academy, Marconi at nineteen had no alternative but to return home. He had no career or ambition for a job that could support him. He arrived at Villa Grifone apparently empty-handed.

Annie prevailed upon a neighbor, Augusto Righi, a physical sciences professor at the University of Bologna, to allow Marconi to attend his lectures. For a year, Marconi remained in limbo. He audited courses, read copiously, and conducted his own experiments at home, all without a stated purpose. Outwardly, Marconi seemed to drift, aimless, unsuited for any conventional pursuit. In Giuseppe's eyes, his son was a failure.

In fact, Marconi was far better trained in the nascent electrical sciences than most. He described himself to Daisy as the "ardent amateur student of electricity." He had been tutored and lectured in physics and chemistry, concentrating on electrology. He had experimented, reproducing where he could demonstrations of principles in the rapidly evolving field. European scientists routinely published papers describing their advances. Marconi could read English and Italian and make sense of French and German papers on subjects that interested him. He devoured scientific magazines, journals, and books. He was familiar

Marconi

with cutting-edge theories and treatises of leading scientists and inventors—Benjamin Franklin, Michael Faraday, Lord Kelvin, James Clerk Maxwell, Edouard Branly, and Thomas Edison.

Marconi hid his true feelings to avoid further shame at the hands of Giuseppe, who ridiculed even successful experiments because none had led anywhere. This humiliation spurred his ambition, as did a natural desire to justify himself to Giuseppe and Annie and himself.

There was an abundance of reasons for positive motivation as well. He had an aptitude and enjoyment in this work. The rewards were obvious—to be known as a scientist in a world awakening to science, in a world being changed by scientists; to have a name among esteemed and respected scientists; to be rich and famous like Franklin, Edison, Morse, and Alexander Graham Bell. A bright young man with high energy and resolve could aspire to these goals. The names of Bell and Edison became legendary while Marconi was growing up. Smart men and practical inventors, they were stellar representatives of the incredible and rapid evolution in the use of electricity and the electric wire.

Marconi burned to prove himself. He later said that since the age of eight, he had had an irresistible feeling that someday he would do something great and new. It was more than a hope. It was a certainty.

CHAPTER 2

The Attic at Villa Grifone

In the summer of 1894, when Marconi was twenty, he and Luigi were on holiday at Santuario di Oropa in the mountains of Biellese in the Italian Alps. At their hotel, Marconi read an obituary by Professor Righi about German physicist Heinrich Rudolph Hertz. Righi described a series of experiments conducted by Hertz from 1887 to 1890. In the experiments, Hertz sent a burst of electricity from one machine across the room to a second machine that caught the electricity. Although previously postulated by mathematicians that electricity could be sent through the air from one point to another without wires, until Hertz's experiment, it had never been done. Righi's article excited Marconi tremendously. He visualized at once that the electricity, properly harnessed, might be used to send signals through the air.

For the balance of the holiday at Santuario di Oropa, Marconi became more and more obsessed with the idea. Physical experiments were impossible until his return to Villa Grifone, but he concentrated on working out equations in his head based on mathematical suppositions with which he was familiar.

The inspiration which sprang from Righi's article was remarkable. It became the center of Marconi's existence for the rest of his life. It drove him relentlessly. It was the lodestone setting all his priorities, even those of his personal life. The inspiration obsessed Marconi until the day of his death.(FN 1)

The moment Marconi reached Villa Grifone, he climbed on the family donkey and hastened over to the university to visit Righi. The

Marconi

professor scoffed. Five years had passed since Hertz's demonstrations. Few people envisioned any practical use arising from the primitive experiments. Some theoretical scientists, Righi being one of them, were investigating possible explanations of Hertz's work, but Righi wrote the article after Hertz's death primarily to commemorate Hertz's life. Clearly, fuller exploration of the difficult concepts required extensive scientific and mathematical knowledge that Marconi did not possess. Some leading scientists postulated that electricity moved in the form of waves and had magnetic properties. Theoretical effort to comprehend the composition of the burst of electricity and how and why electricity moved must precede any practical application. Undeterred, Marconi returned to Villa Grifone and set to work. Over Giuseppe's protests, Annie allowed Marconi to set up a laboratory in the attic using two large rooms connected by a wide archway. Marconi's first task was to re-create Hertz's experiment.

Marconi in effect took a single piece of wire and, bringing the two ends of the wire together, made a circle whose diameter was approximately six inches. He then sent electricity through the circle of wire. Next he detached the two ends of the wire, leaving a small gap of space one inch wide between them. He ran electricity through the circle of wire again, and the electricity jumped across the gap between the two ends of wire. He could see and hear the electricity as it jumped because the electricity made a spark that crackled. Marconi then took another piece of wire and made a second circle with a smaller gap of a half inch between the two ends of the wire. Attaching no source of electricity to the second circle, he placed the second circle on the other side of the room. He then ran electricity through the first circle. The electricity jumped the one-inch gap between the two ends of the first circle's wire, making a spark and crackling as it jumped. On the other side of the room, a spark of electricity flashed and crackled across the half-inch gap of space in the second circle of wire.

Marconi had successfully re-created Hertz's experiment. Hertz stated that the spark in the second gap was electricity released from the first circle. It was released as the electricity jumped across the open space of the gap of the first circle and was caught by the second circle. The electricity, freed from the confines of the wire of the first circle, radiated outwards to the second circle. The electricity radiating through the air was attracted to the second circle of wire because of its material composition.

The first circle of wire was called a "transmitter" and the second one a "receiver" of electricity. Marconi called the space between the two ends of wire a spark gap because of the spark that crossed the gap. Many scientists believed that like light, electricity moved through space in the form of oscillating waves and that these waves traveled at the speed of light—the equivalent of going around the world seven times in one second.

Once Marconi had imitated Hertz's original experiments, he added improvements that others had made. The electricity escaping as it jumped the gap in the transmitter radiated in all directions. Righi placed a curved, metal reflector behind the transmitter to direct as much of the radiated electricity as possible towards the receiver. The small space between the two ends of wire in the receiver had been replaced by a more sensitive collector or detector of the electricity used by Professor Oliver Lodge of London who called the detector a "coherer." The coherer was a horizontal glass tube filled with tiny, loose metal particles. The instant the current entered the second circle of wire and passed through the glass tube, the loose particles suddenly clung together, or cohered to each other.

Working day and night, undistracted by the Apennine mountain views and the sounds of the passing seasons turned now once more into late summer, Marconi focused on improving the receiver. A more sensitive coherer could detect the transmitter's bursts of electricity or electric waves at greater distances. Marconi's primary interest was not to explain how the electric waves worked, but to lengthen the distance away from the transmitter at which the receiver could detect or receive the waves. For Hertz, the distance had been a matter of feet. Marconi substituted for Professor Lodge's coherer a similar type of detector, a tube developed by the Parisian professor Edouard Branly. Sometimes Marconi's Branly tube indicated reception of the waves at thirty feet; at other times no reception was indicated at three feet.

Commencing a long series of experiments, Marconi tried various forms and shapes of tubes, and he filled the tubes with different types of metals. To maximize the sensitivity of the detector, he attempted at least five hundred combinations. In the tube interior, reduced in size to a diameter of one sixteenth of an inch, he created a vacuum by exhausting its air, hoping that the current would meet less resistance. A galvanometer, or voltmeter, which measured current, was added to the circle of the wire of the receiver to measure how much electricity was passing through the circle. The more electricity there was, the greater the likelihood that he could move the receiver farther away or that he could attach an electrical instrument to the second circle of wire and use the electricity to make the instrument function.

As the improvements progressed, it became increasingly apparent to Marconi that if he could invent equipment very sensitive to minimal bursts of electricity, it might be possible to transmit and receive Morse code messages over great distances without wires. He thought of substituting a Morse code receiving machine for the voltmeter he had placed in his receiver and of increasing weak current in the second circle of wire with a booster called a "relay." He went to consult Righi. Righi expressed only grave doubts about Marconi's project. It is not surprising that many years later when Marconi was asked if he had studied physics at Bologna under Professor Righi, he responded that he had studied under the renowned Professor Vincenzo Rosa of Liverno and would be most happy if it were known that Rosa was Marconi's only physics master.(FN 2)

Late one night in September 1895, Marconi's system worked so well he could no longer hide his excitement. For months, locked away in the attic, he had labored in secrecy, forestalling time-consuming visits from family visitors and avoiding further embarrassment from failed experiments. He steered clear of Giuseppe, who regarded this effort as just as much a waste of time and money as the endless obsessions that had preceded it. Barely tolerating his twenty-year-old, parasitic son in his house, Giuseppe contributed no financial support to the project; on one occasion, Marconi sold his shoes to raise money. Since Marconi rarely emerged from his laboratory except for materials or to visit Righi, Righi's laboratory, or the university library, Annie frequently climbed the attic stairs to leave food outside his door or to knock quietly to urge him to rest. She even sacrificed her winter pilgrimage to Florence and Leghorn to support Marconi and fend off Giuseppe's mounting irritation.

This midnight, however, when the air was scented with drying hay and filled with the sounds of crickets, Marconi crept downstairs from the attic to awaken his mother, shaking her shoulder gently but firmly. Instantly she was alert, pulling on her warm bathrobe, aware of the importance of the moment as much from maternal instinct as the urgency of her youngest son's tone. By candlelight, he led her back up the damp, worn stone steps of Villa Grifone to his attic laboratory. As she watched, he seated himself at his working table and bent his head of now darkened blond hair over a telegraph key. He tapped the key delicately with a finger. At the far end of the double room, Annie heard a bell ring. Marconi had placed a bell operated by electricity in the circle of wire in his receiver. He had sent enough electricity from the transmitter through the air to the receiver to make the bell ring. Tapping the telegraph key closed the circuit of the transmitter's circle of wire, allowing electricity to run around the circle and jump the spark gap. Electricity escaping and radiating from the gap reached the detector of the receiver that Marconi had placed at the far end of the second room. Electricity ran around the circle of wire of the receiver and made the bell ring that had been attached to the circle of wire. Marconi had reached the point where he could not only receive electricity consistently across the length of the two attic rooms, but he could also consistently receive enough electricity to make the bell ring.

The next day, Giuseppe's initial reaction was to search for hidden wires. But after finding none, he still was not impressed because the receiver was no farther away than the sound of a voice.(FN 3)

Marconi continued for greater distance. He attached metal plates of varying sizes, a foot square or larger, to the wire on either side of the spark gap, thinking the plates might lengthen the waves radiating from the transmitter as the electricity jumped the gap. He thought longer waves might carry the electricity further if each burst of electricity created the same number of oscillations of the wave being created by the burst, whether or not the wave was longer or shorter. He added identical plates to either side of the detector in the receiver, thinking it would enhance the receiver's receptivity to the longer waves. He called his plates "capacitors," thinking they increased the capacity of his system to send longer signals. Running a wire from the transmitter to the roof, he devised an aerial, always hoping to increase the range. Slowly the distance improved. While the transmitter remained in the attic, the receiver with its bell was placed on the second floor and then the ground floor; finally, Marconi could ring the bell outdoors in the garden.

Despite the gradual improvement, Marconi was worried. He felt his idea was so elementary that he could not believe others were not working on it as well and with more success. It did not occur to him that to others the idea might seem fantastic or impractical or appear to have no

Marconi

commercial use. Frustrated by the lack of money that crippled his progress, a tremendous sense of urgency never left him—and rightly so.

Professor Lodge, who thought the electric waves had no practical purpose, came very close to stumbling onto Marconi's goal of using the waves to send Morse code messages. As early as 1888, Lodge began working on waves called "electromagnetic waves" because the waves had magnetic properties as well as electric properties. In the spring of 1894, he lectured on the principles of electromagnetic waves at the Royal Institute in London. Just as Marconi was returning from Biellese in September 1894, Lodge demonstrated waves publicly at a lecture to the Royal Society in Oxford. He had a Morse printer on the table at the demonstration but never connected it to the receiver. Only years later did he claim that he could have used to the printer to record the burst of electricity. The lecture was reprinted in the *Electrician*.

As far ahead as Lodge and in some instances working on lines very similar to Marconi was Russian physicist Alexander Popov. His electromagnetic wave experiments initiated in 1889 had made little progress until late in 1894, when he read Lodge's lecture. The next May, Popov delivered a paper to the Russian Physical Society describing his detector for thunderstorms. Lightning in thunderstorms released electricity in the sky. It traveled thousands and thousands of feet and could be detected by Popov's receiver. Lightning for Popov was like the spark jumping across Marconi's transmitter's spark gap. It radiated outward, but on a fantastically greater scale. Popov's detector was the first to be described in a scientific publication in which a bell signaled electric changes in the detector.

As with every important nineteenth-century discovery in the field of electricity, Thomas Edison was in the game. In 1875, nineteen years before Marconi began experiments and more than a decade before Hertz's experiments, Edison had accidentally stumbled across electromagnetic waves. Edison mused in the January 1876 *Operator* that the electromagnetic waves could constitute quick and cheap telegraphic transmission, bypassing poles and wires. After several weeks' effort, Edison's attention was distracted, as it often was, by more pressing projects.

By the time Marconi read Righi's obituary on Hertz, William H. Preece, chief engineer of the British General Post Office, led the field in wireless transmission. Because it ran Britain's telegraph system, the General Post Office, known as the GPO, became involved in lighthouse communication following the 1875 sinking of the *Schiller*, an American mail steamship. In a storm off the Scillies, the *Schiller* went down. Three hundred lives and a half million sterling of specie were lost. Had the nearby Bishop Rock lighthouse been connected by telegraph to the lifeboat station at St. Mary's, the lifeboats might have saved many lives. Without telegraph communication, in foul weather when visibility to the mainland was obscured, offshore lighthouses were as isolated as the ships they sought to protect. As a result, the GPO laid submarine cable with telegraph connections wherever feasible from lifeboat stations to lighthouses and to lightships permanently moored offshore near hazardous rock formations where lighthouses could not be constructed.

Due to ocean turbulence and unfavorable bottoms, however, the cable connections were frequently severed. Preece, reminded of his own earlier experiments by reports of Edison's activities, built along the seventy-foot-high cliffs overlooking the Severn River estuary at Lavernock Point, in southeastern Wales, a mile-long line of twenty-foot-high poles that held aloft a copper wire. Three miles across the Severn on Flatholm Island, he raised a parallel copper line a third of a mile long and at Steep Holm Island five and a quarter miles away a similar line. He then sent electricity through the Lavernock wire. Some of it radiated from the copper and was caught by the parallel structures at Flatholm and Steep Holm. Variations in the amount of electricity moving through Lavernock could be detected by Flatholm. This constituted the first permanent wireless telegraphic installation.(FN 4)

A second formidable scientist in the United States had zeroed in on Marconi's goal. Nikola Tesla proposed to send electrical vibrations through the earth so he could transmit a message from an ocean liner to a city, however distant, without wires. In 1894, he tied an aerial to a receiver mounted on the roof of the Gerlach Hotel in New York City and sent it aloft by balloon. He ran another wire from the receiver to the hotel's water main. He claimed to receive electrical energy from his laboratory thirty blocks away.

Born in Smiljan, Croatia, eighteen years before Marconi, Tesla had discovered a rotating magnetic field and developed alternating current. He immigrated to the U.S. in 1884. He was hired by Edison, who had built a network of electrical distribution based on direct current. They soon fell out because Edison refused to adopt Tesla's system. Tesla then sold his patent rights for alternating current dynamos, transformers, and motors to George Westinghouse.

Five years later, Tesla conceived of wireless transmission of intelligence, light, and power. In 1892, he lectured on his concepts before the Institution of Electrical Engineers in London. The audience included Lodge, Preece, Lord Kelvin, Sir Ambrose Fleming, and Oliver Heaviside. Preece sent a horse and carriage to bring Tesla to the hall. The next year in a demonstration Tesla transmitted electric energy from one end of a room to the other. With a transmitter, he turned on a lamp a distance away from him. He began to file patents on the conversion and distribution of electrical energy by mechanical oscillator. Westinghouse lit the World's Columbian Exposition in Chicago with Tesla's alternating current. The following year, based on Tesla's system, Westinghouse won the first contract to generate power from Niagara Falls. Tesla had become well established among New York's leading scientists, industrialists, and socialites.(FN 5)

It had taken Marconi nine precious months to improve the Righi transmitter and Branly coherer to the point where he could transmit from attic to garden. Giuseppe was quick to point out, however, that at this distance it was still a toy. Marconi's accomplishment had been achieved on a shoestring. He had no budget except what he could scrounge. His greatest financial asset was that he had no overhead. Room, board, and the attic were free, courtesy of his parents. He had no other commitments. He could devote all his efforts to his wireless. But he had to build his instruments for experiments. The only sophisticated equipment available to him was in Righi's laboratory and whatever material Righi might lend him. As far as collegial support went, he had none. Righi, still disparaging any outcome from Marconi's work, gave little comfort. Intellectually, as Righi pointed out, Marconi had no mathematical background. He did have access to the journals at the university library in which the latest experiments and theories were expounded by leading scientists.

Material expenses eventually forced Marconi to approach Giuseppe for money. Annie urged Giuseppe to finance his son on faith. Giuseppe required Marconi to prove that he could signal consistently, which Marconi did using the Morse code test letter S—dot, dot, dot—and to explain his device, which Marconi did as well as he could in mechanical terms, not in terms of physics. For the first time, Giuseppe allowed the project might have limited merit, but not sufficient worth for a businessman to invest in. Instead, he lent his penniless son enough to cover immediate needs.

In September 1895, Marconi moved outdoors with his transmitter, receiver, and the four capacitor plates. Marconi's brother, Alfonso, regularly joined him. Alfonso, in the warm days of the late Italian summer, moved the receiver as directed to various test distances and stood by to shout the results to his brother. By exhaustive trial and error, endlessly rearranging the parts and materials, hard-won gains continued. Further gains were thwarted, however, by the enormous amount of electrical power required to transmit a wave even farther. Marconi turned again to increasing the wavelength of the electric bursts. He replaced the capacitor plates with new ones as large as three feet by two feet made by breaking up an old tank of sheet iron. Accidentally, as he modestly said later, he laid one of the transmitter's plate capacitors on the ground and held the other above his head. Alfonso shouted in surprise—the signals had become so strong that he backed away from Marconi again and again. At Marconi's direction, Alfonso did with the receiver what Marconi had done with the transmitter. He left one capacitor lying on the earth while raising the second aloft. With that, the distances increased even further.

It was a major breakthrough. Marconi had made an incredibly important discovery. He had discovered the grounded antenna. He had connected it to an elevated aerial.(FN 6) He did not know it at the time, but this secret would enable him to leap ahead of the pack.

Every configuration was tried again. Other metals were substituted for the iron of the capacitors. Wires of various composition were tried instead of capacitors. Rows of wire were hung—vertically from cross trees or from metal slabs or horizontally on wooden braces made by the estate's carpenter, Marcello Vornelli. Single lines were hung from thirty-foot-high bamboo poles or raised by balloon. An estate farmer, Alto Mignani, was enlisted to dig holes in the ground, some as deep as four feet, in which capacitor plates were buried. Sometimes they were laid horizontally, sometimes standing vertically, to determine if burying the grounded antenna at different depths increased distance. Layers of different metals separated by zinc oxide were connected to the antenna and buried and watered, all in innumerable combinations with different transmitter and receiver aerial designs, in countless efforts to increase the length of discernible signal.

Marconi

The distance increased dramatically. Autumn turned the hills of Villa Grifone to gold. Alfonso, mounting the receiver on a mule and carrying a long bamboo pole to whose skinny peak he had tied a large, white handkerchief, moved further and further away from Marconi. The handkerchief could be seen by Marconi at his terrace station, fluttering in the breeze well beyond the range of Alfonso's hoarsest shouts. Proudly, Alfonso marched through the vineyards and orchards bearing autumn's bright fruit and across the slopes of ripening grain. At each stop, upon the receipt from the transmitter, he raised and dipped the flag in joyous salute until, at last, the gleaming white banner was but the tiniest spot against the foothill foliage.

However, a major test remained. Wireless had but limited utility if transmissions were only to points on an unobstructed, straight line from the transmitter. Marconi knew how little importance his invention would have if it could not communicate across natural objects like hills and mountains. Together, the family selected a distant hill on the estate as the obstacle to be overcome. On the chosen day in the early morning sunlight, the transmitter was grounded in the garden, facing the targeted hill. Once again the donkey was laden with the receiving set and ground capacitor. Hunting rifle in hand, Alfonso led the way. Mignani followed next, watching over the donkey and its heavy load. Vornelli with the aerial, a long pole from whose cross tree hung copper wires, composed the rear guard. The procession trudged through the fields and up the steep hill to its crest, and then one by one each member dropped down out of sight beyond. For twenty minutes, while Alfonso descended the far side, Marconi, Annie, and Giuseppe waited by the transmitter.

A hole was dug to plant the pole and raise the aerial. The aerial grounded, Alfonso arranged the receiver and wired the units together. Tensely consulting his chronometer, Marconi determined impatiently that enough time had passed. He started, manipulating the Morse key. Then he waited. There was a long silence. Annie glanced anxiously at her youngest child, now twenty-one years old, knowing how much was at stake on this test—the future of the invention, the relationship of father and son. Giuseppe stared solemnly ahead at the hill. Marconi pressed the key and waited again. Suddenly a shot from the hunting rifle was heard, fired from beside the unseen receiver on the far side of the hill. The rifle shot reverberated down the long valley and echoed off Villa Grifone behind the trio. Annie and Marconi hugged in excitement.

Giuseppe shook his son's hand in warm congratulations. Now, at last, Giuseppe was convinced that Marconi had a commercially feasible idea, the conviction Marconi had been struggling to establish in his father. But instead of backing his son, Giuseppe concluded that the financial commitment required to obtain a patent and properly develop the concept exceeded his personal resources, or at least what he was prepared to spend. The family must have outside assistance. However, despite his long-standing success in the Bologna community, Giuseppe did not offer to solicit financing from local businessmen or bankers like de Renoli. Patriotically, Giuseppe insisted that the invention should be offered to the Italian government. Annie argued for English development. Out of pride for his country, Marconi agreed with Giuseppe. Above all he wanted a speedy decision because he feared someone else would reach the patent office first.

Through the family doctor, Dr. Roberto Gardini, who was personally acquainted with the Italian ambassador to England, General Antonio Ferrero, the Marconi handwritten offer was conveyed from General Ferrero to Salvatore Sineo, minister of the Italian Bureau of Posts and Telegraphs. Sineo was Italy's key man on communications.

While the family eagerly waited for a response, Captain Henry P. Jackson, Royal Navy, commander-in-chief of the HMS *Defiance*, and responsible for the United Kingdom's torpedo school, was studying wireless communication. Four years earlier, he was the first naval officer to recommend the military use of Hertzian waves. In the prior decade, torpedo boats had been introduced into the navy. In fog or at night as these fast boats sped back from their missions to rejoin the fleet, the fleet had no way of identifying them as friend or foe. Jackson, a thirty-six-year-old torpedo boat commander when he made the suggestion, returned from foreign service to the *Defiance* in 1895, placing him in a position to conduct his own experiments.

Jackson was twenty years Marconi's senior, trim and handsome in a double-breasted naval uniform, four rows of gold braid upon his captain's cuff, and a high-crowned, flat-topped cap with a braided visor upon his head. From photographs it is possible to imagine that at the same young age he and Marconi shared a striking likeness—firm, dark eyebrows, a strong, long but thin nose descending in a straight line from the forehead without indentation between the eyes, and a straight, wide mouth that curled neither up nor down at the corners. Jackson's eyes, however, were narrower at the outer edge, almost slits, and his eyebrows rose away from his eyes instead of following the contour of his skull, giving him a foxier look than Marconi's head-on seriousness.

After what seemed to the restless quartet like a very long several months, the Italian Bureau of Posts and Telegraphs rejected Marconi's offer. The family was shocked. The bureau's position was not necessarily irrational. By 1895, telegraph lines effectively laced the peninsula, and inland communication seemed well covered. Nor was the bureau unthinking. In thanking Marconi for his offer, it asked that all patent rights in Italy be reserved to the government.(FN 7)

Had the bureau or the Marconi family forwarded Marconi's offer to the Italian naval minister or to Italy's king, the outcome might have been different. The Italian navy was aware of the GPO's wireless work. The navy had under review its own special communication needs against the possibility that in wartime the country's submarine cables to Sardinia, Sicily, and Tunis might be cut. Since the 1880s, a naval-industrial complex dominated Italian economic and foreign policy, driving Italy to be an important Mediterranean power. Italy's navy was the world's second largest, behind only Great Britain.

Marconi consoled himself with the thought that at least the Bureau of Posts and Telegraphs had not said that his invention was worthless, only that they had no use for it. Giuseppe was especially disheartened. He had hoped his son would have a solid success, enabling him to buy a lordly property near Pontecchio and settle down to a gentlemanly way.

Annie continued to press for Britain. The United Kingdom was the world's greatest maritime nation. Certainly Marconi understood the potential for wireless applications at sea. Annie wrote to her Irish relatives in England for advice. Back came invitations to London, particularly from her nephew Henry Jameson-Davis, an engineer with a practice in the City of London, London's financial center. If Marconi would come to see him, he would be pleased to assist.

A family decision was reached: Annie and Marconi would go to London. However, departure became impossible as Elizabeth Prescott fell seriously ill in Florence. Annie went to Florence to nurse her, taking Marconi along. Frustrated by the delay, Marconi walked off his anxiety in the streets of Florence, concerned as ever about the race to the patent office.

While Marconi paced, Captain Jackson filled a vital gap in his knowledge. He lacked a sufficiently sensitive receiver. Because of his foreign assignments, he had been unaware of Branly's coherer. However, in the December 1895 issue of the *Proceedings of the Royal Society*, he read an account of Jagadis Bose's experiments at Calcutta University based on Lodge's 1894 demonstrations. Bose had learned telegraphy from courses Preece taught to young men brought from India specifically for that purpose. By year's end, Jackson built Bose's coherer. In March, after reading Lodge's booklet of lectures, the same booklet that invigorated Popov's research, Jackson began experiments to improve the coherer. Attaching long wires to his coherer for handling purposes, he was surprised to discover that the signal received was stronger. It was only a matter of time before he would ground the aerial. Unknowingly, he was honing in on Marconi's devices.

At the same time it dawned on Popov that his detector for thunderstorms could also be used for communication purposes. In January 1896, he published a paper to that effect. Two months later, he demonstrated a wireless communication experiment at Kronstadt to the Russian Physical Society.

As 1895 disappeared into 1896, it was not until February that Marconi and Annie waved good-bye from their carriage window to Giuseppe and Alfonso, leaving them behind with other well-wishers on the Bologna platform, handkerchiefs fluttering, as the train pulled out on the first leg of their journey to London. Among Marconi's luggage was one particularly well cared for large metal box, meticulously packed with his most prized equipment—spark gaps, induction coils, coherers, aerials, all that in a little more than a year he had created out of other men's ideas and his own.

Annie, a matron of fifty, off on a long trip, dressed appropriately in a dark suit and tie shoes, subduing for the moment her hat in a copious veil. Marconi, twenty-one years old, accompanied by his mother from whom he had never been away, was dressed in a dark suit as well with a high-collared shirt. He wore on his head a tweed deerstalker pinched forward and aft at the crown. In his own words, he threw a cloak of dignity about himself to offset his youth. He had become hardened and taciturn, withdrawn deep into himself to avoid criticism and ridicule. But the withdrawal was also a by-product of the ferocious dedication that was a hallmark of his research, the concentration that facilitated the exhaustive, time-consuming trial and error experimentation that at the end of the day yielded the results that prescience had instinctively whispered was there.

Hidden were Marconi's sense of humor and fun, put away for the duration of the drive for achievement. Inside also was a well of humiliation, frustration, and impatience stirred by potent striving and wanting, all sealed from external expression by inhibitions imposed by living at home dependent upon his mother and father and by lack of success. In ways he was naïve, having been sheltered by the comfortable living given to him and spoiled by his mother. In fact, the few women he knew at all had indulged and made much of him.

Although none may have known it as the train station emptied, a family watershed had been crossed. For all the excitement of the moment, in hindsight the moment was touched with sadness. Giuseppe and his son had never been close. In Marconi's teens, the distance lengthened. Marconi was scarred by Giuseppe's acerbity. For some things, Marconi never forgave his father. Yet in his son's twenty-first year, Giuseppe, called a martinet, unyielding, and stubborn (a family trait, whether good or bad), did try to close the gap. Giuseppe was a country man, raised to believe in hard, productive work—his ultimate standard. While Giuseppe had demanded strict family routine and had been harshly outspoken in his criticism, never had he been uncaring. Generously he supported what he understood and loved. What he wanted was the best for Marconi, and that was to live as a country gentleman beside his father in the beloved Apennine hillsides. At last Giuseppe comprehended that beneath what he judged to be eccentric, wasteful, foolish conduct was a serious, realistic undertaking. The parting occurred too soon, only six months after the family had been united for the first time in a single purpose.

The moment was touched with sadness, too, for the beginning of yet another separation in this marriage that had been born in such exhilarating romance. But Giuseppe's and Annie's personal interests pushed them in different directions. His tastes were home and land-bound. She was gregarious; she loved her husband; she loved her friends; she loved everything English; she loved travel, clothes, and social occasions. Not a full year passed when she was not off for sometime somewhere without Giuseppe. As he aged—and he was approaching seventy as Annie left for England with Marconi—he became dour, more fixed in his ways, miserly, the charming dry humor and quick wit less and less in evidence. Yet there is no suggestion that he loved her less, nor was he one bit less proud of her or she of him. Most likely there was no serious disagreement in their marriage other than how to treat their youngest son—though no doubt this wedge divided them. Yet now that their child, a young man of twenty-one, was on his way to England with promises of family support, and there was an opportunity to be together without vexation, Annie saw her place at Marconi's side, not at home with Giuseppe. Nor, apparently, did Giuseppe insist she stay with him.

Marconi was about to land in a country where the leading engineer and electrician of the world's greatest communication system was miles ahead of him in achievement, where a respected university professor/researcher had already publicly demonstrated and published elements of Marconi's system, and where a commanding officer of the world's greatest navy, encouraged by his superiors, was closing in on Marconi's instruments. Over them rose the specter of Edison, the world's greatest inventor, and Tesla, a flamboyant, wildly creative, self-confident intimate of American tycoons.

As determined and ambitious as Marconi was, as accustomed as he was to peering into the future, not even he could have imagined what lay ahead. Preece and Edison pursued a rival method called induction radiation. Popov had but a receiver. Jackson had recently found an effective receiver and like Marconi utilized a spark transmitter. Only Marconi and Tesla had discovered the grounded aerial.

CHAPTER 3

"The Air Is Full of Promises, of Miracles"

Weary from their travel across the Alps by train and then across the English Channel by steamer, Marconi and Annie landed in Southampton, England, in late February 1896. Throughout the trip, Marconi anxiously guarded his large metal trunk. Only he could touch it. But in the customs house he stood helpless as a customs official seized the box. Deaf to Marconi's explanation and pleas, the suspicious officer manhandled the delicate parts. Recently an Italian had assassinated the French president, Carnot. Anarchists, whether Italian or not, had shot at Queen Victoria as she drove up Constitution Hill in the center of London. All British ports were on notice to look for would-be assassins. This inspector would take no chances. Not knowing what the various instruments were and not understanding the explanation by this foreign-looking young man, he dismantled and broke beyond repair in a matter of minutes what had taken more than a year to create. Marconi was devastated.

It was not an auspicious beginning in the land that Marconi hoped would embrace his invention. By 1896, Great Britain had assembled the largest empire in history. Nearly one-quarter of the earth's territory was controlled from London. Investment capital, accumulated from huge overseas returns, abounded in the City of London, the heart of the world's financial systems. That capital was poured into science and technology for the exploding industrial revolution. Many of the world's most prominent electrical physicists and engineers who were at the cusp of new developments and would best appreciate Marconi's invention practiced in London or taught at England's universities. No other country offered so

Marconi

much potential for Marconi. But as he and Annie now boarded the train from Southampton to London, he naïvely feared the richest country in the world would not possess the substitute pieces for his apparatus. The trip would be a failure.

Depressed, Marconi stepped off the train at the crowded Victoria Station, and as promised, the good-humored Henry Jameson-Davis waited to greet them. Nine years Marconi's senior, the debonair Jameson-Davis led Annie and her dispirited son with the metal chest full of emasculated equipment to the lodgings he had arranged for them. Jameson-Davis, himself a civil engineer, assured his cousin that replacement parts could be found, greatly easing Marconi's mind. Jameson-Davis's practice specialized in engineering for grain mills, a business that grew out of the family ownership of Jameson Irish whiskey. The next day the two cousins began the search for repair items, and over the next several weeks, Marconi reconstructed his invention.

Nonetheless, Marconi remained anxious. He was in a race to the patent office, and the pressure he put on himself literally manifested itself in a fever, a reaction he would often suffer when overly stressed. Jameson-Davis hired a patent agent to work with Marconi. As much as Marconi wanted to file the application immediately, he also knew the importance of not overlooking any aspect of his invention. It was an exacting and painstaking process. The trick was to describe what he sought to protect in both broad and detailed terms so that no one could circumvent his claims.

Jameson-Davis had contacts with many of London's engineers and scientists. In the evenings, he invited them to his home to observe Marconi's novel invention. One visitor was A. A. Campbell Swinton. Jameson-Davis knew that Swinton, an electrical engineer, was a close acquaintance of William Preece, the chief engineer at the General Post Office. The GPO was the world's largest communication organization. Responsible for the mail service throughout the empire, the GPO also had a monopoly over the telegraph system and controlled the connection to privately owned submarine cables that crossed the bottom of the English Channel and the Atlantic Ocean. In addition, the British government had recently nationalized the telephone distribution system and placed it under the direction of the GPO.

As an inventor and engineer, Preece himself had developed a method for sending messages without wires. If anyone could understand the significance of Marconi's invention, reasoned the two cousins, certainly Preece should. The chief engineer's opinion carried great weight in the scientific community. Even a simple statement that Marconi's invention had merit might help persuade investors to back Marconi.

Swinton's visit presented what Jameson-Davis had been seeking—an opportunity to introduce Marconi to Preece. Impressed with Marconi's invention, and at the request of Jameson-Davis, Swinton wrote a letter of introduction to Preece on behalf of Marconi. Swinton graciously authorized Marconi to deliver the letter when it best suited him. Marconi feared that if he met Preece at this point, the knowledgeable engineer might detect Marconi's secrets before they were protected by the patent process. Jameson-Davis agreed.

On June 2, three months after his arrival, Marconi filed in the London Patent Office a provisional patent application describing his invention. This, the two men agreed, afforded sufficient protection of Marconi's ideas to permit a meeting with Preece. But still they waited until Marconi was confident that his instruments were in the best possible working order. He might have only one chance to have an audience with someone as important to his invention's prospects as Preece. After four more weeks of testing, refining, and tweaking, he was ready.

The imposing St. Martin's-le-Grand entrance to the GPO's London headquarters dwarfed the country boy who carried Swinton's letter in the coat pocket of his brown wool suit. Behind the imperial façade, a mass of interconnected GPO buildings covered two entire blocks in downtown London. From inside these walls, the GPO exercised its vast power over communications. Preece led his team of thirty scientists in discovering and developing the latest theories and applications of electricity in telephone and telegraphy.

It was early July when Marconi presented Swinton's letter to the receptionist at St. Martin's-le-Grand. Word of Marconi and his instruments had already reached the hallways of the GPO. An intern was dispatched to fetch Marconi and lead him through the bewildering maze of corridors to the office of the chief engineer of the General Post Office. Marconi stepped into an enormous room with tall, grand windows and a very high ceiling. Bookshelves crowded with scientific learning lined the walls. Sturdy work tables supported ongoing experiments and displayed artifacts of Preece's accomplishments and interests over his long and illustrious career. In the spaces not occupied by the tables, several heavy leather Victorian armchairs were scattered about. As Marconi hesitated to get his bearings, he could well have imagined that his two attic rooms at Villa Grifone would have fit into this office several times. Never before had he set foot in an office of such size and magnificence.

Preece stepped from behind his massive oak desk and greeted Marconi in the friendliest manner. The two men shaking hands in the center of the room stood in sharp contrast to each other. The portly Preece was forty years older than the slender Marconi. Preece, fully bearded and august, carried himself with the full confidence and outgoing geniality of a man aware that he was at the height of his career. Not only was he the chief engineer of the world's largest communication organization, but he was also a well-respected leader of Great Britain's scientific community. By contrast, Marconi was unknown, preoccupied with his invention, and struggling to get it launched.

Preece gestured towards a large table that had been cleared of objects. Marconi placed his two black valises there, and with great care he removed their content. Through his spectacles, Preece watched intently. When Marconi gently lifted the six-inch-long glass that was his coherer from its valise, the chief engineer's eyes brightened. As Marconi assembled the transmitter and the receiver at opposite ends of the table, Preece quietly asked questions about the pieces and their assemblage. Despite the imposing surroundings and the stature of his questioner, Marconi calmly continued his preparations at the same deliberate pace. While his hands deftly moved about the equipment, he confidently and openly responded. But when Preece asked about the coherer, Marconi was concerned that Preece might learn too much. Marconi quietly but firmly said he was not in a position to elaborate because of his patent application.

The setup complete, Marconi prepared to demonstrate. The transmitter and receiver were several yards apart on the table. No wires connected them. After one final adjustment, Marconi pressed the transmitter's key, and instantly the receiver's bell rang. A smile spread across Preece's face. He asked Marconi to ring the bell again, and then again, and after the third ringing, he nodded his head in approval. He turned to Marconi and asked if the young man would like to return and continue his experiments in one of the GPO's workrooms.(FN 1)

It was an enormous break for Marconi. It was a response beyond any hopes he and Jameson-Davis had had. Before the meeting, Marconi had worked entirely alone. Except for Jameson-Davis, he had no connections in London. He had no staff or collegial scientific relationships. He was financed entirely by his father.

In one meeting, all that changed. Preece now provided him with a first-class, fully equipped workspace with knowledgeable, technical assistance about him. Preece and he met almost daily. What these arrangements could mean in terms of ongoing support and introductions to other parties with a possible interest in Marconi's invention were subjects avidly discussed by Jameson-Davis and Marconi.

In Preece's mind, he had made no long-term commitment to Marconi. In fact, he immediately wrote Tesla in New York and described Marconi's visit. This spurred Tesla to file further U.S. patent applications relating to his wireless concepts. Most dealt with oscillators generating electromagnetic currents. Tesla immediately offered two of his sets to Preece for experimentation.(FN 2)

Over the next several weeks, Marconi conducted a variety of tests in the mechanic's shop, the GPO's most advanced laboratory for the Telegraphic Services division. After Preece gained sufficient confidence in the equipment, he arranged an outdoor demonstration for senior GPO officials and engineers. On July 27, on St. Martin's-le-Grand's rooftop, Marconi positioned his transmitter to face the receiver located several blocks away on top of the Savings Bank Department on Queen Victoria Street. Behind the transmitter he placed a reflector to focus the waves towards the receiver, and behind the receiver he placed a second reflector to catch the waves. One of the advancements from the GPO's workshop was the attachment of a Morse keypad to the transmitter and a Morse printer to the receiver. Despite taller, intervening buildings, signals from the transmitter were instantly and clearly picked up by the receiver and recorded by the printer.

In front of the gathered officials, Preece publicly congratulated Marconi: "Young man, you have done something really exceptional; accept my deepest congratulations."(FN 3)

Marconi

This official commendation sanctioned further development of Marconi's invention with the support of the GPO. In addition, Preece was now even more confident of the invention. He would demonstrate it to other departments, including the British War Office.

The demonstration was noteworthy for another reason. It marked the first meeting between Marconi and George Stevens Kemp. The forty-five-year-old Kemp, a former naval school chief instructor in electrical and torpedo work, was one of Preece's assistants. On hearing that the test was about to occur, the red-headed Kemp scrambled up to the roof to observe it. Fascinated by the experiment, he congratulated Marconi and offered to assist in any way that he could. Marconi would later take him up on the offer.

Not everyone, however, was enamored of the experiment. Being asked his opinion, Lord Kelvin, the eminent physicist, rendered his considered judgment. "Wireless was all very well," he said, "but I'd rather send a message by a boy on a pony."

Nonetheless, only four months after his dispiriting arrival at customs and only two years after reading Professor Righi's obituary on Hertz, Marconi's patent application was well underway. His research for the moment was supported by the GPO, one of the world's most powerful organizations.

In the course of Marconi's efforts to enhance his system, he tested Tesla's apparatus as well as those of other scientists. Unaware of the correspondence between Preece and the Serbian inventor, he advised the GPO chief engineer that the Croatian American's equipment did not work. Preece, without disclosing his interest to Marconi, notified Tesla of the results and declined to accept his offer to send over his prototypes.

Captain Jackson, meanwhile, was making solid progress. His new receiver incorporated an aerial two feet long and a coherer very much like Marconi's and Popov's. All three men, within the year and without knowledge of each other's work, had hit upon the same coherer. Aboard the HMS *Defiance* at Davenport on August 20, Jackson signaled across the aft cabin, a distance of a few yards. The next day, Jackson received a letter from the Lords Commissioners of the Admiralty. The letter stated that the Admiralty had under consideration an invention submitted to the War Department by Mr. G. Marconi, who claimed to transmit electrical signals without wires. The commissioners directed Jackson to act as the naval representative at a War Office conference ten days hence. With all branches of the military represented, the conference would first witness a demonstration of Marconi's invention and then determine what, if any, subsequent tests should be conducted. Further stimulated by this news, Jackson continued his tests. Before leaving for London, he transmitted signals from the bow to the stern of the *Defiance*, a length of approximately fifty yards. He observed that the signal passed through the ship's bulkheads with no apparent loss of power.

Ten days later at the War Office conference, Captain Jackson, in full dress uniform, found himself staring at Marconi, startled because Marconi looked so much like Jackson himself at the same age. The composed young man was introduced to Jackson and the military's other leading communication experts. It was the first meeting between Jackson and Marconi. Unlike the cordial, easygoing exchange Marconi experienced with Preece when they first met, Marconi stood and formally addressed the seated and grimly silent military representatives.

The moment Marconi concluded describing his invention and before he could begin his demonstration, Jackson bluntly interrupted him. The captain asserted to Marconi and the assembled officers in the most forcible terms that since the prior December he had developed the very same system.

Jackson visibly upset Marconi. It was one of the few times in his life that his imperturbability gave way to his inner feelings.(FN 4)

Marconi had worried for more than a year that someone might be ahead of him. Now without warning the fear had materialized, personified by the redoubtable figure of Captain Jackson, right in front of his face and simultaneously and embarrassingly before a group of formidable experts.

Internally despondent, Marconi had no choice but to continue. With the transmitter and receiver placed twenty yards apart in adjoining rooms, he signaled from transmitter to receiver. Jackson was not impressed. He had outdone Marconi. He disclosed to the group that his own effort just days earlier went fifty yards and through a bulkhead. He reiterated that he was creating the same apparatus.

Marconi, composure recovered, responded calmly. He summarized St. Martin's-le-Grand where he achieved a distance of several hundred yards over a number of blocks and through or around several buildings.

Marconi

Jackson conceded that Marconi might be further advanced in some details. He concluded, however, that Marconi could do no more than Jackson, except perhaps as to distance.

Jackson then stated his overall position. He wanted to make it clear. He was a military man, not an inventor.

He was not competing with Marconi. He had no intention to patent his idea. His primary interest was to improve British naval communication, whether by his machine, someone else's, or a combination.

Marconi, nonetheless, knew he had an extremely powerful rival. That competitor was strategically located in the midst of the government whose support he had only so recently acquired. The War Office, and the GPO itself, might have no interest in proceeding with Marconi when they had a similar invention under development by one of their own employees.

Marconi had been in England only seven months. The trip started on a low point with the destruction of the contents of his trunk at the customs house. As a result of his and Jameson-Davis's hard work, he had recovered to experience success in his meeting with Preece and elation at the results of the St. Martin's-le-Grand rooftop demonstration. Now he sank to a new low. While his equipment could be replaced, opposing Jackson would be much more difficult, particularly if he lost his only backer.

Depressed, but working without let-up, he waited to hear the conclusion of the War Conference. Annie did her best to comfort him.

In less than a fortnight, the response came. Whatever Jackson's invention might be, it did not preclude military interest in a display by Marconi of his system's maximum range. The War Office asked Marconi to schedule a test no later than the end of September. It would be held at Salisbury Plain fifty miles west of London. Over this slightly undulating land, Marconi could signal without building obstruction and with little interference from hills. Because the government used much of the plain for war maneuvers, the receiver mounted on a cart could be readily moved out to a variety of distances away from the transmitter. The field demonstration would allow Marconi an opportunity to show that his invention was superior to Jackson's and worth pursuing in its own right. This he could do if he significantly exceeded Jackson's best effort.

The trial took place promptly in the last week of September within a month of the War Office conference.

It was truly an experiment and an enormous gamble for Marconi.

He had not done a long-distance test of his equipment since he left Villa Grifone. In England, he had had to rebuild his apparatus. Then he made countless modifications. His changes had worked well over short ranges, like the three-hundred-yard GPO rooftop experiment. But he had no idea whether they restricted or enhanced longer range functionality.

This trial was scheduled so rapidly he had no time for preliminary testing. One new untried advancement was a pair of copper reflectors designed in the shape of a parabola to be placed behind the transmitter and the receiver. He also changed the antenna from a cross tree dangling a dozen wires to a two-foot-square tin box held atop a twenty-foot pole. As he tried these out for the first time on Salisbury Plain, he would have no privacy. Every move he would make—every adjustment, every success, and every failure—would be publicly witnessed.

Marconi housed the transmitter in Hill Crest Bungalow on the prominence of Three Mile Hill near Salisbury. He loaded the receiver on a wooden, horse-drawn cart large enough to carry the receiver and several men to operate the machine.

Less than a year earlier, Marconi had stood with his parents in the garden of Villa Grifone. They watched Alfonso, Mignani, and Vornelli trudge over a hill, receiver strapped to a donkey, to conduct Marconi's first long-range test. Now Great Britain's army sealed off a section of Salisbury Plain for Marconi and provided men and transportation equipment. The GPO sent Kemp and other skilled advisors to assist. The audience included an abundance of British officials. Jackson, naval officers, and members of the War Office conference attended. GPO numeraries came from its Postal Telegraphy Department and Preece's engineering group.

As rays of sunshine sporadically broke through autumn clouds that regularly showered the attendees, the plodding horses hauled the cart across the countryside. They progressed methodically from site to site, each further from Hill Crest Bungalow. Marconi at the transmitter signaled every ten minutes. Army cavalry officers accompanied the wagon. They galloped the results back to Marconi. Over the course of the day, before darkness descended, Marconi achieved one and three-quarters mile. He more than doubled Villa Grifone's record. That distance far surpassed Jackson's fifty yards.

Marconi

This time Jackson was impressed. He recommended to the Admiralty that Marconi prepare another experiment with a different goal. The main objective of Preece and the GPO was to beam signals between two fixed points, from a lighthouse to a shore station to summon assistance for vessels in difficulty. Jackson required a system for the navy that would beam signals in all directions. A fleet at sea in bad weather had no way of determining from what direction a torpedo boat might be returning. Marconi must radiate in all directions in order to reach an unseen ship. His transmitter and receiver must also be rugged enough to withstand conditions at sea. The proposed second test would take place once again at Salisbury Plain the following March.

Since the initial confrontation, the relationship between Jackson and Marconi steadily improved. Jackson was genuinely interested in improving wireless's usefulness to the navy, from whatever source. Based on his own technical experience and his perception of what was needed, he was happy to make suggestions to improve Marconi's invention. This assistance, however, did not mean that Jackson would abandon his own work in favor of Marconi. Jackson continued to experiment. In the end, he might surpass or combine with Marconi. In the fall, after lengthening his aerial to eight feet, Jackson's range doubled to three hundred feet.

For Marconi, hope returned. He had leapt far ahead of Jackson. Instead of losing government support, he might gain the Royal Navy as a customer.

Preece also proposed a new trial. He wanted an on-site comparison of his own Severn River signaling near Cardiff in southern Wales against Marconi's wireless. Preece's operation traversed more than three miles over water. That bested Marconi. Preece wanted a head-to-head showdown.

If Marconi did well, the GPO could become a second customer. Preece scheduled Cardiff for May after Jackson's second Salisbury Plain test in March.

Marconi realized how much more he had to do. Distance obsessed him. Weekdays and weekends blurred as did day and night in the course of his pursuit. Since reading Professor Righi's article about Professor Hertz, the twenty-two-year-old had devoted all his energies to sending invisible waves further and further. He had no social life to speak of. Not even bustling London nightlife could distract him. The two major springtime hurdles intensified the pressure. To bring his knowledge of theoretical physics up to date, he spent hours reading current publications from England, Germany, Italy, and America. Did these scientific journals contain any new ideas that might improve his system?

He was keenly aware of increasing competition. News of his success had reached Popov in Russia. He was surprised at how similar Marconi's principles were. This led the Russian to conclude that his own concepts were more effective than he thought. Popov resumed his effort. In Germany, Adolphus Slaby, an electrical scientist and professor at the prestigious Technical High School in Berlin, became aware of Marconi. Slaby was internationally known and well connected. His own wireless experiments had stalled at three hundred feet. He inquired of his English contacts to learn more about Marconi.

December 1896 marked the first exhibition of Marconi's equipment that was open to the public. Preece, the gregarious Welshman, and Marconi, the introverted Italian, collaborated in a lecture. It was hosted by the Royal Society of Engineers at Toynbee Hall in East London. The Royal Society sponsored opportunities generally limited to the scientific community to share knowledge about recent developments. But rumors about Salisbury Plain had been circulating throughout London. Hundreds filed into the gaslight chamber. The press had been invited. A buzz permeated the crowd. Preece's participation heightened interest and added credibility to the talk.

Preece and Marconi were an odd couple. Preece was so robust, so establishment. Marconi, the lone inventor, almost sallow looking, was fiercely intent. His articulations were terse and precise.

On stage, Preece stood behind a table. Before him he had placed a large, black box that hid the transmitter from the audience. Marconi concealed the receiver inside a smaller container that he carried about the hall. He had attached a bell to the receiver. As Preece lectured, Marconi strolled through the audience. Each time Preece wished to emphasize a point about Marconi's wireless, he pressed a lever in the hidden transmitter. Instantly the bell rang dramatically. It did not matter where Marconi stood in the auditorium. Preece embellished the theatrics by announcing that the GPO had decided to spare no expense in developing Marconi's wireless. Preece's statement had no foundation.

The press found the presentation sensational. For years there had been speculation about sending messages through the air without wires.

Marconi

Toynbee Hall marked the first time the press had observed a demonstration. Reporters had not witnessed Tesla's appearances and had never been invited to observe Preece's Severn River system. Conceptualizing messages sent through the air was not novel, but doing it was. After years of fantasizing about the possibility, here it was right before their eyes. Only fifty years earlier, the telegraph had revolutionized communication. It replaced semaphores and horses as the fastest means of communication. What changes would wireless bring? The concept caught the press's fancy. Imaginations soared. Headlines the next morning trumpeted Marconi's success. They called Marconi the inventor of wireless. Preece received compliments from colleagues and fellow physicists for supporting Marconi. The Italian press criticized the Bureau of Post and Telegraph for rejecting Marconi's earlier offer.

The attention paid to Marconi irritated many scientists who had contributed to the study of electromagnetic waves. It particularly upset Professor Lodge. Even if he had failed to see the practical application of Hertz's bursts of electricity, Lodge certainly understood the importance of professional recognition and acclaim for scientific discovery. He felt his lecture at the Royal Institute in London four years earlier in September 1894 had been the first public demonstration of wireless. He had even had a Morse printer on the table but had not connected it to the receiver. No reporters had attended. The *Electrician* subsequently published his paper, but it had attracted no press attention. Why now should there be this outburst of interest and credit to Marconi? Lodge had no doubt that he had formulated his principles over the four-year period leading up to his talk and that Marconi had developed his invention based on Lodge's and other people's efforts. In fact, Marconi's inspiration at Biellese was in the summer of 1894, scarcely months before Lodge's exposition.

Marconi, on his part, never claimed credit for what he had not done. He invariably acknowledged that he worked with other people's ideas. In an interview following the Toynbee Hall lecture, he said, "My discovery does not contain any new principle, but the application and extension of principles already known."(FN 5) In a subsequent interview, he said, "My discovery was not the result of long hours and logical thought, but of experiments with machines invented by other men to which I applied certain improvements."(FN 6)

Lodge immediately commenced work on a patent application after the Toynbee Hall lecture. Marconi was well ahead. On March 2, Marconi completed the arduous, meticulous task and submitted the final draft of his previously submitted application entitled "For Improvements in Transmitting Electrical Impulses and Signals, and an Apparatus Therefore." It included eleven drawings.

The press continued to be fascinated. In an interview with *McClure's Magazine* published in the March 1897 issue,(FN 7) Marconi was asked if he could send a dispatch from London to New York. He always responded to reporters carefully. He did not claim that he could accomplish what he had not yet performed. He replied:

> I would not say that it could not be done. My work consists mainly in endeavoring to determine how far these waves will travel in the air for signaling purposes. I am forced to believe the waves will penetrate anything and everything...(that) they will go through an ironclad... With regard to future developments I am only saying what may ultimately happen; what so far as I can now see does not present any visible impossibilities.

The interviewer reached his own conclusions:

> Such are the astounding statements and views of Marconi. What their effects will be remains to be seen. The imagination abandons as a hopeless task the attempt to conceive what—in the use of electric waves—the immediate future holds in store. The air is full of promises, of miracles. The certainty is that strange things are coming.

Jackson had also been hard at work. He redesigned his aerials, whose importance he had not initially appreciated, to incorporate Marconi's experience and advice. In the first two weeks of March, he fit a transmitter to the *Scourge*, *Defiance's* tender, and extended its aerial to seventy feet. Signals were transmitted two-thirds of a mile. That distance was almost half Marconi's record at Salisbury Plain. The competition was closing in fast. Jackson's progress allowed him to say that his equipment would soon be on a level with Marconi's. Then Jackson set his experiments aside to attend torpedo trials at Weymouth and to observe Marconi's second demonstration at Salisbury Plain.

On March 24, the usually desolate plain came alive. The international coverage following Toynbee Hall had created widespread conjecture. Once again, Marconi found himself on Three Mile Hill. This time hundreds of people surrounded him. It was a major occasion. It had been discussed for months in military, scientific, and press circles. Invitations were eagerly sought. Top military officers assembled in full dress uniform. Marconi personally called Jackson to attend. Scores of high ranking government officials gathered to witness the event. Foreign observers traveled to this barren bit of British countryside to observe what they could not see. Slaby, to ensure his welcome, had had Kaiser William II of Germany intervene through diplomatic channels. Swarming about the guests was the press. Even with this many people about, Marconi remained poised, focusing intently on the immediate task. Characteristically, his face revealed neither what his mind was thinking nor what his heart was feeling. His hands, as always, moved deftly about the instruments.

The primary purpose of the test was to determine the maximum range signals could be transmitted in every direction. It was a true experiment. Marconi had no way to practice beforehand. He had not been working on the plain for months before the spectators appeared to make sure his apparatus would succeed. He arrived when they did. Salisbury Plain was his laboratory. It was a very public one. Crowds watched his every move. Each failed effort would be noted. There was no privacy. And if he faltered, would the Royal Navy and the GPO turn to Jackson to continue the program?

The prior fall on Salisbury Plain, Marconi had placed reflectors behind the transmitter and receiver to focus waves in one direction. Now to meet Jackson's request that the signals radiate simultaneously to all quarters, he removed the reflectors. In the earlier experiment, he had used tin boxes on poles for antennae. This time, to facilitate radiation, he used a single wire from which waves could emit in every direction. A similar arrangement to catch waves was attached to the receiver. Marconi believed that the higher they were, the better the chance to travel new lengths. He planned to raise the aerial over one hundred feet by tying it to a gas balloon.

This was Marconi's initial effort to signal long-distance without reflectors. He had not tried a single-wire aerial before. He had not lifted his antenna more than thirty feet above the ground.

As before, the transmitter sat inside Hill Crest Bungalow on top of Three Mile Hill. While an anxious crowd watched, the transmitter's aerial was fitted to a gas balloon. The day was calm with little wind, only breezes, and intermittent rays of sun. The light rope controlling the balloon was slowly paid out. The balloon lifted the lengthy single wire until it stretched more than one hundred feet up into the sky. A murmur of approval rose from the host looking skyward, watching the balloon's every move as it gently tugged at the aerial.

The receiver again sat in a horse-drawn army cart. A Morse printer was connected to the receiver. The cart moved one hundred yards away and halted. Fitted to the receiver's single wire antenna was another balloon that rose one hundred feet into the air. Marconi emerged from Hill Crest Bungalow to inspect the receiver and its aerial. Then he disappeared back into the bungalow. Minutes later, the Morse printer acknowledged signals from the transmitter. The system was working.

Marconi came out again to inspect the receiver. He supervised the lowering of its wire back down to the ground. The cart moved slowly away, followed by half the assemblage. The rest remained on the hillside. At each stop, the aerial flew aloft. The printer recorded signals at half a mile, a mile and a quarter, and then an astonishing four miles. An enormous cheer burst from the receiver's onlookers. Marconi had shattered all records. A cavalry officer dashed full speed from the site to advise Marconi of the good news. As he thundered up Three Mile Hill, the crowd at Hill Crest Bungalow applauded and shouted in great excitement.

Of all the distinguished guests who had gathered, the one who mattered the most was profoundly affected. Jackson warmly congratulated Marconi. He told his rival that he was very pleased with the results. In his favorable report to the Admiralty, the captain stated that the maximum range reached was seven miles. Reliable signals radiated consistently outward at four miles. He directed his only question to the elevation of the aerials. That could present a problem in squally weather. But he answered his own concern. Masts on warships were ideal for raising nondirectional aerials.

Marconi

Press coverage was worldwide. Letters from readers all over Europe, from America, and from as far away as Japan besieged Marconi. Many came from women. One wrote that his waves made her feet tickle. Numerous requests were made to be his commercial agent. A Milan bank offered to purchase the rights to the invention for an amount sufficient to purchase the Villa Banzi next door to Villa Grifone. Giuseppe sent Marconi a list of Villa Banzi's livestock and advised him to accept the proposal. He wrote of his joy that his son was so successful that he could consider this purchase.

Marconi confided to a friend: *"A calma della mia vita ebbe allora fine."* The calm of my life ended then.(FN 8)

Marconi refused the Milan bank. His invention, he believed, was worth more. Other propositions to enter into a variety of arrangements were made as well. Slaby suggested that Algemeine Elektrizitats Gesellschaft (the German Electric Company of Berlin) manufacture and sell Marconi apparatus.

Jameson-Davis moved quickly. He put forth a general concept, not detailed, that he thought would appeal to Marconi. Jameson-Davis and others members of the Jameson family would form a company to acquire Marconi's invention. In return, Marconi would receive cash and half of the corporation's stock. The consortium would also provide working capital for research and development and patents. Revenue would be generated by equipping ships with wireless. In Marconi's words:

> When one of these devices is fitted in a lighthouse and ships have their receivers, as soon as they come within three or four thousand meters, an alarm bell will ring. This is important in rain and fog, when the lighthouses are not visible. In this way, we shall have an electrically controlled lighthouse, which will always operate, unlike the one depending on light, which is so uncertain. In the same way we shall be able to avoid collisions between ships, and so on.(FN 9)

Marconi's invention had reached a new performance level. It far outstripped its competition. It showed sufficient commercial promise to attract serious, private financial support. Marconi feared, however, that if

Preece heard of these unsolicited offers from someone other than himself, he might conclude Marconi was no longer interested in working with the GPO. The chief engineer might withdraw the GPO's support. Marconi advised Preece of the offers. He assured him that the idea to form a company was not his. The strategy worked. Preece pressed ahead with arrangements for Marconi's experiment over the waters of the Severn River near Cardiff.

As Marconi pondered whether and how to respond to the various business opportunities, he was confronted with an issue that had been simmering on a back burner. Italian reporters began to hound him. When, they asked, would he perform his deferred eighteen-month military service? Marconi knew that if he fulfilled it now, he would seriously derail his momentum. No one else could carry on the work. Rivals would catch up and pass him. Jameson-Davis emphatically warned that even the possibility of such an absence threatened the organization of the company he proposed. He suggested a solution. Annie was a British citizen. By birthright, Marconi could also become one and thereby avoid an Italian military commitment. The British had no such requirement.

Marconi would not consider renouncing his Italian citizenship. He regarded himself as an Italian. He felt enormous loyalty to Italy. He turned for advice to General Ferrero, still the Italian ambassador to England. Ferrero had followed Marconi's progress. He was concerned that the British, not the Italians, would benefit from Marconi's invention. Captain Antonio Bianco, the naval attaché to the embassy, informed Ferrero of the navy's deep interest in Marconi's experiments. It worried them that in wartime an enemy might sever Italy's cable communications to its offshore islands. Ferrero invited Marconi to lunch with Bianco and afterwards advised Benedetto Brin, minister of the Regia Marina in Rome, of the problem.

In May, not long after the luncheon, Marconi boarded a train with Kemp and other GPO electrical engineers and several trunks of equipment for the long trip from London west to Gloucester, then south to Cardiff in southeastern Wales. The coal-fed engine neared the coast, moving along the Severn River's western bank. Crests of lush green hills could occasionally be seen through rifts in low clouds and mists. The journey included many stops and consumed a day. Near Cardiff at Lavernock Point on the Severn River, the party disembarked. It proceeded by horse-drawn carriage for the shore station Preece had constructed for wireless communication to the lighthouses on Flatholm Island and Steep Holm Island. Here Preece proposed the direct comparison between his method of signaling and Marconi's.

Preece's system worked but was highly impractical. A copper line a mile long was suspended twenty feet above the ground by a series of poles. It transmitted across the mouth of the river to similar copper lines a third of a mile long. To satisfy Preece, Marconi's system must only prove it could perform over water as reliably as Preece's. Most lighthouses had insufficient land on which to construct Preece's line. No lightship could carry it. Marconi's equipment could be readily installed on shore and in lighthouses and lightships.

This demonstration was not as well attended as the second Salisbury Plain test. Cardiff was too far from London to provide the same holiday atmosphere of escaping the city for a pleasant day's outing in the country. The weather at Lavernock Point turned out to be despicable. The wind blew up into a gale. Intermittently it poured down sheets of slanting water. The cold was biting. Nonetheless, some military and government representatives were there, including members of the GPO. Preece was not in attendance and nor was Jackson. Reporters and curious hardy locals with flasks ever ready for a warming nip huddled about.

Foreign observers had also made the trip. The Italian navy sent a captain in the naval engineers, Vittorio Malfotti, from London. His mission was "to observe Marconi's work as closely as possible and report back to Rome without making himself conspicuous."(FN 10)

Slaby, on the other hand, ever present, notebook in hand, hovered about Marconi to watch each detail and learn all that he could. Marconi, as he had been with Preece and Jackson, was polite and responsive to the German's constant inquiries, but not to the point he might endanger the pending patent application.

Lavernock Point, like Salisbury Plain, was an experiment. Marconi had not practiced over water or in weather this foul. He housed the transmitter in the lighthouse on Flatholm Island. At Lavernock Point, three miles across the water from Flatholm Island, he placed one receiver. He located a second receiver at Brean Down eight and a half miles from the transmitter.

Because this was a transmission from one fixed point to another, he positioned reflectors behind the transmitter and receivers. He replaced the Salisbury Plain single-wire antenna, designed to radiate in every direction, with a cylinder two yards high and one yard wide mounted on a ninety-foot pole. To maximize height, Marconi situated the receiver on the summit of Lavernock Point, a cliff rising sixty feet above a narrow beach, thereby raising the cylinder one hundred and fifty feet above sea level. He then ran the receiver's ground to the beach below. As a result, he had a ground sixty feet long and an antenna ninety feet high.

He stayed with his GPO team near Cardiff. They traveled by chartered tug back and forth between the three locations until Marconi had set up the equipment to his satisfaction. The effort consumed a fortnight.

Marconi stationed himself at Lavernock Point, ready to see if the arrangements worked. At Flatholm Island, Kemp struck the transmitter's key, a large, wooden handle. An enormous spark jumped across the spark gap that had been enlarged for this purpose. Nothing happened.

For two days, government officials and members of the press and the general public stood about miserable and restless, seeking to shelter themselves from the abdominal weather. They watched Marconi make adjustment after adjustment to the receiver and antenna at Lavernock Point. Despite the pressure and frustration, Marconi never lost his composure. He appeared to block everyone out as if in a lab by himself as he went through mental calculations and conceived of combinations of alterations. He remained cordial in talking to the GPO engineers assisting him and in answering questions from observers, even those from Slaby.

Still nothing happened. Questions arose as to the reliability of the invention. Was it the water over which the electric waves traveled? Was it the weather? Did dampness affect the instruments? Did the wind blow the signals off course? What combination blocked the transmission?

On the third day, in yet another effort to vary the combinations with which he had arranged his apparatus, Marconi detached the receiver from its ground and antenna. He picked it up by himself despite its thirty-pound weight and awkward shape and carried it to the beach below, slipping and sliding down the rough face of the cliff. Marconi manhandled the receiver into a shack on the beach. He directed GPO engineers to reattach the sixty-foot ground to the receiver. He ordered that the unattached end of the ground be carried back up to the top of the cliff and spliced to the antenna. The new configuration resulted in an aerial one hundred and fifty feet high. Marconi grounded the receiver with a new short line. Slaby posted himself in the shack right by the receiver and later reported on what happened next:

> It will be for me an ineffaceable recollection. Five of us stood around the apparatus in a wooden shed as shelter from the gale, with eyes and ears directed towards the instruments with an attention that was almost painful. The hoisting of the flag was the signal that all was ready. Instantaneously we heard the first tic-tac, tic-tac and saw the Morse instrument print the signals which came to us silently and invisibly from the island rock, whose contour was barely visible to the naked eye—came to us dancing on that unknown and mysterious agent, the ether. (FN 10)

A cheer went up from the men in the shed, and then from the men on the beach surrounding the shed, and finally from those still standing in the wet and cold on the summit by the antenna. Transmissions came in without a hitch for the balance of the day.

On the fourth day, Marconi went to Brean Down, eight and a half miles from the transmitter. After the equipment was adjusted to reflect the experience of the past three days, Brean Down, unlike Lavernock Point, received transmission on the first try.

It was a new record. The signals traveled further and more reliably than over the seven miles at Salisbury Plain.

In London, Preece accepted the results. Marconi's system was clearly more practical than Preece's. It was superior to Jackson's that had not yet surpassed a mile. Preece began to consider the best way to obtain Marconi's equipment to fulfill the GPO's obligation to maintain communication with lighthouses and lightships. Marconi was getting closer to having his first major customer.

The popular press once again acclaimed Marconi. The British professional journals, however, sided with Lodge as the inventor of wireless.

They denied any significance to Marconi's improvements. But one of his strongest rivals, Slaby, candidly credited Marconi's contributions:

> Marconi had made a discovery. He was working with means the entire meaning of which no one before him had recognized. Only in that way can we explain the secret of his success. In the English professional journals an attempt has been made to deny novelty to the method of Marconi. It was urged that the production of the Hertz rays, their radiation through space, the construction of his electric eye—all this was known before.
> True; all this had been known to me also and yet I was never able to exceed 100 metres. In the first place Marconi has worked out a clever arrangement of apparatus, which by the use of the simplest means produces a sure technical result. Then he has shown that such telegraphy (writing from afar) was to be made possible only through, on the one hand, earth connection between the apparatus and, on the other hand, the use of long extended upright wires. By this simple but extraordinarily effective method he raised the power of radiation in the electrical forces a hundred fold.(FN 11)

Marconi's invention had arrived at the threshold of being a commercial enterprise. His successful tests had satisfied the requirements of two major potential customers in the Royal Navy and the GPO. Marconi and his cousin also foresaw commercial ships as buyers. The older relative continually lobbied the younger to assent to the formation of a private company once his patent was granted and the question of his military service disposed of. Marconi was not to be rushed. He felt no need to decide until the obstacles were removed. He was particularly concerned about the patent. Could Lodge, who was understood to be preparing his own applications, use his local influence and connections to infiltrate the patent office and thwart Marconi? Could there be unstated prejudice within the office in favor of domestic intellectuals against foreigners? Certainly its officials read British professional journals.

Marconi

Jackson continued experimenting. He accomplished what Preece had failed to do and what Marconi had not yet attempted—mobile communication. With a receiver on the *Defiance* at anchor, he placed the transmitter on *Scourge*, *Defiance*'s tender. As *Scourge* maneuvered about the crowded Davenport harbor, Jackson transmitted at the rate of one word per minute. Varying *Scourge*'s speed, its bearings relative to *Defiance*, and its distance away from *Defiance*, Jackson received signals up to three miles, despite intervening ships. He proved that his wireless worked from a moving vessel. The only disappointment for Jackson was that the test to determine maximum range had to be abandoned. *Scourge* could only steam two miles upriver before the channel became too shallow, and an exception to navy rules would have been required to take the tender out to sea. But his test did help assuage people's fear that this new technology with its spark-emitting transmitter might cause detonators to explode or compasses to go awry or even heart attacks.

No matter for the moment what Jackson's accomplishments were, Marconi's efforts had headway. His distances were greater than anyone's, whether over land or water. Despite disclosing the Jameson-Davis offer to Preece, the GPO relationship solidified. At a crowded Royal Institute lecture attended by scientists and press, Preece countered head-on the criticism that Marconi did not deserve the credit he was receiving for inventing the wireless and that the GPO was giving Marconi undue support. Marconi, Preece said, had produced from knowledge possessed by many a new system of telegraphy that no one else had created. Lodge answered right back. In a letter to the editor of the *Times*, Lodge acidly wrote that Professor Righi and others, including himself, had made the real scientific advances in wireless, not Marconi.

Preece, of course, was not a disinterested supporter of Marconi, nor was Preece any more than Jackson committed to Marconi's best interests. By calling wireless a new form of telegraphy, Preece was not helping Marconi. Two decades earlier, the British Parliament had granted the GPO a domestic telegraphy monopoly. The GPO aggressively protected its exclusivity. If it concluded that wireless was telegraphy, then the GPO might attempt to block Marconi from operating his wireless wherever GPO provided telegraph service. Preece and the GPO had also played an active role in nationalizing the telephone trunk lines. In 1895, Preece had observed that when competing telephone companies hung their major distribution lines on the same street poles, electrical interference resulted, making the voice communication carried on the lines unintelligible. As chief engineer, he recommended that the lines be nationalized under the GPO. Parliament had acted on this advice. In the case of both the telephone and the telegraph years earlier, the British government had permitted private interests to develop the new industries. At the point where the technology's usefulness was established, the government stepped in and nationalized the companies. Preece now foresaw wireless as a threat to the GPO's monopoly. What better place for Preece to watch over Marconi than in his own shop. It was another element for Marconi to consider in his decision whether to go private. He might escape the presence and influence Preece exerted over the direction of his development, but would he antagonize Preece into initiating unfavorable governmental action against Marconi's interests?

An ability to stay in close touch with Marconi was what the Italian government achieved in resolving Marconi's service. Its military was now fully cognizant what the Ministry of Post and Telegraphy had let slip through its hands. In June, at the direction of King Umberto, the navy enrolled Marconi as a cadet. It seconded him to the embassy in London as a naval attaché, an entirely nominal position. This left Marconi free to pursue airborne transmission. On his part, he agreed for no consideration, assuming he was issued a patent, to grant all rights to use the patent in Italy to the Italian government. He donated his monthly stipend as a naval attaché to the Italian Hospital in London, a magnanimous gift as he had no income of his own. The credit for the gesture should have gone to his father. Giuseppe provided Marconi's entire support.

The navy had many reasons to appreciate its association with Marconi. The first became immediately obvious. The Ministry of Marine ordered its new cadet home to demonstrate his apparatus to authorities in Rome and at Spezia, the navy's principal west coast base. Jameson-Davis discouraged his going. The other financial backers of the proposed corporation threatened to withdraw, fearing that their principal asset, Marconi, once back in Italy, might remain there. Marconi asserted that he had no interest in staying in Italy.

Just prior to departing, Marconi received what he had sought so incessantly and diligently. On July 2, 1897, Patent No. 12,039 was granted to Guglielmo Marconi. The patent declared the nature of the invention to be "electrical actions or manifestations transmitted through the air, earth or water by means of electric oscillations of high frequency."(FN 12)

The patent had the full breadth Marconi intended. He had beaten his competitors to the patent office. Whatever their claims, Lodge's included, they had not restricted the scope of what Marconi sought. The document satisfied Jameson-Davis. It was an enormous step forward for Marconi and a major personal relief after months and months of worry.

Tesla, upon hearing of its issuance, obtained a copy. He forwarded it to his lawyer with the observation that the patent was founded on the wrong grounds. He directed his attorney to file in Washington, DC, his first application specifically for wireless transmission. He then purported to send electrical energy without wires from his New York City laboratory to West Point on the Hudson River, a distance several times further than Marconi's record distance across the Severn River. There was no witness, however, to Tesla's feat.(FN 13)

Marconi returned to Italy in great personal triumph. He crossed the English Channel with Annie. They took the train together as far as Milan, where they parted ways, she to Bologna to be with Giuseppe at Villa Grifone and he to continue on to the first stop of his tour at Rome. Not long before, he had been rejected for admission to the Naval Academy. Now he came at the navy's invitation, an attaché, to demonstrate his invention. He must have been laughing quietly to himself. Only sixteen months earlier, with his shiny, black box, timid and unsure of himself and his future, he had left Italy accompanied by his mother. Now in his honor a dinner was to be given, and he had an audience with Umberto I, King of Italy.

CHAPTER 4

The King, the Queen, and the Electrician

Atop one of the seven hills upon which Rome had been founded rose the Quirinal, a grandiose palace of pinken hue whose color deepened in the Roman sunsets. At the center of its enormous façade, which faced the huge Piazza del Quirinal, a grand portal opened onto an interior court-yard with an imposing clock tower. Constructed in the sixteenth century upon the order of Pope Gregory XIII, the Quirinal embodied the influ-ence and riches of the papacy during that time. Three centuries later, it had become the official residence of the Italian monarchy and the center of political power in Italy. It was to the Quirinal that King Umberto had extended Marconi an invitation for an official visit.

Italy had a parliamentary government, but the king in fact enjoyed enormous authority. The parliament was composed of many fractious par-ties, and in order to establish ruling majorities, the parties had to form al-liances. From among the leaders of the numerous factions comprising the majority, the king, as required by the constitution, selected the govern-ment's prime minister. The government lasted only as long as the prime minister held his coalition together. In the nineteen years Umberto had been king, the government had failed almost every other year. Umberto had appointed nine prime ministers. As a result of this frequent interven-tion in the country's most important political process, he wielded consid-erable influence in domestic affairs.

Many Italians supported the monarchy as a matter of principle. It symbolized unity in a country that for centuries had been riven by local rivalries, foreign influences, and disparate political views. The military coalesced around the view of a powerful monarchy, and Umberto fully reciprocated the backing. His monarchy derived from the House of Savoy that traditionally had had close relationship with the army. The Italian king, as the only constant leadership figure in a never-ending rotation of prime ministers, also played a leading role in Italian foreign affairs. King Umberto's role in directing Marconi's appointment as a cadet-in-training had not been a mere royal formality in response to the Italian navy's request. Umberto supported the navy and understood the potential significance of Marconi's wireless in world affairs.

For Marconi, the first six days in Rome had been an exhilarating whirlwind of tours and events. At the Ministry of Marine before top brass, he had demonstrated his wireless. The next night, the Association of Italian Electro-Technicians gave a dinner in his honor, the first such dinner to be held for him. He basked in Rome's sunny warmth, glad to be out of London's damp and dreary weather. It was a heady homecoming. His country, his own country, which had once rejected him, now paid him special attention.

Marconi arrived at the Quirinal for his audience with the king. Under his mother's instruction, he had dressed in his best black suit. He wore a black silk tie that Annie had purchased for the occasion. Unlike his initial meeting with Preece when he had brought in his own instruments, Marconi carried nothing with him. The Italian navy, taking no chances that some piece might be missing, had beforehand carefully set up his equipment in a private chamber next to the king's grand receiving room.

The king wore a tunic heavily laden with medals and crisscrossed with three royal sashes bearing Italy's colors. Even more striking than the decoration of his chest, the king's enormous mustache, unbridled by any cautious cutting of the royal barber, protruded from his upper lip to the outer edges of his face. Although not well read in other subjects, Umberto had an enormous curiosity and detailed knowledge of army equipment and weapons.

Umberto greeted Marconi with genuine interest. Surrounded by his advisors and Marconi's naval sponsors, he attentively watched the demonstration. He asked knowledgeable questions about the materials and mechanics. The naval officers felt that the king had been impressed and considered their endorsement of Marconi a royal success.

In a surprise for Marconi, the elegant and eloquent Queen Margherita granted Marconi an audience after his meeting with the king. She had not been Umberto's initial choice for a wife. His original selection who died before they could marry inadvertently burned herself to death. In surreptitiously trying to enjoy a socially forbidden cigarette, she had allowed the red-hot ash to come too close to her finely spun dress. It burst into flames, and she died from the burns. Margherita was Umberto's first cousin, the daughter of his father's brother. Although generally thought to be a modest and moderate man, Umberto humiliated his wife by conducting open affairs. He appointed a favorite mistress to be one of her ladies-in-waiting. Nonetheless, Margherita comported herself with grace and wit. Many found her far more interesting than her husband. Marconi reported to Annie that the queen was charming and quite aware of his invention.

The king and the naval hierarchy were not merely eager to have Marconi exhibit his wireless in Italy. They wanted to be the first to afford him an opportunity to experiment at sea. The navy put its principal base, St. Bartolomeo at Spezia, at their cadet-in-training's disposal. To reach Spezia, located at the top of Italy's western shore, required an all-day journey by train. As the locomotive thundered northward along the coastline through Leghorn, Marconi might have mused that he had enjoyed his first waterborne ventures in that city's harbor. With Daisy at his side, he had raced his skiff across the bow of the naval academy launch, perhaps carrying some of the officers who accompanied him today.

But he had much more than that to think about. Since leaving England, the future of his invention and the best way to assure its progress had been foremost in his mind. Now that he held a patent and would not be required to perform military service in Italy, he focused on whether or not to accept Jameson-Davis's proposal to organize a company. He went about making the decision much as he conducted his scientific inquiries, methodically looking at it from all angles. However, unlike his experiments, he could not measure the results empirically. He asked himself questions, but he had no one sufficiently knowledgeable and close enough to him to confide in about the answers, other than Jameson-Davis himself. His ambition was not to make money for himself, but rather to advance his wireless. He realized that this decision could be more important than many of the tests he had conducted.

Two questions about Jameson-Davis's offer concerned Marconi.

Marconi

The first involved its backers. Would they attempt to control him and override his current freedom to make decisions? As he later said, the Irish and English "believed at the start that they had a young man of scant experience who could be easily dominated."(FN 1) Marconi, however, was fully aware that he held the better cards. No one else knew how to work his invention. Even if a corporation held the patents, it would be difficult for its directors to further his wireless without his participation. His experience in dealing with dominating figures many years his senior, like Preece and Jackson, and even his father, gave him confidence that he would be the handler. To assure his authority, he decided that he must have majority ownership in the new company.

His second worry was more difficult to assess and solve. If he formed a private company, how would Preece and the GPO react? Would they continue to back Marconi? Would they consider him a competitor to the government's own efforts to develop wireless, or worse, an infringer on the GPO's telegraph monopoly? Preece had not objected when Marconi floated the idea by him earlier. The chief engineer was influential, but he did not make the GPO's final decisions. Also, and this caused Marconi considerable concern, Preece was due to retire soon. If Great Britain believed Marconi to be a rival, how would that hurt him at this stage of his development? He would have his own money to support his research. The GPO had provided a laboratory, the use of Salisbury Plain, and knowledgeable engineers to assist him. That could be expensive to replace. Perhaps more important, the GPO and the Royal Navy were his best prospective customers. Would they turn to Jackson or Lodge instead to develop their own wireless?

On the other hand, if Marconi didn't form his own company, would he be forever beholden to the GPO? Would GPO officials support his effort with the required resources to continue its development? Or would they start to call the shots? Where would he find money for his own personal support? The GPO provided resources for experimenting but did not pay Marconi a salary. How long would Giuseppe carry him? The more Marconi examined his options, the more precarious his financial position seemed to be.

If Marconi did not team up with Jameson-Davis but wished to free himself from the domination of the GPO, what other alternatives did he have? None superior to Jameson-Davis had surfaced. Marconi had full confidence in his patent, but the influential electrical industry journal, the *Electrician*, had mocked its validity. The publication editorialized that many of Marconi's claims had been developed earlier by Lodge. It concluded that if Marconi's patent was "upheld in the courts of law, it will be seen that it is…easy for an eminent patent-counsel to compile a valid patent from the publicly described and exhibited products of another man's brain."(FN 2) Such authoritative, public deprecation of his patent could deter other investors or make them less willing to give as generous terms as Jameson-Davis and his group proposed.

The offer consisted of issuing Marconi 50 percent of the new corporation's stock, an initial bonus that could be as high as fifteen thousand pounds, and funding the company with an even higher amount of working capital. What other investor group could or would top that offer? (Great Britain and the United States were both on the gold standard. One pound sterling was roughly worth five U.S. dollars. Statistically, a dollar was worth twenty times its value in 2004. By numerical calculation, Marconi's fifteen-thousand-pound bonus would be worth one hundred times that in 2004 dollars, or 1.5 million dollars. Such a comparison is overly simplistic as many factors affect a determination of the buying power of yesterday's money today.)(FN 3)

Marconi did not know that Preece had already reached his own conclusions. In his judgment, Marconi had a valid patent. Instead of negotiating a license with limited uses, the GPO should acquire the patent outright. In his official report to the secretary of the GPO following Severn River, Preece outlined his reasoning:

> His patent is a very strong one but its validity is sure to be contested. Professor Lodge claims priority of invention. I have, however, carefully examined Professor Lodge's claims…and I find them baseless. They will, however, have to be submitted to the Attorney General for his opinion. My own view is that…the Government would be justified in acquiring the patent rights for £10,000… Marconi is a very young man. He is a foreigner.(FN 4)

Marconi would not be pleased by such an offer. It fell far short of Jameson-Davis's proposal. Marconi would totally lose control. Preece made the same assumption as Jameson-Davis's backers. Marconi was an easy mark because he was young. Further, a foreigner would find little support in standing up to the English government.

Once the party disembarked at St. Bartolomeo, thoughts about Jameson-Davis and the business proposal could not distract Marconi from the task at hand—experimenting at sea. The yard bustled with sailors, cadets, and launches and steamships belching smoke. He established the transmitter in the dockside equipment shed closest to the open water. The receiver went aboard the cruiser *San Martino*. The officers, who had exchanged their stiff formal dress uniforms worn in Rome to more manageable attire, surrounded him everywhere he went. The very curious and interested group peppered Marconi with questions. He responded in his usual manner—politely answering what he could and deflecting what he could not. Once again, the portability and ease of setting up the wireless, even in new circumstances, became evident. The transmitter and receiver each traveled in three specially designed, carefully packed wooden containers. One man could easily carry a box. Once unloaded from the six boxes, all the pieces being present and unbroken from the trip, Marconi assembled the transmitter and receiver each in less than three hours.

Marconi trained several seamen to operate the transmitter. When the experiments started, their instructions were to transmit a sequence of signals every ten minutes. Marconi and party boarded the *San Martino*. Seven and a half miles out into the Gulf of Genoa, the *San Martino* received signals. At Davenport, Jackson's moving boat had transmitted to a stationary receiver two miles away. At Spezia, Marconi's fixed-base transmitter signaled a moving boat seven miles distant. In the process, he confirmed that Brean Down at the Severn River was no fluke.

More startling, the receiver picked up signals at eleven miles, a new record. The officers became highly excited. At once they expressed interest in acquiring wireless for the navy.

Marconi allowed no outward sign of emotion. In fact, he was perplexed. It did not make sense.

Marconi's experience at Salisbury Plain and Severn River indicated that the higher the antennae, the further away a signal could be received. Accepted electrical theory postulated that Hertzian waves traveled in a straight line. A signal following a straight line over the earth's curvature would require a higher and higher antenna in order to be received.

At eleven miles, the ship was out of sight of St. Bartolomeo. The *San Martino* had passed over the horizon from Spezia. The earth's curvature hid the shoreline.

The cruiser's aerial hung from the top of the mast. At that height, Marconi calculated that the antenna was too far below a straight line from the transmitter to their position beyond the horizon to catch the signal from St. Bartolomeo.

Did the receipt of the signals constitute an aberration or exception to the postulates? Or did it disprove the concepts?

Marconi said nothing to the celebrating officers about his puzzlement. He could not explain what had occurred any more than he could explain why a signal pierced a wall or a building or a hill. He might have theories or a guess, but he had no mathematical proofs or scientifically established answers. It was another phenomenon of the electric waves to be studied.

What happened next was equally perturbing. When the *San Martino* had returned to less than five miles from Spezia, it sailed by two hilly islands; they blocked the line of sight to St. Bartolomeo. The signals became erratic. They did not stabilize until the boat cleared the islands. Once more, Marconi realized he had a lot to learn.

Marconi spent two weeks at Spezia. Before he left to visit his parents at Villa Grifone, he had reached a decision about organizing an enterprise. One criterion stood out above all others. He must be in control of the development of his invention. That would never happen as long as he was tied to the GPO. A private corporation could give him that independence, whatever the consequences with Preece.

Marconi exchanged telegrams with London. He advised Jameson-Davis of his decision to go ahead, provided that he receive a clear majority interest and that working capital be sufficient to support research. He inquired one final time: Did the investors intend to follow his guidance? Did they understand the working capital would be devoted to research? Satisfied by his cousin's reassurances, Marconi consented to the formation of a corporation.

As Marconi traveled from Spezia to Villa Grifone, Jameson-Davis completed the arrangements. The negotiations begun in March following the second Salisbury Plain test culminated with the incorporation of the Wireless Telegraph and Signal Co. Ltd. on July 20, 1897, in London. The

Marconi

"young foreigner" prevailed on each of his points. In return for transferring his patent and know-how to Wireless Telegraph and Signal, which was sometimes called WTS for short, Marconi received 60 percent of the company. The investors paid forty thousand pounds in sterling to WTS for the remaining 40 percent of the stock. As additional consideration to Marconi for his patent and know-how, WTS paid him fifteen thousand pounds out of the forty thousand pounds it received from the investors. WTS retained the remaining twenty-five thousand pounds for research and working capital.

The bonus alone made Marconi a rich man, a U.S. millionaire in today's terms. There were no income taxes. Who knows what his interest in the company was worth. The investors paid forty thousand pounds for a 40 percent interest. Marconi held 60 percent and control. He was twenty-three years old.

Original shareholders included members of the Jameson and Davis families. The families had become related through the marriage of Jameson-Davis's father, A. Grubb Davis, to Annie's second sister. Members of the Saunders and Ballentyne families, who were friends of the Jamesons and Davises, also bought shares, as did corn merchants whom Jameson-Davis knew as suppliers to the Jameson whiskey business. Jameson-Davis had high respect for the business acumen of the merchants, who also acted as commodity traders in the City of London. Marconi and Jameson-Davis became two of the five directors. Marconi had the right, which he subsequently exercised, to name a sixth director. Two of the other three directors were Jameson-Davis family members, and the third was a corn trader. Jameson-Davis became the managing director. He established the company's headquarters at 28 Mark Lane in the city, just a few doors down from his own office at 22 Mark Lane. Marconi held no position other than that of controlling shareholder and director.

Giuseppe did not buy or receive any shares in the company. For the previous three years, he had supported Marconi. He could justifiably conclude that that was enough of a contribution. No records show that Marconi repaid his father any of the money. Giuseppe, of course, would have preferred that Marconi settle next door instead of returning to London.

The unfortunate fact is that Marconi never forgave his father for the slights and insults and lack of encouragement that he suffered at his hands during his childhood. These wounds in their relationship never healed.

Marconi was greeted at Villa Grifone with great enthusiasm. In less than a year and a half following his departure from home with Annie for England, he had become famous. The Bologna papers carried daily accounts of his activities in Rome. Just ahead of his return, a telegram arrived from Jameson-Davis announcing the formation of WTS. As the twenty-three-year-old stepped from his horse-drawn coach, Giuseppe, Annie, Alfonso, household servants, farm laborers, and neighbors smothered him with kisses, hugs, and congratulations. For the first time, Giuseppe treated Marconi with respect. He offered advice instead of instructions.

Marconi was in a jubilant mood, released for a moment from the pressures he incessantly felt. He acknowledged the embraces with hugs of his own, smiling broadly and laughing. For the last month, the quiet young man had been the center of attention. When he disembarked from the *San Martino* at Spezia for the last time, a naval band was playing at a festival full of sailors and civilians in a garden adjacent to the wharf. As Marconi walked down the gangplank, accompanied as always by a swarm of officers, the band announced his arrival with a blare of trumpets and drums. The crowd applauded him and shouted out his name. Guglielmo Marconi had returned home a hero.

But he had one piece of business to attend to. He wrote at once to Preece to explain that many reasons compelled his decision to join a private corporation. He needed capital to convert his prototype into a production model, to pay for exhibitions to prospective customers including most of the European governments, and to defend his patent against opposition from others, notably Lodge. He concluded his telegram fervently: "Hoping that you will continue in your benevolence towards me, I beg to state that all your great kindness shall never be forgotten by me in all my life. I shall do my best to keep the company on amicable terms with the British Government."(FN 5)

Preece's answer chilled Marconi. Acting under the instructions of the secretary of the GPO, Preece immediately answered Marconi by telegraph at Villa Grifone on August 6, 1897:

> I was very sorry to get your letter. You have taken a step that I fear is very inimical to your personal interests. I regret to say that I must stop all experiments and all action until I learn the conditions that are to determine

the relations between your company and the Government Departments who have encouraged and helped you so much.(FN 6)

Preece's response spurred Marconi to return to London at once, even though he had been home only a few days. In addition, the company needed to schedule its first board meeting. Marconi clearly belonged in London. Annie decided to go with him. Rather than remain with her aging husband, she preferred to be in London, looking after the domestic side of her son's life, for which he had no time.

In a very short time, Marconi's prospects and status had changed incredibly. No one could have predicted the degree of his success and recognition. It had been a rapid rise.

As soon as he arrived in London, Marconi called upon Preece in an effort to rectify the damaging breach in the relationship with the GPO. Preece responded by saying that Marconi's contract with WTS was Marconi's own personal concern. If WTS continued to be friendly, then he, Preece, would do all that he could, as he had in the past, to forward Marconi's discovery. Preece went so far as to promise to help future WTS experiments by providing military civil engineers.

On August 12, the directors met formally for the first time. WTS's three-room headquarters at 28 Mark Lane soon filled with the cigar and pipe smoke of the four older board members. Up to this moment, the directors representing the investors had been eagerly wooing the very young superstar from whose invention they hoped to profit. The initial celebratory atmosphere of the meeting, however, soon evaporated. The basic tension between shareholder and scientist quickly emerged. Marconi described the research immediately ahead. The outside members politely but pointedly inquired as to plans for sales. They expressed disappointment at the GPO's reaction and stressed that the relationship required immediate repair. Marconi reported upon his meeting with the chief engineer. The board applauded Preece's statement and reiterated that sales be pressed on all possible fronts, stimulated by well-publicized demonstrations. Efforts at publicity were well underway. The press called Marconi's youth and invention astounding. The *New York World* in a front-page headline named Marconi the "Boy Wizard."

Marconi had won the race to the patent office. But with his fame spreading, the significance of his idea became more widely recognized, stimulating more scientists and their backers, including national governments, to action. The Admiralty approved Jackson's request for money to construct new equipment. The Russian government funded Popov's research, and he sent signals three miles. Slaby solicited investments for research and talked to other German scientists about forming a consortium to build a wireless company.

WTS's effort to rebuild its relationship with the ruling forces at the GPO were met only with silence. Nor did Preece receive any further instructions from his superiors on how to deal with the company. But in September while on sick leave at home in Carnarvon, Wales, Preece learned that the GPO and the War Office were planning to collaborate at Fort Burgoyne near Dover on the English Channel in an experiment using Marconi's wireless. They hoped to signal across the English Channel. If successful, the feat would be sensational. Preece was unaware that the GPO was modifying WTS's equipment without its consent or knowledge. He also did not know that the GPO had instructed the Admiralty that Marconi was not to participate at Dover. Preece advised Marconi of the proposed demonstration and encouraged him to be there. Marconi was about to conduct tests of his own at Salisbury Plain, whose use Preece had quietly and unofficially arranged. Preece had also proposed to lend Marconi Preece's own assistant, George Kemp, and two royal engineers.

Marconi cancelled the tests at Salisbury Plain and informed the GPO that he would be at Dover. The secretary of the GPO promptly responded that Dover was being conducted under conditions of secrecy. Marconi was not welcome.

The board was outraged. In effect, the GPO was appropriating the company's property without authority and without compensation. The Irish directors ridiculed the GPO's pretext of conducting the tests for confidential military purposes. Even Marconi, who rarely permitted himself to be ruffled by adverse events, could not contain himself. With the backing of the board, he fired off a letter to Preece and the GPO:

> If, as I fear, the department does not intend continuing in the friendly bona fide relations as you and I believe it would, I shall be obliged, immediately after settling

experimentally certain little theoretical points at Salisbury
[Salisbury Plain], to proceed to Russia, Austria and other
countries which are very anxious to have extensive experiments carried out at their expense.(FN 7)

Preece hastened to smooth things over. He assured Marconi that
Dover was not the GPO's final assessment of his equipment. He implied
there would be further trials in which WTS would participate. Preece
went so far as to invite Marconi to come stay with him in his English
home at Wimbledon. He extended his offer to lend Kemp and two royal
engineers to Marconi for as long as he needed them.

WTS's fury had no effect on the GPO. It proceeded with its plans.
It ordered Preece to Dover and persuaded Jackson to be present as well.
From the outset, even with such experts, the GPO met with only frustration in its attempt to work Marconi's equipment that it had modified. It
failed to match Marconi's thirteen miles at Spezia or even Brean Down's
eight miles. The GPO's longest signal, five miles, fell far short of the
thirty-two miles needed to cross the English Channel.

While the GPO, Preece, and Jackson struggled at Dover, Marconi
rescheduled his tests at Salisbury Plain. He accepted Preece's offer of
Kemp and the royal engineers. Within WTS, the directors debated
Preece's motivation. Did he have authority to provide these people on
his own initiative, contrary to the GPO's standing instructions that no
assistance be given to the company? Or had the GPO directed Preece
to furnish knowledgeable electricians who would learn from watching Marconi's every move and then report back? Marconi needed the
engineers. He had to accept their help as WTS had not yet hired its
own. But unlike the previous Salisbury Plain demonstrations, WTS
invited no one else from the GPO or the Admiralty to witness the
trials.

The experiments started badly. For ten days, the British weather
wreaked havoc on them. As rain pelted Marconi and Kemp, the blustery
winds out of the west blew so violently the aerials could not be raised
by balloon or specially constructed kits. Finally, the wind abated. This
time no cavalry officers were at Marconi's disposal to relay news of receipt
of signals back to him at the transmitter. Instead, he traveled with the
receiver that was carried over the plain in a horse-drawn cart. One of

Preece's men operated the transmitter at Three Mile Hill and broadcast signals at prescribed intervals. When Marconi arrived at each new location, he listened in at the prearranged times. Marconi's entourage moved west beyond the boundaries of Salisbury Plain, still receiving signals. It kept moving. It rolled through little English farm towns, passing the local markets where people could not contain their curiosity and astonishment. To Marconi's delight, signals carried all the way to Bath, thirty-four miles from Three Mile Hill, more than doubling his record.

Had they originated at Dover, they would have had enough strength to cross the English Channel.

The unprecedented length made headlines in the newspapers. In Marconi's angry letter to Preece, he had told Preece that WTS had certain little theoretical points to settle at Salisbury. Settling the "little points" had resulted in an enormous leap in distance in vivid contrast to the GPO's dismal results at Fort Burgoyne. It would not have been surprising if Marconi, Jameson-Davis, and the other directors had a good, vindictive chuckle at the expense of the GPO.

The GPO, Preece, and Jackson, who were still at Dover, were not laughing. Their collective inability to operate the equipment had become embarrassingly clear. On October 6, 1897, the GPO swallowed its pride and invited Marconi to Dover to improve its results. Considerable sentiment on the board favored declining. Marconi went to Fort Burgoyne, nonetheless, in an effort to restore WTS relations with its former supporter. But when the GPO asked him to attempt the cross-Channel signal, he refused. While he deeply wanted to, he would not do so under government auspices. If and when he successfully surmounted the Channel, full credit would go to WTS, not the GPO.

The Italian navy, after reviewing the impressive results at Spezia, purchased four sets of wireless transmitters and receivers. Given Marconi's deep loyalty to Italy and the company's difficulties with the GPO, it was fitting that Italy be the first WTS customer. In another promising development, Lloyd's of London, the British company that insured maritime risks, opened discussions with WTS to determine how this new technology might benefit the insurer.

Offsetting the good news, Lodge progressed in his efforts to gain the fruits of what he considered to be his original discovery, not Marconi's. In addition to his patent applications, he opened discussions with possible partners. He proposed a league with all other potential applicants to fight Marconi and WTS.

The company's research focused on distance and maritime communication between stations on shore and ships at sea. The Spezia trials provided a model for a permanent flexible experimental platform. WTS established two transmitting stations on the Solent, a large body of water between the southern coast of England and the Isle of Wight, relatively close to London headquarters. The Isle of Wight afforded some protection from ocean weather and also permitted easy access to the sea for long-range testing.

In November, at the tip of the island's long, western finger, on top of a one-hundred-foot-high promontory, Kemp and Marconi positioned a transmitter at the Needles Hotel. The cliff was appropriately called the Needles because the wind had sculpted its soft, chalky rock into tall, thin formations with sharply pointed tops.

Kemp had joined the company as Marconi's assistant and one of its first employees.

Fourteen miles across the Solent to the west at the Haven Hotel, which stood on a sandy spit forming the north side of the entrance to the harbor at Poole, the men established a second transmitter.

The Haven Hotel became WTS's principal research headquarters. WTS rented rooms for Marconi, Kemp, and four electrical experts constituting the research staff. In January 1898, a 120-foot-high mast was raised. It flew an aerial that looked like a fisherman's net, only it was composed of wire. The locals shook their heads in disbelief as they gazed upwards at the strange apparatus.

Once the Needles transmitter became operational, the company hired a tugboat based at Poole to be the receiving station. To maximize the height of the antenna, Marconi extended the tug's mast to a towering sixty feet above the deck. Highly mobile, the vessel constituted a quick method to change the receiver location. It was far more efficient than a horse dragging a cart across the countryside.

For the first time, Marconi had his own research facilities. He could roam about in all types of weather and surface conditions. He could readily vary position and distance. He did away with unreliable and time-consuming balloons and kites.

The inventor relentlessly tested equipment. He ordered the tug out in all kinds of conditions. He tinkered and combined different elements in various arrangements in the transmitter, receiver, and antennae. In the teeth of a gale, bouncing about in high chop, the punishing circumstances suggested by Jackson for naval testing, signals came in free of static and with great sharpness. In Marconi's words:

> The best results we have obtained were on the small tugboat…in very tempestuous weather in the month of November around the Isle of Wight where we had at times about two feet of water in the cabin, and ourselves and all the instruments were practically drenched with sea water. Many of the sailors and engineers of the tug seemed very anxious about their personal safety on that particular occasion. Although it seemed to have a very great influence on the crew it had no bad influence on the instruments which continued to perform their duty and to remain in correspondence with the Island which was eighteen miles away.(FN 8)

It is a picture of Marconi in his element, out in the turbulence, tossing about in some danger, experimenting, fiddling, making progress, suffering setbacks, progressing again, and forever testing and advancing his dream.

The Solent arrangements soon revealed a new and serious problem. Previously, Marconi communicated between one transmitter and one receiver. With transmitters at Needles and Haven, he began to have waves sent simultaneously from each location to the one receiver in the tug. He had not done this before.

The result was an undecipherable jumble. Two signals arriving at the same moment apparently interfered with each other. Neither signal could be identified in the form in which it was sent. Like the Spezia discovery that islands sometimes blocked messages between San Bartolomeo and the *San Martino*, interference became another disturbance. Ironically and irritatingly, just as reception attained new levels of clarity, Marconi stumbled into an unprecedented mess.

Marconi

Despite this adversity, the long workdays, and often atrocious weather, life at Haven had idyllic moments. The seaside resort had been designed for those who sought peace and quiet. The white plaster and brown wood trim building sat at the end of a sandy peninsula. It had its own beach and picturesque views on three sides. To the east lay the open Solent and the Isle of Wight. A scant fifty yards south at the end of the spit, fishing boats, steamships, and sailboats streamed in and out of the harbor entrance. To the west, boat traffic filled the enormous protected body of water. In the distance, Poole's docks presented a faraway backdrop, a jumble of tall masts, steam stacks, and rising smoke. The hotel's large parlor had a huge fireplace. There was a cozy dining room for holiday guests.

WTS normally had eight or nine of its people, including relatives, in residence. Besides Marconi and Kemp, there was the research group headed by Dr. J. Erskine Murray, Marconi's principal experimental assistant. Murray had been an assistant professor of physics at Heriott-Watt College. Marconi had hired Dr. Murray after being impressed by his efforts on several special projects he undertook for WTS. Three skilled electrical technicians worked under Murray—the two Cave brothers and P. J. W. Paget. Dr. Murray had been joined by his wife. Annie moved down from London to look after Marconi. Alfonso, Marconi's brother, frequently visited. Everyone lived and labored together. In the evening, they all ate at a long, wooden table. Madame Poulaine, wife of the hotel proprietor and an excellent cook, served roast chicken, a Marconi favorite. Her husband had a well-stocked wine cellar. Some evenings, before the roaring fire, Dr. Murray played his cello. Alfonso accompanied on the violin and Marconi on the piano. Of course, Annie was thrilled to sing. What a shame that Giuseppe, who had fallen for Annie listening to her beautiful trained voice, was not there.

The dedicated group worked hard at what they loved. They quietly enjoyed a sense of scientific adventure and the excitement their successes generated in the public press. Marconi, younger than any of his men, clearly led. After three years of lone research and experimentation, he nonetheless slipped quietly and naturally into the role of a hands-on manager. He not only directed his staff, but he pitched in enthusiastically to make a piece of equipment if needed or devise a solution to a problem. He had especially adept hands. He could deftly wind a core or raise a kite when others failed. He reveled in what he did. A hard worker, he also dared to go mentally and physically where others might have flinched. Kemp later said, "I remember him having to make three attempts to get out past the Needles in a gale before he succeeded. He does not care for storm or rain but keeps pegging away in the most persistent manner."(FN 9) The persistence and patience Marconi exhibited, and his imperturbability in adversity, a constant companion in experimental research, perhaps contributed as importantly to his success as his scientific creativity.

Signaling across the English Channel remained very much on Marconi's mind. The thirty-two-mile distance from the Needles Hotel due south to Cherbourg in Normandy, the closest land on the continent to Needles, tempted him after the thirty-four-mile signal to Bath.

It wasn't the distance that so intrigued Marconi. It would not be a record. Transmitting over the English Channel would be highly symbolic. The Channel for millennia had been a barrier between Britain and Europe. Like water everywhere, it could be difficult to cross. It was a protector, an inhibitor. Suddenly, by no visible means, it could be spanned in a flash of a split second. It would be such a clear demonstration of a whole new order of possibilities, of things to come. It would be wildly exciting to the imaginative, to the foreseers, to those looking for a story.

The English Channel had another attraction. Submarine cables traversed the width of its bottom, transporting telegraph messages between Great Britain and the continent. Perhaps wireless could carry these electrical impulses of Morse code across the water as easily as the expensive, heavy duty, underwater cables.

Marconi wrote to Jackson. He had been assigned to Paris to assist the French in building a torpedo. Marconi asked the officer to exert British influence to persuade the French to permit the transmission. Jackson was not pleased with recent events. He had been burned at Fort Burgoyne. Perhaps in reaction to that embarrassment, the Admiralty had transferred responsibility for electronic transmissions from the Torpedo School that Jackson had headed to the Signaling Committee. One admiral, who agreed with Jackson that this made no sense, commented that the committee constituted an "estimable body who knew the color of every flag and all about the Morse code, but to whom electricity was a sealed science."(FN 10) For the first time since his outspoken candor at the War Conference, Jackson refused to help Marconi.

Marconi

Undeterred, Marconi proceeded on his own. France turned out to be surprisingly agreeable. But it wanted the continental site to be at Calais, the country's principal port for English crossings, not Cherbourg. At Marconi's range of thirty-four miles, he could reach Calais from Dover, but not from Needles. WTS had no shore station at Dover. Calais was over one hundred miles from Needles. To find and equip a site at Dover, just for this exhibition, would be a distraction and expensive. WTS would certainly not ask the GPO for permission to use Fort Burgoyne at Dover.

In May 1898, the Admiralty took an important step towards adopting the company's wireless. It sent a three-man delegation, the secretary of the Signaling Committee, the commander-in-chief at the Portsmouth naval base, and a technical expert, to observe the Haven Hotel operation. The group reported favorably. Despite the admiral's low opinion of the Signaling Committee, its technical expert noted a possibly crippling deficiency. He observed the same problem Marconi had identified—interference. If the navy equipped two or more ships in a fleet with transmitters, they might cancel themselves out. This weakness, if not solved, severely limited wireless's usefulness for the navy. Marconi said he was working on it. A solution would be found. He had no other answer.

The Admiralty accepted Marconi's response. It continued to be a serious prospective customer. GPO efforts, however, remained stalled. Conversation with Lloyd's progressed significantly. The maritime insurance company proposed a project that could benefit its operations. WTS agreed to establish a transmitter in the lighthouse on Rathlin Island. The island stood among the dangerous, fog-bound western approaches to the Irish coast near Ballycastle. Once past Rathlin, a ship bound eastward for an English port faced few hazards. For insurance purposes, it could be assumed safely home. If Lloyd's insured the value of the boat and its contents, as long as the vessel was at risk, Lloyd's had to put aside some of its moneys so it could be in a position to pay any losses the ship might suffer. The lighthouse, witnessing a vessel's passage through the approaches, could send that information through the air to a shore telegraph station. The station could telegraph the message to Lloyd's in London. Lloyd's could then release the moneys and put it to work insuring other boats days before it otherwise could have. The insurer became WTS's first commercial customer. If Rathlin Island succeeded, the concept could be applied in many places and would be a good source of business.

With two of its major entities, the Royal Navy and the GPO, contemplating contracts for a new technology, the British Parliament requested an exhibition. The directors were delighted at the interest of the elected leaders of the world's mightiest power, who also exercised the ultimate authority over WTS's principal business prospects. To allow members of the House of Commons and the House of Lords to readily witness the demonstration, WTS placed a transmitter in Westminster. Marconi signaled across the Thames to St. Thomas's Hospital. A reporter in attendance noticed that Marconi and his WTS company engineers carried the transmitter with them to Westminster and set it up in only an hour. The reporter thought they could have as easily brought it to a sports event. In a newspaper column the next day, he wrote that wireless could cover competitions at far-away sites and would be first-rate for yacht races at sea. This observation set off a chain reaction. It eventually led Marconi to Queen Victoria and the royal family and to America.

Upon reading the article, editors of the *Dublin Daily Express* liked the writer's idea. It could be used to create enormous publicity for the paper. At the turn of the century, racing regattas were extraordinarily popular. Big yachts, which moved from port to port and raced each week during the summer, were household names. The editor-in-chief asked WTS to provide a running account of the upcoming Kingstown Regatta, the Irish race week off Dublin. The board consented immediately. A tug, the *Flying Huntress*, was hired for the transmitter. Marconi had a field day out on the Irish Sea with the dueling yachts. He flashed seven hundred messages at distances of ten to twenty-five miles to the receiver in Dublin Harbor. The harbormaster relayed the items by telephone to the *Express*. It published hourly special one-page editions and posted them in its windows. Crowds gathered outside to read the latest on what was going on. The *Express* scooped its rivals. They had to wait for each race to end and their reporters to come ashore before they could print their stories. The publicity for the *Express* and particularly for the company was huge.

Queen Victoria, summering at Osborne House on the eastern shore of the Isle of Wight near Cowes, read the race coverage. She was seventy-nine years old. The prior year the "girl-queen" had celebrated her Diamond

Marconi

Jubilee, the sixtieth year since at age nineteen she had ascended the throne. She had grown stout and was nearly blind. The strength of Britain's parliamentary system and her own aging had diminished her governmental role substantially, but her mind remained active, and she did her best to keep a grip on things. She had a problem. Her fifty-seven-year-old son, Edward, the Prince of Wales, the heir to the monarchy, who was waiting impatiently for his opportunity to be king, had fallen down the grand staircase attending a ball at the Rothschild Palace in Paris. He had severely wrenched his knee and was recuperating on the royal yacht, HMS *Osborne*. The prince had carefully anchored HMS *Osborne* out of sight and semaphore range of his mother. Edward led a lively social life and liked to entertain aboard the HMS *Osborne*, especially during the Cowes Regatta. The most famous of the annual regattas, it was to start the following week. The prince did not wish to be chaperoned by his mother. But the queen wanted to remain in communication with her son. She asked Marconi to establish wireless between Osborne House and HMS *Osborne*.

Marconi accepted with true pleasure. The installation for the queen excited everyone in the company. Marconi professed to be interested because it offered him an opportunity to study the influence of hills on transmission. The East Cowes hills lay between Osborne House and Edward's vessel. The problems presented by high land masses had bothered him since the islands off Spezia blocked his signals.

Concentrating on finding the best location for the aerial, he strode about the grounds of Osborne House and into the queen's private garden. A gardener stopped him and ordered him to go back and around. The queen, who liked her privacy, was out for a stroll. Marconi did not care to be interrupted or to go back and around. Instead, he returned to his hotel. The autocratic queen, not amused by the incident, abruptly directed that Marconi be discharged and another electrician be obtained. "Alas, Your Majesty," she was told, "England has no Marconi."(FN 11) Quickly persuaded that this was true, she lured Marconi back. She sent a carriage to his hotel with an invitation to tea once his work at Osborne House was done.

HMS *Osborne* lay two miles offshore from Osborne House. Marconi took no chances. He delivered equipment capable of transmitting ten times the distance. The job complete, Marconi and the queen enjoyed a congenial tea. The laconic Marconi did not have to worry about not having enough to say. The queen was an incessant talker and did not like to be interrupted. She congratulated him and wished him well.

With the transmitter in operation, Marconi boarded the opulent royal yacht, a magnificent black-hulled steamship with gold trim and raked smokestacks and masts. A concealed side-wheel propelled the sleek, one-hundred-foot vessel. Marconi spent considerable time there installing the receiver. Not all those hours, however, were consumed in labor. The ever-social Prince Edward frequently invited him to join the royal party. Edward had overcome his annoyance that his demanding mother now could be in constant touch. In fact, the queen made much use of the instruments. Osborne House and the HMS *Osborne* exchanged over 150 messages during a sixteen-day period. The prince marveled that signals could be sent while underway and through rain and fog. The wireless and Marconi so pleased the prince that he asked them both to stay for race week.

Throughout the festivities, Marconi was introduced to the guests, a steady stream of dukes, duchesses, and cabinet ministers. The audiences Marconi had with King Umberto and Queen Margherita and the tea with Queen Victoria were heady moments. Race week on the royal yacht was an eye-opener. Marconi had had an isolated childhood. Leghorn had been his only social period and time spent with girls. Since his inspiration at Biellese four years earlier, he'd had no social life in Italy or England other than an occasional evening on the piano while Annie sang or relaxing with his men over the evening meal at the Haven Hotel. Suddenly, he became a center of attention. He was questioned by worldly men of importance. Women, beautiful women of all ages, dressed in the latest fashion, elaborately made up and perfumed, teased him and flattered him and made much of his handsome, dark looks and youth. It was his first taste of a way of life that Marconi would find most appealing.

Marconi was maturing rapidly. WTS passed its first anniversary. Unnoticed, because it happened so naturally, Marconi had without difficulty assumed a broader role. He had been a solo scientist/inventor, a lone man much like Thomas Edison, struggling by himself with unlimited energy, vision, and drive, a pragmatist groping his way by trial and error. Then, in his first year in England, he coped effectively with far wiser, more experienced men accustomed to a sophisticated, fast-paced, competitive world—Jameson-Davis, Preece, and Jackson. With the organization of the company, Marconi suddenly had on his hands a board

Marconi

of businessmen who had made their mark in the world's financial capital. Marconi had absolutely no background comparable to the directors who specialized in money matters. Yet, without hesitation, he asserted his leadership. His relationship with Jameson-Davis flourished. Certainly there were disagreements and arguments, but despite Preece's analysis and Marconi's suspicions of his backers' intentions, no one after the incorporation looked down upon him as naïve or "easily dominated." Not only did his board and his managing director deal with him as a peer, but for the first time in his life Marconi had men working for him. Like the directors, these men not only accepted him, but they also respected him for his energy, dedication, and ability. Marconi's maturation was critical. The challenges ahead, the triumphs and the disasters, were to be incredibly greater than what he had already experienced.

Marconi's lifestyle had not changed after receiving the fifteen thousand pounds from the incorporation of WTS. Wireless still consumed him. He had no time to spend the money, live lavishly, or even take a vacation. The company provided room and board at the Haven Hotel and transportation between London and Poole. He had only his quarters and living expenses in London to pay for. Annie looked after his personal arrangements.

Despite Marconi's successes at the Irish regatta and Cowes, excellent publicity, and numerous demonstrations before potential customers, the directors worried. Revenues had been received only from the Italian navy, Lloyd's, the *Dublin Daily Express*, and Queen Victoria. No other negotiations for services or sales had materialized into contracts. WTS's original twenty-five thousand pounds in working capital and research funds was dwindling.

The initial wireless market differed from the first markets for telegraph and telephone. WTS, once organized, had not been swept up in a rapidly accelerating demand for its product. The advantage of telegraph over semaphores and horseback messengers had been phenomenal. Wireless did not perform a new service. It did what telegraph did where telegraph did not do it. Telephone had also provided a markedly different and desirable service. Prospective WTS customers had very specialized needs. They were large institutions—shipping companies, navies, postal departments, and insurance companies. The equipment was elaborate and expensive and required training to operate. It was going to be a long, hard sell.

CHAPTER 5

Chalet D'Artois and the English Channel

In the fall of 1898, WTS faced a growing crisis. No new sales had materialized. The company's intensive research was preoccupying its people and steadily consuming its funds. Within a half year, the company could be out of cash.

Jameson-Davis pulled his younger cousin aside. Marconi should reorder his priorities. Leave research for the moment and focus on selling. If the company did not take in more revenue, it would be forced to raise capital by selling shares. Fortunately, raising capital appeared to be easier and less time consuming than winning a contract from a government bureaucracy. Because of the general excitement over wireless and the high expectations for WTS, Jameson-Davis knew investors eager to own a piece of the company. They were sufficiently impressed by its prospects to overlook the risks clouding its future. However, he warned, if more stock were sold, Marconi would hold a smaller portion of the outstanding shares. If his percentage fell below 50 percent, his control of WTS could be jeopardized.

To Jameson-Davis, the customer outlook was promising, just slow to develop. Rathlin Island had delivered exactly what Lloyd's requested. In its first month of operation, the lighthouse spotted and reported to Lloyd's the safe passage of sixteen vessels not visible through the fog from the shore. As a result, Lloyd's could release money committed to insuring those vessels and use it for other purposes. The Italian navy, reportedly satisfied with its sets, might buy more. The GPO's failure at Fort Burgoyne had weakened the GPO's assertion that the GPO and the Royal

Marconi

Navy could produce wireless without WTS. Pressure mounted on the Admiralty. It could not be pleased that Italy had already ordered company equipment. The Dublin race coverage had been well received and should lead to future business. The benefit to shippers and passengers of ships staying in touch with shore was gaining credence. Marconi need not dilute his control of WTS. From Jameson-Davis's perspective, Marconi could defer research temporarily and concentrate on these opportunities.

Marconi had no question as to what to do. WTS's long-term health in relation to Jameson-Davis's markets depended upon distance, distance, distance—free of interference. Deferral of research was dangerous. Too many scientists and potential competitors strove to catch up to WTS. Someone of whom Marconi might not even be aware could suddenly achieve a breakthrough, a better way to signal, a critical, patentable concept embodied in new materials or configurations. At the moment, the company led the field. Marconi was determined to maintain that position and capture markets with technical superiority. He understood the cash need. To his way of thinking, however, he preferred owning a lesser percentage of a WTS that had resources for heavy research to possessing more of a WTS with limited capacity.

The board reluctantly backed his decision. Issuing more stock diluted all shareholders. The directors wanted revenue, but they honored their commitment to follow Marconi's leadership. Jameson-Davis arranged for the stock sale at more than twice the price per share paid by the original subscribers. Marconi's percentage of outstanding stock was reduced to just above half.

The board now had sufficient funds for a year. Anticipating WTS would soon have equipment orders, the directors leased a warehouse in Chelmsford, Essex, to convert into a manufacturing facility. Chelmsford, thirty-five miles northeast of London and the Port of London, was accessible to both but far enough away to have relatively cheap rents and labor rates.

In addition to the customer types on Jameson-Davis's list, Marconi eyed another category. He believed it could be very lucrative, although it too required distance and freedom from interference. Enormous demand existed for sending messages across international bodies of water between different countries. Over the past fifty years, submarine cable corporations had laid extensive underwater connections between land-based telegraph systems. Cable operated on the same scientific principles as telegraph. The expense of submerging and maintaining waterproof line was far greater. Wireless might penetrate this business. Airborne transmission should have significant cost advantages. A WTS engineer spelled it out:

> Judge for yourself. Every mile of deep-sea cable costs about $750; every mile of land end (land connection) is about $1,000. All that we save, also the great expense of keeping a cable steamer constantly in commission making repairs and laying new lengths. All we need is a couple of masts and a little wire. The wear and tear is practically nothing. The cost of running, simply for home batteries and operators' keep.(FN 1)

The water barrier with the greatest cable traffic was the English Channel. Marconi believed he could carry it from Dover. He needed to prove it, but he felt constrained. The French government's general permission to proceed near Calais did not authorize an exact site. To receive money from the board to construct a new station near Dover, Marconi must have a purpose that satisfied the directors' demand that he spend time on immediate sales prospects. The board would find it too expensive to build, equip, and man sites in France and England just to exhibit a potential capacity to compete with cable across the Channel or to generate publicity.

Jameson-Davis spearheaded WTS's effort to press the GPO to purchase sets to connect offshore lighthouses and lightships to the mainland. Rathlin Island was an excellent selling tool to illustrate what the company could do. As the company sought additional persuasive arguments, it stumbled across an intriguing fact. The GPO did not operate the lighthouses and lightships. Trinity House Corporation, an independent government authority, ran the English Light Service. It contracted with the GPO for submarine cable. Trinity House could just as readily deal with WTS. The GPO's consent should not be necessary, just as it had not been for Lloyd's for Rathlin Island.

Trinity House accepted WTS's offer to exhibit its ability to signal between a lightship and a shore station. For the offshore site, the

Marconi

East Goodwin lightship, twelve miles out in the English Channel, was picked. It was anchored at the dangerous Goodwin Sands entrance to the Straits of Dover. For the mainland station, WTS selected the South Foreland Lighthouse near Dover. It was a tantalizing thirty-two miles from Calais.

The board was pleased. Trinity House agreed to pay expenses. For no cost, the directors had a chance to land a substantial customer and bypass the GPO. Lloyd's would also be impressed and might collaborate with Trinity House. This was marketing.

Marconi must have been grinning to himself. Just as he conservatively overbuilt Queen Victoria's transmitter to assure contacting the Prince of Wales's yacht, he would put more than enough power into South Foreland to assure that its signals would span the Channel.

There was a hitch. The UK Treasury had to preapprove all Trinity House expenditures. The GPO immediately asserted itself. Preece could not help. He had reached retirement age. He was negotiating additional benefits for himself. He was not going to antagonize anyone inside the GPO. The agency asked its lawyers to advise that its monopoly would be infringed by South Foreland. It demanded assurance from WTS, which was given, that messages received by South Foreland for inland transmission would be transferred to the GPO for forwarding on its telegraph system. The GPO solicited objections from the Admiralty and the War Office and alerted the Board of Trade. The board governed trade conditions between Great Britain and other countries, including rules for the landing of goods from abroad on British shores.

Jameson-Davis patiently worked his way through the bureaucratic morass. The GPO was rebuffed on every front. Its solicitors opined that its monopoly would not be violated. Treasury only asked whether Preece's parallel wire system could compete cost-wise with Marconi. The GPO had to answer that it could not. The Admiralty and the War Office did not rally to the GPO's side. The Board of Trade merely imposed non-burdensome restrictions on how WTS might use the foreshore on which South Foreland stood for receiving and sending messages.

In late November 1898, Treasury approved. No response had come from Paris as to what location near Calais might be used. Marconi had South Foreland prepared by Christmas.

On December 19, Marconi sent Kemp out by lifeboat to join the crew manning the East Goodwin lightship. He carried his own food, enough for one week. He noted in his dairy that while he installed the apparatus, the wind came up. It tossed the ship about. For over an hour, it was close to unbearable.

On Christmas Eve, Marconi at South Foreland and Kemp on the lightship established communication.

On Christmas Day, the wind rose to gale force. The sea poured over the bouncing, tethered ship. Kemp managed to exchange Christmas greetings with the mainland. He reported it was as wet between decks as on the deck, but he could still raise a spark. By the twenty-eighth, with no relief from the wind, Kemp had had little sleep. He felt ill, cold, wet, and miserable. On the twenty-ninth, he begged for mercy. Nothing was done. The lightship crew, accustomed to rough weather, had not asked for help. At least when Kemp's week's supply of food ran out, the crew volunteered to share theirs. Some of those in the warmth and safety of South Foreland joked at the ex-sailor's plight. In the lightship captain's view, Kemp was not "as good a sailor as the instruments have proved to be."(FN 2) Kemp was finally taken off on January 9.

In January 1899, the Kingstown Regatta paid off. The *New York Herald*'s publisher, James Gordon Bennett, had had a reporter, Milton V. Snyder, cover the regatta. Cleveland Moffet in Europe for the *Herald* had already been following Marconi's progress. At the urging of Snyder and Moffet, Bennett invited Marconi to New York to provide instantaneous coverage for the America's Cup, the world's greatest yacht race. The opportunity interested Marconi, but it posed a dilemma. To him, the English Channel experiment was more important. To arrive in America in time to prepare for the October start would require departing England in September, allowing for the two-week transatlantic passage by steamer. But Paris had still not granted permission to build out a French site. He did not know how much time might be needed to succeed in sending a signal across the Channel.

American business possibilities excited Jameson-Davis. While aware of wireless research activities in the United States, he knew of no working system comparable to Marconi's. He felt strongly that WTS should establish itself there before others occupied the field. The two men had worked

Marconi

closely together since Marconi's arrival in England two years earlier. This marked their first serious disagreement. They argued with each other, firmly but with respect, first by telegraph and then face-to-face in London when Marconi returned to headquarters from Dover. Marconi insisted on completing the Channel project, whose benefits could be enormous. He also generally favored British and continental projects as closer at hand than those across the ocean. Jameson-Davis, however, pointed out that there could be immediate business prospects in New York and that the American invitation had firm dates. The French reply remained uncertain. Marconi could do the Channel after America, if necessary. Marconi refused. Jameson-Davis deferred for the time being, hoping Paris would answer soon. He asked Bennett to wait as long as he could for the company's response.

As Marconi waited impatiently for the French government, the Admiralty moved forward on its own deliberate course. Following the Signal Committee's visit to the Solent the prior May, the naval hierarchy had authorized Jackson's successor at the Torpedo School, Captain Hamilton, to continue rigorous sea trials of Jackson's equipment. Hamilton improved its operation under sea conditions but not its distance. Despite Jackson's earlier assurances, concern again arose over whether electrical impulses from wireless might trigger explosives aboard battleships or cause heart attacks. This time, the Admiralty sought the expert outside advice of England's best-known electrical and physical scientist, Lord Kelvin. Kelvin no longer preferred boys on ponies over wireless to deliver his messages. In fact, he had helped publicize WTS by paying Marconi to send a wireless message for him from Needles. Without hesitation, Lord Kelvin reaffirmed Jackson—wireless would not inadvertently detonate explosives or cause heart attacks. Preece when asked delivered a similar answer. One last question remained. The Admiralty ordered Jackson and Hamilton to advise whether Jackson's invention being prior in time to Marconi's constituted grounds to invalidate Marconi's patent. It was a remarkable, self-interested pair to put the question to. To the credit of both, they each promptly concluded that Marconi's discoveries preceded Jackson's. They attributed the impression popular among naval officers that Jackson had experimented first to Marconi's reticence to speak about the many matters covered in his patent until it was granted.

With the safety and patent questions settled, and given the navy's continuing failure to build a set equal to Marconi's, the Admiralty had five potential wireless systems to choose among. Jackson's and Marconi's systems were the most developed. Lodge had built a system in collaboration with Alexander Muirhead. Lodge claimed Muirhead conceived telegraphic application of Hertzian waves two years before Preece and Marconi gave their famous black box demonstration in 1896. By merging his work with Muirhead, Lodge hoped to strengthen his own claim of priority of innovation ahead of Marconi. There were also German efforts, one by Slaby and one by Professor Karl Braun, director of the physics department at the University of Strasbourg. These two carried unfavorable nationalistic overtones. The English military had begun to suspect Germany's geopolitical intentions. None of the last three had been tried in practice.

In concluding his report on whether Jackson's inventions preceded Marconi's, Hamilton recommended that trials be held as early as possible to determine the value of WTS's equipment under actual service conditions:

> I would strongly urge that the system is capable of great use to HM Navy, principally for fog signaling and for communicating with scouts, as, if it comes up to anything like the promise of the experiments, it would immensely lengthen the distance to which a line of scouts could be thrown out at night or in thick weather.(FN 3)

The Signaling Committee concurred. The Admiralty asked the company to present its terms for equipping two ships of the fleet. The directors hoped the request marked a breakthrough with the British government, representing potentially the first order from one of its units. The bright spot on the sales front for a moment helped relieve the tension Jameson-Davis and Marconi each felt for different reasons while waiting for a French answer.

On March 2, 1899, Marconi was preparing to speak before the Institute of Electrical Engineers. For the first time, he had been asked to address an English scientific society. In addition to being personally honored, he felt WTS would benefit from the publicity. The institute requested that he describe his own work and invited the public. Advance interest was enormous. Jameson-Davis picked Marconi up to accompany him to the lecture. He had good news. The French government had just telegraphed its full approval. WTS could select any site between Boulogne and Calais. The two men hugged each other in congratulations and in relief. Marconi, however, remained adamant about the American trip. He would go to New York, but only if he finished the Channel work in time. Nevertheless, the two men went off in high spirits.

They arrived at the hall well before the scheduled time. A long queue had already formed outside the entrance. The institute turned so many people away that its chairman announced that Marconi had agreed to give a second address the following week. The institute booked a much larger auditorium for the repeat performance, but it too was oversubscribed. An amphitheater had to be taken. Even then, not everyone gained admission to the second talk.

Marconi turned out to be a natural public speaker. He spoke calmly, clearly, and spontaneously. He needed no notes, the topic being the effort he had been enveloped in for the past five years.

In the first talk on March 2, Marconi credited his assistants for any success he had met with in the practical application of wireless telegraphy. He acknowledged utilizing Righi's oscillator in the transmitter and described as a principal part of his receiver the coherer, also known as the radio conductor, which had been discovered by Professor Calzeechi of Fermo, Italy, and improved by Professor Branly from Paris and others, and in a magnanimous gesture, he even acknowledged Professor Lodge.

In closing, Marconi revealed that he had that day been granted permission by the government in Paris to build a wireless station on French soil. Before month's end, he would attempt to exchange messages across the English Channel.

The dramatic announcement brought the overflow audience to its feet, and the speech ended in a standing ovation. The next day on the London and New York stock exchanges, a flurry of activity dropped the prices of the submarine cable companies as investors reacted to the possibility that wireless might become a competitor.

For the French site, Marconi chose the little coastal town of Wimereux. It lay three miles north of Boulogne, to which Annie had run away from Daphne Castle thirty-five years earlier to marry Giuseppe. On a point jutting out into the English Channel towards Dover, WTS took over the Chalet D'Artois, a small house on the shore. It was a *maison de fleurs*. Wild rosebushes, still dormant in the cold spring, covered the tiny bit of land between the chalet and beach. Clipped rose plants awaited the summer sun in the minute back garden. In the living room, where the equipment had been set up, floral designs decorated the wallpaper and carpet. On March 20, two WTS assistants left London for France, their launch loaded with material for a mast and aerial and boxes full of signaling tools and apparatus. Marconi followed two days later.

On March 27, the day on which WTS and Paris had agreed to attempt the first cross-Channel communication, the wind blew cold and raw. The rickety, hastily constructed mast swayed uneasily in the unpredictable, rain-filled gusts. Undeterred and eager to keep the schedule, Marconi ascended the slippery pole. At midday, halfway up the two-hundred-foot pine, putting his final, delicate touches on the aerial, he looked down in surprise at the early arrival of the French government commission. The delegation swelled with important dignitaries, representing the army, navy, and telegraph services. They in turned reacted with concern upon being advised that the man in overalls perilously high up on the unbelievably tall lumber, stringing wires together, was the Monsieur Marconi. When he finally descended to earth and came over to greet them, he surprised them again, this time by his youthful appearance.

Nonetheless, at five that afternoon in the chalet, the French jammed tightly around Marconi in the overcrowded floral drawing room. Marconi sat at a very large table covered by an overly abundant, flowered cloth that fell to the floor. To the untrained eye, the cluttered table, crowded with equipment, some pieces tenuously wired to others, looked in disarray. If a Frenchman asked the purpose of a large black cylinder, its diameter in excess of two feet, an Englishman politely described it as an induction coil that supplied high-voltage power to the transmitter. Nearby two horizontal rods pointed at each other, their metal ends just centimeters apart. When Marconi depressed a wooden lever attached to one of the pointers, a spark leapt and crackled across the gap between the rods. Next to one of the rods a large, black box concealed the innards of the receiver. A spool mounted on its top fed tape into another instrument the British scientists called a Morse inker.

Marconi

Marconi called for silence. A hush fell over the room. Then Marconi struck the lever not once but repeatedly. Bright flashes and sharp crackles from the spark suddenly filled the room. Marconi completed stabbing out a message. He signed off with the Morse symbol for V. To Marconi and his men, it stood for "Victory."

The French did not have to endure a suspenseful wait for a response. The moment Marconi finished his "VVV," the receiver began to click and the tape recorded a message from South Foreland, thirty-two miles across the English Channel: V [the call letter], M [your message perfect].

It happened so quickly and so effortlessly that for a long moment no one moved. The immediate reply stunned everyone, even Marconi and the WTS engineers. They had all expected anxious hours, days of worried adjustments. But it had been done.

In minutes, the Channel had been crossed twice, once each way.

The room erupted in applause and congratulations. Even Marconi relaxed and exchanged hugs, smiling broadly in the spontaneous celebration. Over the next hours, English and French on either side of the Channel transmitted commemorative and historic messages. Marconi paid respect to his French hosts. Then he tapped out a special message: "Marconi sends M. Branly his respectful compliments across the Channel—this fine achievement being partly due to the remarkable researches of M. Branly."(FN 4) Branly, the Frenchman whom Marconi had acknowledged in his speech at the beginning of the month, had developed one of the earliest coherers for receiving wireless messages. As reported by a guest:

> And there it was, short and commonplace enough, yet vastly important, since it was the first wireless message sent from England to the Continent...And so, without more ado, the thing was done. The Frenchmen might stare and chatter as they pleased, here was something come to the world to stay. A pronounced success surely, and everybody said so as messages went back and forth, scores of messages, during the following hours and days, and all correct.(FN 5)

It seemed so simple; it seemed so easy. Yet it was incomprehensible, invisible, unfelt, not heard. Telegraph and cable had a line leading out of the transmitter and into the receiver. A witness could see the beginning piece of the physical connection between the two instruments and comprehend that an electrical signal ran the course of the wire from one to the other. They were, in fact, connected.

Here, with wireless, two pieces of apparatus sat miles apart, neither attached to anything. Yet they had contacted each other across a formidable body of water. In a flash of a second, unobservable in any way by the human senses, they had exchanged an intelligible message.

Marconi was exactly right. The success filled front-page headlines around the world. The cross-Channel communication caught the public's imagination. The Channel had always protected England and the Continent from each other. Now the barrier could be surmounted instantaneously without ship or cable. The media, fascinated by what had happened, fed on the idea and fed the idea.

The excitement increased a fortnight later when the news broke that the East Goodwin lightship crew had been saved by wireless. Visitors flooded South Foreland and Wimereux. People flocked to the Chalet D'Artois to visit Marconi: journalists such as Moffett and Robert McClure, publisher of *McClure's Magazine*; businessmen and representatives from the Board of Trade; government officials including J. Hookey, who had succeeded Preece on his retirement, and Trinity House board members; scientific colleagues and friends like Major Baden-Powell, one of the royal engineers who had been on loan at Salisbury Plains; politicians and delegations from Australia, Brazil, and China. Among the most interesting to Marconi, high-ranking French naval representatives came in great numbers. They advised Marconi of their interest in his testing WTS equipment aboard one of their vessels.

Women had a certain interest in the accomplishment, as well. Agnes Baden-Powell, daughter of the major, wrote Marconi a letter from Bournemouth near Poole and the Haven Hotel:

> Will you allow me to congratulate you warmly on the grand success you have achieved in actually bridging the Channel? It is a splendid triumph notwithstanding the presence of the group of French skeptics. My mother and I will be here for a fortnight and we hope very much that you will allow us the pleasure of seeing you if you

should come to Bournemouth when we can tell you how much we appreciate what you have accomplished for the progress of science as well as for the comfort of humanity. We are looking forward eagerly to making the acquaintance of the coherer in person and only await your arrival to start on our pilgrimage towards Poole. When might that delightful excursion take place?(FN 6)

Earlier a *Punch* cartoon had depicted the demise of landlines and submarine cables. Now a number of people shared Jameson-Davis's and Marconi's conclusion that wireless could compete with cable. After March 27, the stock of cable companies fell for weeks. Prices did not stabilize until the market rationalized that wireless would supplement, not replace, submarine cable.

Marconi, only a month away from his twenty-fifth birthday, became an international celebrity, a superstar. In 1899, there were no movie stars. There were no professional athletes. There was no radio or TV, only newspapers and magazines. Marconi and his wireless accomplishments became front-page news and the subject of feature articles and cartoons. Marconi found himself among a small, select group of kings and prime ministers, generals and industrial giants, artists and scientists with world renown.

Most remarkably, none of this seemed to affect Marconi. Totally absorbed with increasing the distance of wireless, his growing celebrity status did not seduce him. He pushed himself harder than he pushed his men. He was so focused on his invention's shortcomings that he did not stop to enjoy the fruits of the growth of his inspiration. He was too conscious of how far he had to go.

Following the cross-Channel signals, WTS delivered its terms to the British navy for equipping two ships. The company's success increased its confidence and its price. It advised the navy that WTS would charge an amount for each piece of equipment plus an annual royalty for the use of its patents. The license was a hundred pounds per ship per year. If the navy equipped every ship, the yearly fee would be ten thousand pounds, the same sum Preece two years earlier had proposed the GPO pay for exclusive rights to the entire patent. The proposal far exceeded what the Admiralty had anticipated. Angered by what he considered an outrageous demand, the director of naval ordinance immediately requested a legal opinion on whether WTS's system was exempt from the GPO's telegraph monopoly. He had every intention to better the terms for the Royal Navy by threatening to sue the company for violating the GPO's jurisdiction. However, the Admiralty's solicitor opined that the monopoly applied only within the United Kingdom and not at sea. The Admiralty then inquired of the GPO as to its status in acquiring rights to WTS's apparatus and whether use by the Admiralty would be included. The GPO answered it had not yet been authorized by Treasury to open negotiations. That stymied the Admiralty. The Admiralty's operations group, seeing multiple uses of wireless, pressed it to proceed. But its finance department refused to be out of step with the GPO or to act without Treasury approval.

Despite all WTS's favorable publicity, resentment mounted against what many considered to be the company's commercial appropriation of other scientists' concepts. Marconi's supporters, correctly pointing out that he had constructed and patented the first practical device to use Hertzian waves, argued his entitlement to profit financially from his invention. Marconi openly acknowledged, as he had before the Institute of Electrical Engineers, that he had used others' concepts. But none had been embodied in patented apparatus. Opponents stressed that Marconi based his equipment on public scientific principles. No one, they claimed, could acquire exclusive rights over Hertzian waves. Or, as *Nature* magazine editorialized:

> The fact is that we have in these repeated sensational experiments a pure scientific apparatus boomed by energetic financial speculators for their own individual gain, and not for the benefit of the public—the worst of this money-grubbing age.(FN 7)

The successful Channel demonstration, however, did not solve interference. Indeed, if two messages at a time were to be sent simultaneously across the Channel by using two sets of transmitters and receivers, the signals must be kept separate in some way to avoid disrupting each other. For the better part of a year, Marconi had grappled with this dilemma. Spanning the water with a single transmitter and receiver involved principles and equipment already known and developed. Interference required new theories and new apparatus. If none could be found, the Channel symbol would have limited effect.

Like the early days at Villa Grifone, Marconi spent endless hours testing and tweaking ideas, materials, and apparatus. Aided by a staff and resources that he had not had in his early days, he began to make progress. Kemp told *McClure's Magazine* that Marconi's hard efforts showed signs of hope for a solution:

> Besides the possibility of directing the waves with reflectors, Marconi is now engaged in the most promising experiments in syntony.
>
> I may describe syntony as the tuning of a particular transmitter to a particular receiver, so that the latter will respond to the former and to no other, while the former will influence the latter and no other. That, of course, is a possibility in the future, but it bids far too soon to be realized. There are even some who maintain that there may be produced as many separate sets of transmitters and receivers capable of working only together as there are separate sets of locks and keys. In any event any two private individuals might communicate freely without fear of being understood by others.(FN 8)

The French navy invited Marconi to try his wireless out on its supply ship, the *Vienne.* The choppy, springtime waters of the Channel proved an excellent laboratory not only for ship-to-shore, shore-to-ship, and ship-to-ship tests, which the navy had in mind, but also for simultaneous signals from multiple transmitters within range of multiple receivers, which Marconi intended.

Syntony would permit a receiver when receiving electromagnetic waves simultaneously from several sources to tune into and understand one set of signals and to tune out or block all others. The rejected waves could not garble or interfere with the selected signals. (In today's terms, a radio receives signals from many stations at once, but the listener tunes out all the stations other than the one to be listened to.)

Marconi's syntony device allowed the operation of two transmitters within range of two receivers. One transmitter could send a message to one receiver while the other transmitter sent a message to the other receiver. Marconi proved this. He successfully transmitted from the *Vienne* to South Foreland while Wimereux simultaneously transmitted to the East Goodwin lightship. Both receivers were in range of both transmitters. Each receiver clearly received the message intended for it.

Critical work, however, remained. A single receiver could not simultaneously receive and understand messages sent to it at once by two transmitters. If a ship wished to receive more than one signal at a time, it would have to carry on board more than one receiver.

Nonetheless, the *Vienne* yielded significant results with promise for a complete answer. Marconi filed a preliminary patent application for his syntonic device. Even as a partial solution, it could be a major breakthrough, ahead of the field. His rivals still faltered trying to match WTS's distance. Marconi might be on the verge of a significant second competitive advantage. Interference might be a critical weakness inherent in everyone's wireless. He could be the first to solve it.

Recent accomplishments encouraged Jameson-Davis. He concluded that syntony, as illustrated by the *Vienne*, would eliminate much of the sales resistance WTS encountered from the shipping industry. Ocean liners could send clear messages even when close to other transmitters, whether those transmitters be on shore or on other vessels. He also believed that the new Marconi apparatus would give WTS another strong sales tool. Other systems suffering interference might be unable to deliver clear messages. They might feel compelled to come to the company for a license.

Jameson-Davis was heartened by the quick success at Wimereux. Marconi's schedule should be clear by August to go to America. The inventor concurred. The older cousin cabled the company's acceptance to Bennett.

Marconi's activities aboard the *Vienne* ended abruptly in mid-June. Kemp, who now sported an untidy handlebar moustache to match his uncontrolled red hair, came by Chalet D'Artois to take Marconi by carriage to the ship. At a sharp bend in the seashore road, the horse bolted, overturning the cabriolet. Kemp jumped clear. The vehicle fell upon Marconi and fractured his kneecap.

The accident confined him to the chalet for weeks. To assist his recovery, his engineers twice a day, accompanied by much banter, lifted up their leader and deposited him in an old wine barrel filled with fresh seawater. There he gave his leg a thorough soaking. The strictures of the container forced him to rest momentarily. Otherwise, he would not stop working. He hobbled about day and night, testing and altering the equipment, preoccupied with a complete solution to the interference puzzle and always seeking to increase distance.

One evening, Marconi thought the equipment had gone dead. No response could be raised from South Foreland. He tried everything, checking all the wires, even changing the coherer and rearranging the receiver. He feared he had fallen into a new, awful problem. He limped outside with his men in the pouring rain to examine the aerial. Quickly drenched, his leg throbbing, he gave up adjusting the antenna and returned inside. On the receiver's tape, a message awaited him from the South Foreland operator. He'd been off to dinner and asked if anything had occurred in his absence.

Other than these adverse moments, the spirit at Chalet D'Artois was buoyant and full of bonhomie. The public acclaim lifted the men. All of them were actively engaged in the intensive experimental communications between the Chalet, South Foreland, the lightship, and the *Vienne*. From Marconi's taciturn, purposeful mood, they sensed that the effort on syntony pleased him and that together they were onto something. Similar to Haven, in the evenings the four or five men in residence relaxed together over dinner. Afterwards they gathered around an out-of-tune piano in the parlor. As Marconi played, they all sang the currently popular chorus songs. The men happily became acquainted with an abundance of French table wine. Although Kemp scoffed, pretending not to be that fond of it, he said somewhat wistfully, "The best of the dinner wine remains in the sediment and dregs at the bottom of the bottle."(FN 9) They all laughed, finding his disparagement amusing. The comment became a frequently repeated in-joke. Marconi was doing what he loved best, experimenting, on or by the water, surrounded by like-minded men. At Wimereux, he did not feel away from home. In the conventional sense, he had no home. Home for him was where his work was, where it could be best done. Nor did his long work hours separate him from his social life. The society of his colleagues, to him, happily constituted his social life. A constant stream of visitors called upon him. Among the most frequent were Annie and Alfonso, who often resided with him or nearby.

There was nothing else he would rather do than be in pursuit of his goal, and he was always anxious to move his invention further along. The Admiralty observed Marconi's close relationships with the French and Italian navies with growing concern. The completion of his service as a cadet did not diminish his ties to Italy. The syntonic tuning progress, word of which had gotten back to the Royal Navy, made wireless's naval usefulness more and more apparent. The original concept of signaling between torpedo boat and parent vessel had broadened substantially. Currently, captains communicated with flags or lights. The curvature of the earth and weather isolated ships. To order a change in a fleet's direction or prearranged maneuver became difficult or impossible in fog or bad weather or over the horizon. Without visual contact, ships could not exchange information. Marconi's invention might change all that. It could revolutionize group movement at sea with the possibility of maintaining contact among ships under all weather and nighttime conditions. As its range exceeded the distance of telescopic sight from the height of a crow's nest, its importance for scouting functions expanded as well. The Admiralty had scheduled its annual summer maneuvers for mid-July. The director of naval ordinance, aware that Jackson's tour at the French embassy had ended and that he had been assigned to command a destroyer in the maneuvers, suggested that Marconi's apparatus be tried in that ship. The top brass, eager to test the equipment's performance in real circumstances, determined they could not await the conclusion of the contract negotiations with the company. The Admiralty ordered Jackson to contact WTS.

Up to this moment, the directors had refused to provide the Royal Navy any equipment until terms were agreed, but they found the opportunity to demonstrate in the exercises irresistible. Temporarily deferring insistence on a signed agreement, WTS lent sets to the navy, asking only to be reimbursed for transportation and the expense of WTS technicians who installed and maintained the apparatus. Marconi himself jumped at the chance. He even shut down the syntonic experiments at Wimereux in order to free himself to lead the company participation. In the maneuvers, a convoy of merchant vessels sailed from Nova Scotia for England. At a prearranged time and place, it expected to rendezvous with a Royal Navy fleet charged with escorting the merchants safely to England. A second task group of Royal Navy warships, acting as an enemy force, would try

Marconi

to find the convoy first. WTS installed wireless sets in the first fleet aboard HMS *Alexandra*, the flagship; HMS *Juno* under Jackson's command; and HMS *Europa*, a fast, four-stack cruiser assigned as a scout to move out in front of the fleet to locate the convoy. It was an exhilarating moment for the twenty-five-year-old from Italy. He had once looked up from his tiny sailboat at the jaunty Italian naval officers crossing Leghorn Harbor in a pinnace. A year before, he had chased the racing yachts aboard the *Flying Huntress* and the HMS *Osborne*.

Now he stationed himself on the quarterdeck of the Royal Navy flagship amidst the mightiest flotilla in the world. Surrounding him a powerful panorama of battleships and cruisers sliced through the ocean troughs and swells. HMS *Europa* steamed ahead in the race to find the commercial boats, leaving behind HMS *Juno* and the flagship with the rest of the fleet. HMS *Europa* sighted the defenseless merchants and signaled sixty miles, a stunning new record, to HMS *Juno*. HMS *Juno* in turn relayed the news thirty-five miles to HMS *Alexandra*. HMS *Alexandra* received the message within minutes of the time HMS *Europa* began the transmission. Marconi could not have designed a more dramatic demonstration. Had HMS *Europa* and HMS *Alexandra* each known the precise location of the other, and had they headed in a direct line to meet, both steaming at twelve knots per hour, three hours would have elapsed from the time HMS *Europa* spotted the convoy before it could convey its information by flag to the flagship. HMS *Europa* would have lost contact with the ships the fleet was ordered to protect, and the search would have had to start again. In Jackson's official report to the commander of the fleet, he proposed the installation of WTS wireless in the Channel and Mediterranean squadrons' flagships and scouting cruisers as well as in the offices of the commanders in chief of the principal English homeports.

He recommended training courses, attaching a syllabus drawn up by Marconi, pay increases for the trained seamen, and the assignment of two of these men to each wireless. The fleet commander strongly endorsed Jackson's report, adding in a cover note that from his experience in the past month, wireless telegraphy was invaluable for scouting. Moreover, it could be trusted at night or in fog when no other system was perfectly reliable. At the Admiralty, the Second Sea Lord received the recommendations favorably. In anticipation of the general adoption of wireless, he called for the immediate purchase of eight sets for training.

While this proposal won general approval, the director of naval ordinance pointed out that the GPO and the Treasury still had not informed the Admiralty as to the outcome of negotiations with WTS. Privately, the Second Sea Lord must have exploded. The controller of the navy, who bore responsibility for the design and equipment of ships, but did not have final authority for expenditures, which resided elsewhere in the finance department, concluded that the sensational results of the maneuvers showed wireless to be essential for the navy's fighting efficiency. The Admiralty should equip twelve warships without waiting on the GPO.

The First Sea Lord concurred with the immediate acceptance of Marconi's system. For the moment, he and the Royal Navy were willing to overlook his judgment that the annual royalty of a hundred pounds per wireless was excessive. He pointedly remarked, however, that the amount should not bind the Admiralty in the future.

The sixty-mile signal from HMS *Europa* to HMS *Juno* profoundly affected Marconi. Based on the results at Salisbury Plain and Brean Down, he had concluded that a transmission's length equaled the result of a mathematical equation one of whose factors included the square of the heights of the antennae. HMS *Europa*'s record accomplishment shattered the concept. It was many miles longer than the distance produced by the formula.

In addition, he was puzzled again as he was at Spezia by the scientific theory that electromagnetic waves, similar to light rays, traveled in a straight line. As the earth curved while the signal went straight, the farther the wave traveled the higher it would be above the ocean's surface. In no way could HMS *Juno*'s antenna, hung from the top of the ship's highest mast, pick up HMS *Europa*'s signal. The square of the antenna height equation and the straight line concept each had a calculable limit as to how far from the transmitter a signal could be received. The Royal Navy exercises conclusively exceeded the restrictions of both theories. If neither prescribed wireless's range, what did? How far could these signals really go?

Marconi engineers hypothesized that "Hertzian waves follow around smoothly as the earth curves."(FN 10) The well-respected and knowledgeable *Electrician* magazine flatly discarded such an explanation. It called it ridiculous. Without reservation, the *Electrician* said, "It is an absurdity to suggest that ether waves inherently followed the curvature of the earth."(FN 11)

Marconi's delight and perplexity at the sixty-mile signal received another jolt. Not long after the maneuvers, the Chelmsford factory in Essex received a signal from Chalet D'Artois that had been intended for South Foreland. Chelmsford was eighty miles from Wimereux. According to the square of the height of the mast formula, the chalet's aerial should have been six times higher than it was. In August, Marconi prepared to sail for New York to report on the America's Cup race. He had every reason to be pleased about company prospects. They had never been brighter. He felt confident that he would solve the tuning and interference issue. He had just set another distance record. Lloyd's of London, Trinity House, and the French and British navies all were seriously considering purchasing WTS wireless. Just prior to the inventor's departure, the GPO's secretary advised the board that the GPO only wished to acquire rights to use WTS wireless and not to own it. The directors immediately offered the GPO rights for thirty thousand pounds annually in the United Kingdom or fifty thousand pounds per year if extended to British possessions. The American trip held business promise as well. The company planned sea trials with the U.S. Navy and contemplated forming an American company. Publicity from the America's Cup coverage, which would be far greater than that from the Kingston Regatta, could only open additional possibilities.

Chapter 6

America

Transatlantic travel was booming. The fruits of the Industrial Revolution had spread generously among a swelling bourgeois class of manufacturers, traders, bankers, entrepreneurs, and merchants. They had the time and wealth to enjoy extended periods of leisure. New York to London and New York to Paris trips particularly were socially esteemed. To the end-of-the-century Victorian, the ten- to fifteen-day North American passage offered both entertainment and cachet.

The amenities on such a voyage, due to the vast improvements in ocean vessels, had reached a luxurious stage. Over the past forty years, commodious steam-driven boats had come to replace uncomfortable, cramped sailing ships. First it was iron; then steel supplanted wooden structures. Remarkable design advances in propeller propulsion quickly outmoded side wheels that powered early steamships. Coal-consuming engines, increasingly efficient and reliable, reduced the time and uncertainties of the voyage. Further advances were promised by an internal combustion motor just invented by the German Rudolf Diesel. First-class passengers lived in a world of luxury and comfort. Uniformed maids and valets attended the spacious upper-deck cabins, and continental chefs served Parisian cuisine in the elegant dining salons.

A half dozen steamship lines, coveted customers for WTS's ship-to-shore marketing, competed for transatlantic passenger business. North-German Lloyd built extra cabins on the *Trave* to meet demand out of Southampton. Hamburg-American claimed its twin-screw steamers between Cherbourg and New York held the record for the fastest time on that route between the two continents. Cunard dedicated six ships for the transatlantic route departing from either Southampton or Liverpool. Estimates for the number of Americans visiting Europe in 1895 reached as high as two hundred thousand, spending upwards of two hundred million dollars. WTS booked Marconi on Cunard out of Liverpool for the trip to America. The bustling, heavily trafficked commercial port stood at the mouth of the Mersey River that flowed from the industrial English Midlands to the Irish Sea. Since the 1700s, Liverpool had played a principal role in western commerce with Ireland, the British West Indies, and North America.

It was a time of high excitement for Marconi. He loved the sea. Although he had traveled across the English Channel a number of times, this would be his longest voyage, his first across the Atlantic, and his initial visit to America.

The trip placed enormous pressure on him. His experience aboard the HMS *Osborne* indicated the social curiosity that might swirl around him. The America's Cup would attract far more attention than the Dublin Regatta. At the time of that contest, Marconi was virtually unknown. Now his reputation circled the world, and the *Herald Tribune*, to advance its own publicity, trumpeted his role.

Jameson-Davis had scheduled trials with the U.S. Navy following the conclusion of the yacht races. Marconi had arranged to meet and address the New York electrical scientific community. A subsidiary was to be organized and funds raised by selling shares to the American public.

For all these activities, Marconi's equipment must perform well. Future revenues depended on it. The opportunity to raise money for working capital and research relied upon his technical ability. Now that he personally enjoyed enormous prestige, that too he risked.

Despite his success at Wimereux and at the British naval maneuvers, Marconi worried. In negotiations with the U.S. Bureau of Equipment to arrange the U.S. naval tests, the bureau asked how WTS would handle interference. Marconi wrote back that he had an apparatus that came close to solving the problem. But at the last moment before embarking, he concluded that until a patent was issued, the danger in allowing knowledgeable U.S. observers to study his invention's operation must be avoided. To remove the temptation to display his discovery under the pressure to which he feared he would be subjected, Marconi did not bring the syntonic tuning device with him. On this important American trip, he would be unable to demonstrate that two of his transmitters could operate simultaneously and intelligibly within range of the same receiver.

On September 11, 1899, five company representatives boarded Cunard's *Aurania* in Liverpool. When the organizers incorporated WTS two years earlier, they had given Marconi the right to appoint one director, and he had chosen William Woodcock Goodbody. Goodbody now joined Marconi for the trip to America. Before departing, the board authorized Goodbody to make arrangements with New York banks to float an initial public offering (IPO) of shares of the proposed American subsidiary. The third member of the party was William W. Bradfield, an expert electrician who had won high marks for his work at Wimereux. Two technicians, Charles Rickard and William Densham, completed the group. Considering the overall finances of the company, this entourage represented a very expensive undertaking, but it reflected Jameson-Davis's high ambitions for its outcome.

In anticipation of the trip, Marconi had grown a mustache. Perhaps after his experience with the French at Chalet D'Artois he felt he should try to look older. He also thought he would create a more mature impression if not accompanied by his mother. Though Annie longed to go, she failed to persuade him that she could make a vital contribution to the outcome.

After the ten-day crossing, Marconi looked over the *Aurania*'s rail at the dockside overflowing with people who had come to meet the ship. He spotted the crowd of reporters clustered together. The *Herald*'s publicity had alerted them to his arrival. Most of them failed to recognize Marconi as he filed down the gangplank amidst the other passengers. Too youthful, almost boyish-looking, he could not be the famous man they envisaged. He responded to their questions about his coverage of the America's Cup by saying, "We will be able to send the details of the yacht racing to New York as accurately and as quickly almost as if you could telephone them. The distance involved is nothing nor will hills intervene."(FN 1)

He did not win over all the journalists. Several found Marconi's attitude towards them to be glacial and inflexible. His short worded answers they considered curt and assertive rather than helpful. This style of response, they concluded, reflected a conviction on Marconi's part that he was to be an historic figure. Two other reporters had different perspectives.

Marconi

The first wrote that Marconi was a serious, somewhat self-centered young man who spoke little but then always to the point. The second shared a number of observations: He is no bigger than a Frenchman and not older than a quarter century. He is a mere boy, with a boy's happy temperament and enthusiasm, and a man's nervous view of his life work. His manner is a little nervous and his eyes a bit dreamy. He acts with the modesty of a man who merely shrugs his shoulders when accused of discovering a new continent. He looks the student all over and possesses the peculiar semi-abstracted air that characterizes men who devote their days to study and scientific experiments.(FN 2)

Marconi later wrote of his view of the interview:

> I arrived in New York on 21 September and had to run the gauntlet as soon as I descended the gangway of numerous reporters and photographers who awaited me. The following day full and detailed reports of my arrival, my appearance etc. come out in dozens of newspapers together with more or less accurate accounts of what I had accomplished as regards wireless telegraphy until then. For some reason or another it seemed to come as a shock to the newspapers that I spoke English fluently, in fact "with quite a London accent" as one paper phrased it, and also that I appeared to be very young and did not in the slightest resemble the popular type associated with an inventor in those days in America, that is to say a rather wild haired and eccentrically costumed person.(FN 3)

From the boat, Marconi's group went to their hotel, the elegant Hoffman House on Broadway and Twenty-third Street. But before they had unpacked, the boiler in the basement exploded. A hysterical guest blamed it on the wireless apparatus they had brought into the building. To soothe the man and show him that the equipment would have no effect upon the furnace, the technicians opened their boxes. To their dismay, they discovered the trunk containing the coherers missing. For once, Marconi's cool demeanor disappeared. The pressure on him burst out. He flew into a rage and announced his return to England on the next ship. Without coherers, the receivers would not operate. The races could not be covered. The U.S. Navy trials would be impossible. Bradfield quieted him down and then rushed off to the customs house with the horse drawing the cab galloping the entire way. After an extensive search, the trunk remained missing. Then a bright idea struck Bradfield. A liner headed for Boston had steamed from Liverpool on the same day as the *Aurania*. A *Herald* reporter volunteered to take the train to Massachusetts to search that liner for the trunk. A day later, he telegraphed that he had found it. The news restored Marconi's humor.

With the equipment recovered, Marconi, Bradfield, and the two assistants hired a tug. The little power boat headed directly south, leaving the Upper Bay of New York Harbor to cross the vast Lower Bay past Sandy Hook to the Twin Lights Lighthouse. The dual beacons stood on the Navesink New Jersey Highlands overlooking the ocean to the east, where each of the best of seven races constituting the America's Cup would start. While the light keepers and signalmen silently watched, the technicians raised a mast for an aerial. They installed a receiver in the lighthouse next to its telegraph equipment. In the words of a reporter, "When Marconi explained that buildings and hills would not interfere with wireless, the Signal Servicemen spat scornfully and gazed at the inventor as they would at a madman."(FN 4) The tug then took the WTS crew back to the Upper Bay, where they set up sending instruments on a new steamship, the *Ponce*. From this boat, Marconi would follow the racing yachts. They also placed a receiver on the cable ship *Mackay Bennett* moored off New York City over the New York-London transatlantic submarine cable. At the time of the race, the *MacKay Bennett* would raise the cable from the bay bottom, splice into the line, and then with a telegraph key immediately relay Marconi's narrative to London and Paris.

There was tremendous excitement in New York. Every day the newspapers carried articles on the America's Cup competitors, *Shamrock*, the challenger led by the flamboyant Sir Thomas J. Lipton, and *Columbia II*, defender of the cup. In the midst of all the publicity, the *Oceanic*, the world's largest ship at 704 feet long, landed in New York on her maiden voyage. Thomas Peary's attempt to reach the North Pole filled the daily news. Commodore George Dewey, fresh from his victory over the Spanish at Manila in the Philippines, arrived triumphantly on his flagship, *Olympia*. To salute the commodore, a parade of vessels of all types passed by the *Olympia*. Marconi in the *Ponce* joined the long line, his wireless

Marconi

describing the scene. As the *Ponce* pulled alongside the *MacKay*, which was also in the parade, a woman guest aboard the cable ship picked up a megaphone and shouted towards the *Ponce*, "Three cheers for Marconi!" The passengers aboard both ships took up the cry until the *Ponce*'s captain, also by megaphone, explained that Marconi was too busy in the cabin sending messages to acknowledge the cheers. The scene repeated itself more than once as the *Ponce* passed the armada of ships witnessing the parade.

The U.S. Bureau of Equipment had assigned a naval officer to be aboard the *Ponce* to size up Marconi and his equipment. By wireless from the *Ponce* to Navesink, the observer dispatched his report to be forwarded by telegram to Washington. He concluded that Marconi had passed the stage of uncertainty. The value of his wireless that he felt sure to be adopted for use at sea could not be too highly estimated.

The day of the first race in the series was beautiful, if a bit wintry. The breeze whistled in the rigging of the hundreds of boats that glided past the Statue of Liberty into the Lower Bay. They gathered for the start at the Sandy Hook Lightship moored off the Navesink Highlands. The course was fifteen miles from lightship to the outer mark and back. Marconi trailed the dueling *Shamrock* and *Columbia II*, transmitting a steady stream of fifteen words per minute. The Navesink station received the messages and retransmitted them by telegraph to the *Herald*. A word tapped out on the *Ponce* arrived at the *Herald* seventy-five seconds later. The *Herald* scooped all of its rivals. The receipt of four thousand words during the second contest moved the *Herald* to editorialize the following:

> The possibilities contained in the development of telegraphy without the use of wires are so important that any step tending to bring the system before the public and to show what it is capable of accomplishing in a commercial way must be of interest not only to those interested in science, but also to everyone who sends a telegram.
>
> The tests stimulate the hope that the man of the coming century may be able to "halloo his name to the reverberate hills" and irrespective of distance or material obstacles "make the babbling gossip of the air cry out" in intelligible speech.(FN 5)

Some reporters still viewed Marconi askance. One aboard the *Ponce* filed this report:

> When you meet Marconi, you're bound to notice that he's a "for'ner." The information is written all over him. His suit of clothes is English. In stature he is French. His boot heels are Spanish military. His hair and mustache are German. His mother is Irish. His father is Italian. And altogether, there's little doubt that Marconi is thoroughly a cosmopolitan.(FN 6)

Marconi's appearance did not put off the passengers aboard the *Ponce*. They crowded about the door to the cabin where he had established his wireless. Few women who asked for an explanation of the wireless did not receive a thoughtful, polite answer. A reporter observed that some of these women seemed more interested in Marconi than his wireless.

Lipton, a self-made millionaire with an Irish mother like Marconi, and Marconi saw each other frequently over the course of the races and at the attendant social events sponsored by the *Herald* and the American Yacht Club. From the first, the two men instinctively liked each other and would remain lifelong friends. Although Lipton lost in five races, he was popular among the Americans. The victors gave him a gold loving cup, a token of their esteem for his sportsmanship and charm. Dewey's victory in the Philippines earned him a promotion to admiral and a house in Washington from his grateful country. For Marconi's role in the America's Cup, the *Herald* awarded him a newspaper accolade; in a feature article it acclaimed him a U.S. national hero.

Marconi had a chance to meet Tesla while he was in New York. The twenty-five-year-old was introduced to his senior at Manhattan's New York Science Club by Michael Idvorsky Pupin, a professor of electrical mechanics at Columbia University. Pupin had been born in Serbia near Belgrade. The professor subsequently took Marconi to Tesla's lab, where Tesla explained his wireless transformer. "That's impossible," Marconi is reported to have said. Pupin ushered Marconi out before the conversation could become heated. "Time will tell," was Tesla's parting shot.(FN 7)

As soon as the races concluded, Marconi turned to the tests commissioned by the U.S. Bureau of Equipment. The Bureau controlled U.S.

military equipment procurement. It had heard from U.S. naval officers of WTS's extraordinary Royal Navy results. U.S. military wireless testing fell to the U.S. Army Signal Corps. Its best signal to date spanned the twelve miles from Fire Island to the Fire Island Lightship. When Jameson-Davis sought to demonstrate to U.S. governmental authorities, the bureau quickly offered to provide U.S. naval vessels for tests in the Lower Bay. After the America's Cup, WTS electricians transferred transmitters and receivers from the *Ponce* and *MacKay Bennett* to the battleship USS *Massachusetts* and the cruiser USS *New York*.

The U.S. Navy clearly understood the need for a wireless system. To communicate with his own commanders in Washington, DC, Dewey in the Philippines had to send dispatch boats back and forth between his flagship at Manila and Hong Kong, the nearest port with submarine cable connections. Between Hong Kong and Washington, the U.S. government relied on privately owned cable companies to handle confidential and sensitive U.S. military information and orders. Once Dewey had left Hong Kong pursuant to President Theodore Roosevelt's final cabled instructions to attack the Spanish in the Philippines, Dewey had to act on his own as events rapidly unfolded. He had no way to confer with his superiors on a timely basis.

Marconi's coverage of *Columbia II* and *Shamrock* was a huge success. From the moment he stepped off *Aurania*, he was lionized, questioned, photographed, written up, cheered by crowds, and flattered by countless women. Two months earlier, he was in the midst of two twenty-five-ship fleets, on the flagship's quarterdeck with the commanding admiral, impressing the world's number-one sea power. Before that, he had been at sea with the French and Italian navies. He had reason to be confident as he boarded the USS *Massachusetts*.

For its part, the U.S. Navy in its short history had not lost a war. Representing the globe's greatest industrial power, it was enjoying a building program buoyed by its country's expansionary mood. Its crushing, lopsided victory against the Spanish had occurred scarcely a year ago, and Dewey's hero's welcome in New York City still echoed in naval ears.

The USS *Massachusetts* and the USS *New York* began the tests in the New York Harbor, and then they steamed out to sea in blustery, wet weather. Aboard were admirals, generals, and captains of the U.S. Navy, the U.S. Army, and the Army Signal Corps, as well as representatives of the Bureau of Equipment and a host of reporters. Marconi transmitted thirty-six miles through the wind and rain to the Navesink station, vastly exceeding the Signal Corps' distances at Fire Island. He transferred to the torpedo boat USS *Porter.* The equipment operated effectively despite the twenty-four-knot speed in the choppy sea and severe vibrations from the massive engines.

But when the USS *Porter* and USS *New York* transmitted simultaneously to Navesink, the signals intermingled. Messages from both ships became unintelligible. What Marconi feared most when he left the syntonic tuner in England began to unfold before him.

He tried to avert the disaster but could not. The Americans wanted to know why he could not control the interference. Marconi explained that he could. He had a device under development. In tests with the French navy, it overcame the difficulty. He described his invention in general terms. He said that he could not be more descriptive because of a pending patent application. This perturbed the admirals, who were annoyed that Marconi did not have the equipment and would not discuss details of its operations. Like Preece, Slaby, and other inquirers, the U.S. Navy discovered that Marconi would not speak about his unpatented apparatus. He would not jeopardize his secrets. Particularly upset were bureau officials. They felt that WTS, in negotiating for the demonstrations, had promised the new device would participate. Their frustration escalated. Marconi would not permit any of the U.S. representatives to make a complete inspection of certain pieces of the equipment he had brought. Disgruntled, the navy filed a critical report:

> During the tests the instruments were open to the naval board, except certain parts which were never dismantled, and these mechanics were explained in a general way. The exact dimensions of the parts were not divulged... Mr. Marconi although he stated to the Board before these attempts were made that he could prevent interference, never explained how, nor made any attempt to demonstrate that it could be done.(FN 8)

Marconi's failure to bring the syntonic invention he had tested with the French navy clearly nettled the U.S. Navy. Could the French navy, an inferior force compared to the U.S. Navy, be more trustworthy?

Marconi

Marconi did not act capriciously. The sea trials aboard *Vienne* in the broad waters of the Channel, with wireless stations at Chalet D'Artois, the East Goodwin lightship, and South Foreland, offered a better research platform than the Solent. There Marconi had only Haven, Needles, and a tug to work with. Once he developed the instrument to the point where he became satisfied that it worked, he did not wish to expose it to further French observation. That was one reason for closing down Chalet D'Artois, the other reasons being its expense and his preoccupation with the Royal Navy exercises. The lesson learned from Fort Burgoyne with the GPO and the British navy remained fresh in his mind. No one could be trusted.

The Bureau of Equipment, despite the shortcomings in Marconi's performance and disclosures, understood that what he exhibited surpassed any equipment available in North America. The bureau also realized that he might have a solution for interference. It asked WTS at the end of the trials to submit a bid to provide wireless for the U.S. Navy. Marconi hoped that he had talked his way through the absence of the tuner. The bureau's quick response also raised hopes that the U.S. government was more efficiently organized than the British government and that WTS would not have to endure protracted discussions. WTS responded immediately. It proposed to equip twenty vessels for a price of ten thousand dollars to cover the cost of the apparatus and installation plus an annual royalty of ten thousand dollars.

In addition to the financial terms, the company imposed a restriction. When the U.S. Navy communicated with shore, except in emergencies, it must signal only to a WTS shore station, no one else.

This condition addressed what the board viewed as a fundamental problem in the structure of the wireless business as compared to telegraph. Governments, railroads, and private companies had wired just about every town and train station in the United States and Europe for telegraph service. A vast market existed for telegraph transmitters, receivers, parts, and line. Wireless did not enjoy a similar outlook. Naval and commercial ships, lighthouses and lightships, and shore stations composed its short customer list. Relying solely on equipment sales to this narrow group limited the company's profit horizon, particularly in light of the strong bargaining power of these heavyweight potential buyers.

The directors perceived for wireless what Alexander Graham Bell's financial backers immediately understood about Bell's telephone. Significant long-term money lay in providing a service over the years. In the case of the telephone, the switchboard was the heart of the service. Without someone to connect one caller to another, telephone had limited bilateral use. Whoever owned and operated the switches controlled the telephone service market.

Airborne transmission lacked this element of control. The essence of wireless, mechanically and economically, was that a signal could travel from sender to receiver, anywhere within range, without an intervening mechanism or person. No switch was needed.

To emulate the telephone system, the company sought an artificial system of control.

First for commercial customers, WTS planned to install equipment on a ship and furnish a man to manipulate and maintain it. The apparatus would not be sold or leased. It would remain company property. The operator would be a WTS employee. WTS would charge the shipowner an annual fee for the use of the equipment and the services of the operator. In addition, there would be a charge for each message, or Marconigram, as they came to be known.

Second, and thus was the key to high profit, WTS would build and run shore stations to connect maritime wireless and inland telegraphy. The coastal sites would be the switch between sea and land. Without access to mainland communication, the board doubted there would enough demand for shipboard wireless. If WTS provided a comprehensive interconnection and structured its use appropriately, the directors foresaw an opportunity for significant revenue.

Assuming Marconi could raise reliable wireless performance to a hundred miles and if ships were to be in constant land communication while within seventy-five miles of a coast, there would have to be a shore station approximately every fifty miles. Each would consist of a building, tall mast and aerial, and sending and receiving set and be staffed seven days a week, twenty-four hours a day with trained operators. Substantial capital would need to be spent to get such a system up and running. To help pay for this, customers would be required to use WTS stations wherever they were in range.

It was initially envisioned that the stations would communicate with everyone. The board quickly recognized that would significantly benefit its competitors. Even if there was a charge for processing messages to and from non-WTS apparatus through company facilities, other equipment manufacturers would in effect be subsidized because they had not incurred this major investment. The directors concluded that except in emergencies its coastal sites would exchange messages only with WTS operators.

If the company were the first to build along the English Channel and out into the Atlantic a comprehensive series of stations in England, Ireland, and Wales that its customers were required to use and its competitors were not allowed to access, the directors hoped to establish a high degree of control over prices that would enable WTS to recover its investment and be very profitable.

The company modified these terms for the U.S. Navy. Navy crews could operate the sets. Lower rates were offered to avoid tempting the U.S. government to build its own shore stations. But, and this point stuck in the navy's craw, the directors would not relent on its condition that the navy not communicate with non-Marconi shore stations. This might not have upset the U.S. if it had not just been dependent in the Philippines on private submarine cable companies. From the navy's point of view, why did WTS care where the navy sent its signals as long as WTS received the same amount of revenue?

The board was not going to set a precedent with the U.S. Navy that would be hard to explain to commercial customers whom the company intended to require to use WTS shore stations. Nor were the directors going to disclose their strategy to the U.S. government.

The U.S. objected. The directors refused to yield. Unable to resolve this difference, despite the bureau's recommendation, WTS sold no sets to the navy.

The failure to bring the syntonic tuning device to the U.S. Navy trials did not appear to be the determining factor in the navy's refusal to proceed with WTS. But the negative buzz in New York financial circles surrounding the failure to overcome interference and Marconi's attitude on disclosure had an immediate, adverse impact on the directors' ambitions for a subsidiary. With the formation of the Marconi Wireless Company of America, they planned to raise over eight million dollars.

Of the two million shares to be issued, WTS would own 365,000 (approximately 15 percent). Marconi would receive 600,000 (30 percent). The remainder would be sold to the public at eight dollars per share, or a total of $8,280,000 before expenses and bankers' commissions. With that money, the new company would buy the U.S. rights to Marconi's patents from WTS for seven million dollars.

These were incredible amounts of money. The public had to invest eight million dollars to own slightly more than 50 percent of a company with rights only in the United States. These rights came from a UK corporation that to date had produced virtually no sales and had mounting losses. The moneys received by selling the stock to the public would generate much-needed working capital for WTS and establish an adequately capitalized U.S. operating company. The increase in the paper value of Marconi's shares in WTS and the American company would be huge. He had negotiated well for himself.

The controversy over interference and WTS's unwillingness to provide information about its systems, however, chilled the investment community's enthusiasm for the IPO. The bankers found the share price too high to support. The board refused to lower it. The directors had reached a judgment. Eight dollars might seem exorbitant. It might be arbitrary. But they had confidence in the value of wireless over time. In offering the public a majority of the new company's shares, the directors realized WTS would be disposing of half of its future in the U.S. market. Potentially, that could be worth far more than eight million dollars. They did not want to surrender it for less. A compromise could not be reached. The board shelved the offering. Assuming that the directors' assessment about the degree of American appetite for an interest in Marconi's wireless had been realistic at the outset of the trip, the events at the U.S. Navy trials had hurt WTS and Marconi financially, at least in the short term. The investment community had lowered its valuation. An opportunity to raise substantial working capital and research money had been missed.

Instead of incorporating a subsidiary, the board registered the name Marconi Wireless Company of America. The offering abandoned, WTS deferred any start-up or operating activity. Marconi, focused on WTS's many problems, did not allow whatever changes might have occurred in the paper value of his holdings to divert his attention. He had no intention of cashing out any of his interest and no time to enjoy his paper wealth in activities that did not enhance his wireless.

The U.S. tour terminated abruptly. Marconi had intended to stay in New York to see the IPO through. Once cancelled, he did not wish to expose himself to further rounds of questions that he would not answer. It only engendered additional ill will. The visit that began with a triumphant debarkation ended less than two months later in a fizzle. The board wanted Marconi back in London as well. Business conditions there had also become turbulent.

The Boer War had broken out in South Africa between Great Britain and the Boer republics, Transvaal and the Orange Free State. If WTS could demonstrate wireless's usefulness in this conflict, other countries might consider systems for their armies. The company lobbied the British Army to test wireless in the battlefield. The army agreed. However, the company's vision of the best military application differed from the commanders'. Wireless, the directors felt, should be carried behind enemy lines to report on enemy activity or be located at headquarters to direct overall troop movements. Instead, the sets went to the front line. To raise the aerials, the army provided jointed, fifty-foot-tall bamboo poles. They could not withstand the cyclone force winds. In lieu of bamboo, WTS deployed six-foot-tall box kites and fourteen-foot-diameter balloons. The gales tore these apart as well. To make matters worse, the wind stirred up dust and sand that clogged the receivers. For weeks the equipment was out of service.

While negotiations dragged on between WTS and its large prospective customers, competitors closed in. They were granted numerous patents. Lodge, himself, received four. They strengthened his syndicate with Muirhead and bolstered his standing in the English scientific community, which continued to favor the professor over Marconi. The patents did not impinge on Marconi's, but they did hem him in. They blocked him from areas in which he might have discovered improvements for his system, particularly for syntonic tuning.

Lodge had many goals. He wanted to profit from his ideas as Marconi was doing and to garner the prestige the Irish-Italian inventor had gained. Lodge would not think of himself as jealous or bitter. Rather, he truly believed that the recognition rightfully belonged to him as a matter of priority of invention and exhibition. From his perspective, the situation had to be rectified.

Rumors also reached WTS that the Germans, Slaby and Braun, in their separate efforts had attracted investment money in collaborative efforts with other scientists. WTS, however, could not acquire specific intelligence on their status. The French navy, despite its assistance to Marconi, appeared ready to adopt the system of Popov, the Russian scientist, even though he had achieved only ten miles. WTS could only speculate that the French wanted a system not closely tied to British interests.

The directors struggled for a major sales breakthrough. Negotiations with each of its principal prospects were stalemated. The GPO still had not reacted to the proposal that they had requested and that WTS had delivered before Marconi left for America. Seven months after requesting and receiving a price for two sets, the Royal Navy still had not responded to WTS. Lloyd's could not have been more pleased with Rathlin Island and the East Goodwin lightship experience, which vividly demonstrated the utility of the WTS equipment. But now, a year later, no order had been placed by Lloyd's, and only silence came from Trinity House.

Unbeknownst to WTS, the secretary of Lloyd's, H. M. Hozier, who was responsible for negotiating with the company, had traveled to Strasbourg, Germany, to examine Braun's work. From Strasbourg, Hozier wrote to the First Lord of the Admiralty that Lloyd's was not completely satisfied with the Marconi tests. Hozier recommended that the Admiralty defer purchasing WTS wireless until it judged Braun's and Marconi's relative merits. The director of naval ordinance agreed: "In view of the prohibitive price asked by Marconi it would be very desirable that we have an alternative."(FN 9)

The director of naval contracts concurred as well, noting, "The terms proposed by the Company are preposterous, and they refuse to sell instruments exclusive of royalty [and] leave the amount of royalty to be settled afterwards."(FN 10) In its offer, WTS had priced the equipment just above cost (one hundred pounds per set) and relied on a proposed royalty of a hundred pounds per set per year for the profit. The navy's frustration at dealing with a sole supplier spilled over into its vehement comments on the company's pricing. But the directors concluded that the government, being the most powerful organization in the world, had overwhelming bargaining power. If the Royal Navy gained possession and use of the apparatus at cost and deferred determining the amount of royalty to some future time, WTS would lose its bargaining power to negotiate a desirable royalty.

Despite the opinions of the directors of naval ordinance and contracts, the Admiralty's top hierarchy did not want to wait for Braun. They wanted eight Marconi sets immediately. Once more the Admiralty inquired if the GPO had progressed with WTS, and once more they received a negative response. Having studied WTS's alternate prices, one for the right to the system in the UK alone and the other for the entire British Empire, the GPO answered the Admiralty saying that "the Company has made a proposal, but it is of such a nature that the Postmaster-General does not think Her Majesty's Government could possibly entertain it."(FN 11) Treasury not only concurred but found the proposed charges so excessive that it recommended the GPO suspend discussions with WTS.

The Admiralty seethed with frustration. It had been moving down this interdepartmental road for some time and was getting nowhere. It wanted the strategic advantage of wireless. But it believed it should not agree to terms that a sister agency found unacceptable. Aware of the Admiralty's plight, WTS as it had done for the summer maneuvers offered to lend eight sets until terms were agreed. This arrangement no longer satisfied the Admiralty's finance department. It would be improper to accept equipment while similar negotiations were underway with another governmental unit. At the time of the maneuvers, when a loan of sets was accepted, WTS had not yet submitted its bid to the GPO.

The Admiralty tired of waiting. It had another route to follow. It had authority to circumvent the bureaucratic purchase process. Under the Patents, Designs and Trade Marks Act, a government department, over a patentee's objection, could manufacture and utilize a patented device on terms to be settled later by Treasury after hearing all interested parties. WTS patents appeared to be too strong for the Admiralty to break. At the moment, no acceptable, alternative product existed. WTS would not back down on its price. The Admiralty exercised its power under the act. As Marconi demonstrated on the USS *Massachusetts*, the Admiralty ordered Jackson to the HMS *Vernon* to initiate building transmitters and receivers based on Marconi's patents. While Jackson obeyed the orders, he immediately alerted Marconi. Despite the irritation of Fort Burgoyne, the captain had developed an attachment and feeling of loyalty towards Marconi. He thought it only fair that WTS be aware of the Admiralty's action. The directors angrily criticized the Royal Navy's decision as totally unjust. They feared Treasury under the act would award WTS inadequate terms. The board had a dilemma. It did not have that many potential customers. For its profitability, to recover all that it had invested in research and development and to invest in the shore stations, the company needed a high enough price structure. If it gave reductions to the Admiralty, it would do no better with the GPO. Other customers would inevitably hear of the lower pricing and hold out as well.

Internally, the board and officers sharply debated the high-pricing strategy. The decision to require ships at sea to communicate only with WTS shore stations also caused dissension. It was very tempting to sacrifice these policies to attain an immediate sale, particularly when the company had generated so little revenue. In theory, if WTS did not stick rigidly to its overall game plan, it would lose its opportunity to be a powerful and profitable communications service organization, like the telegraph, telephone, and cable companies. It would be an equipment manufacturer, struggling to keep its market share and its margins. On the other hand, as a practical matter, if WTS had no sales, plans for market domination became irrelevant. Marconi and Jameson-Davis adhered to the long-term plan. The new chief operating officer, Major Samuel Flood-Page, whom the directors had recently hired in August to run the company on a day-to-day basis as the deputy to Jameson-Davis, wanted results. He was brought aboard to make things happen. Nothing was happening. He argued to cut the price.

In a compromise between the warring factions within the company and in an effort to head off the Admiralty without undermining its pricing goals, WTS changed its offer to the Royal Navy. Inasmuch as the board had also learned from Jackson that the Admiralty now wanted eight pairs of transmitters and receivers, the new terms covered the higher number. WTS increased the charge for each set from a hundred pounds to a thousand pounds but dropped completely the annual per set royalty of a hundred pounds. Jackson thought it still an expensive proposal. Nonetheless, he recommended it for the eight sets because, as a customer, the Royal Navy would be advised of WTS's improvements and new products. The Admiralty rejected the revision. Jackson then advised the Admiralty that while the apparatus the Royal Navy had developed on its own did not yet equal Marconi's, he believed it would in a few months. Based on that expectation, as a stopgap until the navy sets came up to an acceptable standard, the Admiralty advised WTS, the GPO, and Treasury that the Royal Navy would manufacture Marconi sets under the act.

Exhausted, Marconi boarded the *St. Paul* on November 9, 1899, for the return to London. The demands on him were enormous. Although he had hired technically qualified support, he still conceived the scientific advances necessary to effect the much-needed improvements in range and to overcome the debilitating problem of interference. He conducted the tests. Clearly his efforts and inspiration underlay the company's technical progress. In addition, no other company officer or director could sell or conduct promotional demonstrations as convincingly as Marconi. As majority shareholder, he stayed on top of the business and financial decisions.

Marconi was unlike the other principal inventors of his time. He retained the roles of inventor, salesman, and principal businessman. Once Bell completed his invention of the telephone, the demand for the product carried its sales efforts, and Bell turned his back on management issues. Edison, a full-time inventor and sales demonstrator, had performed his telephone and telegraph work under contract for Western Union, which managed the business and sales implementation. The growth and complexity of the electric industry, once Edison had developed light bulbs, power generation, and distribution to a level of commercial practicality, exceeded any one man's capacity to oversee. He soon lost control of their management and ownership.

Marconi had departed for America on a high. He had pulled off the English Channel public relations sensation. He had set a new distance record while the eyes of the entire Royal Navy had focused upon him. WTS had just submitted major contract proposals to the GPO and the Admiralty. The directors planned to make a fortune in the IPO of a new American subsidiary. Marconi seemed invincible. Now, two months later, the stock sale was on indefinite hold. The U.S. Navy had spurned a company bid. Two and a half years had passed since the formation of WTS. Despite significant scientific advances, WTS still had not yet landed a significant order. Suddenly Marconi appeared very vulnerable.

On his voyage home, Marconi had a great deal to think about.

CHAPTER 7

The Siren Call of Cyrus Field

Marconi boarded the *St. Paul* for the return to London on November 9, 1899. The public criticism of his refusal to disclose details of his inventions rankled him. He particularly did not appreciate charges made within WTS that blamed him for the failure to launch the American subsidiary. No one confronted him directly, but he understood from Jameson-Davis that the two directors who were corn brokers thought the decision not to bring the syntonic tuning device a naïve mistake. It was the type of mistake that the more sophisticated investors had feared in allowing the young and inexperienced Marconi so much latitude in the management of WTS. Scientists, they quietly murmured to themselves, rarely exhibited good business judgment. A good businessman would have been forthcoming with a potential customer the size of the United States government.

Despite the adverse circumstances under which Marconi departed New York, the homeward voyage turned out to be unexpectedly enjoyable. The isolation for ten days at sea from everything and everyone save his fellow passengers and his own thoughts relaxed him.

Although late in the year, Americans filled the steamer. They were hastening to London or Paris, perhaps for a shopping spree, before returning to their New York townhouses and country mansions for the Christmas social season. With the frequent and rapid transatlantic crossings, Paris became more and more accessible and an enormous draw for fashion-conscious women. To return home with a Parisian wardrobe certainly enhanced one's prestige. The upper circles regarded London as preeminent for establishing social standing. Presentation at the Court of St. James to the Queen of England, particularly since Victoria herself had become such a venerable institution, became the ultimate goal. If one could not return from the capital of the British Empire confidently asserting acceptance by its society, at least one could discreetly drop the names of parties attended and people met. Leaders of this grand movement to England and its ranks of royalty included such well-known socialites as Consuelo Vanderbilt, who had by marriage become the Duchess of Marlborough, and Pauline Astor, daughter of John Jacob Astor. The thirst for a taste of the grand life permeated as far inland as Chicago, elegantly represented by the delightful Mrs. Potter Palmer, and to other hinterland cities as well.

Ms. Josephine B. Holman, caught up in the spirit of the times, traveled by train from her provincial hometown of Indianapolis to New York City for her maiden voyage. Young, slender, and attractive, she arrived on the *St. Paul* with a small party of Midwesterners. They had scheduled London as the first stop on their itinerary. Also on board headed for that city, H. H. McClure, co-publisher with his brother of *McClure's Magazine,* perhaps the most highly regarded periodical of the day, traveled with a coterie of business associates and friends. His magazine specialized in feature articles and interviews with the leading figures of the day. His brother, Robert, had already covered Marconi at Wimereux.

The pleasantness of the daily shipboard routine surprised Marconi. On his outbound journey to New York, he had been preoccupied and stressed, preparing for the many upcoming activities and readying his equipment. On the homeward passage, the pressure momentarily lifted. An enormous amount had to be done on his return, but no immediate trials awaited. No lecture had to be given. No swirl of appointments ladened his calendar.

On his first day, he unpacked enough of his apparatus to set up a makeshift transmitting and receiving station. WTS had not previously had an opportunity to demonstrate aboard a transatlantic liner. With the market for wireless on commercial ships, particularly passenger ships, very much in mind, Marconi had cabled headquarters before departing. Near the end of the voyage, he would signal Needles as the *St. Paul* approached the Isle of Wight. For docking as well as insurance arrangements, it would be useful if a ship, which had not been heard from since departing New York more than a week earlier, could advise Southampton of its estimated arrival time hours before it actually appeared. Passengers could learn of news in London and Europe and exchange messages of urgency in advance of coming ashore. For purposes of conducting important business or social affairs, the ability to communicate twelve hours before landing in effect shortened the trip by that much time. The novelty of the communication would create a stir, and the press was sure to pick it up.

But until the *St. Paul* approached England, Marconi had no one to receive his signals. There were no land stations en route until Needles, and no other ships at sea were equipped with wireless. Without anyone to transmit to, he could not test for distance or interference. He had no WTS business to attend to. He had not been so idle for a whole week since his inspiration at Biellese more than five years earlier. He could think. He could worry. But there was little else he could do for WTS. Instead, he could sleep, eat at leisure, read, and stroll on deck. Unexpected activities presented themselves as well.

The company aboard the *St. Paul* turned out to be most entertaining. McClure, always in search for another story, could not resist the opportunity to meet Marconi himself and quickly sought him out. Marconi welcomed a second opportunity for major coverage for WTS in the preeminent magazine. The two quickly became friends. McClure enveloped Marconi in the comings and goings of McClure's companions. One of his compatriots knew Josephine. Who would not be eager to introduce the darkly handsome, famous foreign bachelor to a charming, unattached lady? The stature of the world-renowned inventor overwhelmed the girl from Indiana. The days passed with Marconi and Josephine frequently together in McClure's circle. In amiable conversations over candlelit, five-course dinners, which the group enjoyed in the richly decorated state dining room, or gathered together in discussion bundled up against the cold in clusters of deck chairs, Josephine delighted Marconi. She captivated him. He quickly became infatuated, if not enamored. Not since Leghorn as a teenager had he spent this much time with a woman. The last time he had had a crush on a girl, it was Sita Camperio, the older sister of his close friend Giulio. Josephine, lithe and tall, dressed fashionably. Her hats in a funny way reminded him of Annie's in Leghorn. She was talkative but not lordly or condescending as some of the Prince of Wales's guests on HMS *Osborne* had been. Marconi had had little experience in handling sophisticated, worldly women. But his exposure to society and social events in New York, particularly with the friendly and relaxed Lipton at his side, had increased Marconi's confidence and made him less shy, especially of women. Josephine's relative naïveté and her quiet manner suited his growing self-assurance in female relationships.

Marconi walked the decks daily, invigorated by the brisk November winds. Invariably he focused on WTS. He fretted over the slow pace of revenues and the frustrations with the Admiralty and the GPO. As he gazed about, the surrounding ocean constantly reminded him of the difficulties its vast distances posed to communication. Only submarine cable companies had found a way to operate rapidly across the seas.

Over land, telegraph and telephone satisfied demand for fast interchange. In the United States, major companies provided this service. In Europe, government monopolies occupied the field, protected by laws prohibiting private competition. The infrastructure of telegraph and telephone lines, telegraph offices, and telephone switching facilities had been built and amortized. Wireless did not have a significant cost advantage over inland telegraph and telephone. Few profitable opportunities to enter land markets appeared available to WTS.

For information exchange at sea, nationalistic navies and their governments exhibited a preference for domestic suppliers. The British, Germans, French, and Russians each proved to be a difficult sales prospect. This forced WTS to be more dependent on revenue from commercial shipping interests. Marconi believed that once he solved interference, which he hoped would be soon, sales would follow. But he worried over when this revenue would materialize. To be effective, ship-to-shore wireless required the construction of many shore stations, an expensive program just underway. He doubted that the magnitude of the shipping market could carry WTS to profitability.

The transoceanic market excited Marconi. Unquestionably, the costs of wireless fell far below those of laying and maintaining submarine cable. Demand appeared to be enormous. Most important, free enterprise flourished. The most significant crossings were international seas and waterways that separated countries. The authority of individual governments ceased a short distance off shore. No government could impose a monopoly beyond its own territorial limit or on the opposite shore controlled by another country. As a result, private corporations laid cable in international water free of regulation. They negotiated shore landing rights with governments where the cable emerged from the water and interconnection agreements with local telegraph systems. Best of all, companies could set their own prices. Because of the enormous capital required to lay a cable and maintain it, few were willing to undertake the risk. On most underwater routes, only one or at most two corporations provided the service. They had no competition. The submarine cable businesses were geographic monopolies or oligopolies, charging the maximum the market could bear. High margins and high profits went to those entrepreneurs with the courage and luck to successfully lay a cable.

If WTS could enter this market, it should have the same rights as cable. A wireless company should be able to receive permission from governments for shore stations and be allowed to contract with telegraph operations for interconnections. The wider the body of water and the longer the distance spanned, the greater wireless's cost advantage should be over cable. Although the English Channel had the heaviest cable traffic, Marconi suspected providing cross-Channel service would be more symbolic than profitable because of its narrow width.

Over the past fifty years, the transwater cable market had grown rapidly. In 1849, two brothers, John and Jacob Brett, raised two thousand pounds and obtained a concession from France for a telegraph line across the English Channel. On August 28, they successfully laid the first submarine cable. Messages were exchanged that night. The next day, a fisherman's anchor severed the wire. The brothers had nothing to show for their expenditure and had to start over. The next year, they put up three thousand pounds more and dropped another line from Calais to Dover. This time, it remained in operation. Over the course of the 1850s, cable companies sank additional lines in the English Channel from Dover to Calais as well as new lines from London to Belgium and the Netherlands. From Spezia in Italy, a line ran due south on the bottom of the Ligurian Sea to Corsica, then across the Strait of Bonifacio to Sardinia, and finally under the Mediterranean to Algeria. A short line submerged at Italy's toe crossed the Strait of Messina to Sicily. In the Crimean War, cable lines tied British interests in Constantinople to the rest of Turkey across the Sea of Marmara as well as to Russia in the Crimea across the Black Sea. The 1860s saw cable in the Persian Gulf. By 1870, the technology extended to India and Singapore. In the 1870s, ships laid cable in the south Atlantic from Madeira to Puerto Rico and laced the South American eastern coast to Rio de Janeiro, Sao Paulo, and Montevideo. At the same time, new connections stretched from Singapore to Djakarta and Darwin and northward to Hong Kong, Shanghai, Vladivostok, and Japan.

At midcentury, a message required twelve days to travel by boat between London and New York. Frederic N. Gisborne, an English engineer who had constructed a telegraph line from Montreal to Cape Breton, Nova Scotia, became obsessed with reducing that time. He proposed sending telegraph messages from Cape Breton to Cape Ray on Newfoundland's western shore by steamboat or carrier pigeon. From Cape Ray, he would hack eastward through two hundred miles of Newfoundland wilderness, clearing a way for a telegraph line to the port at St. John's. That harbor was Newfoundland's and the North American continent's easternmost port and the closest to Europe. From St. John's, fast ships could cross the North Atlantic to Galway, Ireland. From there, telegraph would retransmit the messages to London. By reducing the boat trip of thirty-five hundred miles from New York to London to twenty-one hundred miles from St. John's to Ireland, Gisborne hoped to reduce the overall time to deliver a message across the Atlantic by as much as four days. He petitioned Newfoundland, a British territory, for authority to establish a corporation to build a line between St. John's and Cape Ray. The legislative council granted Gisborne exclusive telegraph rights in Newfoundland. The terrain and weather proved more difficult than anticipated. In 1853, after just forty miles of construction across the rugged landscape, his enterprise exhausted its financial resources and went bankrupt.

Gisborne appealed to Cyrus W. Field, age thirty-four, a New Yorker who had made a fortune in wholesale paper. Gisborne's project intrigued Field. The New Yorker proposed eliminating the use of ships altogether. He favored submarine cable between Cape Breton and Cape Ray and most audaciously between Newfoundland and Ireland. On inquiry, he had discovered that the U.S. Navy had just conducted the first systematic soundings between the two islands. They revealed the bottom to be basically a plateau, at no point deeper than two and a half miles. Fragile, microscopic shells covered the ocean floor. To oceanographers, this indicated that no hostile currents or terrain at the bottom would disturb a cable. Samuel Morse, inventor of the telegraph, advised Field. In his judgment, an electric current could traverse twenty-three hundred miles of submarine cable, more than the expected maximum distance from Newfoundland to Ireland, taking into account undulations in the level of the ocean bottom. Field formed the New York, Newfoundland, and London Telegraph Company and raised 1.5 million dollars, or three hundred thousand pounds (at that time five dollars bought one pound), among Peter Cooper and other New York City industrialists. He acquired Gisborne's organization and paid off its debt. From the Newfoundland legislature, Field received a grant denying anyone else the right for the next fifty years to touch Newfoundland with a telegraph wire or cable. Field finished Gisborne's cross-island telegraph line and submerged a submarine cable from Cape Ray to Cape Breton. In the process, he used up all available capital, and his venture, like Gisborne's, went under.

Nonetheless, Field persisted. In 1856, he traveled to London and won the financial backing of John Brett, the first person to lay cable across the English Channel and now a cable magnate. Field retained some of England's best physicists and electricians, including Lord Kelvin and Charles Bright, who in 1853 had laid the first successful cable across the Irish Sea. Morse and British scientists collaborated in experiments that confirmed Morse's earlier opinion that battery-driven current would travel the cable length and deliver messages at a commercially acceptable rate of eight words per minute. Assured by the world's leading specialists, Field with Morse petitioned the British government for support. Provided that Field raised three hundred and fifty thousand pounds, Treasury committed to furnish ships to take further soundings and assist in laying the cable. It agreed to pay at a minimum fourteen thousand pounds annually for its cable messages. In return, the British government must have priority in sending messages. It would share this priority with the United States government if that country made a comparable commitment. Field organized the Atlantic Telegraph Company to continue New York, Newfoundland, and London Telegraph Company's service to Ireland. He raised the required capital by public subscription in London, Liverpool, Glasgow, and Manchester. Brilliantly, he capped his efforts by obtaining a matching contribution in Washington.

In 1857, the two governments made good on their promise to assist, lending two warships to the expedition. USS *Niagara* and HMS *Agamemnon* undertook to lay the cable, paying it out first from the stern of the USS *Niagara*. The outing failed. The paying-out machinery braked too firmly, halting the cable at the same moment a swell lifted the stern.

Marconi

The line snapped under the pressure. In 1858, after two more failures, the cable was finally landed. The London *Times* rated the significance of the accomplishment:

> Since the discovery of Columbus nothing has been done in any degree comparable to the vast enlargement which has thus been given to the sphere of human activity. More was done yesterday for the consolidation of our empire, than the wisdom of our statesmen, the liberality of our Legislature, or the loyalty of our colonists, could ever have effected.(FN 1)

The *New York Herald* called it "the great work of the age." President James Buchanan and Queen Victoria exchanged messages. In celebration, a hundred-gun salute fired in New York, church bells pealed throughout the city, and at night the proud, surging metropolis was illuminated to such an extent that City Hall's cupola caught fire. Poems were written, speeches given, sermons delivered. Everywhere the message proclaimed that peace had come closer to hand. On the cornerstone of the new Cathedral of St. Patrick, the clerics carved Field's name alongside those of the saints. On September 1, a solemn service at Trinity Church attended by city authorities, representatives of foreign governments, and an immense concourse of people began the official day of celebration. At noon, the USS *Niagara* landed in New York from Newfoundland. Field and the ship's officers led a six-hour-long procession, which wound from the Battery to the Crystal Palace at Forty-second Street. The queen knighted Bright and would have done so for Field, but he declined the honor as inappropriate for a U.S. citizen. On the evening of the parade, at an extravagant assembly at the Crystal Palace, its aisles and galleries filled, speaker after speaker honored Field. The captain of the USS *Niagara* accepted a gold medal. A spectacular firemen's torchlight parade crowned the gala occasion.

But the night ended in disaster. The transatlantic cable sputtered its last signals. The cable went dead. No one ever knew why. Did the engineers apply too much voltage to the line? Did the cable, which had been left outside in the sun between the 1857 and 1858 voyages, dry out? Whatever the reasons, it devastated the stockholders. Nothing remained of the total five hundred thousand pounds committed to the scheme but the experience gained. Public sentiment immediately turned against Field. Former enthusiasts doubted that signals had ever been received. Unsubstantiated charges arose that the announcement that signals had been received was nothing more than stock manipulation to allow insiders to sell out at the height of the August excitement.

Even after that debacle, Field labored indefatigably for the next five years to revive the project. The Civil War, however, significantly hindered U.S. fund-raising. But the value of transatlantic cable had become clearly understood, and the ability to lay the cable had been demonstrated. The Atlantic Telegraph Company forged ahead, aided again by Britain's best engineers and scientists, who improved the design and manufacture of the cable and laying apparatus. In 1863, Thomas Brassey, who built railroads on every continent but Antarctica, offered to pay one-tenth of the next expedition's cost. The Gutta Percha Company, which made the waterproof insulation, and Glass, Elliot & Co., the world's principal sea cable manufacturer, merged to form TCM, the Telegraph Construction and Maintenance Company. TCM underwrote a major portion of the cost. Altogether, five hundred thousand pounds was raised, in part by public subscription, the price per share being reduced to five pounds to attract wider participation. Into the *Great Eastern*, a six-masted, five-funneled paddle steamer, the world's largest vessel, TCM loaded the cable, one single strand twenty-seven hundred miles long and weighing seven thousand tons. The *Great Eastern* carried five hundred men, eight thousand tons of coal, one milking cow, one dozen oxen, twenty pigs, one hundred and twenty sheep, and flocks of ducks and geese. Three times unidentified hands aboard the *Great Eastern* sabotaged the cable by driving a steel wire into its core. This action caused the current to leak out of the cable into the ocean. After the third act of sabotage, the *Great Eastern* attempted to lift the cable two and a half miles up from the ocean bottom to repair the leak. The great ship drifted backwards over the cable and severed it. The broken end sank to the ocean floor and could not be retrieved. The *Great Eastern* returned to port.

The next year, 1866, the undaunted Field organized a new company. Of its six hundred thousand pounds capital, a hundred thousand pounds was subscribed for by TCM, ten thousand pounds each by twenty individuals including Field, and the balance by the public. This time the laying succeeded uneventfully. In addition, the *Great Eastern* grappled on the ocean bottom and recovered the cable lost the prior year. The year 1866 ended with two transatlantic cables in operation. The endeavor to lay the transatlantic cable had taken thirteen years since Gisborne first went bankrupt hacking his way through forty miles of Newfoundland wilderness.

By the end of the century, far below the deck of the *St. Paul*, a dozen cables now crossed the ocean floor between the two continents. Cable linked the world. On the London market, the stocks of a dozen companies reflected a prosperous industry that manufactured, laid, and operated cable. Government, industry, and the public spent enormous amounts of money to speed their messages under the world's waters. Marconi believed that wireless could send messages over the water as quickly and clearly and at far less cost. Traffic between London and New York dominated all other routes in dollar or sterling volume. Before the voyage ended, Marconi carefully weighed each WTS sales opportunity. He reached a firm conclusion. WTS must enter the North Atlantic market.

When the *St. Paul* neared England, Marconi executed the experiment he had planned at the outset of the voyage. Needles Hotel was reached at a distance of seventy-six miles. The success affirmed the eighty-mile record transmission from Wimereux to Chelmsford and Marconi's judgment that signals did not travel forever in a straight line, shooting over the horizon into endless space farther and farther above the earth's surface. Over the course of the next six hours, the *St. Paul* entered the Solent, passed by Needles, and steamed up to Southampton. The liner and the Isle of Wight station exchanged a constant stream of messages. Needles described major news of the day. The captain collaborated with McClure and printed a one-page newspaper that they distributed about the ship. A quarter of a day before their arrival in port, the several hundred voyagers who had been completely isolated from the world for the length of the passage had information about principal events onshore. They landed fully informed, to the astonishment of those who greeted them. It became major publicity for WTS's ship-to-shore marketing effort.

The camaraderie of the Atlantic crossing and the afterglow of Marconi's popular reception in New York burnished by his celebrity status among the passengers no doubt warmed his heart. The shipboard introduction to Miss Holman had blossomed into romance that promised to continue in London. The onboard newsletter identified McClure as publisher, Marconi as correspondent, and Josephine as treasurer. They had a grand time with it. She hinted to Marconi that she might prolong her visit in London while her companions continued on to Paris. There was a suggestion among some of those with McClure of a possible engagement.

Marconi debarked, rejuvenated by the voyage and the fabulous communications with Needles. Already, though, the challenges posed by his decision to enter the transatlantic market preoccupied him. A massive spark and incredible power would be required to propel the electronic waves thirty-five hundred miles. No one had ever built a machine on the scale he envisaged. That constituted a unique challenge. Such a spark would produce a huge number of powerful waves that might well flood receivers within hundreds of miles of the transmitter with unintelligible signals. The solution to interference he had devised at Wimereux and aboard the *Vienne* he believed should tune out even the strongest of these waves. The Atlantic project reinforced the pressure already on Marconi to perfect his syntonic tuning device.

Even if he thought he could solve these problems, Marconi needed the director's approval to proceed. The board had scheduled a major meeting for February 1900 to review the year and WTS's status. The directors were in a truculent mood. WTS had failed to budge the GPO, who was stonewalling contract discussions. Trinity House stubbornly followed the GPO's lead. Relations with the Admiralty were a disaster.

The fault may not have all lain with the government's and the GPO's intractability. WTS's high price demands generated resistance. Dissension within WTS's management ranks rose to the surface. Major Flood-Page, despite having been brought in the prior August to assist Jameson-Davis as secretary and deputy managing director, struggled to get things done. He did not have final authority to set price or important terms in negotiations with customers. This power remained firmly in the hands of the directors. He felt they frustrated his efforts. In an outspoken conclusion to a lengthy memorandum reviewing WTS sales efforts, he lashed out at the board's negotiating techniques:

> I feel that as long as the Board are undecided as to the royalties to be charged for the use of the instruments then no business can be conducted with satisfaction to anyone working in this office be he Managing Director, Secretary, or otherwise engaged. Moreover it appears to me that as

soon as the directors find that their offers are acceptable
and people come forward to close the bargains they have
invariably imposed fresh conditions and tried to raise the
price and this does us harm.(FN 2)

Marconi pressed individual directors to agree to build the unprecedented supertransmitter. The eager young Italian persistently
pestered the cigar-smoking elder statesmen with an array of scientific
data that they made little effort to comprehend. He encountered stiff
resistance. They understood sterling and pence. The project would
consume vast amounts of time and money. It would distract WTS
from the urgent need to realize immediate sales. Flood-Page displayed
a total lack of interest in the project. The more the inventor discussed
it, the more opposed the manager became.

Marconi gave way to the pressure. Already annoyed at the niggardly
results of his prodigious efforts at the prior summer's Royal Navy maneuvers and the frustrating, nonresponsive government negotiations,
he became infuriated at the British Army. He believed WTS's men in
South Africa performed bravely under the arduous circumstances of the
Boer War and were unfairly blamed for WTS's instruments' performance.
The army's poor assignment and support of the sets, he believed, caused
their failure. Marconi outspokenly defended his engineers and dared to
attack the army. In the British public's eye, the army was sacrosanct,
despite a succession of bloody losses and the inability to relieve sieges
at Ladysmith, Mafeking, and Kimberly. In a Royal Society lecture in
February, Marconi lambasted the government. The War Office had not
provided suitable aerial masts. His men had volunteered to carry wireless
into Kimberly through Boer lines, but the army had refused their offer.
Kimberly, Ladysmith, and Mafeking should have been equipped with
wireless before hostilities began. Irritated by Marconi's outburst and the
fact that it came from a foreigner representing a commercial interest, the
army retaliated. It ordered the sets dismantled and returned. That ended
a brilliant opportunity for WTS to have demonstrated to armies everywhere the advantages of wireless on the battlefield.

Some matters, however, began to move in WTS's direction. The
Royal Navy's effort to manufacture Marconi wireless devices aboard the
HMS *Vernon* proceeded unsatisfactorily. Under Jackson's supervision,

naval personnel built tappers, tuners, and coherers based on Marconi's patented designs, while private subcontractors copied other components. The navy then assembled the parts. The resulting apparatus field-tested at a maximum range of twenty miles, far short of Marconi's. In the midst of the tests, Jackson was transferred to command HMS *Vulcan* in the Mediterranean. At the same time, Flood-Page, taking matters into his own hands and wishing to change the tone of the negotiations, called on the Admiralty. He offered assurances of friendly relations and renewed the offer to lend equipment and WTS technicians. This time, the top brass overrode its financial advisers. It concluded that the sets it built did not approach WTS standards under active service conditions. It could no longer be without Marconi wireless. In February 1900, an agreement was reached to accept the loan and to pay WTS engineers to operate the equipment at the rate of three pounds salary a week. The informal, partial understanding constituted a small step forward. It had no immediate effect on the stalemate over the purchase price and royalty for the equipment. Nonetheless, it satisfied Flood-Page. Something at least had been accomplished. It strengthened his arguments for more personal authority.

In the weeks before the February board meeting, Marconi progressed remarkably in his tuning efforts. When he had advised the U.S. Bureau of Equipment prior to the American trip and the U.S. Navy at the New York sea trials that he had a solution to interference, he was referring of course to the syntonic tuning apparatus developed at Wimereux and on board the *Vienne* for which he had filed a patent application. While it eliminated interference in most situations and encompassed the elements of a full solution, by Marconi's own standards it fell short. He continued searching for a comprehensive answer. In February, he felt he had arrived. He sensed he had achieved a major breakthrough. The instruments were at last performing satisfactorily. The science of his solution seemed complete and novel in application. He was aware of no competing product or concept as effective as his. He awaited only the recognition of his pending application by the patent office to confirm his private judgment. Tight-lipped and noncommittal as always, he had, nonetheless, in the last month been unable to entirely contain himself as the final pieces fell into place. He exuded an air of excitement discernable to his WTS scientific colleagues. He was in the hunt. It was contagious. It lifted them all.

Marconi

The startling new distances achieved the prior summer resulted from two years of experiments with transformers called jiggers. Jiggers, housed in small, black cylindrical containers, changed the form of the electricity that passed through their circuitry. Marconi placed jiggers in the transmitter and receiver. In the transmitter, the jigger reduced the voltage from the spark and boosted the current that propelled the waves and therefore increased the distance of the signal. In the receiver, Marconi reversed the jigger's role. The jigger reduced the current from the received signal and boosted its voltage. Higher voltage made it easier for the coherer to detect the wave. Marconi and his team of research assistants tested more than five hundred combinations of jigger and circuit arrangements. What a difference WTS meant to Marconi. At Villa Grifone and in London in the early days, he labored alone. He could not have experimented to this extent by himself. The records set at the Royal Navy maneuvers resulted from installing the best of these combinations in the equipment used for the exercises.

Remarkably, the jigger not only enhanced distance but also facilitated syntonic tuning. In his effort to increase distance, he added similarly configured jiggers to both the transmitter and receiver and discovered that he attained superior results if elements of the transmitter and receiver were in harmony with each other—that is, if they had identical electric characteristics in some of their essential components. He had not arrived at this result by the application of a preconceived theory. Nor did he fully understand why it worked. As with many of his advances, he hit upon the startling new concept by combining by trial and error different elements not previously arranged together. Once he saw promising results, he tweaked the relationships between constituent parts until he maximized performance. In his jigger patent application, Marconi spoke of adjustments in the transmitter and receiver that the small transformer experiments indicated contributed to syntony between the instruments: It is desirable that the induction coil [of the receiver] should be in tune or syntony with the electrical oscillations transmitted, the most appropriate number of turns and most appropriate thickness of wire varying with the length of wave transmitted.(FN 3) The syntony benefits to distance reduced interference. Marconi's focus on transmission length unexpectedly laid the foundation for a tuning system that tuned out or excluded unwanted signals.

On his return from New York, Marconi immediately sought a final solution for tuning centered on the jigger's harmonics. The effort begun at Wimereux and aboard the *Vienne* and deferred by the Royal Navy maneuvers had been halted by the American trip. The moment Marconi stepped off the *St. Paul*, experimentation resumed. On December 19, 1899, he filed an improved specification to the tuning application. It represented a giant step forward by bringing more elements of the transmitter and receiver into harmony. In the specification, Marconi said, The best results are obtained when the length of the wire of the secondary of the induction coil [of the receiver] is equal to the length of the vertical wire used at the transmitting station.(FN 4) Following these instructions, a receiver could select which incoming message it would receive by making the receiver's secondary wire equal to the length of the transmitter's vertical wire or antenna. Similarly, a receiver could tune out messages from other transmitters by making its wire a different length than those transmitters' aerials. This was true in almost all cases except when the transmitters of the messages were equidistant from the receiver. Unfortunately, such a situation could occur numerous times among ships in a fleet equipped with wireless.

As a result, the solution still did not satisfy Marconi. He pressed on. He looked everywhere for ideas, including the syntony patents granted to Lodge in 1897 and 1898. Lodge had succeeded in tuning the apparatus he built based on those patents, but the equipment could not send and receive signals at any appreciable distance. Just before the February 1900 board meeting, Marconi arrived at a new combination of adjustments not covered by Lodge's patents. At the center of both the transmitter and receiver, Marconi placed the end of the wire that ran down to the ground near the beginning of each instrument's wire that ran up into the air as the aerial. Next he constructed the antennae in both the transmitter and receiver so that each could be adjusted to the same timing or periodicity of the electronic waves produced by the transmitter's spark. That is to the time required for the wavelength to repeat itself. Then he examined the condensers attached to the transmitter and receiver. These condensers had the capacity to accumulate and hold only one amount of electric charge. He substituted condensers whose capacity could be adjusted to hold various amounts of electric charge. Marconi did not invent variable condensers. But no one had previously utilized them in the way he did in wireless circuitry.

Marconi knew that he had arrived at the solution. In both the transmitter and receiver, he could vary two key elements—the periodicity of the antenna and the capacity of the condenser. Marconi had created two controllable variables. Operators could now adjust their transmitters and receivers to a unique combination of periodicity and capacity so that they could communicate only between themselves. In effect, they blocked out any signals not tuned precisely to their combination.

WTS rushed to the patent office with a master patent application for the newly configured tunable transmitters and receivers. The application embraced all of Marconi's ideas that contributed to his unprecedented and effective instrumentation.

Marconi prepared for the upcoming February board meeting highly confident that a patent would be issued. The solution incorporated in the patent should end the complaints of interference that caused shipping companies to defer purchases. Furthermore, Marconi had written the application as broadly as possible. He expected that WTS's competitors would have difficulty finding tuning solutions that did not infringe on his hoped-for patent.

Most exciting to Marconi, he had satisfied one of the prerequisites for transatlantic transmission. The new tuning devices should eliminate interference from the super powerful signals that would have to be generated for the crossing. Transmitters and receivers within the enormous range of that signal need only be tuned to a periodicity or capacity not being utilized by the huge transmitter.

The day for the much-awaited February board meeting arrived. Serious matters filled its agenda. The year's results depressed everyone. Disappointments on the sales side far outweighed successes. The lack of revenue and the rapid rate at which WTS spent its capital worried even the optimists. The cash-conscious directors feared that Marconi's transatlantic proposal could bankrupt WTS.

From Marconi's scientific viewpoint, however, the year had been the best ever. Distance had tripled. He had cracked tuning. He fully expected to signal from England to the United States. Revenue would then follow.

The board meeting started calmly enough. Indeed, to outward appearances, little had changed since the organizational meeting two years earlier. Outside it was the same, dreary wintry weather in London. Inside the directors gathered in the room in which they first met. The mature, wise financiers puffed on their cigars, quickly filling the small chamber with acrid smoke. Marconi talked enthusiastically of his plans. The only indications of WTS's remarkable progress were pictures of some of the more astounding events that hung on the mahogany walls and the presence of Flood-Page at the crowded oak table.

In its first piece of business, the board voted to add Marconi's name to that of the WTS. The directors acknowledged that Marconi was known everywhere and WTS was not. WTS now became officially the Marconi Wireless Telegraph Company (MWT). Only Marconi voted against it. He believed completely in his wireless. Its performance and reputation would provide the organization's identity. When the corporation had been formed, Giuseppe had argued strenuously that Marconi's name be included. But to Marconi, the company was not his personal thing. It was not a vehicle to promote him. He was genuinely modest, whatever critical American reporters may have thought on his arrival six months earlier in New York. Even in this year in which he had achieved worldwide celebrity status, he was not interested in it for himself. He remained, as he had been from the first day of his inspiration at Biellese, devoted to achieving long-distance signals. Nonetheless, he did not veto the change. Perhaps he was not totally adverse to the recognition.

The next action personally saddened Marconi. Jameson-Davis formally stepped down as managing director. In his place, the directors elected Flood-Page. The move had been expected since August. For close to three years, Jameson-Davis had juggled organizing and managing MWT and running his own engineering firm. As a result, his engineering practice had suffered. MWT needed a full-time managing director, and Flood-Page had proved himself to the board as Jameson-Davis's assistant. Although he removed himself from day-to-day activities, Jameson-Davis would remain a very active director.

Nonetheless, it was a watershed event for Marconi. Since his arrival in England four years earlier, Jameson-Davis had been Marconi's counselor, adviser, and supporter. Jameson-Davis would still perform these functions. But MWT now had a professional, full-time manager with his own agenda.

Flood-Page's priorities were more short-term, bottom-line oriented than Marconi's. For Marconi, the company should be a research vehicle.

Marconi

Its success in creating a competitive product would over time assure its maximum profitability. For the new managing director, the future was now and profits came first. In his struggle for authority and achievement, Flood-Page articulated his views, often with more candor than tact, and politically sought to align sales-minded directors against Marconi's cash-consuming research. Marconi led by example, by accomplishment, by determination, and by his position in the company. For the moment, the two men's professionalism obscured their differences in styles and goals.

In his initial act as managing director, Flood-Page delivered a state of the company analysis to the board, particularly emphasizing income. It culminated in a question. Should MWT accept an offer from a shipping company to be its first commercial liner customer? To the directors' amazement, Flood-Page, despite being so pro-revenue, opposed the sale. The subject provoked animated debate. Professor Slaby—in collaboration with a countryman, Count von Arco, and with the support of their government—had developed a wireless system. It worked but could not compare with Marconi's. The German navy, however, had adopted the Slaby-Arco platform. Surprisingly, the German shipping line, Nordeutschen Lloyd of Bremen, sought Marconi wireless. It intended to install MWT equipment aboard its ship *Kaiser Wilhelm der Grosse* and on the approaches to its harbor in the North Sea at Borkum Island lighthouse and on the Borkum Riff lightship. Flood-Page argued adamantly against the sale. Why did the increasingly nationalistic and militaristic authorities not insist that Nordeutschen support Slaby-Arco? Flood-Page had no doubt that they only wished to acquire the sets to break them down and steal their secrets. Given the dismal state of sales, and Flood-Page's own persuasive arguments on other occasions for revenue, the board could not resist the offer. The directors approved allowing the *Kaiser Wilhelm* access to MWT apparatus.

The last item on the agenda was Marconi's transatlantic proposal. Flood-Page led the numerous, persuasive arguments against the idea. As managing director, his duties required him to bring the company into the black, pumping up sales and cutting down costs, particularly research expenses. Flood-Page bluntly attacked Marconi's penchant for development and his obsession with distance. He should be restricted to realistic endeavors consistent with sales goals. MWT needed immediate revenue sources, especially naval procurement and ship-to-shore agreements like

Nordeutschen, much as Flood-Page disliked that contract. The company already had the battery-driven equipment in working order for these businesses. The apparatus was simple and relatively inexpensive. Marconi should make sure he had resolved the basic problem of interference and then lead the marketing effort to the world's shipping lines and navies. This strategy would benefit MWT far more than rushing off in a new direction with a host of new scientific problems. Enormous generators and antennas with which MWT engineers had no experience would be required to carry the Atlantic. The energy input, the size, the complexity, and the cost of transoceanic transmitters had no precedent. The design and construction of such generators called for enormous capital at a time of eroding company reserves. If MWT should actually create a superpower transmitter, it would present a new danger. The electromagnetic waves released from its mammoth spark might drown out the company's ship-to-shore signals for hundreds of miles, ruining the potential commercial shipping business. And while Marconi might have applied for his master tuning patent, the fact was its effectiveness when confronted with waves from a mega-generator had not been tested.

Flood-Page saved his most telling objection for last. By the great weight of electrical and mathematical theory and in the opinion of almost all current knowledgeable scientists, what Marconi proposed could not be done. Maxwell's fundamental conclusion that electromagnetic waves obeyed the same laws of reflection and refraction as light waves, differing only in frequency, had been verified again and again. Light travels in a straight line. When the sun sets below the horizon, the earth becomes dark. When Marconi's waves traveled beyond the horizon, they would not return to earth. They would be too far above the surface to be received. Instances where Marconi's transmissions had exceeded distances impossible under this theory, but only by a small amount as at Spezia, Flood-Page could disregard as insignificant. He had a more difficult time dismissing recent months' signals. The Royal Navy maneuvers, Wimereux to Chelmsford, and *St. Paul* to Needles covered sixty to eighty miles. All doubled the possible range projected by the optical rules. Each, in theory, should have been far above the reach of the receiving antenna. Flood-Page could not credibly challenge their veracity, particularly when witnessed by the Royal Navy and passengers and crew aboard the *St. Paul*. There were too many received signals to disclaim them as one-off aberrations.

Marconi

Flood-Page could point out, however, that no scientific theory explained or supported these extraordinary transmissions. Therefore, to protect the company's assets from waste on theoretically unsound experimentation, Flood-Page conservatively and reasonably argued that he and the directors were compelled to accept the prevailing scientific view. No signal sent from England's shore could be received in the United States.

Marconi had two simple answers. First, for all of the board's efforts, Flood-Page's efforts, and his own efforts, MWT had failed to attain the necessary sales. The company was doomed if it continued on its present course. In contrast, the private cable companies had handsome profits. They literally sat on the shorelines, on the outer borders of the government telegraph monopolies, not prohibited but rewarded for operating their interconnections to the inland telegraph services. Wireless would enjoy the same privilege and would dramatically outperform submarine cables. The estimated cost of building wireless generators would be far less than the multimillion-dollar costs of manufacturing and laying cable. The expense of maintaining transmitters would be substantially less than maintaining cable. The demand for transwater messages already existed. MWT did not have to try to create a new market as it did with ship-to-shore. With its potential price advantage over cable, wireless should capture substantial revenue.

Nor did MWT have to fear wireless competitors. Given its technical superiority and patent protection, MWT might be the sole transatlantic wireless company. Marconi did not have to spell it out.

The board might be able to establish a monopoly in long-distance, transwater, rapid communication. He did not address the consequences if he failed.

Marconi's second answer in the eyes of some consisted of no more than his long-standing, almost blind faith in the feasibility of long-range signaling. Wireless seemingly had the ability to penetrate hills and steel buildings. The curvature of the earth across the Atlantic, if likened to the hill that he surmounted at Villa Grifone, constituted a colossal mountain between London and New York, a mountain 150 miles high and far thicker. But Marconi did not have to penetrate that mass. Now that he had disproved the optical analogy that waves went out in a straight line and had demonstrated that his signals followed or clung to the curvature of the earth, no theory limited how far signals might travel and be received. All he needed was power.

Marconi had an ever-present third argument, which he did not need to articulate. He was the largest shareholder and the driving technical mind. He wanted to do it. MWT, like Queen Victoria and England, had no other electrician like Marconi.

With serious misgivings and fear for the company's remaining capital and ability to survive, tentatively and conditionally, the board approved Marconi's proposal. First, however, he must build a superpower transmitter that worked. Then he must prove that it would not annihilate the company's nascent ship-to-shore commercial shipping business by drowning out MWT's other transmitters. Having met those prerequisites, he must surmount the ultimate challenge if all this effort and expenditure were not to be in vain.

Could he really hurl an invisible, electromagnetic wave thirty-five hundred miles and prove that he had received it?

CHAPTER 8

Preparations for a Preposterous Gamble

Not yet twenty-six years old in February 1900, Marconi had already traveled a long way. Now he demanded that his loss-burdened, undercapitalized company with an unpretentious board and small staff undertake a high-risk venture. When submarine cables arrived at the same critical juncture in their development, the cross-Atlantic gamble had required the backing of a dozen major capitalists and investment capital exceeding ten million dollars, more than a decade of effort, involvement of some of the world's most eminent electrical engineers and scientists, and support from two major governments. More than one company went bankrupt in the process.

Marconi's solitary enterprise had expanded to seventeen people. The new managing director, Major Flood-Page, did not always consult with Marconi as Jameson-Davis had. The chummy, single department "band of brothers" at the Haven Hotel had been replaced with organized divisions of labor. In the former furniture warehouse at Chelmsford, a condenser and winding shop, a carpenter's shop, a mounting shop, and a machine shop all came under the supervision of a works manager. Below Edison light bulbs, well-groomed women in long-sleeved blouses and ankle-length dresses, some wearing aprons, stood at two long workbenches, their nimble fingers manipulating the intricate wiring An increasingly competent staff did research and demonstrated to customers.

Flood-Page, having been overruled by the directors in his opposition to the contract with Nordeutschen Lloyd of Bremen, reversed direction and moved immediately to install the ordered equipment. The day after the board meeting, he sent Kemp off to the Borkum Island lighthouse. By February 28, Kemp had wireless stations operating at the lighthouse and the Borkum Riff lightship. He boarded the *Kaiser Wilhelm der Grosse* as it steamed out of Bremen. *Kaiser Wilhelm* easily contacted both lightship and lighthouse. Once into the English Channel and heading westward, the German passenger liner picked up Needles and Haven and stayed in constant touch as it moved towards the Atlantic to a distance of fifty miles.

With his heart perhaps warmed by the success of the company's first commercial passenger liner contract, Marconi introduced Josephine to Annie. The romance had blossomed in London while Marconi shuttled back and forth between headquarters and his syntonic research at Haven. Annie, who had gone home to be with Giuseppe to overcome her disappointment at missing the trip to America, had returned to London to look after her son. She quickly learned about Josephine. The threesome dined near Annie's London residence, the Grand Hotel on Trafalgar Square. Annie magnanimously suppressed her fear of losing her special relationship with her famous child to this American beauty with whom her son had become so infatuated. Whatever their respective internal apprehensions of the role the other might play in the future in Marconi's life, the two women graciously accepted each other's company. On many subsequent evenings, the trio attended the theater together, followed by a late supper. Before Marconi's twenty-sixth birthday on April 25, Josephine and Marconi announced their engagement.

In addition to his absorption in wireless and his fascination with Josephine, Marconi became increasingly preoccupied with his health, particularly with sleep and what he ate. He developed a regime, perhaps to give himself stability and a daily touchstone in a life where he felt relentless pressure. Every morning he breakfasted at precisely the same time with the same menu. He insisted upon soft-boiled eggs, bread with butter and marmalade, and tea. No matter what time he climbed into bed, and if late he then worried about lack of sleep, he roused himself to be at the table by eight o'clock sharp. He ate well, but sparsely, a habit he first developed in childhood when Annie fretted about his skinny frame.

Marconi's birthday coincided with the incorporation of a new MWT subsidiary, the Marconi International Marine Communication Co. Ltd. Flood-Page, anticipating more commercial maritime business following the success of the *Kaiser Wilhelm*, organized the subsidiary to specialize in commercial shipping contracts. He also wanted to isolate the shipping business from other MWT activities. In the event sending telegrams from ship-to-shore transgressed local telegraph monopolies, like the GPO's, Flood-Page hoped to insulate MWT's other affairs from any sanctions imposed on Marconi International Marine for the violation.

The next day, Marconi received a magnificent gift, one that he had eagerly sought for more than two years. The London Patent Office granted his syntonic tuning device Patent #7777. Marconi celebrated at dinner with his two women. He embraced his new fiancée with such uncustomary enthusiasm that she could well have wondered where his priorities lay. Annie he grasped as emotionally as the day he signaled over the hill at Villa Grifone. The board of directors congratulated him at a luncheon the next day. Jameson-Davis carried on effusively about all the implications Marconi had seen before the February board meeting. Even Flood-Page acknowledged that this patent represented a huge step forward in favor of the transatlantic project. They all hoped the device would effectively eliminate interference as longer and more powerful signals came into contact with more and more unintended receivers. Marconi, a rare smoker, permitted himself a cigarette.

Years later in the resolution of a patent suit involving MWT that reached all the way to the top of the American judicial system, U.S. Supreme Court Justice Wiley Blount Rutledge acknowledged the magnitude of Marconi's accomplishment:

> Schoolboys and mechanics now can perform what Marconi did in 1900. But before then wizards had tried and failed. The search was at the pinnacle of electrical knowledge. There, seeking among others, were Tesla, Lodge and Stone, old hands and great ones. With them was Marconi, still young as the company went, obsessed with the youth's zest for the hunt. At this level and in this company Marconi worked and won."(FN 1)

Upon hearing the news of the issuance of Patent #7777, the commanders of the Royal Navy fleets could no longer contain themselves. They pressured the Admiralty. At last it acted to override its financial department. In emphatic tones, it formally sought Treasury authorization to acquire Marconi equipment on MWT's terms. The capitulation was total. The application confessed:

> My Lords, however, feel so strongly as to the absolute necessity of obtaining the free use of this invention for HM Navy that…they see no alternative but to accept unconditionally the proposals of the Company.(FN 2)

On May 13, thirteen months after the company delivered its first proposal, the Admiralty informed MWT of the Royal Navy's decision to buy thirty-two pairs of transmitters and receivers.

It was an enormous breakthrough. The equipment still needed to pass rigorous tests before the acceptance of the installations and, more importantly, before payment. Satisfactory communications had to be maintained by naval seaman aboard two vessels, one anchored at Portsmouth and the other at Portland sixty-two miles away, including eighteen hilly overland miles. Nonetheless, the order vindicated the company's pricing structure. For each set, the Admiralty agreed to pay £196 plus a £100 annual royalty. The high revenue level the board desired had been realized. The royalty achieved the directors' goal to earn income into the future, bringing the corporation closer to synthetically emulating the telephone industry's model of creating a long-term cash stream. Absent the royalty, MWT would receive no further payments subsequent to the sale. Jameson-Davis, Marconi, and the rest of the directors congratulated themselves on holding out for such confirmation of their business plan. They vowed to continue to press for this pricing with the GPO and Treasury. The uniqueness and desirability of MWT's product gave its customers no choice but to accept MWT's terms.

With the one order, the Royal Navy tripled MWT's total sales since its organization. The purchase sent a message around the world as to the acceptability of Marconi's wireless. It forced navies to reconsider their plans. It endorsed MWT in shipping company boardrooms. Japan's navy acted first. The Japanese ordered five sets for installation aboard the *Fuji,* the *Yashima,* the *Asama,* the *Akashi*, and the *Yaeyana*. The Italians followed by equipping shore stations at Leghorn and Viareggio. Although the Admiralty would not pay MWT until all thirty-two sets were manufactured and accepted, a process that might consume a half year, the three naval orders reassured the board.

The purchases were certainly timely. They brightened the company's financial prospects just as Marconi initiated heavy expenditure to build a giant generator of a size he had not yet determined. He only knew it must be enough to shoot signals thirty-five hundred miles across the ocean.

Marconi's attempt to create and apply huge voltage power to delicate transmitter electric circuits and mechanisms constituted an engineering challenge never before contemplated. It rivaled the effort to overcome interference. Up to this moment, only laboratory-built battery packages with a minute amount of electricity sparked signals. Batteries had insufficient energy for what Marconi had in mind. He needed a power plant. Marconi had no exposure to generators. He did not understand what effect the amount of electricity a generator produced might have on the workings of the jiggers, the coherer, the ground and aerial, and other parts of the wireless apparatus. In an oversimplified analogy, Marconi proposed to increase the water pressure in a fire truck one hundred fold to propel water from its hose forty-five times farther than had ever been done before. The new level of force would challenge the strength and working mechanics of every water line and piece of equipment in the truck.

Marconi, however, knew Dr. J. Ambrose Fleming, a professor of electric technology at University College in London. Fleming had studied electromagnetic waves since the first writings of Professor Hertz and had followed Marconi's progress with great interest, even defending Marconi against his critics. The two men had collaborated in a publicity stunt before Marconi left for America. Fleming was scheduled to lecture on *A Centenary of the Electrical Current* at the British Association's three-day annual meeting at Dover's town hall. On the same dates, the Association Scientific Française convened at Boulogne and the Italian Electrical Congress at Como. With Fleming's backing, the British Association allowed Marconi to attach an aerial mast to the town hall. He arranged a wireless relay from the hall to South Foreland to Wimereux and telegraphic relay from Wimereux to the Boulogne and Como conventions. As Fleming addressed his British peers, Marconi conveyed the speech simultaneously to their French and Italian counterparts via the relay. The interchange between the gatherings caught everyone's fancy. All three assemblies exchanged countless messages with each other throughout their sessions, generating an exciting buzz among the scientists and a wealth of press coverage.

What piqued interest was not that wireless did something that before only cable could do, but the way in which the new method operated. Messages exchanged without physical connection between the points of communication presented intriguing possibilities. Information might become instantaneously exchangeable between any two locations far more readily than had ever been imagined.

Now, nine months later, Marconi invited Fleming to tea at company headquarters. Marconi knew that the highly respected doctor of physics had been an early experimenter with voltage and had successfully supervised the installation of a high-voltage land cable between London and nearby Deptford. Marconi described his unprecedented proposal to the attentive professor, whose tea went cold as he comprehended the magnitude of the undertaking. Marconi asked if Fleming would lead the project to build a super-powerstation and harness it to wireless transmission. Fleming eagerly accepted. In July, he became MWT's scientific advisor while still retaining his professorship.

Marconi, however, was not the only premier-class scientist/inventor interested in the Atlantic. Tesla conceived a worldwide electromagnetic system. He would send energy to circle the globe, contact the stars, and cause rain to fall in the desert. He was a formidable rival with two significant advantages over Marconi. There was no question about his expertise in large generators. He intended to harness sufficient power at Niagara Falls to transmit through the upper air strata, cause mechanical resonance, and create terrestrial currents.(FN 3) He also had his own financial resources and was well connected in New York money circles. John Jacob Astor was his current financier.

As soon as Marconi consummated the arrangements with Fleming, Marconi turned his attention to selecting a site for the supergenerator. In order to minimize the cross-ocean distance, the two scientists agreed the location should be as much west as possible. That would be Ireland's far coast. But Marconi and Fleming both wanted to be able to visit the construction whenever appropriate while continuing their other activities in London and, in the case of Marconi, at Haven. A trip to western Ireland consumed two days. It could be more if the Irish Sea passage should be delayed by bad weather. That was too often the case. Cornwall in southwestern England, however, could be reached with a long day's train journey. Although Cornwall added more than one hundred extra miles onto the route to the United States, the directors agreed to it.

Marconi, Flood-Page, and a company engineer, Richard Norman Vyvyan, booked a first-class compartment so they could plan in private and departed London. They established goals: a site as far south and west as possible and high on a promontory with no obstacles between it and America. They also hoped for accommodations nearby.

All this they found at Poldhu Cove. It was a barren headland almost at the tip of Cornwall. It had an uninterrupted shot across the Atlantic. A modest, small hotel at the tiny village of Mullion near Poldhu provided rooms and meals.

Two major concerns preoccupied everyone. First, could Fleming, in consultation with Marconi, design and build a machine that generated a spark so powerful that it could hurl electromagnetic waves thirty-five hundred miles and yet not burn up the sensitive wiring of the transmitter and aerial? Second, would these powerful waves drown out other transmitters? Marconi argued his syntonic tuning prevented the latter. But no one knew for sure. They needed a practical test. Fleming and Marconi wanted to build an experimental station close to Poldhu's massive generator/transmitter. At this new site, they would attempt to receive signals from a third station at the same time Poldhu transmitted. It would be a realistic measurement of whether Poldhu's powerful signals would overwhelm the third station's transmissions.

Flood-Page argued strenuously against the proposal. MWT had to build another major station in America for the transatlantic project. Now, before any building had even started, the research-orientated engineers demanded additional investment simply to test the effect of their work. He grimly warned he could not control expenses on this basis. Potential interference from Poldhu, he argued, could be observed at an already existing location like Haven.

Fleming and Marconi overruled the managing director. Results at Haven, more than 160 miles from Poldhu, would not be meaningful. At that, range Poldhu's waves might be weak or nonexistent. If Poldhu did not interrupt reception at Haven, it would be difficult to conclude that syntonic tuning, not distance, had prevented interference. Flood-Page did not take well to the decision. Personally, he did not like being countermanded. Professionally, it undermined his authority as director. Ultimately, he would be judged on how well he executed his responsibilities. No one would remember, or care to remember, how many times his recommendations had been thwarted by Marconi and the engineers. Flood-Page's disposition soured.

Marconi and Vyvyan settled upon a site for the experimental station at Lizard Point, six miles from the massive transmitter at Poldhu.

As Marconi became increasingly preoccupied with the transatlantic project and further testing of syntonic tuning at Haven, his relationship with Josephine deteriorated. He had less and less time to be with her at dinner and on other occasions. In his effort to keep the transoceanic work a secret from his competition and critics, Marconi did not tell even Josephine what he was up to. Instead, after the initial Poldhu trip in July, he simply advised her that he would be spending major time in Cornwall. They did not confront each other with the adverse implications his announcement held for their relationship. Josephine put the best possible face on it. It was a good time for him to be busy, she consoled herself, for she had to return to America to prepare for the wedding. Before she left for Indiana, however, she broke down and criticized him for not having time for her. In defending himself, Marconi could not resist hinting at his dream and the demands it placed upon him. When Josephine arrived in Indianapolis, after giving the subject considerable thought, she wrote her fiancé with a touch of bitter skepticism:

> I shall wait eagerly to hear from the results of your experiments with the "great thing" which I do not read about in the newspapers. You must have a magnificent way of managing the Press to have succeeded in keeping even a line of it from the public ear.(FN 4)

In July, the Royal Navy once more held its summer maneuvers. Unfortunately for the company, none of the thirty-two sets scheduled for August arrival were ready. Instead, the Admiralty equipped its two warring fleets with Jackson's wireless. On the first day of the exercise, all his equipment failed. The dismal performance confirmed the Admiralty's wisdom in selecting MWT. But it also led the navy to undertake an urgent and comprehensive overhaul of the Jackson apparatus with the mission to bring it up to Marconi standards. In September, MWT made its initial delivery. The sets passed the rigorous inspection required by the contract. They were immediately placed in service.

Flood-Page, eager to capitalize on the Royal Navy order and promote the commercial shipping business of the Marconi International Marine subsidiary, prevailed upon Marconi to demonstrate publicly the effects of syntonic tuning. Marconi felt sufficiently comfortable in the results of Haven's field tests to consent. MWT, and particularly Marconi, had become skilled in the use of exhibitions to manipulate the press and others to promote the company's technology. Reporters were personally called. Flood-Page invited potential corporate customers. Officers of the Royal Navy and Italian and French military and officials at Trinity House and Lloyd's were targeted.

Approximately one hundred observers assembled in two locations, one at the Haven Hotel and the other at MWT's new St. Catherine's station at Niton. Niton, on the southernmost point of the Isle of Wight, had replaced the Needles Hotel site. Two operators on two adjacent transmitters at St. Catherine's simultaneously transmitted different messages across the Solent. The signals, on two distinct bandwidths, had been carefully matched to the identical periodicity and capacity of the two receivers at Haven. In the past, the transmissions would have interfered with each other. The receivers would have picked up only garbled messages. But Marconi's new invention tuned one transmitter and one receiver to a narrow band of wavelengths and the other transmitter and receiver to a separate bandwidth. The two receivers immediately and accurately printed the two Morse code messages. Applause and commendation from the crowd of witnesses at Haven greeted the chatter of the automatic inkers typing out the Morse symbols. It could not have been a more vivid demonstration that two transmitters could operate right next to each other. This moment had been the one eagerly anticipated a year earlier by the U.S. Navy and Bureau of Equipment. At last it had arrived. From Marconi's perspective, the wait, despite its costs in lost business and adverse publicity, had been worthwhile. The syntonic process now had full patent protection, and the demonstration had been flawless.

Marconi had a surprise. He proposed another, more dramatic experiment. For the first demonstration, each receiver had had its own independent aerial hung from the Haven Hotel mast. Now Marconi placed the two receivers at the hotel literally on top of each other and attached both receivers to the same aerial. The two operators at Niton, side by side, tapped out two messages on their respective transmitters, one in French and the other in English. The two sets of signals printed out simultaneously and perfectly on the corresponding receiver's tape at Haven. MWT had made its point to its astonished visitors.

The next day, the press, in incredulous tones, reported what it had witnessed.

Fleming, in a letter published by the London *Times*, marveled at the demonstration. Two distinct sets of printed dots and dashes had resulted from simultaneously but separately sent intermingled electric waves. The electromagnetic waves, which travel at the speed of light, had rushed thirty miles across the Solent and had been picked up by a dangling, single, forty-foot wire. Two separate receivers disentangled the waves caught by the sole aerial into exact replicas of their respective transmissions. The wonder of it all, Fleming mused, could not but strike the mind. Nothing done on one current affected the other.

In seeking an analogy to illustrate the accomplishment, Marconi engineers pictured ripples from a stone thrown into the water, and then the ripples from two stones thrown into the water simultaneously. The invention permitted each stone's ripples to be separately identified, even when cross ripples from the different stones passed through the same point at the same moment. Newspaper acclaim was enormous. Flood-Page pressed ahead eagerly with his shipping prospects.

In November, MWT completed the final delivery to the Royal Navy. The Admiralty installed sets throughout the Channel, Mediterranean, and reserve fleets, at the principal UK home ports and at the Torpedo School at Davenport.

At last, MWT could be paid. It was good thing. Three major projects, two underway and one waiting to start, threatened to consume what remained of Flood-Page's precious horde of capital raised two years earlier. The transatlantic project and Marconi's endless syntonic and distance research on the Solent demanded constant investment support.

The managing director and board wanted to begin building shore stations to service the fledging Marconi International Maritime business. Now that MWT had clearly established its solution to interference, potential customers had only one remaining objection to signing up. Ships could only communicate with Niton and Haven, close together on the Solent, and South Foreland near Dover. To shipping companies, such few contacts did not justify the price asked for the systems. Many more shore stations were required.

The board, however, hesitated to commit the sums necessary to build numerous shore stations without a clear understanding of the GPO's reaction to the commercial ship-to-shore, shore-to-ship service envisioned. The GPO might attempt to assert its monopoly and prohibit the activity. The directors could not afford to invest huge amounts into shore stations only to discover they could not be used. Given the GPO's and MWT's unfriendly relations, the directors feared asking the GPO for advice. A direct inquiry would likely provoke an adverse response.

MWT needed a test case. Flood-Page inadvertently found it. He persuaded the Belgians to consider a MWT wireless system. Responding to the managing director's insistence and board pressure to engage in activities immediately related to sales, Marconi sacrificed his other undertakings for two days. He traveled to Belgium to exhibit to the royal family and government officials. As a result, Belgium awarded Marconi International Maritime a license to build a wireless station at Ostend, Belgium, to communicate with Belgian mail packet ships on the cross-Channel Ostend-Dover route. In accordance with the business plan that MWT had adopted for the U.S. Navy negotiations a year earlier, Marconi International Maritime leased Belgium a complete system of wireless equipment for the packets. It provided operators for the ships and the Ostend site. The MWT subsidiary did not charge for individual telegrams.

On November 3, the Belgian packet *Princess Clementine*, equipped with Marconi wireless, exchanged messages with South Foreland near Dover and Ostend from the moment the mail boat left the continental coast to the moment it arrived in Dover. It relayed messages from South Foreland to Ostend and from Ostend to South Foreland.

The GPO reacted immediately. It forbade the packet from interchanging messages between South Foreland and Ostend within British territorial water. But the GPO raised no objection to such interchanges occurring more than three miles offshore.

The MWT board convened at once to assess the GPO edict's effect on the shore station commercial shipping business.

Marconi

The directors first noted that the GPO had raised no objections when MWT received messages at its shore stations for Lloyd's and from Wimereux as long as the messages were intended for recipients at the shore stations or were forwarded to the GPO for transmission by GPO telegraph to their ultimately intended recipients. The board also observed that the GPO had permitted the submarine cable companies to operate on that basis for the last half century.

The board then considered the GPO's reaction to the *Princess Clementine*. The directors concluded that MWT could not relay messages between two of its UK shore stations or between one of its shore stations and one of its operators at sea within three miles of the UK shore. But it could relay messages between a shore station and one of its operators beyond the UK's territorial limit. Assuming two English ships each four miles off the coast were out of range of each other but within in range of Niton, Niton could relay messages between them.

Based on these conclusions, the board felt MWT could proceed with shore station construction without undue risk of violating the GPO's monopoly. Flood-Page commenced work forthwith.

The directors had to be pleased. They had devised and under adversity adhered to a plan that they felt over time maximized MWT's opportunity to build a high-margin, very profitable business. The Royal Navy capitulated to a steeply priced royalty structure. The Belgian government acceded to the leasing arrangement. That format maximized long-term profits from commercial shipping without violating the GPO's monopoly. And finally, Marconi's patented tuning appeared to solve interference.

Now the company had to execute its plan. The profit structure called for lofty prices that generated sales resistance and opened the door to competition. Construction of a sufficient number of shore stations to satisfy customer demand required heavy capital investment. These expenditures promised to outstrip sales revenues for some time and to impose heavy demands on MWT's dwindling cash reserves. For Flood-Page, trying to determine how many months that would last was next to impossible. Fleming's enormous generator had no precedent. Fleming himself could give no meaningful cost estimate or even a time schedule to completion. As for Marconi, he had embarked on an entirely novel design for massive aerials at Poldhu and in the United States. It was premature to guess at a final budget. Uncertainties abounded in constructing so many shore stations. By December, Flood-Page had begun work at seven coastal locations.

Josephine, meanwhile, began to fray under the separation and lack of attention from Marconi. In one letter she wrote:

> You say that you have been ill but that you are well again and of that I have my doubts as I fancy that I could detect a bit of a dreary tone in your letter which, not being caused by disappointment or discouragement, must have meant the presence of this illness.(FN 5)

Or perhaps writing Josephine bored Marconi. In another missive, after signing "always your own true and loving Jo," Jo said in a postscript, written in Morse code as her postscripts often were, "Your long silences have made me very unhappy."

In early January 1901, five months after the Poldhu site selection, Vyvyan, Fleming, and Marconi successfully completed their collaboration to erect a supertransmitter. It was massive, a series of hulking pieces of black machinery, haphazardly arranged to the unknowing eye and sewn together with fat, dark electric cable. Its parts included Fleming's generator, transformers, and a bank of condensers. All were housed in one building near a gigantic new aerial. The transmitter employed one hundred times more power than any previous MWT machine. The engineers had redesigned every element to handle the incredibly increased load.

The nearby antenna had a design radically altered from the aerials at Haven and Niton. Those consisted of wires, woven together in a mesh like a fishnet, suspended from the crosstree of a tall mast one hundred twenty feet high. At Poldhu, four hundred individual wires, each one hundred ninety feet long, hung from a cable at the top of twenty masts two hundred feet high. They stood in a huge ring with a two-hundred-foot diameter. The bottom of the wires came within ten feet of the ground. There they were gathered together at the center of the circle and spliced into a single wire that went to the supertransmitter. From a distance, the aerial resembled an enormous, inverted cone soaring into the sky. Altogether the aerial contained seventy-six thousand feet of wire.

Fleming, with care, fired up the generator at low power. He feared voltage peaks. They could return to the transformers and alternator. The consequent surges might break down the insulation. Fleming and Vyvyan watched anxiously as Marconi struck the transmitting key for the first time. An enormous spark with a thunderous crackle leapt like lightning across the spark gap. No explosion occurred in the machinery. No wisps of smoke suddenly rose from the wiring. The system appeared to work. The members of the MWT team at the site cautiously congratulated each other. Then they turned immediately to begin the inevitable trial and error adjustments to remove flaws and fine-tune the colossal system.

On January 21, Vyvyan pronounced the new experimental station at Lizard ready for testing as well. Immediately Marconi's relentless efforts at Haven to improve distance and syntony paid off. From Lizard, Vyvyan signaled 186 miles to St. Catherine's at Niton on the Isle of Wight. That shattered the distance mark by 100 miles. It more than doubled the old record. Equally astonishing, Vyvyan had sent two sets of signals from two transmitters at Lizard to two receivers at Niton. The startling length had been achieved using syntonic signaling.

The engineers exchanged excited congratulations. Fleming understood that Marconi's particular pleasure arose not just from the confirmation of the results of his refinements. More importantly, in Marconi's mind the 186 miles buried for good the theory that electromagnetic waves traveled in a straight line. If the waves had traveled to Niton in a straight line, the 120-foot aerial on the Isle of Wight should have been 6,500 feet high. The theory had conceptually limited how far Marconi could send messages. It no longer applied. Clearly, signals followed the earth's curvature. Marconi did not know why. While understanding the science behind his success could be helpful, he did not stop to inquire. Whatever the concept was, it appeared to impose no limit on how far electromagnetic waves might go. He accepted the results and forged ahead. Distance was a question of power. How much did Marconi need to cross the Atlantic? Could Fleming produce it? Could Marconi's sensitive transmitter handle it?

The Lizard test did not answer one major question. The supertransmitter was not yet ready to send out signals. When it did, when it was operating at full power, would it drown out Lizard and MWT's ship-to-shore transmissions?

While Marconi's confidence increased, Fleming's decreased. He became more and more displeased with the results of the adjustments to the supergenerator. The attempts at refinement revealed serious design problems. He ordered the power plant torn apart while he considered his next move. Fleming's action did not discourage Marconi. He had lived in this experimental world of one step backward, two steps forward for almost seven years. To him, the initial January results of the generator and Lizard confirmed his expectations. No serious new problem had arisen since the board authorized the transatlantic project.

With the various pieces of the English side of the equation falling into place, Marconi announced his departure for America to begin the western end.

The women in Marconi's life now for a moment shared a common interest. They conspired to achieve their goals. Josephine desperately desired her fiancée to come to Indiana on his American trip. Annie, who had missed the first voyage, very much wanted to be a part of the second. Josephine invited Annie to Craigmor, Josephine's family home in Indianapolis. Certainly, the thinking went, Annie could not be at Craigmor without Marconi. Marconi would feel compelled to go to Craigmor if his mother were invited.

The combined female power, however, failed to penetrate Marconi's preoccupation with the transatlantic project and his dedication to accomplishing it at the earliest possible moment. MWT funds were running dry. The shore station construction program and the transatlantic project consumed money at an alarming rate. Compounding that concern, MWT had received no new naval orders from any country. The shipping companies insisted the shore stations be operational before they would commit to orders. Transmitting 186 miles from Lizard to Niton might be a celebratory experience, but it represented only one-sixteenth the distance from Poldhu to the United States. Marconi could not afford the time to go to the Midwest. He declined Josephine's invitation to Indiana. He did not invite her to New York. Once again, he did not ask Annie to accompany him. Josephine changed tactics. She wrote a letter to her fiancé, hinting that another man had entered her life. The threat moved Marconi no more than the conspiracy. He remained oblivious to all but the "great thing."

Without any publicity, Marconi, Kemp, and Vyvyan departed England. No fanfare greeted their New York arrival, and they immediately proceeded to Cape Cod. The trio had selected the glacial sand

Marconi

spit because from its eastern face across the Atlantic to Cornwall not a single piece of land rose above the surface to obstruct the signal's passing. Soon after they established temporary headquarters on the Cape, Marconi met Ed Cook, a wrecker who lived by salvaging flotsam from the sea and beach. Cook, not a man of letters but a bit of a pirate, operated entirely at the edge of maritime law. If he spotted a drifting boat, he would tow it to shelter and refuse its release until adequately rewarded. With the proceeds, he bought land along the dune-crested coast. Nothing, he reckoned, could be finer than to stand on his own Cape hilltop, look to the next, and say, "That's mine, too." He quickly sized Marconi up as an opportunity.

The wily Cape Codder, protected by oilskins from the elements, took the Italian-Irishman in his buttoned-down, fur-lined coat prospecting for a site. The rain-filled, raw March winds buffeted the two explorers. Marconi must have felt like he never left Cornwall. On the inner bay lay Barnstable, a village of white clapboard rectangle cottages with gabled, shingled roofs and sturdy center chimneys. While easily accessible to supplies shipped across Cape Cod Bay, Marconi rejected it. He feared the arm of dunes running up to Provincetown. They lay between Barnstable and Poldhu and might block transmissions. At the tip of the arm, the Provincetown Highland Light, the first landfall for ships making for Boston, seemed ideally suited for advising shippers and insurers of vessel arrivals as well as for transatlantic signaling. The Yankee keepers of the light, however, like the men at Navesink on the New Jersey highlands, viewed Marconi suspiciously. Marconi was foreign to their sight. His wireless appeared nonsensical. Cook, who had no financial interest in the lighthouse, could not persuade them to deal with Marconi.

Near South Wellfleet, a site overcame all objections. It had a high bluff, a heath-clad cliff of sand and clay that rose 130 feet above the ocean, and it looked east, unhindered, to Cornwall. At this narrow neck of the Cape, materials from Boston could be unloaded on the bay side and hauled across the mile width. Its purchase was assured as Cook owned it.

Marconi prepared to return to England. The task before him was formidable. He now knew its dimensions. There were three thousand miles of ocean to cross between Cornwall and Massachusetts. He asked Vyvyan to remain behind and lead the South Wellfleet construction.

Josephine's efforts to arouse Marconi's jealously had failed to bring him to her side. She reversed course. She wrote that the man to whom she had referred had become engaged. But to no avail. Marconi had no time to travel to the Midwest or even to see her in New York. He felt too much urgency, too much pressure.

Marconi was not the only one to select a U.S. site. After a three-month negotiation, Tesla convinced J. Pierpont Morgan to finance a tower whose energy, inexpensively and abundantly powered by Niagara Falls, would cross the Atlantic. Morgan made a down payment. He received a 51 percent interest in the project and in Tesla's wireless patents. Tesla had moved his personal living quarters into the plush and socially prestigious Waldorf Astoria Hotel, home to many magnates. Without telling Morgan, Tesla decided he did not want to spend time at the falls building and testing and signaling. He preferred a location to which he could commute daily and return to his luxurious surroundings each evening. He bought a site he named Wardenclyffe a comfortable train ride away from New York City just past Port Jefferson on Long Island. He retained the renowned architect Stanford White of McKim, Mead & White to design the World Telegraph Center.

Flood-Page had warned persistently that at current spending and revenue rates, MWT would be out of funds in a matter of months. In the previous cash crisis, Jameson-Davis had been confident he could raise additional capital through stock sales. Now he was not. He no longer had a list of investors eager to buy. Nor did he believe anyone would lend MWT money. Too many uncertainties threatened its future. MWT was in an increasingly desperate race against the clock to bring in revenue before it exhausted its resources.

While Marconi explored Cape Cod, the Royal Navy completed its comprehensive upgrade of the Jackson sets. Unbeknownst to MWT, the Admiralty sent one of the thirty-two Marconi sets to Ediswan Light Company, a leading British electric corporation, to be copied. Ediswan secretly manufactured fifty copies for the navy. (The fact that the Royal Navy had ordered the copies made by Ediswan did not come to light until years later when it was discovered by a MWT director who also was a director of Ediswan.)(FN 6) The Admiralty never advised MWT nor compensated it for these illicitly manufactured sets.

Marconi

After improving the Jackson equipment, the Royal Navy tested Jackson and Marconi apparatus under comparable conditions at sea. It is not known whether Ediswan copies or wireless features owned by MWT had been illegally incorporated into the Jackson sets. The navy reported to MWT that of seventeen different features, naval operators preferred seven of Marconi's and ten of Jackson's. From what MWT knew, the survey, assuming it had been fairly conducted and reported, unfortunately indicated that the Admiralty's self-manufactured units had attained parity with MWT's. The Admiralty then ordered from itself fifty-two more Jackson sets. MWT received no orders. It had lost the Royal Navy contract. The astonishing, if not infuriating, change in Royal Navy preference occurred less than one year after the navy could not restrain its desire for the company's system. Had the Admiralty, possessor of the world's greatest navy, unchallenged ruler of the earth's oceans, concluded that the navy could not be dependent on someone it did not control for something so vital to its interests?

Altogether, the navy ordered twice as many sets from itself as MWT had sold to everyone since its inception. What a difference such an order would have made to MWT's worsening cash crunch. Had the Admiralty's initial MWT order been promptly filled, at a mutually acceptable price, there might have been no need for the Admiralty to explore self-construction. Had the Royal Navy promptly ordered Marconi wireless for use throughout its fleet, other nations, in order to keep pace with Britain, might have felt compelled to outfit their navies as well at a time when the world had no operable system other than Marconi's. While it is easy to criticize Treasury's recalcitrance and the GPO's stubborn attitude throughout the Admiralty's negotiations, the high price uncompromisingly demanded by the company had been a major stumbling block to effect a deal. When a year earlier the Admiralty ordered the thirty-two Marconi sets at MWT's original pricing, the order appeared to vindicate the company's pricing policy. Now it looked like that policy might be a mistake. Insistence on high profit per unit may have cost the company dearly in long-term volume.

The unexpected setback increased pressure on marketing to commercial shipping firms. To Marconi, who did not believe that the shippers could sustain the company, the adverse development underscored the absolute necessity to enter the transatlantic communication market.

It is no wonder then that, in response to the ever-mounting pressure, he fretted more and more about his sleep and clung to his dietary order. Annie thought his worrying about his health was a growing concern. It could not have been inherited. Neither she nor Giuseppe carried on about themselves. But she fretted that his lack of sleep would affect his mental capacity and his attitude towards his work.

Marconi held no rancor against Jackson personally for the Royal Navy developments. Jackson had little, if any, role in the decision. And Jackson had always been open in his goal: to obtain the best possible wireless for the Royal Navy. No record exists of who ordered the Ediswan copies. At the time, no one at MWT knew of the copies.

The Lloyd's discussions encountered a peculiar and unexpected turn. Colonel Hozier, Lloyd's representative in the talks who had encouraged the Admiralty to investigate Professor Braun's German apparatus and to purchase the same system as Lloyd's, had acquired a system of his own. Negotiating with Flood-Page, Hozier promised to recommend MWT's wireless to Lloyd's if MWT bought his wireless system. Hozier's device had no value to the company, but the Lloyd's contract MWT prized highly. Despite finding Hozier's offer odious, the directors authorized Flood-Page to strike a deal. The board purchased Hozier's wireless for £3,000, a substantial sum particularly in light of MWT's increasingly dire financial circumstances, plus fifty MWT shares the company acquired from Marconi for £150.

Shortly afterwards, Lloyd's awarded the company a handsome contract. Lloyd's ordered MWT service at ten coastal sites to be equipped with transmitting sets and operators. The company would train the operators to spot at sea ships which Lloyd's had insured and report to Lloyd's by wireless on their safe passage. The transaction promised MWT future positive cash flow, but not immediately. First the company had to cut into its remaining resources to outfit the lighthouses. Then when all was ready, Lloyd's would not pay the company a large amount but would begin the payment of monthly fees for the service. It would be some time before MWT recovered its investment.

At South Wellfleet, Vyvyan constructed and equipped the receiving shed and replicated Poldhu's aerial. Now at the edge of each continent stood a gargantuan ring of twenty, two-hundred-foot-tall masts. From each circle hung the inverted, four-hundred-wire cone. These antennas

Marconi

held enormous significance for Marconi. Not only must he propel electromagnetic waves three thousand miles to South Wellfleet, but there he had to catch them. At Poldhu, the aerial's elevation and mass enhanced the transmitter's ability to radiate over the ocean.

If the signals actually managed to reach Cape Cod, Marconi did not know how weak they might be on arrival. The likelihood of intercepting them, he reasoned, depended upon the height and amount of wire in the receiving antenna. While convinced that electromagnetic waves skimmed the earth's surface, following its curvature, he did not known at what altitude they might fly or how far apart they might be spaced. The more wire in the receiving antenna and the higher it stood, the better the odds the aerial would intercept a wavering pulse of energy. To Marconi, the vast array assembled at South Wellfleet, seventy-six thousand feet of suspended wire, mounted on a 130-foot bluff and reaching upwards another 200 feet, ready to catch at any point in its web the weakest indication of an expiring wave from Poldhu, was critical to MWT's chance of success.

The massive aerials had a fault. Metal supporting lines held the huge masts in place. Ropes were neither strong enough nor stiff enough to anchor the two-hundred-foot timbers. But these guy wires, being metal, competed with the wires constituting the actual aerial in attracting and absorbing the electromagnetic waves. In an effort to reduce the energy diverted by these supporting lines, the engineers had deployed only one horizontal cable to link the poles together and only one external guy line to run from each mast to the ground outside the circle. The poles had no buttressing on the inside of the circle. The barely supported formations resembled out-of-scale apparitions from another world, especially at dusk in the gray half-light when mist and fog swirled through their upper reaches. Vyvyan worried about the masts' strength. He feared that at some point during the hurricane season gale force winds would tear ferociously at them. He cabled London for permission to reduce the height and add buttress cabling. The design engineers strenuously argued for the highest possible aerials at South Wellfleet and Poldhu to maximize sending and receiving capability. Marconi made the final decision. He took a calculated risk that the current antenna construction on both coasts had sufficient reinforcement to withstand possible storms. Height was critical, and he wanted as much as possible.

By midsummer, Fleming had reconstructed the generator. This time it satisfied him. Cautiously, in trial after trial, Fleming turned the power up, a little more each time. Again, the system did not self-destruct. The sparks became stronger, more thunderous, the flaws fewer. At the end of August, Marconi sent the first signals from Poldhu. No problems surfaced. Fleming and Marconi conferred. Were they at last ready to test whether the supertransmitter would drown out reception at other stations? Could they satisfy the board's insistence that transatlantic transmission not interfere with local operations? Would Marconi's syntonic tuning permit simultaneous signaling as close as Lizard?

It was time to find out. Fleming brought up the generator. Marconi transmitted while Niton sent Lizard messages. All of Niton's signals were clearly received at Lizard. No interference occurred. The serious problem everyone had feared did not materialize.

Marconi had been right. The powerful waves generated by the lightning-like, explosive spark of the super Poldhu generator did not drown out Lizard's simultaneous receipt of electromagnetic waves sent by Niton. Marconi's tuning solution worked even under these extreme conditions. Marconi and Fleming celebrated their satisfaction of the board's preconditions to the transatlantic experiment. They had created a supertransmitter with extraordinary power that had record-breaking range but did not interfere with nearby receivers. They were ready to test Marconi's preposterous proposal.

While Fleming and Marconi congratulated each other, Tesla was enjoying a fine summer morning. Sipping his hot coffee in the dining car on his way to Wardenclyffe, he was enjoying one of his favorite pastimes, reading the latest issue of the *Electrical Review*. Deep into the magazine, he came unexpectedly to an article written by Marconi. The Irish-Italian described his syntonic device. He reported that it incorporated a Tesla coil. That was not a new idea, Marconi said. It had been used by Preece and mentioned in patent applications by Lodge and Braun.

Tesla exploded. It was clear that Marconi had stolen the Croatian's concepts. He was incensed. He had been informed by Preece based on Marconi's advice that his, Tesla's, apparatus did not work. Now here Marconi was using Tesla's coil in what Marconi was brazenly claiming to be Marconi's invention. Furious at Marconi, Tesla, in the words of one of his biographers, decided to scrap the trivial idea of sending mere Morse code across the Atlantic. He would inaugurate a world communication enterprise "to pulverize the vermin [Marconi] as a pachyderm would crush a toad."(FN 7)

In early September, with the Poldhu generator at three-quarters strength, Fleming and Marconi attempted its first long-distance transmission. A wave carried 225 miles to Flood-Page's new shore station at Crook Haven on Ireland's west coast. Great excitement swept through MWT. As Fleming applied more power, the signals received at Crookhaven became clearer and sharper, an indication that the electromagnetic waves surged well beyond Ireland's west coast. The full distance of Poldhu's transmission could not be measured. No stations lay west of Crookhaven. No one knew what a fully powered Poldhu could do. The latest record, because it emanated from the new generator, particularly encouraged everyone. To Marconi, it further confirmed that electromagnetic waves followed the curvature of the earth.

Despite the general knowledge of the project throughout the company and the intense activity, no word had slipped out to the general public. No newspaper called.

More than eighteen months had been devoted to this scientifically inadvisable project. The company had almost exhausted its capital and could not go on much longer. The transatlantic construction had been completed. The shore stations had been built as well and stood ready for business. Lloyd's made its first monthly payment. Flood-Page had at last begun to sign up shipping companies. As soon as Marconi International Marine could equip the vessels and provide trained operators, revenues would begin to flow, some as early as mid-fall.

But as Marconi feared, it would be a long time, if ever, before these contracts alone would catch up to operating costs. MWT had two super-stations, ten shore stations, and the Lloyd's sites to maintain. It had to pay operators to man the stations, the lighthouses, and the ships. It had payrolls for manufacturing at Chelmsford, for research at Haven, and for headquarters in London. MWT desperately needed another source of revenue. The board looked to Marconi and Poldhu.

Full readiness for the transatlantic trial fast approached. The aerials on both continents were in place. Vyvyan was making the final adjustments at South Wellfleet. Fleming ran the Poldhu generator almost up to full power without destroying the transmitter or spark. Even at that level, nearby Lizard could simultaneously send and receive without interference. The supergenerator had passed all of its run-up tests. In a matter of days, all would be ready.

Then disaster struck. On September 19, a hurricane slammed Cornwall with its full fury. Gale-force winds, high tides, and driving rain devastated the western coast. Poldhu took a direct hit from the storm. The company paid dearly for the risk it had taken. The winds ripped through the antenna, flailing the wires about and tearing them from their couplings. Tied together in a vast circle, not supported from every side, the forty masts, each two hundred feet high, creaked and groaned and swayed in the savage, gusting air, and then they cracked and collapsed, the first to fall tugging at the others to follow.

The wreckage was total, an unsalvageable tangle of cables and broken timbers. Surveying the site, the engineers gloomily predicted at least three months would be needed to clean the debris, repair the generator, and rebuild the aerial. Depression swept the ranks. The directors, deeply discouraged, despaired. They doubted the company's cash could last the three months.

Marconi, the youngest member of management, did not lose his characteristic composure. He attempted to soothe the board, accepting full responsibility for the aerial's design flaw. He would build a new one. It would be shorter, just 160 feet high. Only two masts, buttressed on every side, would support far fewer wires. Height and the number of wires, he rationalized, really mattered at the receiver side. There the two-hundred-foot-high poles and four hundred wires were essential to receipt of the signals. He could transmit with less. The newly designed aerials would substantially reduce the three months required to reconstruct Poldhu. Under Marconi's leadership and exhortation, engineers and laborers cleared out the timbers and wire within a week. Work immediately began on the new aerial. Fleming moved into the Mullion Hotel, where he promised to stay until he had restored the supergenerator.

It was a most anxious moment for the company. For the last five years, since Marconi had arrived in England, he and his devices had led the field, far more advanced than the competition. Still MWT had only bled losses, inciting its rivals. The pack bayed at the company's heels, funded by governments and well-financed capitalists and supported by nationalistic interests. Marconi's transatlantic dream seemed close to ruin.

Marconi

Under the pressure, Marconi wrote to Josephine, telling her that he did not know when he would ever be able to marry her. Every bit of his concentration must be devoted to the company.

Shipping contracts continued to flow in. Marconi International Marine fitted a Cunard liner, the *Campania*, with Marconi wireless, then a second, the *Umbria*, then a third, the *Etruria*. The subsidiary accepted an order for a French liner, *La Savoie*. A Belgian company, Cie de Telegraphie sans Fils, formed just to develop Marconi systems on the continent, delivered two more orders from sister ships of *La Savoie, La Lorraine* and *La Touraine*. The Beaver line installed the first wireless on a British ship, *Lake Champlain*. On its maiden voyage between Liverpool and Halifax, *Lake Champlain* exchanged signals with MWT shore stations at Holyhead in Wales, Rosslare in southeastern Ireland, and Crookhaven in west Ireland. In a very exciting moment, the *Lake Champlain* and the *Lucania,* which had been previously equipped, exchanged messages with each other in the mid-Atlantic, the first far offshore exchange between two commercial vessels. The groundswell of orders for which the company had worked so assiduously at last began.

By mid-November, Marconi fulfilled his promise. The new, simpler, shorter aerial stood ready at Poldhu. Fleming finished his repair work. Once more the supergenerator's signals came in sharply at Crookhaven. Monthly leasing revenue from the shipping companies began to build at Marconi International Marine, but still at a level far below MWT's operating costs. Little cash was left. Once more only a few days of preparation remained before commencing the transatlantic test.

Then unbelievably a second catastrophe struck Marconi. This time a hurricane swept across Cape Cod and tore the South Wellfleet station to shreds. The pine masts came thundering, tearing down. They pierced the roof of the receiving shack, nearly killing Vyvyan inside.

In sharp contrast to these overwhelming setbacks, construction of Tesla's World Telegraph Center was underway. Reacting in ire to Marconi's alleged pirating, Tesla doubled the planned height of his tower to six hundred feet, almost four times higher than Poldhu's makeshift structure. Once more, however, Tesla failed to advise his financial partner. Morgan on his own discovered this expensive modification and Tesla's location at Wardenclyffe, not Niagara Falls. The banker cut off all further financing. Tesla was not perturbed. He had his own money. Morgan could be replaced. Although the financier owned 51 percent, or control, of the project and Tesla's wireless patents, Tesla was confident that would not be an insurmountable problem.

Marconi faced his grim reality stubbornly. The South Wellfleet antenna could not be rebuilt with the amount of money remaining to the company. But he refused to surrender. He needed another aerial, fast. He would improvise. He would fly a kite. Or he would raise a balloon. It did not matter. It would be like the old days on Salisbury Plain.

But a kite or balloon could only lift a single wire. How could an electromagnetic wave traveling more than three thousand miles across the Atlantic Ocean from Poldhu possibly find a solitary wire over Cape Cod? Where could he fly a kite closer to Poldhu but on the opposite side of the Atlantic?

Marconi consulted an atlas. He saw what Field had seen: Newfoundland. Newfoundland was North America's closest shore to Cornwall. Telegraph and submarine cable connected St. John's, the island's capital, to Canada and the United States. He could send a message from Cornwall across the Atlantic via the Canadian province to New York for all practical purposes as fast as underwater cable and clearly at a lower cost. Canada's east coast lay twenty-one hundred miles across the water from Poldhu, nine hundred miles closer than South Wellfleet.

Marconi spoke to Fleming about his decision. Fleming brought the Poldhu supergenerator up to full power. Crookhaven consistently and clearly received Poldhu's signals. Fleming said he was ready.

The twin catastrophes had no effect on Marconi's confidence that signals would follow the curvature of the earth as far as they could travel. They would go ten times farther than Crookhaven. He announced his plan to a stunned board and managing director already traumatized by the second calamity.

The outspoken Flood-Page found it incredulous. Marconi, of all people, thought a solo wire aerial, perhaps one hundred feet long, swinging from a kite over Newfoundland, twenty-one hundred miles from Cornwall, could pick up a signal from Poldhu.

Marconi himself had been the one insisting upon seventy-six thousand feet of antenna wire at South Wellfleet. Flood-Page bitterly rued the transatlantic project. The money wasted at Poldhu and Lizard and Cape Cod could instead have kept MWT alive until his shipping revenues and other income brought the company into the black.

Marconi

The directors could not believe that the scientist who had called this project vital to the company's survival had authorized aerials that could not withstand gale-force winds. The terrible bad luck of suffering two hurricanes in one season on two continents shocked them.

Most incredible to the board, how could MWT be teetering at the brink of collapse? Only two months earlier in mid-September, the business plan had been in place, the shore stations built, sales at last growing, the supergenerator setting records without the anticipated problems.

The directors looked unsuccessfully for alternatives to Marconi's wild, scientifically unfounded, last desperate grasp to survive. MWT's money had run out and with it time to affect more practical solutions.

Uncomfortable and fearful, the board reluctantly acquiesced to Marconi's proposal. As soon as Marconi could be ready, he would depart for St. John's, where he would attempt to receive signals from Poldhu.

There was to be no public disclosure of Marconi's intentions. If he failed to receive signals in Newfoundland from Cornwall and that became known, it would dash any pretense that wireless could compete at significant distances with submarine cables. MWT's competitors would perceive the company's fatal economic weakness. They would step in to crush MWT and pick up its pieces for their own benefit.

Marconi now fully realized how daunting Field's task had been. He painfully perceived firsthand how companies who had dared to lay submarine cable across the Atlantic had been bankrupted in the effort.

CHAPTER 9

Dot...Dot...Dot...

On November 26, 1901, Marconi boarded the liner *Sardinian* at Liverpool, accompanied only by Kemp, his most trusted personal assistant, and Philip W. Paget, a technician expert in receivers and aerials. For equipment, they brought just three wooden crates, each meticulously packed with receiving apparatus and copper antenna, and an oversized wicker clothes hamper in which lay two carefully selected balloons and parts and materials to make six kites. Marconi's and MWT's fate rested on this aerial support, a meager substitute for the two-hundred-foot masts and seventy-six thousand feet of wire that lay in ruins at South Wellfleet. Annie, in an effort to provide moral support for her beleaguered son, had tucked into his personal luggage a copy of Isabel Judson's biography of her father, *Cyrus W. Field*.

Ten days later, on Friday, December 6, 1901, after picking its way through icebergs in the damp, chilling fogs of the Grand Banks, where frigid Labrador currents mixed with the warmer, eastward flowing Gulf Stream, the *Sardinian* made landfall. Newfoundland's east coast, the desolate, remote Avalon Peninsula, was in its wintry conditions just as severe and depressing as it had been for Gisborne and Field.

With their breaths crystallizing in the air, the three men watched from the rail as the *Sardinian* steamed into St. John's harbor. Marconi, grim and determined, wearing the slightest hint of a mustache, had his overcoat buttoned up to his neck and his tweed deerstalker fedora pulled down to his eyebrows to ward off the cold. Kemp and Paget both bore thick walrus mustaches popular in the British Army. For protection from the wind, Kemp hid his red hair and ears beneath a heavy, black wool hat while Paget shielded himself with a cloth cap. Looming over the harbor entrance, dominating it and sheltering the port from the Atlantic gales, was Signal Hill, a promontory six hundred feet high, rising abruptly from the water. Its height immediately attracted Marconi's attention as a possible launching site for the antenna. On its crest stood a new signal tower, the Cabot Memorial Tower, which celebrated Giovanni Caboto's discovery of Newfoundland. St. John's nestled on the harbor's opposite shore. Quays and warehouses for fishing fleets and oceangoing vessels ringed the waterfront. Above them two rows of shops and tier after tier of simple wooden houses clung to the steep hillside. St. John's housed the provincial government, but to anyone accustomed to the comforts of English and Italian cities, it constituted a bleak, frontier town, not a capital. Instead of reassuring the band of three, the arrival in the freezing cold, remote port chilled their hearts, a stark reminder of how distant they were from Poldhu and of the raw elements of nature to be overcome by their frail expedition.

Field on his final thrust to lay submarine cable across the Atlantic stood aboard the bridge of the *Great Eastern*, in command of a British crew of five hundred, with millions of pounds invested and the last two years devoted to preparations for the fourth leg of his travail. He possessed the most advanced laying and testing apparatus available. The critical cable had been designed specifically for its task by the world's foremost cable manufacturer. Two Royal Navy frigates accompanied the *Great Eastern*. A government contract assured revenues. The scientific and engineering community and years of experience endorsed his concept.

Marconi came to this desolate land to play his last hand. If internally he felt desperate or frightened, no evidence remains to show it. Since the second hurricane, he had exhibited only sangfroid. Back at Poldhu, Fleming brought the supergenerator up to full power. The new aerial had been hastily lashed together after the first storm. The engineers had not had time to match its wavelength to that of the transmitter. Its masts, three quarters the height of the original, preferred design, bore far fewer feet of wire from which to radiate than initially intended. The equipment at Newfoundland, now the location for the western reception, fell far below the standards of the decimated Cape Cod apparatus. That gigantic antenna had had a far better chance to gather in electromagnetic waves from Cornwall. At St. John's, Marconi had no aerial of substance. A single wire bouncing about irregularly below a kite provided no comparable alternative. Over the course of his two-year preparation, Marconi had constantly asserted that he needed huge transmission power and a massive receiver to achieve his goal. Unlike Field, for this effort on which all rested, Marconi lacked one of his own prerequisites, and few experts even acknowledged the theory on which his experiments were based.

Marconi never wavered. He complained to no one about the bad luck. He refused to second-guess himself or anyone else. He still believed in his concept. Without flinching or sharing with anyone his awareness of the risks surrounding him and MWT, he stepped forward with confidence.

No one greeted them that Friday, not even the sole reporter on hand, a *New York Herald* writer who had traveled to St. John's under the general impression that MWT hoped to establish communication at greater distances with steamships at sea. Marconi had created this expectation as a diversion to conceal his real purpose. Saturday, Marconi, Kemp, and Paget formally called upon the British colonial governor, Sir Cavendish Boyle, the premier, Sir Robert Bond, and other ministry members. Marconi told them he had been shocked reading in a provincial bulletin that over the last decade eighty vessels had sunk off the island's coasts with six hundred people lost. He expressed his conviction that wireless could save lives. Continuing with the cover story, Kemp cabled Liverpool requesting the schedule of outbound liners headed towards America equipped with wireless.

Sunday, the party scoured the area for sites for their receiver. To Marconi's delight, the governor offered unrestricted use of facilities at the summit of Signal Hill. Its six-hundred-foot height fit Marconi's new tactics. From the moment he heard of the Massachusetts calamity, he knew that, with the time and money remaining to the company, he would be unable to build a significant replacement aerial. In this cold territory whose earth had frozen hard and deep, he wasted no time considering a mast and cross tree for a multiple-wire antenna. Instead, he intended to make the single-wire aerial, which he would raise with a kite, as long as he could, and he would fly it as high as possible. After consulting Paget, Marconi and Kemp agreed they would try to lift a six-hundred-foot strand. If they succeeded in this effort from the top of Signal Hill, the antenna would be twelve hundred feet above sea level, six times the height of the defunct

Marconi

American masts. In short, to replace South Wellfleet's vast array, Marconi proposed a single wire. Its length would cover the altitude between six hundred and twelve hundred feet. It would be nine hundred miles closer to Poldhu than Cape Cod. It was the best strategy he could devise.

On Monday, the *Herald* reporter climbed to the freezing, exposed pinnacle of Signal Hill, grumbling to himself as the biting wind tugged at his outer garments. He found the MWT trio in a gloomy, dark, unused, and unheated one-room building. It stood on frigid ground adjacent to abandoned barracks, all depressingly built of the same gray-brown rock. The company men busily unpacked hamper and crates, gingerly handling the sensitive coherers and cylinders of hydrogen gas for the balloons. A single window looked northeast to Cape Spear, the continent's easternmost point. The dirty glass barely provided sufficient light to organize the equipment. With great care, Marconi assembled the receiver and earphones on which he planned to hear signals from twenty-one hundred miles away. Outside, local labor cleared away the snow. It was arduous work to bury earth plates under frozen dirt and to prepare the surface for a zinc covering. In a hole chopped through the ice with a pick axe, they planted a tether pole to hold the balloons and kites in flight. Kemp laid in a supply of whiskey and cocoa to fortify the scientists against the bone-chilling cold of their quarters.

On Tuesday, the weather was fair enough to launch a kite. Marconi without hesitation went immediately with six hundred feet of copper aerial as a preliminary test. The boxed frame kite, skillfully managed by Kemp, ascended to an altitude sufficient to pull the entire length of antenna off the ground. The kite had to lift as well the rope guideline by which Kemp controlled the kite and the insulated electric tie line which would carry any signals caught by the aerial back to earth, a total load of three lines—antenna, guideline, and tie line. Encouraged by the result, Marconi cabled Cornwall to begin daily transmissions the next day. Every day between ten o'clock in the morning and four in the afternoon Newfoundland time, Poldhu would continuously tap out the Morse letter S—dot dot dot. This Morse letter, the simplest to transmit, placed the least strain on the sending apparatus. More importantly, in the heavy static and stormy weather expected to prevail over the long Atlantic distance and above Newfoundland, the three dots constituted the easiest combination to identify on the receiver. The engineers calculated that the signals would cross the Atlantic in one ninety-third of a second.

Wednesday, the team was as ready as it could be. Kemp and Marconi had been together for more than five years, since the day Marconi first demonstrated to Preece on the rooftops of the GPO's St. Martin's headquarters. Few words needed to pass between them. They trusted each other, and Kemp intuitively anticipated Marconi's needs. Paget, a taciturn professional, competently carried out instructions with little need for explanation. They talked sparsely, when required, as to the power of the wind, the tension on the kite, and adjustments to the receiver and with self-deprecating humor about how cold they were. They were a proud team, experienced and accomplished. They would not admit to themselves or to each other how desperate they were to succeed.

Marconi put himself on the line. Later he wrote:

> I was at last on the point of putting the correctness of all my beliefs to the test. The experiment had involved risking at least 50,000 pounds to achieve a result, which had been declared impossible by some of the principal mathematicians of the time. The chief question was whether wireless waves could be stopped by the curvature of the earth. All along I had been convinced that this was not so, but some eminent men held that the roundness of the earth would prevent communication over such a great distance as across the Atlantic.(FN 1)

With one thousand cubic feet of hydrogen gas, the men inflated one of their two balloons to a diameter of fourteen feet. They sent it aloft trailing five hundred feet of copper wire weighing ten pounds. The weather had turned foul. It had deteriorated all morning with the wind rising steadily and the temperature dropping. Inside at the receiver, Marconi sat straining his ear, adjusting and readjusting the tuning receiver, having no sensible idea as to the wavelength of the signal. Again and again, as often as four or five times a minute, by trial and error, he sought to match the electrical characteristics of the antenna, changing incessantly with every bounce and gust of wind, to the configuration of the incoming waves, which he could only believe were reaching Newfoundland. He tried to pick three dots out of all the crackling, rushing sounds captured by the flapping, airborne wire and sent through the tie line back to his earphone. The volume of the static, confusing and meaningless noise, rose and fell in the headpiece. Could all this irrelevant noise be concealing, drowning out, the faint signal S? With his free hand, he covered his open ear to muffle the sounds of the fierce wind that howled outdoors and rattled the joints of the dilapidated building.

Outside, Kemp struggled to hold the balloon steady, both to reduce the unwanted noises generated in Marconi's ear by the irregular movement of the aerial and to prevent the skinny guideline from alternating dangerously between moments of slack and then extreme pressure when hit by a gust. But he could not. The treacherous winds sweeping unchecked over Signal Hill whipped and flailed the totally exposed balloon.

Marconi heard nothing he could positively identify as the letter S. He abandoned a special tuning receiver, which his longtime, boyhood friend Solari, now an officer in the Italian navy, had developed for use with Marconi's wireless. Marconi suspected the antenna's rise and fall caused its capacity, the amount of electric charge it could hold, to fluctuate too much to permit him to harmonize the receiving circuit. Harmonizing or tuning required him to match the capacity of his receiver to that of the aerial and to the electric charge of the incoming wave. Given the turbulence of the air, such a match, he concluded, was highly improbable. He substituted for Solari's device an older coherer that did not require tuning. But it made no difference. Before Marconi could try a third instrument, Kemp's guideline slackened as the balloon experienced a moment of quiet air. Then a ferocious gust hit the balloon. Like a piece of cotton, the fibers of the guideline pulled apart where it attached to the balloon. The tie line simultaneously snapped. The balloon disappeared into the dark storm clouds. The day's effort ended abruptly. The alarmed crew's flying arsenal now consisted of only one balloon and six kites. Kemp and Marconi exchanged looks of deep chagrin, knowing balloons were much easier than kites to fly in extreme weather.

The next morning, Thursday, December 12, the weather worsened. The vicious gale no doubt surpassed anything Marconi had experienced tossing about on the Solent. Marconi decided not to chance the second and last balloon. Instead, Kemp and Paget prepared a kite with two, five-hundred-foot copper antenna wires and launched it into the wild wind. They raised it to four hundred feet, but the bottom one hundred feet of each aerial dragged on the ground. The experiment lasted only an hour before the savage wind ripped the four-sided kite to shreds.

Fiercely stubborn, undaunted, refusing to back off and wait for a better day, Marconi ordered up another kite, this one trailing a six-hundred-foot antenna. With great difficulty and skill, letting the line out and then pulling it in, attempting to keep it under firm tension, Kemp and Paget played the kite into the turbulent sky until the entire length of the aerial cleared the icy grounds. At every moment the wind threatened to tear the guideline out of their numbed, mittened hands. The kite reared and dived and skidded sideways, constantly changing the height and angle of the aerial. The antenna's receiving properties constantly fluxed. Marconi, in the hut below, tried to make meaning out of the frustrating crackling in his ear. He raced mentally through every combination of variables, every option, every adjustment he might make to realize his rapidly fading dream. Rising from his chair, he shook off his discouragement and went outside to trade places with Kemp and Paget. Perhaps the cold, fresh air might clear his head and ear. Kemp might have better luck listening.

Shortly after half the day's allotted signaling time had passed, Marconi called Paget back outside to handle the guideline. Marconi returned indoors to take over the earphone from Kemp but asked Kemp to remain to work the receiver's controls under Marconi's direction while Marconi focused on listening. MWT engineers all acknowledged that no one could match Marconi's deft manipulation of the receiver, to coax it to acknowledge receipt of the faintest electromagnetic wave. The scientist/inventor, the man who had bet his reputation and company on this daring or ridiculous effort to span the Atlantic, placed the single earphone to his ear and started once more to listen. Before him in the cold, dimly lit room on the bare wood table lay the instruments he had so dramatically improved. Wired together in circuit were coherer, condenser, and electric coils. From that configuration a copper wire snaked through a small hole bored in the window frame. It ran across the open ground to the tether pole, where by a splice it joined the tie line. That line then ran up to the kite and by a second splice attached to the flailing antenna.

Marconi glanced through the window into the driving rain and mist-filled air. Had it been clear, he might have seen Cape Spear's hulking

CHAPTER 10

"Can You Hear Anything, Mr. Kemp?"

Seated at the stained, decrepit work table, his right hand pressing the earphone hard against his right ear, shivering in the cold, Marconi strained to hear the signal S, three dots, radiating from Poldhu. He had no doubts that the signals filled the air about him. He badly wanted the wildly flapping antenna to catch one or two or maybe even three of the electromagnetic waves with enough strength remaining to be heard over the terrible static. He watched Kemp adjust the receiver. Marconi removed his left index finger from his left ear canal, where it helped block out the sounds of the wind rushing about the building, only long enough to direct Kemp to another adjustment. Kemp removed his right mitten and delicately adjusted the cold, black metal dial that controlled the capacitor, all the time intently watching Marconi. Marconi had closed his eyes to focus his entire concentration on the noise of the receiver in his ear. Without opening his eyes, he nodded curtly when what he heard satisfied him. Kemp removed his hand from the knob and returned it to the mitten as quickly as he could.

Already more than half the time allotted for this day's signals from Poldhu had passed. The wind seemed to rise even more. Kemp went over to the narrow table under the little window that provided the room's only light and looked wistfully at the bottle of whiskey that was their last defense against the cold. He worried that the kite might soon tear away. He dared not make a sound that might divert Marconi's attention. Earlier they had all grimly agreed that they could expect no break in the weather in the days ahead. Tomorrow's gale could well be worse.

169

Marconi

Without warning, Marconi stiffened. In his own words:

> Suddenly, about half past twelve there sounded the sharp
> click of the "tapper" as it struck the coherer, showing me
> that something was coming in and I listened intently.
> Unmistakably, the three sharp clicks corresponding to
> three dots, sounded in my ear.(FN 1)

Marconi turned at once to Kemp, eager to have his assistant's cor-
roboration. Kemp positioned the earphone.

"Can you hear anything, Mr. Kemp?" Marconi asked.

Could this be the moment for which Marconi had worked so feverishly for the last two years? Was this to be the confirmation of what
MWT so desperately needed?

The loyal Irishman vigorously nodded his head in affirmation.

Marconi ordered Kemp to get Paget. Outside, Kemp took over handling the guideline while Paget scrambled inside. Known to be a little
deaf, he listened intently, first with one ear, then the other.

Paget heard nothing. In disappointment, he shook his head.

Sharply Marconi instructed him to listen harder. Upset, Paget listened as intently as he could. Still he did not hear three dots.

Marconi seized the earpiece back and slammed it to his own ear.
Paget sat frozen in fear. Marconi listened with such absorption he stopped
breathing. But after a moment he acknowledged that he could no longer
hear the signal.

Marconi remained seated, fixed at his position, longing for confirmation of what both he and Kemp believed to have been the signal from
Poldhu. Paget replaced Kemp outside. Kemp stood by Marconi's side,
hoping to affirm again whatever Marconi next heard.

At 1:10 p.m. Marconi was sure three more distinct clicks came to his
ear. When Kemp placed the headset to his ear, he heard only static.

Again at 2:30 p.m. Marconi heard three more. Kemp tried his best.
However he could attest to no more signals.

Marconi and Kemp assured each other that they had heard the signals. Faintly, through the crashing static, each had picked out three clicks
and a pause, three clicks and a pause until the barely discernable rhythm

faded away, lost amidst all the other competing noises in the earphone. Between the two of them, they had heard the signal S twenty-five times.

But curiously the record contains no scene of rejoicing on that Thursday, December 12, at the accomplishment of Marconi's incredible dream. In later written accounts of Marconi and Kemp, when each had time to reflect and fully record all the events of that momentous day, neither notes down a celebration. Not a single word or handshake of congratulation passed between the three men.

Marconi's small pocketbook, in which he only occasionally made entries, merely noted on December 12, "Sigs. at 12:30, 1:10, 2:30." Kemp, himself a detailed daily journalist, described the hearings as of no more interest than any other scientific data transcribed from experiments. At dusk that fell early in that northern region, particularly as the winter solstice approached, the three men trudged down the hill through the snow towards the city whose lights glimmered in the twilight.

Strangely depression, not elation, affected Marconi. He expressed disappointment at such a faint showing instead of a continuous sound of strong, steady signals. They said not a word to anyone. Kemp checked again on ships with wireless that might be in the vicinity. None had been scheduled to be within signaling distance of St. John's on that day.

Friday the thirteenth they woke early and tramped back to their station. The weather had degenerated even more. Snow, sleet, and hail pelted their efforts. Three kites fought their way into the dark sky only to retreat shortly thereafter and fall back to the ground under the storm's irregular assault of extreme gusts and unexpected lulls. However, during one brief period, Marconi was certain that he heard the signals again, although if possible even fainter than the day before. Finally, frustrated by the difficulty of maintaining the kites aloft, they surrendered for the day. On their return to their quarters that evening, the European contingent once more said nothing to anyone about the signals. Saturday would be better, they told each other with little conviction.

The three fared no better on Saturday. In desperation, Kemp led the gang of local laborers to the edge of Signal Hill. He had them fix an aerial from the cliff-top to an iceberg beached six hundred feet below. He hoped this tactic would save the day as a similar trick had once rescued Marconi at Lavernock in the Bristol Channel. Still no signals sounded in their ears. No improvement from the day before occurred in the kites' performance.

Marconi confronted a serious dilemma. No written record existed of the signals he and Kemp were convinced they had heard. Marconi had feared that electromagnetic waves after the long transatlantic journey would be far too weak to power the tapper and the inker. If the electric energy remaining in the waves had to trigger both instruments, it might be dissipated between the two to such an extent that it would fail to trigger either. As a result, the signals would never give any evidence of their arrival. The tapper required less power than the recording device. Therefore, Marconi had decided to attach the tapper, not the written recorder, to the receiver. As a consequence, they were without written proof of the signals' arrival.

If only they could hear a constant stream of vibrant signals, then he might dare attach the inker and have a writing made by the signals. He far preferred to have an objective record for support rather than to assert to the world that he and Kemp had heard signals without any proof other than their self-serving assertions.

With the winter weather worsening, Marconi could not tell when he might hear the signals again, much less whether they might be strong enough to power the recorder. The three men badly needed a stationary antenna. They could erect one at Signal Hill or Cape Spear where a site might be suitable for a shore station. Given MWT's financial condition, however, they didn't even discuss such a project.

Every day that passed without an announcement of their success would lessen Marconi's credibility if and when he did let the world know. Why had he waited after he first heard the signal to disclose this fantastic event, this receipt of signals, unless he needed confirmation, unless he was not that sure? Daily Marconi received cables from headquarters, anxiously seeking news of results and advising that little cash remained.

If Marconi broadcast to the world that signals had been received, with the only proof his word and Kemp's, people would have too many sound reasons not to believe him. Scientific theory postulated that it would be impossible; electromagnetic waves, like light waves, traveled over the horizon in a straight line, and a signal traveling twenty-one hundred miles would be too far above the earth's surface to be caught by the receiver's antenna. The existing distance record stood at two hundred plus miles. A claim they had gone ten times farther lacked credibility. Prior records had been established with written proof. Why not this time? Realistically, even following the curvature of the earth, could a signal survive two thousand tumultuous miles of stormy Atlantic air filled with static electricity? There had not been time to tune the giant transmitter or to learn precisely the syntonic elements of its transmission. Only by chance could the receiver be matched to the Poldhu wavelength. The kite's antenna was flung about so erratically, its movements so rapid, that it seemed unlikely to capture signals that at best after traveling such a distance must be faint. Both witnesses to the receipt of the waves were biased. The third attendant to the scene, also a company employee but the least involved with the company's affairs, had heard nothing. The most skilled telegraph operator with the best intentions could be easily misled as to what he thought he recognized.

There was every reason not to believe signals had arrived at Signal Hill but one. Marconi. Marconi believed he had heard signals. Unlike Edison, Marconi had never publicly claimed a result unless he had actually achieved it. He had never had to withdraw a public announcement of an accomplishment.

That Saturday, the three men abandoned their efforts before the end of the day. Marconi had reached a decision. Despite all the reasons that he might doubt himself, he remained convinced that he and Kemp had heard Poldhu's letter S on Thursday and he again ever so faintly on Friday. He seriously questioned that the waves would become strong enough to record on the inker. He concluded that the longer he waited, if he received no new affirmation, the less credible his revelation would be.

Flanked by his two engineers, Marconi marched down the hill. They went straight to the telegraph office and told the world their news. Over the Anglo-American Cable Company's submarine cable, Marconi sent a cablegram to his London office:

> St. John's Newfoundland. Saturday 14.12.01 Signals are being received. Weather makes continuous tests very difficult. One balloon carried away yesterday.(FN 2)

Notably, he did not disclose he had waited to make the announcement.

Marconi

Headquarters rejoiced. At Poldhu, the engineers ran out of the transmitting shack and danced about in the rain, hugging each other and shouting hurrah. Caps flew in the air. Congratulatory cablegrams flooded back to St. John's. MWT immediately telegraphed the London and New York papers to advise them of the historic event. Jameson-Davis sent Marconi his personal congratulations. Fleming and Marconi applauded each other. The governor of Newfoundland came personally to the telegraph office to commend the three men who had remained there receiving the messages from London.

Sunday, as Marconi and his assistants attended services in St. John's Cathedral followed by a party thrown by the provincial government in their honor, the *New York Times* broke the astonishing news. The *Herald* reporter, after being the only foreign reporter on the scene, missed the story. Under the headline "Wireless Signals Across the Atlantic—Marconi says he has received them from England," the *New York Times* reported:

> St. John's, N.F., December 14. – Guglielmo Marconi announced tonight the most wonderful scientific development of recent times. He stated that he had received electric signals across the Atlantic Ocean from his station in Cornwall.(FN 3)

On this announcement, leading reporters and magazine writers scrambled out of New York to St. John's to interview Marconi in person. The accomplishment, if true, had historic implications. It dwarfed the sensational communication across the English Channel less than three years earlier. That demonstration hinted at what wireless might do. This achievement represented the first actual fulfillment of that promise.

On a more immediately practical basis, the reporters knew that to lay and maintain a single transatlantic submarine cable cost millions of dollars. The first newsman to arrive at St. John's asked Marconi how much he had invested in his experiment. With an eye towards the cable companies, Marconi said MWT had spent only two hundred thousand dollars for wireless to cross the ocean. Although that sum represented a staggering amount to MWT, bringing it to its knees, it was so much less than underwater cable costs that it immediately represented a challenge to the ultimate competitiveness of submarine cable. Cuthbert Hall, a company engineer who would soon replace Flood-Page as MWT's managing director, deepened the adverse implications for underwater lines. He asserted to reporters that wireless could send messages at the rate of twenty-five words per minute compared to cable's fifteen-word pace. Further, airborne communication had potentially infinite capacity compared to the finite limits of copper wires. This drew an immediate, angry retort from the Commercial Cable Company, operator of one of the fourteen cables that crossed the Atlantic. Its president attacked Marconi's credibility. He told reporters, "Signor Marconi had mistaken the action of ground current or lightning for signals."

Many joined the criticism. Preece, of all people, Marconi's former sponsor and advocate, led the charge. He authoritatively stated that three dots for S had strong similarities to the type of noise most commonly caused by atmospheric interference. He also suggested that Marconi may have picked up a signal from a passing liner. The *Daily Telegraph* sardonically wrote that "the view generally held was that electric strays and not rays were responsible for actuating the delicate recording instruments." Another pithy critic opined that "one swallow does not a summer make." Tesla was in a state of shocked disbelief. At least no unfriendly reporter publicly reported the fact, apparently missed by Kemp, that the *Luciana* that carried wireless had left Liverpool for New York on Saturday, December 7. St. John's might well have been within range if the ship had been transmitting on Thursday the twelfth.

The *Western Electrician* filed its story, the most damaging of all:

> It is reported from Orange, NJ, that Mr. Thomas Edison without casting any aspersion on Mr. Marconi is doubtful of the reliability of the published statements. The newspapers thus report Mr. Edison: "I do not believe that Marconi has succeeded as yet. If it were true that he had accomplished his object I believe he would announce it himself over his own signature."(FN 4)

Edison's curious litmus of veracity may have said more about the incorrigible promoter's standards than about Marconi's.

But Marconi had proponents as well. Michael I. Pupin, who had introduced Marconi to Tesla, stated the following:

Marconi

> I fully believe that Marconi succeeded in signaling between the coasts. Marconi deserves great credit for pushing this work so persistently and intelligently, and it is only to be regretted that there are so many so-called scientists and electricians who are trying to get around Marconi's patent, and thus deprive him and his people of the credit and benefits of the work to which they are fully entitled.(FN 5)

Professor Amos Dolbear, an American wireless inventor who had claimed at the time of the America's Cup that MWT infringed on his work, nonetheless graciously accepted Marconi on faith, stating "if Marconi says he has, why should I not believe he has fully solved the problem." The editor of the *Electric World* said he always thought Marconi would do it but did not anticipate that it would be this soon.

Most importantly, Edison reconsidered his original reaction and reversed himself, publicly stating that his faith in Marconi's integrity offered sufficient ground for accepting his claim.

Edison's revised reaction marked a curious anomaly. In the United States, where fewer knew him, Marconi's accomplishment found more ready acceptance. In England, where he had worked for five years, many doubted.

The *New York Times*, like everyone else required to rely on Marconi's word as the only proof, after reflection waxed eloquent. In an editorial reminiscent of the London *Times* accolade at Field's transatlantic cable accomplishment, the New York paper under the headline, "The Epoch-Making Marconi," rhapsodized:

> If Marconi succeeds in his experiments with intercontinental wireless telegraphy his name will stand through the ages among the very first of the world's great inventors.
>
> The thing he is attempting to do would be almost transforming in its effect upon the social life, the business and political relations of the peoples of the earth. The animating spirit of modern invention is to overcome the obstacles of time and space, "to associate all the races of mankind," by bringing them nearer together.

> The initial success of Marconi appeals powerfully to the imagination. It will be the fervent hope of all intelligent men that wireless telegraphy will very soon prove to be not a mere "scientific toy," but a system for daily and common use. The men of science point out the obstacles. They have commonly been deemed insuperable. The first triumph is an augury of future conquest.(FN 6)

Marconi had placed himself and MWT in a most precarious and dangerous position. He had trumpeted his accomplishment to the world, unconditionally, without reservation or qualification. He had left himself no out if in his next transatlantic attempt he could not demonstrate receipt of signals. If he was wrong, his eager critics would destroy his and the company's credibility. In its exhausted financial condition, MWT would not have time to recover the confidence of the investment world. Jameson-Davis had been unable to find financial supporters before. This would be the end of the company. It would be bankrupt.

How certain was Marconi that he had actually heard signals? Far more to the point, now that he had publicly declared his achievement, how could he prove it to a curious and doubting world? Particularly, how in the tumultuous Newfoundland weather could he emulate what he believed he had scarcely heard?

The demand for proof came immediately. His hosts wanted to hear for themselves. At the Sunday party, they asked if they might listen to Marconi's instruments for the now world-famous *dot...dot...dot*. He had to consent. He had no choice.

After the Sunday celebration, an official government announcement stated that Marconi proposed that on Tuesday Governor Boyle and Premier Bond examine his tests to satisfy themselves of the proceeding's absolute genuineness. Marconi had not yet flinched. But under the circumstances, he had made an audacious commitment. The release professed the colony's warmest support for Marconi, disclosing that he attracted such general admiration owing to his achievements at such a young age.

The next morning, Monday, only ten days since the *Sardinian*'s arrival, a morning of both blizzard and fog, Marconi, Kemp and the minister of lights and fisheries reconnoitered Cape Spear as a potential site for a new permanent station. Perhaps if the governor and premier could not clearly hear a signal given the instability of the kites, Marconi could persuade them, and the waiting world, to allow MWT time to build a stable antenna that would permit clear evidence of the receipt of the signals. Such an explanation would not satisfy MWT's critics. Nor would it convince investors to lend support. The wretched visibility prohibited any visible survey of the land, and no decision could be made.

The weather did not bode well for Marconi's demonstration the next day. Tuesday could be a disaster. It could be the day of reckoning Marconi had been striving so desperately to avoid. But externally he still showed no hesitation.

On Marconi's return from Cape Spear, an officer of the law, a process server, awaited him. The Crown official brusquely thrust into the hand of the surprised inventor a written ultimatum from Anglo-American Cable Co.:

> Unless we receive an intimation from you during the day that you will not proceed further with the work you are engaged in and remove the appliances erected for the purpose of telegraphic communication, legal proceedings will be instituted to restrain you from further prosecution of your work and for any damages which our client may sustain or have sustained; and we further give you notice that our clients will hold you responsible for any loss or damage by reason of your trespass upon their rights.(FN 7)

Marconi laughed aloud when he read the threat. Although witnesses to the unfriendly delivery of the demand may have thought his outburst to be Irish-Italian bravado, it was in fact a sound of relief and delight. Marconi immediately perceived that Anglo-American had unwittingly solved his excruciating dilemma. If Marconi yielded to the belligerent declaration of rights, which of course he must, everyone would understand that Anglo-American had rendered it impossible for MWT to proceed with the next day's demonstration to the governor.

The threat was serious. Anglo-American possessed a monopoly over all telegraphic communication in Newfoundland, the right originally given to Gisborne's telegraph company. Gisborne had assigned this exclusivity, which the Newfoundland legislature extended to run for fifty years from the date of assignment, to Field's New York, Newfoundland, and London Company. Field's corporation subsequently passed the grant on to Anglo-American.

Marconi promptly informed Governor Boyle of the letter. The governor reacted indignantly to Anglo-American's ungraciousness. The monopoly still had two years to run. No one suggested that Anglo-American could not enforce it or that the Newfoundland legislature would or could abrogate it. Marconi might have argued that his transmissions constituted experiments and not messages within the exclusionary ban. If Marconi's argument did not prevail, however, the damages to Anglo-American from MWT's Newfoundland activities could be easily measured. Marconi's announcement had already caused a substantial decline in the value of the submarine cable company's stock. Under the circumstances, Marconi had no interest in even raising such an argument.

On Tuesday, Marconi cabled his London office. Because of Anglo-American's threat, he permanently ended the St. John's experiments. Transatlantic operations would be renewed where no possibility existed of legal interdiction. He then advised the government officials and reporters at St. John's of the decision.

At once an outcry arose against the obstructive attitude of Anglo-American. The governor, accompanied by the full cabinet, marched up Signal Hill in solid support of Marconi. Regretfully, the scheduled but legally prohibited wireless demonstration to verify Marconi's claim had to be cancelled. Instead, a grand luncheon honored Marconi. The governor cabled King Edward VII, praising the wireless. The St. John's Council adopted a resolution expressing gratification at Signor Marconi's success, marking the dawn of a new era in transoceanic telegraphy. The council's resolution also expressed displeasure at Anglo-American.

The newspapers aligned themselves with Marconi. The *New York Times* assaulted Anglo-American in a full broadside blast:

> The more the incident of the proceedings of the Anglo-American Cable Company against Signor Marconi is considered, the more evident it becomes that the management of that company is in the hands of short-sighted, narrow-minded, unprogressive persons who are much in

need of supplementing the Lord's Prayer with a petition to be taught to know their daily bread when they see it. Marconi could have been helped in no better way than by recognizing his system as a dangerous competitor before he had ventured to make that claim for it himself.(FN 8)

All week long, the stocks of the cable companies plummeted. The newspapers became the company's best marketing agents, broadcasting to the world at no cost to MWT the advantages of wireless over cable. An editorial in the *St. John's Evening Herald* illustrated the points:

> "A transatlantic cable represents an initial outlay of at least three million dollars, besides the cost of its maintenance," explained Mr. McGrath. "A Marconi station can be built for $60,000. Three of these bringing the two worlds into contact will cost only $180,000, while their maintenance should be insignificant. What his success will mean can best be grasped by considering the extent of the property which would be displaced thereby, although it is only since August 5, 1858, forty-three years ago, that the first Atlantic cable was laid. There are now fourteen along the Atlantic bed, and in the whole world 1,769 telegraph cables of various sizes, with a total length of almost 189,000 nautical miles, enough to girdle the earth seven times.
>
> "These require a great number of ocean-going cable steamers for their laying and repairs, and while the total value of cables cannot be computed easily, it is known to be a fact that British capitalists have $100 million invested in cable stocks".(FN 9)

Marconi pressed the advantage. The cable companies, he pointed out, charged twenty-five cents a word across the Atlantic. He predicted wireless charges would be only one cent. Anglo-American, stung by the storm of criticism and unfavorable publicity for cable its ultimatum had generated, fought back. Its London solicitors cried foul. Anglo-American's letter had not caused Marconi to stop experiments and withdraw from

Newfoundland. They challenged the significance of Marconi's Tuesday cable to his London office. They quoted from a letter that Marconi had already written on Monday, the day before, to the solicitors wherein Marconi had said, "I may mention that, prior to the receipt of your letter, I have decided to discontinue the tests and to remove the instruments tomorrow." When queried about the quotation, Marconi brushed it aside. It referred to a temporary measure, taken to await instruments arriving from England, and not a permanent withdrawal. Anglo-American's defense came too little, too late. The press continued to side with Marconi. The daily stories starred Anglo-American as the villain. Since his first public success at Salisbury Plain five years earlier, Marconi had lived with the fourth estate, not naïvely as a pure scientist might, but as an astute businessman. Just as he had with his transatlantic announcement, Marconi wrung every sales opportunity that he could out of Anglo-American's embarrassment.

Acuity marked the twenty-seven-year-old whom four years earlier the seasoned WTS founders had wrongly assumed they could dominate. This man acted upon empirical evidence he observed. While his scientific peers clung to historical theories contrary to Marconi's observations, he staked his reputation and his assets on his own judgment. Correspondents pointed critically at his foreignness or his nervous energy. Below the surface lay courage, insight, and a very steady hand. MWT's survival rested on this transatlantic gamble. Marconi played his cards for all they were worth. Any internal doubts about whether he actually had heard the signals did not break through his countenance.

Once Marconi announced MWT's withdrawal from Newfoundland, offers of relocation besieged the company. Bell proffered his summer retreat, a Nova Scotia peninsula on Cape Breton he had christened Breinn Breagh. Canada's eastern provinces and its federal government eagerly wished to assist. While MWT considered the choices, Marconi decided to visit South Wellfleet and then return to England from New York. Ray Stannard Baker interviewed Marconi before he left St. John's. Baker's summation caught the excitement of the moment and the man:

> A cable, marvelous as it is, maintains a tangible and material connection between speaker and hearer; one can grasp its meaning. But here is nothing but space, a pole with

a pendant wire on one side of a broad and curving ocean, an uncertain kite struggling in the air on the other and thought passing between. And the apparatus for sending and receiving these transoceanic messages costs not a thousandth part of the expense of cable...

One of the first and strongest impressions that the man conveys is that of intense activity and mental absorption. He talks little, is straightforward and unassuming, submitting good-naturedly—although with evident unwillingness—to be lionized.

Another writer elaborated on Baker's theme:

In his public addresses he has been clear and sensible. He is reluctant to write for any publication; nor does he engage in scientific disputes, and even when violently attacked he lets his work prove his point.

One factor that has endeared him to the world is his acceptance of success with calmness, almost unconcern; he certainly expected it. Boastfulness is not in his make-up. Opposition is his keenest spur to greater effort.

There has never been the least doubt that Marconi embarked on experimental research because he loved it. No amount of honor or money could tempt him from the pursuit of the great things in wireless, which he sees before him. Besides being an inventor, he is a shrewd businessman with a clear appreciation of the value of his inventions and of their possibilities when generally introduced. What is more he knows how to go about the task of introducing them.(FN 10)

The celebrated trio of MWT engineers departed St. John's on December 24. Paget returned to England, instructed to conduct detailed experiments to improve the effectiveness of the transmission. Marconi knew he had gained a reprieve to prove that he had heard signals. He would waste no time in taking every step he could to assure that he would not fail. He and Kemp traveled across Newfoundland by private railway carriage on Christmas Eve and Christmas Day. The trip proceeded like a royal progress. Everywhere the train stopped, locals from the farms and tiny hamlets en masse pressed up against their car in an effort to see them. In a blizzard on Christmas night, they boarded the steamer *Bruce* and crossed Cabot Strait to the town of North Sydney on Cape Breton, Nova Scotia. Alec Johnston, publisher of the Sydney *Record* and a member of the federal parliament at Ottawa, intercepted them as they changed from the steamer to the train for Boston. Johnston tried to persuade Marconi that Cape Breton's coast would serve Marconi just as well as St. John's. Johnston argued that the three hundred additional miles from Signal Hill to a Nova Scotia site should not be significant. Most important, Cape Breton had no communication monopoly that would challenge Marconi.

The train left without Marconi and Kemp. Instead, the next day, Boxing Day, the two—accompanied by the head of Nova Scotia's provincial government, the general manager of the local coal company, and Johnston—boarded a special train, consisting of only a locomotive and their parlor car, which slowly chugged along the eastern coastline. Near Glace Bay Marconi spied Table Head, a headland whose high cliffs overlooked the ocean. They stopped the engine. The party clambered out and inspected the lofty bluff. The coal company general manager offered on the spot to donate the site to MWT for a new wireless station. After a brief conference with Kemp, Marconi accepted. At that night's celebration back in North Sydney with officials from the provincial government, the coal company, and the railroad, the excitement, Johnston reported, reached even the staid Marconi.

The transatlantic success engendered new confidence and excitement in MWT. As evidenced by the Nova Scotia coal company, people were ready to lend the company support. Already in London MWT stockholders approached Jameson-Davis to put additional sums into the company. In the frenzy of excitement over the transatlantic signals, new investors appeared at the doorstep. Jameson-Davis and the board began discussions as to the most advantageous way for MWT to receive new capital. Acceptance of fresh investment would only increase the pressure on Marconi to have been right in what he thought he heard. Flood-Page acknowledged that Marconi's gamble would likely save the company, but he persisted in his position that MWT would not have been in such desperate straits if the transatlantic money had been spent instead on sales.

The Nova Scotians insisted that the federal government would assist with the payment for the construction of the new station. The next day Marconi's contingent, now swelling in numbers, left by train for Ottawa, seat of the Canadian colonial federal government. On the year's next to last day, Marconi met the governor general and prime minister of Canada. They quickly hammered out a draft agreement for building the Glace Bay station, including seventy-five thousand pounds in assistance from the federal government. Marconi estimated that the sum, enormous by MWT standards, would suffice to construct a superstation at Glace Bay Table similar to Cornwall. Canada demanded nothing in return, expecting the publicity to enhance Nova Scotia's attractiveness in the minds of prospective settlers and investors.

Kemp encouraged Marconi to go next to New York City, where Cuthbert Hall had been urging Charles Steinmetz, chairman of the American Institute of Electrical Engineers, to organize a dinner in Marconi's honor. Steinmetz had been stalling. A number of his members refused to attend because they did not believe Marconi. MWT's London headquarters wanted the endorsement of the institute and the publicity of the dinner. For Marconi, this appearance before his peers could only increase his personal embarrassment if he had mistaken static for signals.

Before he could commit to be in New York, Marconi had another, more immediate problem. It would do little good to receive signals at Glace Bay if MWT had no means of relaying the messages onward from Nova Scotia to their recipients in the United States. The Canadian Pacific Railway, headquartered in Montreal, had telegraph lines on its railroad rights-of-way from Cape Breton across upper Nova Scotia and lower New Brunswick to the Maine border. Instead of heading to New York, Marconi reversed the direction from which he had just come and traveled eastward to Montreal to arrange with the railroad for the use of its telegraph lines.

Marconi had not heard from Josephine following his letter in late November regretting that the company's tumultuous affairs did not allow him to consider marriage at any time in the foreseeable future. If possible, he was now even more preoccupied. The eyes of the world were upon him. MWT's future remained at stake. Even if he managed to convincingly demonstrate receipt of transatlantic waves, he must convert his experiment into a viable money-making service.

Rumors swirled about the couple. The press, cognizant of the engagement, assumed the wedding would soon follow Marconi's astounding accomplishment. But Josephine, deeply upset and angry, reviewed her options. She concluded she could no longer tolerate Marconi's behavior. In Montreal, a telegram arrived from New York: "From Hall to Marconi. The *Herald* told me Holmans would serve writ on your entering United States."

An engagement, in 1900, constituted a contract to marry. To break an engagement was a breach of contract for which damages could lie. Josephine presumed Marconi to be as rich as he was famous. At this particular moment, MWT's value could be anywhere from close to zero to some unimaginable amount, depending upon confirmation of St. John's.

Marconi did not pause to consider whether this shy, young girl from an American provincial city would really sue him and what personal value of his might be at risk. He would go to New York City if his business interests required him to do so, whatever her course of action might be.

In New York, Steinmetz was overcoming the resistance to a dinner in Marconi's honor. Steinmetz had been in a very peculiar position. Perhaps one of the most important events in electrical history had just occurred. How could the leading American society of electrical engineers not recognize the responsible scientist? On the other hand, if these prestigious, supposedly knowledgeable engineers feted the claimant and in fact the record-shattering breakthrough had not happened, they would look foolish. Edison's change of heart had helped. C. Comerford Martin, editor of *Electric World*, backed the testimonial and publicized it widely. Finally when Elihu Thomson endorsed Marconi, acceptances begin to come in. Thomson wrote a strong letter in support of Marconi for Steinmetz to circulate. In the electrical world, Thomson stood only a step behind Edison. His electric arc lighting company merged into Edison General Electric. Unlike Edison, Thomson remained a consultant to the entity when Edison General Electric became General Electric. Thomson specialized in alternating current motors, electric welding, high-frequency generators, and transformers. Ultimately, he collected 700 patents to Edison's 1039.

Marconi successfully concluded the Canadian Pacific negotiations and arrived in New York. He had brushed aside any threat Josephine

Marconi

might make. The dinner in his honor had become a major event in the life of the city, eagerly looked forward to not only by the scientific community, but also by the press and general public. Forgotten in the mind-boggling excitement of a transatlantic communication was criticism that two years earlier Marconi had not brought his syntonic tuning device for the U.S. Navy trials. Instead, news articles fondly recalled his coverage of the America's Cup. Staying again at Hoffman House, he called a press conference there before the testimonial. It was jam-packed. Reporters thronged about him, shouting to attract his attention and peppering him with wide-ranging questions. They spared nothing. When would he demonstrate transatlantic receipt of the waves? How did he know it was not static? What did he think of the aggressive behavior of Anglo-American? How would he deal with the cable companies? Where was Josephine? When would they marry? Calm as ever, Marconi answered that he and Kemp had heard the waves numerous times and made a record in their workbooks. The submarine cablers might act as they wished. MWT would go ahead with business as it thought best. He then announced that MWT planned to construct four stations, two on each side of the Atlantic. Nova Scotia and Cape Cod would be the North American sites, Belgium and Cornwall the European ones.

Despite the early anxiety concerning the dinner, the evening came off splendidly. The Astor Gallery of the Waldorf Astoria Hotel sold out even after a last-minute change advanced the date two days earlier to January 13, 1902. Three hundred dinner guests crammed the banquet floor. Above them, three levels of galleries overflowed with standees. The memorabilia menu designed by the thoughtful hosts bore a medallion of Marconi framed in the Italian flag. On one wall of the magnificent hall a tablet had been mounted bearing the name Poldhu, and on the opposite side a sign said St. John's. Between the walls a string of little, bright white Christmas lights flashed out "S S S." Above the speaker's table, larger lights spelled out "Marconi." As the pièce de résistance, following the main course, all the lights were dimmed. A profusion of waiters poured out of the vast kitchen. Each carried a tray above his head bearing candlelit dessert ices in the form of telegraph poles, a somewhat curious memento as wireless ultimately aimed to replace telegraph.

As toastmaster, Martin brought the highly excited guests to order. He then read portions of letters and telegrams he had received celebrating

Marconi and his accomplishment. The *Electric World* editor expressed everyone's regret at the absence of the master of electricity, but then he paid Marconi an enormous compliment. Among them that night, the knowledgeable commentator said, one guest in one field had gone beyond Edison. Martin then read a letter from the grand inventor:

> I am sorry not to be present to pay my respects to Marconi.
> I would like to meet that young man who has had the monumental audacity to attempt and succeed in jumping an electric wave across the Atlantic.(FN 11)

The master of ceremonies went on to recount his conversation with the irrepressible Edison, who had said:

> That he thought that some time there might be daily signals across the Atlantic without wires, but that he did not know when, and being preoccupied he did not think he would have time to do it himself. He said to me, "Martin, I'm glad he did it. That fellow's work puts him in my class. It's a good thing we caught him young."(FN 12)

Martin concluded his opening and introduced Marconi. A crescendo of applause greeted the honoree as he rose to his feet. No doubt those who saw him for the first time looked on in disappointment for the long, wavy hair of a young Edison, or the professional fullness and dignity of a Bell. If they had passed the man they saw before them on the street, they would not have taken note. If they had engaged him in cocktail conversation, they would have thought him shy. Some appraised him as thin-lipped, frail, or bearing a sad look. His keen eyes, however, stood out. Altogether, his neatly trimmed, well-brushed hair, the careful fit of his clothes, and the diffidence in his bearing suggested a clubman or a city worker. Only attention to a brisk step displayed the enormous energy, the enthusiastic drive that lifted his coworkers with him in his ceaseless, lifelong fascination of wireless.

Standing before this highly expectant audience teeming with experts, peers, compatriots in the quest for scientific advancement, competitors, critics, and press, Marconi raised his glass above his head and wordlessly

Marconi

toasted the diners. In silence, they instinctively stood en masse and returned the toast. Then cheers and applause thundered through the gallery. When the tumult at last died down, Marconi spoke. Without notes, he addressed them earnestly and modestly, exhibiting neither anxiety nor bravado. He held them entranced for half an hour. The *New York Times*, two days after the Institute of Electrical Engineers dinner, captured the tenor of the speech and the character of the man:

> Signor Marconi is not a stranger to the representative men of his profession in the United States, but it may be truthfully said that he leaves our shores with the respect and good wishes of every electrical engineer and the confidence of everyone financially interested in the telegraph business.
>
> At the banquet given in his honor Monday evening by the American Institute of Electrical Engineers he made his first specific statement of the results claimed by him as already achieved and of his hopes as to the future of his work. This statement was so modest, so free from every trace of exaggeration for business purposes, so generously just in its recognition of the obligation to the pioneers in experimentation along the lines he had followed, so frank in acknowledging the claims of the living as well as the dead, and the withal so conservative in its predicting of what may follow the work he now has in hand, that everyone present realized that to Marconi was not only due the honor of his discoveries in the field of mechanics, but the still higher honor which belongs to one who can subordinate all professional jealousies and rivalries to the truth.
>
> From the wreath woven for his own brow he borrowed enough to make wreaths for his predecessors and colleagues in the study of electrical waves—Clerk Maxwell, Lord Kelvin, Professor Henry, Dr. Hertz, Alexander Graham Bell and others—and by what he took from it his own was rather enriched than impoverished.

It cannot have escaped the notice of those for whom the subject of wireless telegraphy has even a news interest, that to establish the fact that the feat of transmitting intelligible signals in pre-arranged order and frequency of occurrence no other evidence was needed than Signor Marconi's unsupported and unverified statement. Immediately on receipt of telegraphic intelligence from Newfoundland that his feat had been accomplished and representative engineers of the world were interviewed, and without exception their response was: "If Marconi says it is true, I believe it."

There have been few great facts in science thus accepted with unquestioning confidence on the authority of one known to be anything but disinterested. In Marconi's case all that he claimed was conceded even before the details were known. No higher tribute could have been paid by the world of science to an inventor than was paid to Marconi by this unquestioning acceptance of the announcement that he had succeeded in accomplishing the seemingly impossible.

Concerning the commercial value of Marconi's work, his own claims are all that can safely be made at the moment. He hopes to give his system commercial value: if he does it will undoubtedly facilitate and cheapen electrical communication. He makes no boasts, and indulges in no extravagant promises. He does not understand the art of promotion, perhaps, but he has established a character for truthfulness and conservatism, and when he makes the announcement that his system can compete successfully with cables and land wires for business, we venture to say that he will have no need of the services of a promoter to capitalize his invention.(FN 13)

After a trip to South Wellfleet, Marconi departed the United States on January 22, 1902, disappointing public expectations that a wedding would first take place. No writ had been served. Josephine had given him one more chance to come to Indianapolis—he had no time.

Marconi

Marconi boarded the *Philadelphian*. A huge quantity of mail accompanied him, received from all kinds of people, congratulating him, asking for advice, seeking favors, or asking him to speak, write, or lecture. He was twenty-seven years old. Less than six years before, he and Annie had left Bologna with a black trunk and a letter of rejection from the Italian government. Only a little more than two years ago, on another ocean liner also embarking from New York, he had met Josephine and conceived the audacious idea to signal across the Atlantic.

Now to him Josephine was a thing of the past. His most recent laurels—the dinner, the acclamation, the *New York Times* tribute to his credibility and integrity—had been granted on faith. All rested on twenty-five sets of dots he and Kemp claimed to have heard. With his principal support a company whose financial lifeline depended entirely on what Marconi believed to have occurred, he must now provide tangible evidence of his accomplishment to a waiting world.

CHAPTER 11

The Quest for Transatlantic Signals

Marconi's second voyage home from New York contained none of the excitement of the first. No H. H. McClure and coterie of friends entertained him in a whirl of evening soirees. Infatuation for a pretty young American lady did not sweep over him. Unlike the first return, the wintry decks offered little solitude for contemplation. Everyone on board knew who he was, and few could resist approaching him. The worry that he must prove he heard signals at St. John's consumed him, for he knew too well the consequences if he did not. Stacks of letters asking him to speak, seeking a job, proposing deals, and so forth, littered his cabin. He did his best to cope with them as he was conscientious about answering his mail, but he spent the better part of his time planning what he must do next.

On landing at Southampton, Marconi unsuccessfully attempted to duck the throng of reporters and photographers awaiting him. It was the British press corps' first opportunity to question him about St. John's. As soon as he finished the interview, coldly deflecting questions that bristled with doubt about his achievement, he headed to Annie's latest London residence, 67 Talbot Street, in Bayswater. Her new address was not publicly known, and Marconi hoped for some momentary privacy there. Annie welcomed him home joyously. His room had been carefully prepared, and a fire roared in the drawing room. Solari soon joined them in celebration. What emotion, Solari asked, had Marconi experienced over his transatlantic signal? "I am never emotional," Marconi answered, consistent with his public persona. Then he must suddenly have remembered in whose parlor he sat. "I did feel strongly when I saw my mother

191

again. She's the only person on earth who understood my misgivings and trepidation when I left for Newfoundland."(FN 1)

The two friends talked late into the night, taking turns tending the fire and provoking it into brilliant outbursts of flame. The next transatlantic demonstration needed to produce clear, objective evidence to convince the world that signals had crossed the ocean. When the electromagnetic waves arrived at the receiver, they must possess sufficient energy to operate a machine to record their presence. Anglo-American's monopoly rights in Newfoundland precluded Marconi's return to St. John's. In his eagerness to verify his experiment, he did not want to wait to construct an antenna at Glace Bay or to reconstruct South Wellfleet. Nor did he wish to risk the additional transmission distance those sites required. Instead, he confided to Solari, he would receive signals aboard an ocean liner bound for New York. The proposed plan posed new dangers. The position of the ship would not be under Marconi's control. The receiver would be a constantly moving target, further and further from the transmitter. Marconi would be unable to stay in one spot while he adjusted his instruments. But the bold plan allowed him to undertake the confirmation exercise almost immediately. A special mast could be readily raised aboard a vessel. Improvements to Poldhu had been underway since Paget returned from St. John's with Marconi's detailed instructions. Furthermore, while the waves might not print out aboard ship at twenty-one hundred miles, the distance from Poldhu to St. John's, they might at a somewhat shorter distance that could still prove his point.

Typical of Marconi, his thoughts ranged far beyond the immediate necessity to bear out his claims. He wanted to establish commercial service between America and Europe. To achieve this, he intended to upgrade the Cornwall supergenerator to send unmistakable messages on a reliable basis across the Atlantic and then to replicate that machine at Glace Bay and South Wellfleet. All three locations would require major new antennas.

Scientifically, now that he believed his waves had flown thousands of miles, Marconi worried about a host of new problems. What might adversely affect signals over such a long distance? Would they be more exposed to electrical interference from light and solar disturbances? They had crossed the ocean from east to west, counter to the direction of the earth's spin. Would west to east be more difficult? Could they pass over land with mountainous terrain as well as over water?

Marconi had no efficient way to experiment over these extraordinary lengths and obstacles. The British Royal Navy, however, remained eager to have access to his latest accomplishments. It asked if he would like to explore these questions on a cruiser while it carried out its missions at sea. The directors, still perplexed and angry that the Royal Navy had not ordered any company sets the prior spring, considered the offer warily, skeptical as to the Admiralty's motives.

Marconi personally would rather experiment aboard an Italian vessel. Despite four years in southern England with both private and government support, Marconi continued to feel intensely loyal to Italy. But the relationship with the Italian navy had also been frustrating. In response to his appointment as a cadet attaché at the London embassy, Marconi had transferred his patent rights in Italy to the Italian government. The navy was among the first purchasers of MWT wireless. Subsequently, though, it had bought few additional sets. Instead, its behavior paralleled the Admiralty's. Utilizing Marconi's grant, Italy's navy attempted to improve the equipment in direct competition with Marconi. This irritated the company and personally annoyed and embarrassed Marconi. The Italian navy ordered Solari, as one of its officers, to participate in the effort. Even in that awkward position, Marconi's friend did his best to rectify the MWT estrangement. Arguing strenuously, Solari convinced his superiors that Marconi's developments far surpassed everyone else's, including his own and his own navy's, and to try to catch up was futile. The Italian authorities finally agreed and directed Solari to mend fences. Italian assistance for testing, Solari suggested to Marconi, might be possible. He understood that the new king, Victor Emmanuel, who had recently succeeded his father, was also a Marconi advocate. The possibility of an Italian warship tempted Marconi, who longed to work with his country. He authorized Solari to try. He also thanked Solari for the use of his receiver at St. John's. It had not proved useful, but it reminded Marconi that his receiver was too slow and needed improvement.

The day after his arrival, Marconi met with his fellow directors at MWT's new headquarters located at 18 Finch Lane between Threadneedle Street and Cornhill. The office was only a brisk walk away from the Bank of England and the center of the financial district. The location delighted

Marconi

Flood-Page. Not being in the immediate vicinity of Jameson-Davis's office, as the previous space had been, made him less susceptible to constant oversight by the former managing director.

On the surface, the board meeting was an enthusiastic, celebratory gathering. Thick cigar smoke filled the boardroom. Jameson-Davis reported that, on the assumption Marconi would substantiate the signals, investors had been lined up for a significant new share offering. Relief that MWT should now apparently be able to escape from its perilously close brush with financial disaster mingled with awe at the magnitude of the averred accomplishment.

But the directors were keenly sensitive to the many challenges to Marconi's assertions. In response to their repeated inquiries, he could only answer that he and Kemp were satisfied that they had heard signals.

Jameson-Davis's capital raising would replenish the company's exhausted cash account and allow the company to pay off its overdue bills. Once more the stock sale would dilute Marconi's ownership of MWT, bringing his share down to only 40 percent of the outstanding equity. Again he did not hesitate. MWT could not survive without fresh capital, and he would remain the dominant stockholder. No one else's holdings came close to his. Although the company employed other scientists and consultants such as Fleming, Marconi clearly continued to be MWT's guiding genius. While not possessing majority ownership, he still held practical control of the company.

Marconi informed the board that as soon as he completed Poldhu's improvements, he would corroborate the St. John's signals aboard a steamship headed for New York. Flood-Page lauded Marconi's achievement, but criticized the plan. He argued that a constantly moving receiver significantly reduced the chances to catch the signals. There were enough uncertainties inherent in any demonstration that a substantial new variable should not be added. Flood-Page then pointedly reminded the directors that Jameson-Davis's financing was predicated upon Marconi's success. Failure would instantly return MWT to December's dire financial condition. He recommended building a new receiving antenna at Glace Bay. Marconi disagreed. He wanted to get on with it. But the world-famous scientist would conceal the purpose of his trip to New York by saying he was en route to South Wellfleet and Glace Bay to oversee new construction. If he did not receive signals that supported St. John's, he would not announce it.

Marconi then described his proposal to prepare the three stations for transatlantic commerce. Again Flood-Page opposed the controlling shareholder, contending that Marconi's ideas were imprudent, the cost of the construction he contemplated was unpredictable, and the company had no experience by which to judge what quality of transmission would win customers or whether operating revenues would exceed expenses. Building out three stations might well deplete Jameson-Davis's new funds, and the service could run in the red. Flood-Page concluded that MWT should concentrate on its ship-to-shore business. The directors deferred a decision until Marconi landed in New York and advised them of the voyage's outcome.

The board also faced an international diplomatic crisis. The Germans were in an uproar. Kaiser Wilhelm's son, Prince Henry, had traveled to New York aboard the *Kronprinz Wilhelm*. On the outbound voyage to America, the luxury liner carried a syntonic Marconi receiver. By special arrangement, it received simultaneous messages from Poldhu and Lizard when the ship passed south of Cornwall. The prince was impressed. The volume of wireless traffic off the English and Irish coasts surprised him.

On the return trip, however, the prince sailed on the *Deutschland*. Its transmitter, developed by Professor Slaby, Ferdinand Braun, and Count von Arco, was owned by Telefunken, a new company formed to develop German wireless. The corporation was supported by the German government. It quickly became MWT's most formidable European competition.

Deutschland transmissions were not acknowledged by MWT's shore stations. Following the 1899 U.S. naval trials, the company had instituted its policy not to communicate with vessels utilizing competitive equipment except in the case of emergencies. MWT had paid the entire cost of establishing its seashore locations. It had by far the most. If others were allowed to use its system, the company would be surrendering a valuable advantage.

The kaiser regarded MWT's refusal a personal slight. The Germans bitterly attacked the company procedure. Telefunken accused MWT of pique. But the board dug in its heels. After the sale to the Nordeutschen line that Flood-Page had hotly resisted, the German shipper had not purchased another set. The directors suspected that Nordeutschen had given its Marconi devices to Telefunken to copy. MWT had not sued because the board doubted its rights would be protected by German courts. MWT ridiculed Telefunken. Its range barely exceeded one hundred miles. The directors blamed faulty Telefunken gear for the failure to exchange signals. Angered, the Germans would not let the incident drop. They would find a way to disrupt MWT's growing control of the ship-to-shore market.

Following the board meeting, Marconi wasted no time in preparing to confirm St. John's. He headed straight off to Cornwall to supervise the Poldhu adjustments. One month later, all was ready. At midnight on February 22, 1902, he secretly boarded the *Philadelphia* at Cherbourg. He had chosen the French port, due south of Southampton across the English Channel, and the nighttime embarkation to avoid attention. Joining him were seven company men. Saunders was to represent the board. In the event *Philadelphia* results were disappointing, Saunders would attempt to minimize adverse publicity. Marconi replaced Kemp and Paget, who had accompanied him to Newfoundland, with Vyvyan and C. S. Franklin. Both were more qualified engineers. For additional support, Marconi brought along two mechanical operators and his personal secretary.

In contrast to St. John's, where the aerial bounced about under unstable kites and balloons, the *Philadelphia* antenna hung from the top of a 170-foot fixed mast built to MWT's specifications. That height, however, was nine hundred feet less than the altitude to which the kites had managed to climb at stormy Signal Hill. Marconi connected the *Philadelphia* aerial to a tuned conventional dust-metal coherer housed in a warm cabin on the deck. In the circuit with the receiver he joined a Morse ink-on-tape printer capable of producing visible, written evidence of the receipt of signals. This inker would provide the objective proof he lacked at St. John's. There he could only attest that he had heard the sound of waves in his earphone. To furnish unbiased verification, the ship's captain and first mate agreed to witness what transpired. Marconi scheduled Poldhu to transmit for an hour every sixth hour—at noon, six o'clock in the evening, midnight, and six o'clock in the morning. Poldhu's super dynamos now generated a controlled spark that was a foot long and as thick as a baseball bat.

On the twenty-third, the *Philadelphia* steaming below Needles picked up signals from the Isle of Wight at a distance of seventy miles. At noon it then tuned in on Poldhu for an hour, receiving and sending messages until two hundred and fifty miles beyond Lizard and Land's End. Marconi labeled the tapes on which the Cornwall messages were recorded Message No. 1. That night at midnight, at a distance of 464 miles from the super-generator, a flurry of receipts set a new world record for signals evidenced by an inker. With satisfaction, Marconi marked the printed record of these communications as Message No. 2.

At six o'clock the next morning, however, the tapper printed nothing. Quiet once again permeated the hour between midday and one o'clock. Marconi's assistants bravely climbed the pitching mast to adjust the aerial. Marconi fine-tuned the instruments. Vyvyan and Franklin went over all the connections in the circuit. Saunders was visibly flustered, saying little to the *Philadelphia* captain and first mate, who stood by patiently. From six to seven o'clock that evening, the inker sat motionless. The enormous, unnerving silence was a severe setback and raised serious questions about the validity of St. John's.

In consternation, the group waited for midnight. The engineers whispered among themselves about the combinations of variables most likely to catch waves. They considered temporarily replacing the inker with an earphone because it was more sensitive to the electromagnetic impulses. Marconi rejected the idea. Just before midnight, the first mate informed the anxious party in the cabin that they were 1,032 miles from Poldhu. All eyes focused on Marconi at the receiver. The tapper suddenly broke through the heavy gloom. A steady stream arrived over the next hour. With no display of the relief he must have felt, Marconi recorded them as Message No. 3. At six in the morning at 1,164 miles, the machine pecked away for another hour (officially Message No. 4). The MWT party relaxed slightly. Optimism seeped back into the men's conversation.

But again during the two scheduled hours of daylight transmission at noon and six o'clock at night, the recorder remained still, causing confusion and concern once more. At midnight, however, it chattered away and for an hour printed dots and dashes constituting official Message No. 5. At the end of the allotted time, the ship was 1,551 miles from Poldhu.

Nothing came at six o'clock the next morning. The captain informed the puzzled MWT group that at midnight that night they would be more than two thousand miles from Poldhu. At noon, no signals were received. Marconi could not rationalize the daytime failures. It was similar to the experience at Spezia. There he could not comprehend how he picked up waves over the horizon. Here he could not explain reception at night but not by day. At St. John's, he had not tried to listen after dark. He had heard signals only during the day.

Saunders began to argue that the prior night's distance of 1,551 miles would be sufficient proof of St. John's. The world would have to acknowledge they had confirmed Marconi's claims.

No signals came in at six o'clock.

As midnight approached, the captain, first mate, and company party huddled over Marconi at the instruments. No one spoke of either their fears or their hopes. Marconi quietly conferred with Vyvyan and Franklin as he made minute final adjustments.

At midnight, the inker sprang to life. A roar went up from the assembled men. Marconi smiled broadly. Saunders slapped everyone on the back and broke out the cigars. Cheer after cheer went up. The captain had champagne brought to the cabin. Congratulations were exchanged all around.

As the hour ended, at 1:00 a.m., February 27, 1902, at latitude 42.01 N, longitude 47.23, 2,099 miles from Poldhu, the letter S, the familiar single dot of St. John's, printed across the tape, only seventy miles short of the official distance from Poldhu to St. John's. The *Philadelphia* voyage confirmed Signal Hill.

Bounding down the gangplank in New York, Marconi eagerly thrust the tapes at reporters. "This," he coolly declared, "merely confirms what I have previously done in Newfoundland. There is no longer any question about the ability of wireless telegraphy to transmit messages across the Atlantic."(FN 2)

One newsman noted that while Marconi did not appear astonished by the result, nonetheless he seemed to be a very happy young man. Saunders aggressively underscored the inventor. "We are prepared to meet anyone who may dispute our claim on this trip, and confront them with unconvertible proof of what has been done."(FN 3) Asked if a message could someday be transmitted round the world and back to its starting point, Marconi thought it possible. But he wryly allowed that he did not think it a paying investment. Cable company stocks that had stabilized after falling for weeks following St. John's sagged again upon publication of the interview.

Neither Marconi nor Saunders disclosed to the press the failure to receive daytime signals. The intentional omission reflected their deep concern over this new problem. Marconi privately attributed the adverse results to "daylight fog," or atmospheric conditions that interfered with the transmissions. Not having a fix on the cause, he did not have a clear grip on a solution. He later said:

> It was during the trials on the *Philadelphia* that I discovered a marked and detrimental effect of daylight on wireless transmission, and the greater ease with which messages could be sent over long distances at night. I was of the opinion that weak signals during the daytime might have been caused by the loss of energy at the transmitter due to the diselectrification of the highly charged elevated aerial under the influence of sunlight.(FN 4)

As word seeped out to the scientific community of the strange pattern on the *Philadelphia,* others had opinions as well. Oliver Heaviside, an English physicist and telephone engineer, theorized that a layer of ionized air high in the atmosphere acted as a mirror reflecting waves back to earth. Harvard's Professor Arthur Kennelley agreed, believing the mirror to billow up and down like a tent-top in a gale. But few recognized the Heaviside-Kennelley layer. The solution to the newly discovered difficulty, Marconi believed, was more power. All three stations should have double Poldhu's current voltage. This immediately added to the financial burden of building a transatlantic service.

The *Philadelphia* recordings permitted Jameson-Davis to consummate the stock sale. The daytime difficulties, while troubling, had not deterred private money excited by potential business suggested by transatlantic transmission.

Marconi had gambled the company. He had gone to the brink in the belief that long transmission was MWT's best route to a highly profitable future. Since his inspiration at Biellese more than seven years earlier, distance had been his driving instinct and close to total preoccupation. Preposterous as his proposal had seemed, unsupported by any scientific theory, tenuous as his verification had been at stormy St. John's, electromagnetic waves could and had in fact crossed the Atlantic.

For the moment, Marconi had won. Enough investors had accepted his vision. The credibility of MWT's future had been restored. The viability of meaningful electromagnetic communication had been verified, and the extraordinary expansion of its range evoked new concepts of what wireless might do.

The riches that might come to Marconi from his company ownership did not spark a lawsuit from Josephine. She acceded to what had become increasingly apparent. Marconi's work meant more to him than she did. She had returned to Indianapolis to prepare the wedding festivities and had joyfully told all her friends that she was to marry the famous Marconi. Now, facing the fact that it was over, she was deeply embarrassed. Still, she tried to salvage some pride. A relationship with Marconi would not be one with which she would be satisfied. She broke it off. She wrote her absentee fiancé, saying that she could never marry him. Annie, while publicly disappointed, was privately relieved. There would be no wife to usurp her cherished role with her child. Her son had no time to reflect on his loss.

As soon as the directors received news of the *Philadelphia* success, they authorized Marconi to build Glace Bay as he had proposed, despite the financial and scientific risks that Flood-Page had voiced. Considering the excitement generated at London headquarters by the confirmation voyage, it was hardly politic for the managing director to press his concerns. Meanwhile, Marconi's engineering party did not linger in New York, but headed straight off for Nova Scotia. Although others under similar circumstances might have been flushed with enthusiasm, Marconi matter-of-factly inspected the Glace Bay site and approved construction plans for the costly superstation. Leaving Vyvyan at Table Head to supervise the new project, Marconi finalized the Canadian agreement in Ottawa and returned to the United States. At South Wellfleet, he inspected the four 210-foot wooden towers that had replaced the fallen circular antenna.

In New York at the end of March, Marconi witnessed the completion of the organization of MWT's U.S. subsidiary. On November 22, 1899, following the America's Cup race, MWT had registered the corporation as the Marconi Wireless Telegraph Company of America. Most people called it American Marconi for short. On April 1, MWT had American Marconi formally incorporated. The parent transferred its U.S. rights in Marconi's inventions to American Marconi. In return, the subsidiary promised to pay MWT fifty thousand pounds, the same price intended to be paid in 1899. The company directed American Marconi to sell its shares to the public when appropriate and pay the debt out of the proceeds. Until stock could be sold, MWT would provide American Marconi with operating capital. The subsidiary's functions were to run South Wellfleet and to build shore stations for ship-to-shore business. Nantucket was to be the first such station.

Although the American ship-to-shore market was in its infancy and several years behind Europe, American Marconi was not the first to enter the field. United Fruit operated a fleet of boats bringing produce from South America to the East Coast. Aware of the perishable nature of its products, it wanted to reduce the time required to offload and make deliveries to grocers by giving ports and buyers advance warning of a ship's arrival. United Fruit originally developed wireless for its own use. Another commercial enterprise had been organized by Lee de Forest, an inventor. He and Abraham White, a promoter, had teamed together to raise money to develop de Forest's concepts. National Electric Signaling won a contract to build shore stations for the U.S. Navy utilizing Professor Reginald Aubrey Fessenden's instruments. In technical terms, none of these competitors came close to MWT, but de Forest was approaching Telefunken's levels.

De Forest had competed with Marconi representatives the prior fall to provide press coverage for Lipton's second attempt to capture the America's Cup. The American de Forest Wireless Telegraph Company was authorized to sell three million dollars of capital stock to invest in the business. It had two shore stations on New York Bay, three on Long Island, and construction was underway at Atlantic City, Key West, and Havana. De Forest had signaled to the *Deutschland* one hundred miles at sea as it approached New York. He had thirteen patents pending and was feverishly working on a receiver or responder that would be superior to the coherer Marconi was using. He clearly had Marconi in his sights.

After almost three months living out of suitcases, always on the go, Marconi returned in May to Poole. He needed to address the weakest point of his system, the one identified by de Forest. The coherer worked, but too slowly. An integral part of the receiver, the coherer consisted of

Marconi

a vacuum tube filled with tiny metal particles scattered loosely about inside. When an electromagnetic wave arrived, the metal bits all adhered or cohered to each other. This adhesion allowed the electric current generated by the wave to pass through the tube to operate an ink printer or whatever device evidenced the arrival of the signal. To prepare for receipt of the next wave, the coherer had to be tapped to separate the metallic particles and spread them about again. The inventor wanted to eliminate the tapping step. At Poole, he conceived a new instrument that would utilize a magnetic field in place of the coherer and tapper.

On a gorgeous June morning, Marconi straddled his bike at the Haven Hotel and pedaled through the pines and flowering rhododendrons of New Forest to Bournemouth. He inquired of the local merchants for a special type of wire that he hoped to use in his magnetic field. In a flower shop, he thoughtfully examined the very thin wire used to bind floral arrangements. Judging it appropriate for his purpose, he purchased it and then cycled back to Poole at full speed. In his workshop, he coiled the fine wire with his long, skilled fingers around an empty glass tube. He connected one end of the wire to an antenna and the other end to a ground. Next he wound a second strand of the florist's wire around the first coil and attached both ends to a telephone receiver. Then he created a magnetic field where the two wires were coiled together by placing the tips of two horseshoe magnets on either side of the tube. He transmitted an electromagnetic wave to the antenna. The wave went through the antenna and into the first coil of wire. The interaction of the wave in the first coil passing through the magnetic field generated a burst of electric current in the second wire wrapped around the first wire. That current produced a sound in the telephone receiver. The noise evidenced the arrival of the electromagnetic wave. It was a form of a signal. Once the energy created by the electromagnetic wave had passed through the system, the receiver was immediately ready to receive another wave or signal. No further act was necessary to prepare for the next signal. Marconi's invention had eliminated the tapping step.

He nicknamed his most recent invention the "Maggie"; it was his abbreviation of magnetic. The Maggie was an enormous advance. Without having to prepare for each signal, the number of words received jumped to thirty a minute, doubling the coherer's word count, but more importantly equaling cable's. In one brilliant move, the scientist/inventor had doubled MWT's capacity to communicate between its shore stations and ships carrying its wireless. The device had other attractive features as well. Its parts were more resistant than the coherer's floating particles to the pounding receivers endured at sea. Simpler mechanics meant fewer operating troubles. Durable magnets and wire coils had longer lives than coherers. No competitor's receiver came close to the Maggie.

Marconi proceeded at once to obtain a patent for the Maggie, which would rank among his most significant inventions. For the next twenty years, it became standard equipment in wireless receivers. Marconi had not conceived the scientific concept. Its roots were in an 1842 demonstration by Joseph Henry. Further advancements were made in the 1890s led by Lord Rutherford and Professor E. Wilson. But just like his original work creating workable wireless communication, Marconi grasped the significance of others' efforts and converted them into practical instruments. That adaptive ability was the heart of Marconi's inventive genius.

While Marconi had been traveling in America, Solari pursued his own suggestion that Italy provide a ship for long-distance testing. He boldly worked his way up through the Italian naval hierarchy. His effort culminated in an audience with King Victor Emmanuel. The monarch delighted the lieutenant by immediately granting his request. Under royal direction, Admiral Morin, the minister of the navy, invited Marconi to conduct his tests aboard the *Carlo Alberto*, a new first-class cruiser. Marconi accepted without hesitation. Yielding again to his instinctive, deep love of his native country despite its aggressive use of his first patent grant, he transferred to its government the right to use in Italy his most recent developments. To Solari's surprise, an Italian professor at the University of Pisa in a widely publicized lecture asserted that Telefunken had a more advanced system and produced better results. The naval officer took it upon himself to respond. In a letter published by a Genoa newspaper, he adamantly disagreed with the professor. His writing incensed Admiral Carlo Mirabello, commander of the *Carlo Alberto*. The admiral could not believe that a lieutenant in his navy would challenge an acclaimed professor. He called Solari in. In Solari's words:

> He asked how it was that I, a young ship's lieutenant, felt free to contradict an eminent professor of physics on a scientific question. "I know I'm right, sir." "Then prove it.

Marconi

Sail with me to England on the *Carlo Alberto*. If it turns out as you say, I'll be one of Marconi's greatest supporters; if not, you will be posted to Africa."(FN 5)

The *Carlo Alberto* with Solari aboard picked Marconi up at Dover at the end of June. Admiral Mirabello had been ordered to Kronstadt near St. Petersburg on the Gulf of Finland for a meeting of the Italian and Russian monarchs, Victor Emmanuel and Czar Nicholas. Marconi fitted the cruiser with a four-wire cage antenna, receiving equipment, and a Maggie. The second day out in the North Sea, the ship received signals from Poldhu. The waves had traveled 250 miles over England, the longest distance Marconi had transmitted over land, as well as another 250 miles over the sea. But to Marconi's and Solari's disappointment, the signals quickly faded away.

Solari worked well with Marconi. He was creative and resourceful and not afraid to act on his own. He was an enjoyable companion, as gregarious as Marconi was reticent. Being Italian himself, Solari understood and shared Marconi's deep love of their homeland. He was dedicated to wireless, as well. The two men worked feverishly round-the-clock in an effort to improve the reception. On this trip they climbed the bucking, towering mast to adjust the antenna while the admiral powered the *Carlo Alberto* at full speed, slamming ahead in the narrow, choppy passage around Jutland. But like the *Philadelphia*, the *Carlo Alberto* succeeded in detecting long-distance signals only at night. "Damn the sun," Marconi said, frustrated at the Maggie's failure to solve the Hertzian fog. "How long will it torment us?"(FN 6) As the ship passed the Baltic island of Gotland, east of Sweden, eight hundred miles from Poldhu, half the miles being over land in England, Denmark, and Sweden, the night signals disappeared.

On July 12, *Carlo Alberto* entered the canal at Kronstadt, its skyline a mysterious combination of forts, gun batteries, and eastern-style, onion-shaped Orthodox spires. Despite the social blandishments offered by the occasion and by the welcoming Russian fleet, Marconi and Solari resisted all temptations. Three days later, their diligence paid off. Night signals came in from Cornwall over twelve hundred miles of land and water. But immediately a more awkward problem arose. Victor Emmanuel announced the next day that he had invited Czar Nicholas aboard the following morning to visit the wireless. Marconi knew the two crowns would expect to witness the receipt as well as the transmission of wireless signals. Marconi had not received a single daytime signal since the North Sea. He could hardly ask the king to defer the czar to evening. Solari volunteered a partial solution. Before daybreak, he would hide in the ship's stern a small transmitter/receiver perfectly suited for exchanging messages with Marconi's forward cabin.

Czar Nicholas and King Victor Emmanuel pulled alongside in the czar's yacht, *Alexandra*. Russian warships fired round after round of booming cannon, sending clouds of smoke across the harbor, followed by choruses of hurrahs shouted by the thousands of deep-throated seamen. The Italian national anthem accompanied Victor Emmanuel's brisk ascent to the *Carlo Alberto*'s foredeck, where he stood amidst its snapping pennants. The two monarchs reviewed the Italian sailors and then proceeded to the wireless station. Marconi explained the instruments and showed the thirty-four-year-old czar, only six years Marconi's senior, taped messages from Poldhu. Marconi then transmitted messages to nowhere but the stern. He received in return a laudatory message to the czar secretly tapped out by Solari one hundred feet away. Where, asked the czar, had the message come from? In answer to the czar's direct question, Marconi, half with wry humor and half in embarrassment, explained his difficulty. Smiling, Nicholas asked Solari to join them. The four men chatted away amicably about wireless for the next half hour.

This had to be a happy time for Marconi. He adored Italy. Being aboard a ship and at sea appealed to him enormously. No activity entranced him more than to be experimenting with his long-distance wireless. Here for a period of several weeks he was totally immersed in his favorite things. It brought out in him the sense of humor that his cousin Daisy had enjoyed in his boyhood. The fun in him had been buried by years of endless responsibility and pressure. The night following the demonstration for the monarchs, Marconi in a civilian suit and Solari in full dress naval uniform attended a reception ashore given in honor of Victor Emmanuel by the top Russian military brass at the request of the czar. The imperial military band played throughout the evening. The daughter of a Russian general asked Marconi what role he played aboard the *Carlo Alberto*. He said he was a soldier. What then is your rank and why are you not in uniform, the militarily wise young woman inquired.

Marconi

"I am his orderly," Marconi replied with a straight face, pointing to his regal looking friend.(FN 7)

With diplomatic duties completed, the *Carlo Alberto* returned to Italy. On entering the Mediterranean Sea, it would pass the Rock of Gibraltar. Marconi hoped that at that moment he could answer a question that had been plaguing him. Since installing Queen Victoria's wireless at Osborne House among the East Cowes hills, he had wondered if mountainous landmasses would block long-distance electromagnetic waves. Marconi scheduled nighttime transmissions from Cornwall at the hour when, according to Mirabello's estimates, the *Carlo Alberto* would sail close by the Rock of Gibraltar. Its thirteen-hundred-foot-high, precipitous pinnacles would lie directly in the path of signals between Poldhu and the ship. Before encountering that obstacle, the waves would have to span Spain from north to south, including its Cantabrian mountain range, whose peaks thrust above eight thousand feet.

Crossing the Bay of Biscay, the *Carlo Alberto* encountered a major storm. Mirabello, Marconi, and Solari had closeted themselves in the wireless cabin, preparing for the Gibraltar experiment. At the receiver, intent on hearing an incoming message, Solari tried to ignore the ship's bucking and rolling. An old seadog unperturbed by the relentless, unpredictable, heaving motions, the admiral puffed away contentedly on an enormous cigar. Marconi noticed that the thick smoke and heavy waves were about to make Solari sick. "Admiral," Marconi asked, "don't you know that a German professor has declared that a pillar of smoke can act as a screen to electric waves?"(FN 8) Startled, the admiral opened the cabin door and pitched out his cigar. Marconi could not restrain his laughter. Mirabello looked at Marconi and then saw the look of relief on Solari's face and joined in the merriment.

At two o'clock in the morning on September 4, in the midst of swirling patches of fog, the *Carlo Alberto* reached the Straits of Gibraltar. The sheer cliff, unseen in the dark, towered massively over the ship. In the wireless room, Mirabello and Solari watched Marconi don the earphones and adjust the receiver. The admiral sensed the tension. Not wishing to divert Marconi's attention by his presence, he left the cabin. Half an hour later, an upset inventor joined the commander on the bridge. He reported that he had heard nothing and went on to say the following:

We have to wait for Poldhu's next signals at three o'clock. The station may have had some slight mishap that would account for the silence at two. If there is still nothing at three, I am afraid we will have to conclude that the European continent is an insuperable obstacle to the propagation of electrical waves.(FN 9)

Mirabello acceded to the request. He ordered the helm to slowly circle in the soupy dark. At the moment of three, the printer sprang to life, stamping Vs on the tape. Solari ran for the command post. As he scrambled across the deck, a searchlight from another ship unexpectedly raked the *Carlo Alberto.* Then a dozen beams danced through the mists to play on the Italian naval warship, bedazzling Solari. The Italians had not notified the British authority governing Gibraltar of their presence and peculiar course, fearing they would be ordered to move out. The hulking shape of a British cruiser and even nearer the outline of a pilot boat, blurry in the vapors, closed in on the Italian warship. Blinded, Solari groped his way to Mirabello to inform him of the wireless success. Disregarding the British commands to halt, the admiral ordered full speed ahead to open water and then casually joined Marconi in the wireless cabin. Together the former cadet, the lieutenant, and the commanding officer perused messages streaming in from Poldhu. One reported that the Empress of Russia had miscarried. Strange, the admiral remarked, that a great failure should confirm a great success.

The next day, as the ship passed Sardinia, Marconi fell into bed with a severe fever. Solari called it exhaustion. When they neared Spezia, however, he struggled to his feet to direct Poldhu to send a message to Victor Emmanuel care of the *Carlo Alberto.* It would be the first wireless message to cross not just the Iberian Peninsula but a substantial portion of the European continent as well. In recognition of the event's significance, Marconi wanted special words to honor his royal sponsor who had made the Italian vessel available for experiments. To his horror, only gibberish came over the tape. Clearly the Cornwall operator had insufficient knowledge of Morse code. The normally self-contained scientist flew into a rage. Temper flaring, he smashed a case of glass jars and attacked the receiving equipment. Solari rushed to Marconi's side to restore his friend's composure. With light humor, the naval officer reproached his boyhood companion by saying that the Italian navy would hold its present officer, not its former attaché, personally responsible for the wreckage. Somewhat sheepishly, Marconi repaired the injured equipment and arranged for an appropriate message.

The *Carlo Alberto* docked at Spezia. Mirabello and Marconi exchanged warm farewells. Mirabello had been elevated with a prize promotion to command the entire Mediterranean fleet. True to his word to Solari, the admiral numbered himself among Marconi's greatest advocates. Once ashore, Marconi called upon Victor Emmanuel. Only five years Marconi's senior and in office scarcely more than a year, the relaxed king swapped stories with the scientist about incidents aboard the *Carlo Alberto*. Marconi advised Victor Emmanuel that the Canadian station neared completion. Marconi would shortly travel there to commence MWT's commercial transatlantic business. To Marconi's delight, Victor Emmanuel understood at once the prestige that would accrue to Italy if the government supported the establishment of the revolutionary, unprecedented communication link between the two continents. He authorized the navy to transport Marconi to Nova Scotia aboard the *Carlo Alberto* and to have the ship stand by for the inauguration of wireless service at Glace Bay.

Eight months after the confirmation of St. John's aboard the *Philadelphia,* Marconi and Solari crossed the Atlantic aboard the *Carlo Alberto.* It received nighttime signals from Cornwall the entire distance. On October 31, decks laden with snow, the cruiser steamed through the ice clogged waters off Table Head promontory. The new site's aerial, four hundred copper wires hung from cables suspended between four stout towers set in a square, rose dramatically 210 feet above the transmitting and receiving hut. Onshore, Marconi took charge of the final adjustments to the powerful new transmitter. He hoped it powerful enough to eliminate daytime "fog." The length of the electromagnetic wave had been increased to five thousand yards, almost three miles long. Marconi believed the longer the wave, the more efficiently it would slice the air. He recognized immediately the difficulties remaining to bring the service on line and the arduous conditions under which the men labored. Borrowing from what he had learned on the *Carlo Alberto,* he imposed taut naval discipline on his crew of eight. Each night at eight sharp, the team met for dinner. Marconi, the youngest, sat at the head. The others found their places down the table. The more important their function, the closer their seat to Marconi. Vyvyan, as station head, was on Marconi's right and Solari, as his principal assistant, on his left. The men called Marconi "sir," which came most naturally to Solari, and each other by last name.

For twenty-nine days, no signal passed in either direction between Poldhu and Glace Bay. Representatives of the world press, alerted to the commencement of the novel service, had traveled north. Now they watched critically, writing querulous articles, kept at bay by Marconi, who had nothing to report. Finch Lane constantly queried Marconi, cabling for signs of progress. The new commander of the *Carlo Alberto* advised Marconi he could not stand by indefinitely. Further, he reported that the king, having lent his prestige to the endeavor, was anxious for results.

On the night of November 28, after numerous Glace Bay modifications, Cornwall reported receipt from Nova Scotia of "weak signals for the first half-hour, nothing during next three-quarters, last three-quarters readable and recordable." The jubilation at the first intelligible west-to-east readings ever recorded, however, dissipated in a day. The next night Poldhu received no signals. Yet the adjustments and positions on both sides of the ocean had remained identical to those of the prior evening. Again the following night Marconi ordered no changes. Still nothing arrived in England. A depressing reality slowly sank in. Unseen, immeasurable, unidentifiable forces adversely affected wireless performance at night as well as in daylight. The influences acted erratically. Marconi and his frustrated scientists could not predict or respond rationally to their consequences. The settings for one effective message did not assure the success of the next. No matter at what distance a signal might be received from time to time, the painful possibility remained that Marconi might never achieve reliable long-distance wireless communication. Apparent accomplishments at any moment could fade into nothingness.

In this critical period, Marconi, in Solari's words, "showed all the geniality of his mind, all the authority of his character and all of the activity of his organizing genius."(FN 10) He needed every bit of his strength. Glace Bay was depressing. The color stretching in every direction from the isolated, dreary location was dismal gray. Leaden clouds filled the sky. To the east, the headland looked out over frozen ocean. To the west, snow covered the flat, barren interior, relieved occasionally by a stand of dark

Marconi

fir trees, until the land met the horizon. The weather at best could be described as frigid, and the near arctic November days were short. The most important work had to be done in the middle of the night, every night. None of the men could escape the unspoken knowledge that if Glace Bay failed, Marconi's invention had limited commercial value.

Increasingly, headquarters worried. A year had passed since St. John's. Yet once more in the frozen northern lands, in the grips of winter's blasts, the future of Marconi's invention and the fate of the company lay uncertainly in his hands. Throughout his career, Marconi had achieved pinnacle after pinnacle of success. Each new height conquered, however, revealed a new, more formidable obstacle to surmount. Each time the failure to achieve the next level threatened the overall significance of his inventions. How many times could he rise to the challenge?

On December 14, at seven o'clock in the morning Nova Scotia time, Cornwall acknowledged that it had received steady signals from Glace Bay for an entire two-hour transmission period. The men who, in the heat of the transmitting shed generated by the enormous electric sparks, had stripped off their upper garments ran outside half-dressed and joyfully danced about in the snow, oblivious to the cold. Marconi hesitated. At St. John's, he had believed he had heard Poldhu. Now he knew he could transmit steadily for a period of time, but was a steady transmission of 120 consecutive minutes sufficient to establish reliable transoceanic service?

London demanded a public demonstration. Marconi agreed. He invited Sir George S. Parkin, professor at Upper Canada College and correspondent for the *Times* of London at Ottawa, to be an impartial observer of the first message to be transmitted over the new system. Officers came from *Carlo Alberto* as well to attest. Parkin reported that everyone assembled at midnight for a light supper. He could feel the tension mount. Just before one o'clock, in bright moonlight, they all tramped across the snow to the operating shack. Following are Parkin's own words about the occasion:

> The machinery was carefully inspected, some adjustments made, and various orders carried out with trained alertness. All put cotton wool in their ears to lessen the force of the electric concussion, which was not unlike the

successive explosions of a Maxim gun. As the current was one of most dangerous strength, those not engaged in the operations were assigned to places free of risk...A brief order for the lights over the battery to be put out, another for the current to be turned on, and the operating work began. I was struck by the instant change from nervousness to complete confidence which passed over Mr. Marconi's face the moment his hand was on the transmitting apparatus—in this case a long, wooden lever or key...Outside there was no sign, of course, on the transverse wire from which the electric wave projected of what was going on, but inside the operating room the words seemed to be spelled out in short flashes of lightning. It was done slowly, since there was no wish on this occasion to test the speed. But as it was done, one remembered with a feeling of awe—that only the ninetieth part of a second elapses from the moment when he sees the flash till the time when the record is made at Poldhu.(FN 11)

Poldhu acknowledged the message. Transatlantic commercial service had begun. In the first gloaming of day, in the freezing cold, the resolute band of pioneering engineers and scientists at their desolate outpost marked that initial formal communication with a simple ceremony. *Carlo Alberto*'s sailors bearing an Italian flag marched to Table Head. At dawn, the small contingent of Britons, Canadians, and Italians, led by a bareheaded Marconi, gathered at the foot of one of the towers and together raised their national flags.

Over the Christmas week, nighttime messages to Poldhu continued, but not without difficulty. Sometimes a transmission required two dozen repetitions to assure full and accurate receipt. Clearly, sufficient transatlantic service had not yet arrived. At the opening of the New Year, 1903, the *Carlo Alberto* could no longer stand by waiting for a fully satisfactory service. It departed with Solari. As a gift for his friend, Marconi inscribed a photograph of himself. Solari found the inscription "so flattering and affectionate that I was deeply moved."(FN 12) The gift represented Marconi's way of thanking Solari for his unfailing support for the past twelve months.

Marconi

Marconi's further efforts at Table Head had no appreciable effect, so he decided to depart for South Wellfleet, which lay six hundred miles from Glace Bay. That distance was too far from Table Head to receive day messages. There was an apparent five-hundred-mile daylight limit that Marconi had failed to pierce. The barrier made Marconi's receipt of waves at St. John's in the daytime seem incredulous and raised further questions as to whether he had received signals there. But such questions had no significance now that Glace Bay and Poldhu regularly received signals at night. The restriction, however, limited Glace Bay's role to that of a nighttime relay station for messages crossing the Atlantic. The messages would have to be received from Poldhu at night, then resent to South Wellfleet at night by wireless or forwarded over the Canadian Pacific's telegraph lines to the United States. By mid-January, the system became operational. Poldhu sent communiqués to Glace Bay that then retransmitted to South Wellfleet. American communications to England reversed the route.

On Friday night, January 18, 1903, Cape Cod signaled Glace Bay with greetings from Teddy Roosevelt to Edward VII for relay to Poldhu. To everyone's great surprise, the South Wellfleet signals carried all the way to Poldhu as well as to Glace Bay.

It marked the first full transatlantic crossing by wireless.

Unfortunately for public relations, Edward's response had to cross the ocean by submarine cable. The Mullion telegraph office, where the Poldhu station sent and received its telegraph messages, had closed for the weekend by the time the king's reply had been readied. MWT had no means to deliver the king's message from Sandringham to Poldhu for wireless relay to the United States.

Nonetheless, the Roosevelt transatlantic transmission merited celebration. Mrs. Doane, at whose boarding house the South Wellfleet Marconi men resided, provided a luncheon of oysters followed by turkey and trimmings, cranberries, turnips, and squash, finished off by Indian pudding. She also recorded the local effect of the new accomplishment:

> After the news of the establishment of communication was made known extra operators in Provincetown and Wellfleet had to take care of the messages which came in by telegraph. Telephones on the Cape...were rare. The

King of Italy sent half a page of congratulations. It came via Provincetown telegraph office and by telephone to the little store at South Wellfleet. The fatigued storekeeper and his pretty clerk had been standing most of the day by the wall telephone with a pencil in one hand, trying to take down the names of men of importance it was stunning to contemplate.

The London *Times* printed a letter of congratulations to the British people from the Canadian premier. The cable stocks that had recovered as MWT's Nova Scotia difficulties mounted sagged again. Marconi received the Italian Order of Merit. The Italian government contemplated ordering a super wireless station.

The publicity did nothing to enhance Tesla's mood. He was forging ahead with his World Tower but had not yet reached completion or conducted preliminary tests. Morgan remained adamant about not advancing further funds. Tesla had not secured another financing source. His own funds were close to exhaustion. Westinghouse, who had built the tower's equipment to Tesla's specifications but had not been paid, threatened to remove it.

Despite the Cape Cod to England fanfare, Marconi and the directors worried that the quality of transatlantic service, with patches of messages undecipherable and delivery times unpredictable, would hurt the long-term credibility and reputation of wireless. Nor could the inefficient night service be economically competitive with cable operating around the clock.

The directors, overruling Marconi, decided to close Glace Bay until further improvements permitted profitable twenty-four-hour operations. The decision deeply upset Marconi. It was a blow to his pride and a reversal in his scientific progress. The London *Times* insisted the station remain open to provide transatlantic news service. MWT assented, but shortly thereafter the weight of ice built up on the four hundred Table Head copper wires collapsed the entire antenna.

In thirteen months, the performance of Marconi's invention had strengthened incredibly from St. John's questionable, tenuous, faintly heard letter S. Signals had been clearly received under Gibraltar's formidable rock wall. Electromagnetic waves spanned the full Atlantic from

Marconi

South Wellfleet to Cornwall. Waves for substantial periods of time at night conveyed steady streams of communication over two thousand miles of ocean.

A host of serious problems, however, accompanied these scientific advances. MWT remained undercapitalized. Poldhu, Glace Bay, and South Wellfleet, as Flood-Page had predicted, had consumed almost the entire amount of money Jameson-Davis's sale of shares had raised a year earlier. Yet the three transatlantic sites had earned only minimal revenue. Company engineers still had no solutions to the puzzling daytime and erratic nighttime barriers to long-distance transmission. Marconi's suspicion of solar disturbances did not suggest a remedy. Nonetheless, he insisted the supergenerators have more power, which required additional capital, even while he admitted that commercial service and contracts remained a far-off prospect.

Here was a bitter pill for Marconi to swallow. He was fascinated to the point of preoccupation with achieving long-distance wireless. It was the driving, predominant thrust in his life. He had persuaded the board that MWT could not be a significant, profitable corporation, perhaps could not survive, on short or ship-to-shore signals. High margins lay in the field owned exclusively by cable. Real money would be found in wresting away that control and becoming the dominant transoceanic provider. Since Marconi's return from the America's Cup race at the end of 1899, MWT, in reliance on his conviction, had poured enormous resources into his endeavor. His expenses had repeatedly exhausted the company's cash and brought it to the verge of bankruptcy. Now in 1903, after three full years of effort and expenditure, his great scientific successes had brought no financial return but only demands for more money and new solutions. He could offer no ultimate assurance of success. Endless expenditure might never lead to worthwhile commercial enterprise. The directors had to begin to ask themselves if Marconi's tunnel vision could be leading the company in a wrong direction.

Ironically for Marconi, it was the ship-to-shore business that had grown and that for the moment kept the company afloat. For the fiscal year that ended September 30, 1902, MWT's revenues modestly exceeded total company non-investment costs. The ship-to-shore business slowed the cash drain from the heavy spending projects. With this operating profit and the bit remaining from the share sale, MWT entered 1903 with a small amount of capital.

MWT's wireless network consisted of twenty-five shore stations servicing seventy ships. The low ratio of sets to land installations reflected the reality that MWT had to have an infrastructure to process messages before shipping companies would purchase equipment. The company had invested heavily to obtain the business. The investment was beginning to pay off. The large number of stations had in fact created the market.

MWT was poised to overwhelm its competitors as long as they could not access what the company had built. No rival had more than a handful of shore stations. None manufactured transmitters or receivers that approached Marconi's level of performance. With a sufficient coastal network and superior equipment, the board looked forward to selling additional sets without further substantial expenditure for construction. The profits and positive cash flow from ship-to-shore should multiply. The directors considered commercial shipping's immediate prospects to be favorable and more attractive than transatlantic business. While this was good news for the company, for Marconi it meant winning board support to invest more in Poldhu, Glace Bay, and South Wellfleet would be more difficult.

Long-distance wireless did achieve one sale. The mileage from South Wellfleet to Cornwall approached the length from Italy to some of its foreign interests. The Roosevelt transmission impressed the Italian Ministry of Posts and Telegraphs. At last the bureaucracy that had rejected its native son's first offer saw a use for his wireless. The ministry awarded MWT a major contract to build a thirty-two-thousand-pound high-power station at Coltano and operate it for fourteen years. Land for the station, 175 miles north of Rome, was donated by the king.

As would be expected, the company organization expanded with its sales. Operators and installation engineers worked at more than thirty locations. Hall, who had handled Marconi's arrangements in New York following St. John's and had the internal political touch so absent in Flood-Page, succeeded him as the company's third managing director. Although Flood-Page's insistence on promoting ship-to-shore was about to bear fruit, the traumas endured by MWT during his brief tenure of less than two years had worn him out. His attempts to conserve MWT's capital had repeatedly pitted him against Marconi. He could not remain managing director and be in constant opposition to the company's dominant force.

The transatlantic signaling cemented Marconi's stature as a top, world-class celebrity. One publication called the twenty-eight-year-old the globe's most interviewed man. In February 1903, *Scientific American* profiled the scientist inventor:

> When you meet him for the first time you know that he is not a cordial man; and yet you feel that he will not rebuff you, that he will probably do for you what he can. His manner is that of chilly reserve. In the press he is referred to as "the young Anglo-Italian" who has done some startling things which are not very clearly explained. A cool, calculating man of the North is this so-called Anglo-Italian.
>
> For a successful inventor Marconi appears the least joyous of men. His features are melancholy in expression. They are those of a man fast approaching forty—not those of a man of twenty-eight. His face is impassive, his eye almost cold. When he smiles he half shuts his eyes, wrinkles the muscles of his cheek and draws up the corners of his mouth. It is not a pleasant smile.
>
> He talks of his magnetic receiver almost objectively, as if it were the production of some other inventor's mind, which is all the more noteworthy because the instrument in question is, probably, the most valuable contribution to wireless telegraphic apparatus made since the invention of the coherer. He admits his receiver's great speed and its general merit, and expresses his opinion of its recent remarkable performance at Cape Cod in terms of mild approval, which are, however, not utterly devoid of a tinge of pleasure. It is difficult to picture Marconi waxing enthusiastic even over a very great achievement. It is significant that the newspapermen who saw him after his wonderful feat at Cape Cod merely reported him to be in exceptionally good humor.(FN 13)

The pressures of the almost nine years since his inspiration at Biellese were catching up with Marconi. He fought many battles alone. He took positions harshly criticized by colleagues and peers. Only he had the genius to create practical instruments that broke through barriers in useful ways. The company's scientific existence he had generated. Its success or failure still lay in his hands. The experience of reaching the highest levels of achievement and recognition had not swollen his head, but it had hardened and matured him. Few other than his cousin Daisy in his childhood and Solari recently had seen his joyous, ebullient side. Now it was buried deep inside him.

CHAPTER 12

The Pace Thickens

In April 1903, not nine years after his inspiration at Biellese, Marconi returned to Italy at the invitation of the Mayor of Rome. The ancient capital wished to confer honorary citizenship upon its country's celebrated, twenty-nine-year-old inventor. En route Marconi stopped at Villa Grifone for the briefest of visits with his aging father and Annie, who had returned from London to be with her husband. Another stop was made in neighboring Bologna. He had once sat in on classes in the city's university and made some use of Professor Righi's laboratory. The people welcomed him enthusiastically at a public reception that filled the university's Littoriale Gymnasium. Between Annie and Giuseppe, he sat happily, quietly amused at being honored by the venerable institution that had refused him admission. Annie smiled proudly at the outpouring of accolades. Giuseppe, now past eighty and in failing health, wept with joy. The hometown tributes touched even the outwardly stoic son. Rising in his turn to respond, he found himself so choked with emotion that he retreated in great embarrassment, returning to his seat unable to utter a word of acknowledgment or thanks.

After the ceremony, Marconi and his parents headed straight to Rome. For the trio to be together was a rare occasion. Giuseppe, unlike Annie, seldom attended events with his famous son. But on May 2, the three Marconis arrived in Rome to a thick welcoming crowd greeting them at the train station. Leading his petite mother and frail, elderly father by the hand, the son pushed his way through the surging throng to reach the four-horse state coach personally dispatched by the mayor for their personal benefit. Marconi had scarcely settled in the carriage, his fatigued parents safely beside him, when the vehicle was surrounded and jostled by students eager to catch a glimpse of their national hero. Greatly excited, the students unharnessed the horses and delightedly pulled the Marconis all the way to the Grand Hotel.

Two days later, Marconi delivered a speech before a gathering of the king, the queen, government officials, and scientists invited specifically to hear him. In it he described his fundamental belief that in developing the use of electromagnetic waves for wireless communication, he followed the universe's most fundamental concepts:

> In truth telegraphy without wires is no more than a simple consequence of observing and studying the means employed by nature to obtain her effects of heat, light, of magnetism across space. As the heat and light of the sun upon which depend the life of our planet are transmitted across millions of kilometers of space, as the light of the most distance stars, as the electrical and magnetic perturbations of nature are manifested to us after having crossed the most immeasurable distances, it appeared to me by adopting means similar to those adopted by nature, it should be possible to transmit these effects at our will.(FN 1)

The following night, Victor Emmanuel honored Kaiser Wilhelm II at a state function in the Quirinal. The king invited Marconi and introduced him to the German emperor. Wilhelm had made a number of inimical public remarks about Marconi and MWT following MWT's refusal to exchange messages with the emperor's son, Prince Henry, on the prince's return to Germany on the *Kronprinz Wilhelm*. The remarks had been circulated by the London press and had not been appreciated by the inventor. The kaiser still smoldered over the well-publicized rebuff. During dinner, the leader of the German nation turned to Marconi and pointedly said, "Signor Marconi, you must not think that I have any animosity against yourself. It is the policy of your company I object to." Without hesitating, Marconi fired back, saying, "Your Imperial Majesty, I should be overwhelmed if I thought you had any personal animosity against me. However, it is I who decided the policy of my company." (FN 2)

The confrontation between the German interests and MWT did not end at dinner. The board's policy to deny service to ships not equipped with Marconi wireless irritated its competitors, led by Telefunken. They resented the company's monopolistic grip on the ship-to-shore business, particularly the lucrative Atlantic route. They wanted access to MWT's shore stations without having to reimburse the Marconi shareholders for their heavy capital investment in the extensive communication system. In August, the Germans succeeded in convening in Berlin an international radiotelephone congress. Delegates attended from Great Britain, Germany, Russia, Austria Hungary, France, Italy, Spain, and the United States. No MWT representatives were invited to participate on behalf of the UK. Solari, however, headed the Italian delegation. As expected, the convention roundly criticized the company's policy. At a critical juncture, Solari vigorously protested against the relentless attacks and to underline his displeasure stormed out of the conference. The gesture was personally enjoyable but ineffective. Before adjourning, the congress adopted a formal resolution recommending to its constituent governments that all coastal stations be mandated to accept and send messages from and to all ships, regardless of what apparatus the vessels carried.

The resolution appealed to many countries. As its distance and reliability increased, mobile, point-to-point, airborne communication's significance grew as well. Wireless did not respect national borders. It entered countries or crossed over them without stopping at customs and entrance barriers. Over both earth and water, wireless messages permitted an empire's geographically far-flung parts to stay in contact without relying on telegraph lines controlled by others or submarine cables vulnerable to enemy sabotage during wartime. Admirals on land gained the ability to direct fleets offshore. Improved communication facilitated commerce. Nationalistic and military implications multiplied. Recognizing these issues, governments wanted not only access to the new technology, but to control it as well. The conference marked the first effort to regulate wireless.

In Great Britain, Parliament reacted by opening a review of its laws relating to wireless. The board saw the action as an opportunity to push for legislation that would favor the company. It boldly seized the initiative and proposed that MWT be granted permanent authorization to work wireless in the country and that initially the right be exclusive. Further, it asked that the General Post Office act as receiving and forwarding agents for MWT's transatlantic service, just as the GPO did for cable. Finally, MWT requested exclusivity in wireless communication between England and her colonies. To the directors, the proposal was farsighted. To critics, the last demand was overreaching since MWT's superstations could not reach many member countries, such as India and Australia.

The Royal Navy's self-manufactured Jackson sets lagged dangerously behind Marconi's. The Admiralty's efforts to reestablish itself with MWT by offering a ship for experiments had been thwarted by Italy's provision of the *Carlo Alberto*. From a strategic point of view, British military feared Rome's close relationship with MWT. Jackson's wireless range of several hundred miles would be at a distinct disadvantage against the Italians, who could communicate thousands of miles utilizing Marconi's technology. The Royal Navy wanted Marconi's developments. It could no longer tolerate being bound by the inaction of other government departments like the GPO. At long last, from the company's view, the Admiralty opened comprehensive negotiations.

Despite the past difficulties, the board very much coveted a meaningful relationship with the world's leading naval force. It made clear business sense that the British navy should be a major, long-term customer. The company also speculated and hoped that, in an effort to stay abreast of the improved British technology, other national navies would feel compelled to purchase MWT's system as well. Both sides came to the table, eager for a transaction. The negotiations were frank, to the point, and successful. MWT granted the Admiralty full use of its patents (except the right of assignment) and first call on supply of Marconi apparatus. As Captain Jackson had earlier advocated, the Admiralty contractually guaranteed itself a right to stay abreast of company advances. In addition, the arrangements entitled the Admiralty to exclusive use, for twenty minutes each day, of a super-powerstation and priority of messages on the company's existing shore stations, now numbering thirty-two. In exchange, the Admiralty paid MWT twenty thousand pounds up front, a royalty of five hundred pounds per station, and five thousand pounds per year. Although not discussed, this arrangement may have in effect partially reimbursed the company for the fifty sets the Ediswan Company surreptitiously copied for the Royal Navy.

Invigorated, Marconi exerted renewed pressure on the board to develop transatlantic service as rapidly as possible by focusing on long-distance experiments and aerial configurations. The board's focus, however, had shifted to the U.S. Heavy volumes of commercial shipping and passenger traffic moved along its eastern seaboard, creating the potential for a vast market for wireless. Equally important, no governmental permission was required to establish and operate shore stations. It was just that freedom that originally attracted Marconi to the transatlantic market. In the U.S., there was no version of the GPO. Private companies ran the internal telegraph system. MWT could conduct its business as it thought best without government regulation, negotiate for interconnections with the telegraph companies on terms that it wanted, and arrange its relations with its customers in the most efficient way.

Tesla was no longer a formidable foe. He had failed to raise sufficient money to stave off his creditors. In July, he experimented at Wardenclyffe for the first time with his completed apparatus designed to transmit signals across the Atlantic. Late one night at midnight, the crown of the gigantic World Tower emitted dramatic electric flashes. The next morning, Westinghouse representatives arrived at the Long Island site with a legal writ. They removed critical pieces of the manufacturer's equipment for which it had never been paid, rendering the project inoperable.

The American de Forest Wireless Telegraphy Company was MWT's principal American competition. It had established a rapidly growing lead in the U.S. market. It operated a Newark manufacturing plant. It had added shore stations at New Haven, Connecticut; Galilee, New Jersey; Cape Hatteras, North Carolina; and Galveston, Texas. While the U.S. Army awarded Telefunken business, de Forest won orders for naval installations at Pensacola, Florida; Guantanamo, Cuba; and in Panama. De Forest planned to enter the west coast where a new competitor, Pacific and Continental Wireless Telephone and Telegraph, was building a pair of sites in San Pedro and on Catalina Island.

Money poured into American de Forest. Flamboyantly promoted by White, the piecemeal offerings of stock from the corporation's three million dollars of authorized capital were eagerly subscribed by the public. The sales effort combined de Forest's technical skills and White's showmanship, as described by the *Electric World*:

> A "latest model" 1902 automobile ran about the streets of New York carrying a demonstration de Forest apparatus; its spark gap crackled daily before gaping crowds, and every afternoon it invaded Wall Street and stopped before the Stock Exchange to telegraph the "closing prices" to mythical listeners. At Coney Island, the city's amusement resort, a high mast went up and there, too, hundreds were introduced to the new telegraphy.(FN 3)

Brochures depicted a worldwide chain of stations. The Pacific would be an American lake. To foster the global impression, de Forest went to Europe and experimented from the Eiffel Tower. He installed his wireless on the yacht of Marconi's friend, Thomas Lipton. For the GPO, he demonstrated across the Irish Sea between Holyhead and Dublin. British Army field trials included de Forest as well as the Lodge-Muirhead syndicate that ran a franchise in India.

The board deliberated as to how to slow de Forest. Marconi consulted legal advisers. They concluded that de Forest's equipment infringed the Irish-Italian's patents. The directors had been reluctant to challenge Telefunken in the German judicial system for fear it would favor its own nationals. They had greater confidence in the impartiality of U.S. courts. The company also now possessed the financial resources to mount a lawsuit. MWT decided to attack de Forest in his headquarter city, New York, and filed an action there.

The decision provided Marconi a welcome opportunity. The American lawyers invited him to their offices to assist in readying the papers. Whenever there was a lull in the work, he intended to head for Nova Scotia. Although he had no new funding from the board, he continued to seek technical adjustments to boost power at Poldhu and Glace Bay. He also hit upon an idea for a dramatic demonstration to emphasize again to the directors and customers the usefulness of long-distance wireless. Before departing on the *Lucania* in August, he installed a receiver on the ship. Now that relations had been reestablished with the Admiralty, he invited Royal Navy officers to join him on the crossing to witness the experiment. Solari was also there representing the Italian navy. For the first part of the crossing, the *Lucania*'s receiver recorded transmitted messages from Poldhu. Before Poldhu's waves faded, Glace Bay's signals reached the *Lucania* and were received for the remainder of the trip, even as the vessel docked in New York. The voyage marked the first Atlantic passage in which a ship stayed in constant touch with shore stations. The meaning was not lost on the naval observers. The demonstration did not, however, move the board.

Unexpectedly, the *Lucania* turned out to be far more than a testing ground. Marconi fell in love again and once more with an American. Inez Milholland's beauty stunned him. Her personality intrigued him. Highly intelligent, she was articulate and passionate in her views, of which she had many and many of which were unconventional. Before the *Lucania* docked, the smitten inventor could not resist proposing to the New Yorker. His impetuosity, which he had also displayed with Josephine, contrasted markedly with his methodical and deliberate approach to science. Inez accepted at once. The object of his affection surprised Marconi's acquaintances. She was hardly his type and loudly vocalized concepts Marconi disfavored. Her declarations of female equality brought only a wry smile to his face. The fact that in championing her cause she had ridden a white horse up Fifth Avenue, however, may have piqued his interest. He certainly understood the character required to stand publicly for an unpopular position. He respected her frankness and honesty. Nonetheless, his daughter, Degna, later wrote with a trace of criticism:

> Marconi lost his heart…with fair regularity but this one seems to me the most unlikely attachment he ever formed. Except for her beauty, Inez Milholland embodied everything he basically disapproved. She was a confirmed bluestocking and a feminist.(FN 4)

Marconi traveled indefatigably between Nova Scotia and New York. Having no research facilities or headquarters in the city other than the limited offices at American Marconi permitted him much more free time in the evening to spend with this fiancée than he had ever had with Josephine. The couple was very much in demand in New York social circles. Years earlier, Lipton, over the course of the America's Cup festivities, had first introduced Marconi to society. Now with Inez as his constant companion, the taciturn bachelor became much more confident and at ease in the constant round of parties. As he had matured into an adult, Marconi had had very little exposure to social discourse and entertainment. The man, who as a teenager playing hide-and-seek always chose to hide with the prettiest girl, quite enjoyed his newfound activity.

The Glace Bay operation was not going as well. Nothing he did raised reliability of communication across the Atlantic to competitive commercial standards. With great reluctance, he concluded that Glace Bay power should be raised above his previous estimates. The resulting additional expense heightened the board's reluctance to proceed with the project.

That fall, St. Louis held a World's Exposition that displayed many modern inventions. De Forest and his wireless tower starred. Under White's unrestrained direction, the American inventor installed his instruments in a glass house one hundred feet above the ground, the tallest structure at the fair. In de Forest's words, the purposely unmuffled spark brought curious crowds swarming from all over the grounds. Wireless communication was established between the tower and Springfield, Illinois, and to a receiver in the downtown office of the *St. Louis Dispatch.* The paper headline called it a "miracle of Science." Subscriptions to American de Forest Wireless Telegraph Company stock swelled. The board, prodded by Hall, felt Marconi should attend to counter de Forest. The managing director arranged for the convention to invite Marconi as an official guest and well-publicized speaker. At the luncheon preceding his talk, he drank several mint juleps in rapid succession, unaware that they contained alcohol. Not surprisingly, the sweet Southern drink made his world swirl. When it came time for his speech, he could not rise to his feet. Not knowing what was happening, he suspected that someone had poisoned him.

Upon returning from Missouri, Marconi visited Edison at his Orange, New Jersey, home. It was the first meeting of the two electrical geniuses. Marconi, younger, meticulously dressed, and well groomed, deferred to his disheveled elder, whose reputation preceded and eclipsed his. Engrossed in their conversation, Edison never thought to offer luncheon. Finally Marconi's hunger overcame his Victorian politeness, and he inquired if they were to eat. Being the help's day off and with his wife away, Edison rummaged about, discovering only cheese and crackers. The sole beverage in the house was water. The two celebrated inventors, among the greatest scientists of their time, munched away amidst the chaos of Edison's laboratory, totally absorbed in their dialogue. This plain lunch did not upset Marconi, who was still suffering from the mint juleps. Following their meeting, Edison, in a gesture of respect for Marconi, assigned for a small consideration his wireless patent to MWT. It was a field of inquiry for which Edison had no available time. The transfer foreclosed a potential weakness in Marconi's patent claims.

Impressed by the *Lucania* experience, the Admiralty requested Marconi at the outset of 1904 to join Jackson aboard his ship, HMS *Duncan*. The high command wanted Marconi to demonstrate under actual conditions the reliability of signals from Poldhu to Gibraltar and to ships en route to Gibraltar. Such long-range communication excited the Royal Navy. With an understanding of the overall battle picture, the home port could more effectively deploy warships far distant at sea. The Admiralty could keep its fleets, or more specifically its commanders, under its immediate control. Otherwise, it had no choice but to rely on freelance operations like U.S. Commodore Dewey's action in the Philippines when he was no longer in communication with his superiors. Long-distance wireless could also end Gibraltar's dependence on submarine cables that could be cut in hostilities.

Once back on shore from a successful voyage aboard HMS *Duncan*, Marconi found 1904 degenerating into a depressing and ambiguous state of affairs. Inez, engrossed in her feminist activities, would not leave the United States to be with her fiancé in London. The de Forest lawsuit at its current stage did not require his presence in New York. The directors refused for the moment to authorize any further money for the transatlantic project. Consequently, Marconi could find no business excuse to travel to New York. The board avoided a decision on his long-distance wireless proposals by calling for a study of what sites were best suited for transatlantic signaling. Until the review was concluded, it ordered the three superstations to stop experimenting and engage only in ship-to-shore traffic. The decision was reasonable. Marconi's Canadian and Cornwall expenditures had drained all the cash MWT had generated from operations, Jameson-Davis's stock sale, and the Royal Navy contract.

To fund itself, MWT sold thirty-nine thousand new shares to International Marine, MWT's ship-to-shore subsidiary that it controlled.

Marconi

The stock sale to International Marine raised MWT's outstanding shares to almost two hundred thousand. Marconi's percentage ownership fell below 40 percent. Again he did not oppose the sale because he had no choice. MWT had no other financing alternatives, and Marconi would not give up his goal of transatlantic service.

The adverse course of events deeply discouraged Marconi. The vexing, unsolved problem of daylight fog combined with the lack of funds to experiment with new power levels stalled his long-distance wireless quest. And the board no longer shared his vision of the company's most strategic goals.

In March, Giuseppe died of pneumonia. Marconi, in England at the time, professed he was too busy to attend the funeral in Bologna and the burial in the family vault in the city's ancient cemetery of Certosa. For a man who crossed the ocean on business on a moment's notice, Marconi's absence sadly commented on his parting relationship with his father. As he grew older, Marconi's few remarks on the matter indicated a clinging bitterness over his boyhood relationship with Giuseppe. Marconi evidenced no warmth or regard for Giuseppe's better intentions, the considerable support Giuseppe did in the end lend, and the obvious pride and affection Giuseppe ultimately expressed. Even if Marconi would not go to Bologna for his father's sake, he might have gone to support Annie.

Giuseppe surprisingly left Villa Grifone to Marconi rather than to either of his two other sons. Annie moved out of both Villa Grifone and the Palazza Albergatti on the Via Saragozza in Bologna where Giuseppe had stayed in the winter as he grew older. She remained for some time in smaller quarters in Bologna. Marconi apparently did little to help her. She wrote MWT's London headquarters inquiring if they knew whether her son was receiving her letters and where he might be.

Perhaps Marconi's rejection of Giuseppe and disturbing disregard for Annie marked the first outward signs of depression. He lamented to Solari that man could not live on glory alone. Something had changed. For ten years, Marconi had been intensely active, producing astonishing results, one development after another, under unrelenting scientific and financial pressure, more and more in the public eye. Suddenly the rate of advance had slowed. The number of scientific discoveries declined while technical difficulties increased. New insights did not come so simply. Achievements were more complex and were not as readily understood as an increase in distance or clarity of signal. Advancements required more collaboration than just the small band of brothers at Haven. Competing scientists made sophisticated discoveries in new and related areas. The concept that Hertz identified and Marconi and others developed had expanded in many directions. Marconi could no longer keep abreast of a spreading industry by an intense reading of periodicals as he had once done. MWT, itself, had changed. The adrenaline of a start-up had faded as the company matured. No longer could Marconi deal primarily with Jameson-Davis or Fleming. Management grew bureaucratic and more bottom-line orientated. The inherent conflict between Marconi's scientific drive and MWT's commercial goals became more acute.

Marconi could have been mentally and physically exhausted. He had been traveling extensively, relentlessly. For years, he had called no place home. The challenges of hostile governments, better-financed competitors, and expanding far-flung geographical markets diffused his attention and energy. The pace had thickened. Press attention had lost its novelty. He was recognized. He was celebrated. But that had never been his goal. Growing up, he had had no clear direction. He faltered. At Biellese he had found his inspiration. Now after ten years of exhilarating achievement, he felt let down and unproductive and worried that the route to his goal was blocked. His remark to Solari captured his mood.

Over the first half of 1904, Marconi spent most of his time in England. He embarked on only one short Atlantic trip, and otherwise did not see Inez. En route, he received daylight signals up to twelve hundred miles, but nighttime signals ceased at a disappointing seventeen hundred miles. That further depressed him. Staying at Haven and headquarters for more extended periods, alone and without being totally absorbed by MWT activities, Marconi began to accept the many social invitations that came his way. Once word spread that he was actually available, he was very much in demand. Thirty years old, famous, and attractive, he made a most welcome addition to any hostess's list. Inez was not known in English social circles. His engagement, if anyone was particularly aware of it, did not detract from the excitement his presence generated. He found that even without Inez by his side, he managed quite well, particularly with women, who swarmed about him. In fact, his reputation as a social lion in London's fashionable circles soon abounded. He drove his Mercedes, one of the very first new luxury automobiles, from Haven to London for

CHAPTER 13

Beatrice O'Brien

Awarm, offshore breeze gently ruffled her brown hair. The late-blossoming teenager blushed self-consciously at meeting such a celebrity. This further flushed her already high coloring. Marconi did not know that the wholesome young woman standing before him, dressed in a simple summer frock that naturally revealed her fulsome Victorian figure, traced her lineage to the first and only king of all of Ireland. In 1002, Brian Boru, or Boroimhe, consolidated the island under his rule. In 1014, he was killed in battle and his power dispersed. His descendants, Beatrice's ancestors, subsequently ruled portions of western Ireland as monarchs titled Baron Inchiquin and Marquis of Thomond. Twenty-seven generations after Brian's demise, the sweet, innocently flirtatious Beatrice O'Brien stood before the world-famous inventor. She was not impressed.

As he had done several times before, Marconi in his launch had crossed the short distance from MWT's research center at the Haven Hotel to Brownsea Island to lunch with the socialite Florence Van Raalte. She and her husband, Charles, had only recently acquired the island that lay just a mile from the hotel inside the mouth of Poole Harbor. They restored its mid-Victorian castle, where they loved to entertain their London acquaintances, of whom Marconi was one. Lady Howard de Walden, who lived in Chirk Castle a few miles from Haven, was a frequent guest. Mrs. Van Raalte knew that Lady de Walden had invited Beatrice and her mother, Lady Inchiquin, for an extended visit. The Van Raaltes had three children, the oldest, William, being just younger than Beatrice. Mrs. Van Raalte, well aware of the social prominence of the O'Briens, could not let

231

Marconi

the opportunity pass. She asked Lady de Walden if Beatrice would like to come to Brownsea for the last fortnight of summer. Lady de Walden recommended the Van Raalte family to Lady Inchiquin. The Irish lady and her daughter agreed. Bea might enjoy a visit at the sea island before returning to their townhouse in Marble Arch in London.

On Bea's arrival, her hostess could talk only of Marconi, whom she called a dear friend. In fact, she expected Marconi the very next day and asked Beatrice if she would like to walk with her to meet his boat at the dock. The request puzzled Beatrice, for she felt Marconi to be too old and too worldly to find her of any interest.

The following noon, Beatrice and Mrs. Van Raalte strolled through the castle gardens and island woods down to the boathouse to greet Marconi's small craft. When he stepped ashore, Beatrice's windswept, fresh, natural beauty struck him at once. Throughout the luncheon, he directed his attention to her as well as to the island's proprietress. But his efforts had no affect other than to affirm the young woman's reservations. Marconi had had his thirtieth birthday. To the eyes of the nineteen-year-old Beatrice, he appeared to be even older.

While Marconi had no knowledge of Beatrice O'Brien, her parents, or her lineage, she knew a great deal about him. Living in English society with her sisters and mother in a London townhouse near Marble Arch, she could not help but be aware of his huge popularity. Her mother often spoke of the demand for his company. The Duchess of Sutherland sought him for her soirees. Rumors linked him to the Viscountess Falmouth, at whose mansion he was a favored guest. Beatrice had heard firsthand from Lady de Walden that Marconi had raced in his Mercedes against her son, Lord Howard de Walden. Beatrice had once ridden with Howard. At top-speed, fully fifteen miles an hour, they had struck the castle's stone buttressing. Fortunately, only the car suffered a scratch.

More than a half dozen years earlier, when few knew of Marconi, Beatrice's father told her about the young scientist with the startling invention. Together with her favorite sister, Lilah, just younger than she, they had been walking with their father in the forests of their home, Dromoland, a gargantuan Victorian castle built over the site of the ancestral O'Brien home. Ax in hand, her father marked trees to be cut down while Bea and Lilah buzzed about him in play. As they ambled about in the woods, he described Marconi's sensational signals.

That he had time to read about the inventor's accomplishments was a wonder. Beatrice's father, Lord Inchiquin, in fact the thirteenth Lord Inchiquin, fathered fourteen children. Despite being the tenth child, Beatrice still felt quite close to him. In a sketch drawn by John S. Sargent to celebrate the government members of the House of Lords on the occasion of Queen Victoria's silver anniversary, Edward Donough O'Brien wore an enormous black beard and appeared appropriately somber and stern. Born in 1839 and educated at St. Columbia's College, Dublin, Ireland, he had by his first marriage three sons and a daughter, the eldest being Lucius, Beatrice's stepbrother. On his wife's death, Beatrice's father married her mother, Ellen Harriet White, daughter of Lord Annaly of Luttrellstown. They had three sons and seven daughters.

By the end of the lunch, Marconi found Beatrice irresistibly appealing. Thereafter, he sought any excuse to frequent Brownsea Island. Initially he returned every other day to see Mrs. Van Raalte or her husband. Then he gave up all pretence and came daily specifically to see Bea. She was still not that taken with him. He was so much older. Only slowly did she begin to warm to him. Not far removed from her tomboy days when she kept pace with her brothers in sailing, tennis, and cycling, she preferred the company of the Van Raalte children to that of Marconi. She remained in his presence only as long as politeness dictated. Then she would escape to join the three young siblings in the castle's schoolroom at games and tea. They were so much more like her sister Lilah, to whom she was so close, than the awesome visitor from the Haven Hotel. Requesting permission to take leave from his more than understanding hostess, the celebrity suitor would solemnly follow after Bea as persistently as an important experiment. Soon he discovered their common ground—sailing. Together they raced happily about Poole Harbor in the castle's small sloop, tacking, heeling, and running before the wind.

Shortly into the second week of Beatrice's late summer fortnight with the Van Raaltes, Marconi informed her that he would immediately ask Inez Milholland, his American fiancée, to release him from his engagement. He had learned from Josephine Holman of the potential perils of unilaterally breaking an American engagement. He confessed to Bea that all he wanted was time to be with her. When the moment came for her to return to Marble Arch, he pressed Mrs. Van Raalte to permit him to drive Bea back to London, a day-long journey in the early days of motoring on frequently unpaved roads occupied by horse-drawn traffic. Whatever Bea's sentiments about the driver, the prospect of such an outing in a Mercedes excited her. But as much as Mrs. Van Raalte had been encouraging Marconi, the suggestion that a young, unchaperoned lady accompany a gentleman in an automobile all the way to the city shocked the proper Victorian matron, as she knew it would Lady Inchiquin. Instead, pouting all the way, accompanied by her maid, Beatrice traveled home by train.

Once Beatrice left Brownsea, Marconi abandoned Haven and followed her to London. Her initial emotional disinterest was fading. Their common love of sailing had been a fortunate icebreaker for Marconi. She found enjoyment in their times together. But her feelings were still mixed. He was nothing like the carefree young men to whom she was accustomed. Her male acquaintances were her brothers and their friends, mostly schoolmates in their late teens or early twenties. Marconi was far more suave, worldly, mature, and serious. Although he was half Irish and spoke impeccable English, he did not appear to be either Irish or English. He looked dark, Italian, and foreign. Beatrice had grown up sheltered from people not from her world, surrounded instead by O'Brien brothers, sisters, aunts, uncles, and cousins and their titled contemporaries. Her upbringing was like a late-nineteenth-century fairy tale. Dromoland butlers, coachmen, and maids waited upon her. On holidays the castle reverberated with the merriment of the older boys' university classmates, who were particularly attracted to Dromoland by its riding and the shooting, which was renowned. At night the halls filled with light-hearted songs and laughter and dancing. The baron's fourteen children alone made a large, joyful party. In summertime, the family, accompanied by a full retinue of servants, traveled by train to Holkham Hall in Norfolk to visit Viscount Coke, their Coke cousins, and Aunt Alice Leicester. Sandringham, a royal family residence favored by Queen Victoria's offspring, was not far from Holkham. Her grandchildren, including Edward, Ena and George, often came to Holkham to play with the Cokes and O'Briens. There had been no Marconis in this world.

Despite the differences, many underlying similarities also existed. Notwithstanding contrary external appearances, Marconi was half Irish. Both had grown up on beautiful rural estates that required farming for their sustenance. Both had been tutored at home for many years. The

O'Briens were dedicated Anglicans. Although baptized and nominally Catholic, Marconi's religious instruction had been administered by his Anglican mother.

What seemed to weigh on Beatrice the most, however, was the age difference. She was a very young nineteen, he a very old thirty.

Marconi was handling his ardor with uncustomary control. Weeks had passed since he was introduced to Bea, and he had not yet asked for her hand. In his first two engagements, he proposed within days of meeting. A letter arrived from Inez. Unlike the experience with Miss Holman, there was no threatening intimation of litigation. The tenor of the epistle was quite to the contrary. Inez amicably consented to their disentanglement. Her own interests more than absorbed her. If Marconi had not have been so obsessed with his pursuit of Beatrice, he might have been upset with Inez's readiness to grant his request.

Now there was nothing to restrain him. He could hardly contain himself. He sought an appropriate opportunity to express his heart's desire. Lady Inchiquin had organized a charitable ball at the great, red brick Victorian landmark, Albert Hall. Despite the furor of Marconi's courtship, the lady had chosen not to recognize his interest in her daughter. He was not Beatrice's escort to the dance. He bought his own ticket and came alone. Desperately he searched everywhere for his beloved amongst the huge, milling crowd. He found her at last, sitting at the top of the marble stairs surveying the elegant scene below her. Fortunately for him, she was unattended at the moment. He plunked himself down beside her. Unable to wait a minute longer for a more suitable time or spot, Guglielmo asked Bea to marry him.

Beatrice felt honored by his proposal. She was flattered by his affection. Despite the many fun moments together, however, she often felt restrained, rather than relaxed, in his presence. His all-out pursuit of her, while it warmed her heart towards him, was at times overwhelming and even frightening. She was ambivalent about his world fame. It was exciting, but notoriety was not a goal sought in her family. Everyone was familiar with the Irish Jameson whiskey family and their excellent standing in business in London, but they were trade. No one had the slightest knowledge about his father or had ever heard of Poretta or Pontecchio in the Apennines. She felt she hardly knew Marconi. It had all happened so extraordinarily quickly. Even the lilting tunes of the band and the romance of the evening could not bring her to respond favorably. She could only say that she needed time to think about it. She would have to talk to Lilah. She did not tell him that Lilah had already left for Dresden.

Marconi could not stand by quietly. He flooded her with hand-delivered letters. His anxiety induced a fever. Ten days went by without a response. At her young age, Beatrice had never before been so coveted, and she enjoyed it. But it did not persuade her or help her make up her mind. Finally, she told Guglielmo she would talk to him about his proposal. She invited him to tea at the Marble Arch townhouse. There she announced her decision. She did not care enough for him. In fact, she did not love him. She followed her heart and declined his proposal.

This had not happened to Marconi before. Never had he wooed so arduously. He had had no need to. Josephine and Inez had both readily accepted his proposals. True, growing up he had constantly faced rejection from his father, in his academic endeavors, and among his classmates. Since his inspiration at Biellese, he had been rebuffed in his scientific endeavors and publicly criticized by his peers. But as an adult, as a famed scientist, his offers of marriage had not been refused.

He reacted, Degna later wrote, like the jilted suitor in a romantic Victorian novel. Wearing his broken heart on his well-pressed sleeve, he took off for Turkey, Bulgaria, and Rumania. Unlike his fictional prototype, he did company business in these far places.(FN 1) Turkey, Bulgaria, and Rumania each had ports on the Black Sea and were potential ship-to-shore customers. Only the burning desire to escape London, the site of his heartache, drove Marconi to travel to these countries to make sales calls. But while in Rumania, he contracted malaria. In addition to his unfortunate, already existing proclivity for fevers, the disease left him with a lifelong exposure to sudden chills and even more severe high temperatures. Recovering from the illness in Rumania protracted his trip. He then stopped in the Balkans on the Adriatic coast to inspect the wireless station MWT was constructing at Antivari in Montenegro where a large Italian population lived. Earlier in the year, in July, MWT had opened Italy's superstation at Coltano in Italy. The Italian government wanted Coltano to communicate directly with its Balkan populations rather than rely on unsecured telegraph messages that had to pass through Austria by landline. To accommodate this desire, MWT agreed to install the Bari and Antivari stations. The Coltano station, the world's most powerful, turned out to be a huge success. To the delight of Italian officials, it could transmit not only to the Balkans, but also to Italian East Africa, 2,238 miles away. The station raised the prestige of Italy, MWT, and Marconi.

Mrs. Van Raalte unexpectedly rescued Marconi from Montenegro and his two months' malaise over Beatrice. The matchmaker summoned him to return to England, and he obeyed at once. She had invited Bea to a pre-Christmas visit to Brownsea Island. The trusting teenager accepted on the condition that Marconi not be told. Her hostess immediately dishonored the commitment. Marconi's arrival at the Brownsea castle shocked Bea. She threatened to depart at once, but the conspirators cajoled her into a better humor, and she agreed to stay on. Bundled up against the frosty mists and fog, the couple took long walks in the island's beautiful woods and along the seashore and meadows sloping gently down to the water's edge. When the clouds temporarily lifted, they even sailed in the harbor, despite the winter cold. They ate with the Van Raaltes, but afterwards sat alone by the fire when the understanding family retired early. Guglielmo's unflagging interest impressed Bea. She relaxed and tried to allow her sentiments to deepen for the man a decade her senior. She even felt "contrite at her lack of feeling."(FN 2) One afternoon, as they sat together on a hillside overlooking the harbor, Marconi asked her again to marry him.

This time she accepted, but only if Lilah approved.

Lilah remained in Dresden. Marconi, however, now knew she was there. He offered to go to Germany to pursue his cause, but Bea said that would be unnecessary. Instead, on December 21, 1904, she wrote Lilah from Brownsea:

> [I've] begun this letter one hundred times and torn it up...Can you guess it—I am engaged to be married to Marconi...on these conditions: Only, only if you like him, darling Luzz, you must try for my sake. I don't love him. I've told him so over and over again, he says he wants me anyhow and will make me love him. I do like him so much and enough to marry him...I don't even know how mamma or any of them will take it and as for you my own darling Luzz, if you don't like him a little I shall die.(FN 3)

Marconi

Beatrice's younger brother Barney arrived at Brownsea for dinner the next evening. Afterwards, alone before the fire in the sitting room, Bea nervously revealed her secret. She did not know if she could stand disagreement. Barney reacted favorably. He recommended that she tell their mother and their eldest half-brother, Lucius. Upon the death of their father, Lord Inchiquin XIII, in 1900, Lucius, as the lord's oldest son, had inherited his father's estate. He moved into Dromoland Castle. He was now Lord Inchiquin XIV and head of the family. Lord Inchiquin XIII's widow, Beatrice's and Barney's mother, and her children still living in the castle, moved out. With her deceased husband's assets now belonging to her stepson, the widow depended financially upon him. He consequently held considerable influence over her. Delighted with Barney's reaction, Beatrice agreed to his advice. Marconi left for London the next morning. He intended to ask Lady Inchiquin for permission to marry her daughter. However, he first had an important purchase to make. Beatrice ended her visit at Brownsea shortly thereafter. As soon as she returned home, Marconi arrived at the doorstep. To her delight, he presented her an enormous engagement ring. He could not wait to call upon Lady Inchiquin in her Marble Arch residence.

The highly proper lady gave the world-famous suitor no encouragement. She granted no consent. She referred Marconi to the fourteenth baron, who she said spoke for the family on such matters. In fact, Lady Inchiquin was highly displeased. She opposed the union. Her reaction paralleled the Jamesons' on hearing of Annie's proposed betrothal to Giuseppe. The Inchiquins were scarcely acquainted with Marconi. Whatever his fame and Irish Jameson parentage, he was a foreigner in their eyes. The O'Briens could not overlook their Irish royalty. Certainly they expected at least established, prominent English lineage for their marriages. Whatever one might think of the number of Italian princes, dukes, and nobles, Marconi did not even have one of these titles. With such shortcomings, Lady Inchiquin found it unnecessary to even have to refer to the difference in age.

Lucius confirmed the reaction. He commanded Beatrice to break the engagement and return the ring. Like Annie before her, Beatrice refused. She would marry Marconi. No longer would she even wait for Lilah's opinion. But Marconi did not know that. Upon hearing Lucius's decision, he immediately departed for Italy. Word of him soon arrived back in London in the form of a newspaper report from Rome. He had been seen constantly with Princess Ciacinta Ruspoli. The news worsened. The next gossip item said that the couple had a box together at the opera and had become engaged.

This conduct proved the case to Bea's mother. Such behavior could be expected of a foreigner and should pour cold water on Bea's infatuation. Instead, the teenager dug her heels in, defending Marconi's fidelity. In Lady Inchiquin's opinion, Bea's reaction warranted a visit to Beatrice's tough-minded aunt, Lady Metcalfe. Over tea, in Bea's presence, the old woman scolded Beatrice's mother for permitting the child to even become engaged to someone with a foreign background.

Marconi, however, also read the newspaper account of his rumored engagement to Princess Ruspoli. Canceling his business in Rome, he sped back to Bea in the Marble Arch townhouse to tell her it was not true. That made an impression on Lady Inchiquin, upon whom he called next, turning on all his attentive and smiling persuasiveness. He was convincing. Following his visit, Beatrice's mother and Lucius changed their minds.

Degna later offered an explanation of the sudden, dizzying reversal:

> Marconi was accepted, even lionized, by society, the darling of duchesses in Mayfair, a familiar figure in the great houses of Fifth Avenue, commanded to dine at the Quirinal, and followed by the Press wherever he went. Though marriage to an eldest—preferably titled— son was every mother's dream for her daughters, Marconi was internationally considered a brilliant second best. However agonizing his worries about company capital, in terms of personal income he was comfortably well off, was believed to be rich, and expected to become richer. For some years now women had thrown themselves (or their daughters) at his head and for the rest of his life they went on throwing themselves at him.(FN 4)

Such sentiments may help to explain the Inchiquins' sudden about-face. But the probable, unspoken reason was economic. In the first quarter of the nineteenth century, Sir Edward O'Brien, Beatrice's great-grandfather, had taken thirteen years to build the grandiose Dromoland pile in the gothic revival style sweeping the prosperous UK. This effort seriously depleted the family's wealth. Her grandfather then carefully husbanded the land's resources to restore the fortune. But the potato famines in the 1840s decimated the O'Briens, as well as most of Ireland. The castle's cash income depended upon its tenant farmers, who suffered severely. In 1870, 1881, and 1902, Parliament passed Irish land acts limiting rents that landlords could charge, restricting forfeitures for failure to pay rents and granting tenants rights to purchase their leased lands at government prescribed rates with financing provided by the government. Dromoland's farm receipts, like that of other landed estates, fell drastically. As required by his social and titled standing, Beatrice's father had six sons to educate at English universities and eight daughters to marry off with proper dowries. At his death, he had exhausted the estate's cash fulfilling those commitments.

His widow, his second wife, Lady Inchiquin, did not live in London with her daughters by choice. On Lord Inchiquin's death, his title had passed immediately to Lucius. Lady Inchiquin, being only Lucius's stepmother, had no right to be mistress of Dromoland. He had no obligation to support her and little wherewithal from the estate to assist her voluntarily. Lady Inchiquin needed income. In fact, she had a secret job in London. She anonymously wrote a newspaper gossip column under a pseudonym, with information innocently supplied by her friends and daughters. At the time Marconi courted Bea, her mother still had five unmarried daughters. An unpedigreed Italian would not have the same expectations about a dowry that an Englishman might. Beatrice's mother and the fourteenth baron decided it was time to get on with it.

The family scheduled a March wedding date. Marconi gave Beatrice two presents. Bea suspected her mother prompted the first, a coronet of Brazilian diamonds. The second, a bicycle, could only have come from Marconi, who knew her love of the sport. "That," Bea said with a smile, "was really his own idea."(FN 5) Crusty old Lady Metcalfe, who had scolded Lady Inchiquin for allowing Beatrice to meet the Italian, swung over admirably. She gave Bea a complete trousseau. As if that were not enough, she added a parure of diamonds and opals. Even Marconi's rivals honored the couple. Popov, Russia's leading wireless scientist, gave the groom a silver samovar and the lucky bride a sealskin coat.

While the women happily focused on the ceremonial arrangements, MWT news that winter of 1905 cheered Marconi. Profits for the fiscal year that ended September 30, 1904, ten years after Biellese, increased to £12,681 from £10,607 the prior year. Particularly important, Parliament passed favorable telecommunication legislation. The new law permitted wireless organizations to collect messages through the domestic post offices and to be paid on a per-message basis. At last the company had achieved its goal of a strong shore station system coupled to the active British telegraph system.

Germany, however, relentlessly pursued its campaign to break MWT's tight grip on the ship-to-shore business. It arranged another Berlin international conference to promote the regulation of international wireless. The first had had no effect on the company. MWT, pressing the advantage of its predominant shore stations, had ignored the convention's proposals and continued to refuse messages from non-Marconi equipment except in emergencies.

The company had such a strong order book that Chelmsford, running two full shifts a day, fell behind. A search began for a new factory. Sixty shore stations now served wireless on sixty passenger vessels with fourteen more ship installations scheduled. The *Daily Telegraph* proposed that all eastbound ships for three days before landfall wire in their weather conditions for publication in the paper. The government's London Meteorological Office followed suit and requested the same information for its weather reports.

The directors' annual report to the stockholders cheerfully concluded "the business of the company is making satisfactory progress all over the world" and predicted that when the new stations for transatlantic telegraphy came into operation, "a new era in the company's affairs may be anticipated." The board, however, had not yet concluded its study on the best sites for the new superstations and continued to refuse to provide funds to upgrade the existing installations as Marconi desired. In fact, MWT's growing businesses absorbed the cash they generated, requiring that it be reinvested in their operation and leaving no money for expansion. Once again, more capital had to be raised. The company offered another thirty thousand shares for sale to the stockholders. The subscription sold out, further diluting Marconi's holdings.

Marconi

While the directors contemplated their investments in wireless stations, the wedding planners focused on the size of the ceremony. Beatrice proclaimed to Lilah that "nothing on earth could induce her to have a large wedding."(FN 6) It would be simply her mother, Lilah, and Barney. That is, nothing could persuade her but her mother and the Inchiquins. Royalty did not have small weddings. The nuptials were held on March 16, 1905, in St. George's, Hanover Square, "then, as now," Degna said, "the most fashionable church in London."(FN 7) The Inchiquin coach bearing the royal arms, a hereditary right, last used at Queen Victoria's diamond jubilee, had since been given up. In its place Viscount Coke lent his smartest carriage. His daughter Marjorie attended Beatrice as did Lilah, Maude Lyttleton, and Eve Trefusis. Beatrice wore a lace veil and a satin wedding dress covered with lace and followed by a great train. The bridesmaids wore billowing, cream-colored dresses with Parma violet hats and bouquets. Bea's quiet little gathering became a mob scene. Marconi even received a death threat, resulting in detectives being posted at the church portals. Billboard headlines that morning proclaimed, "Marconi to Wed Daughter of Irish Peer." The crowds swamped Hanover Square. Three hundred and fifty congratulatory telegrams were delivered from around the world. Lady Inchiquin had hoped to give a modest reception at Marble Arch. The number of guests could not be controlled. The wedding had too many constituencies. The Inchiquins had a host of social obligations. The Jameson-Davises were not to be overlooked. The world-famous inventor could have filled several townhouses. Then there was the bride. This was her wedding. She wanted a party. All of her beaux and friends must be there. There was standing room only at Marble Arch.

After the ceremonies, the viscount's carriage whisked the happy newlyweds to the Great Western Railway and a first-class cabin on the boat train that crossed the Irish Sea overnight. The next morning, they pulled out of Dublin for the west. Lucius, who lived with his family in London, had made Dromoland available for their honeymoon. Only Mrs. Simpson, housekeeper for fifty-one years, was there to greet them. Beatrice had not been home since her father's funeral, five years earlier, when the house became Lucius's. How different it felt to return to the grand estate so peculiarly deserted. She was no longer a young teenager but a bride with her world-famous, older husband in tow. It was unsettling to be assigned to stay in the visitor's part of the castle instead of the room where she had grown up. She led her groom on a tour along the castle's imposing gallery and up its grand stairs past the many ancestral portraits. A 1690 Jan Van Wyck oil pictured Donough O'Brien, thirteenth-century king of Limerick and Thomond, in full armor on a rearing steed. Nearby Queen Anne, first cousin to Catherine Keightley, wife of Donough O'Brien, stood regally in her coronation robes. Beatrice pointed out Morrough O'Brien who made submission of the O'Brien lands and title to Henry VIII in the first half of the sixteenth century. Nor did she overlook Red Mary, Moira Ruadh. Widowed when her husband died fighting the English, she then saved the family estate from confiscation by marrying an English officer.

The handsome couple explored the grounds, the gatehouses, barns, dairy farms, and sawmills. Fifteen hundred acres were all that remained in the family after eight hundred years. Once, the O'Brien domains stretched westward from Dromoland to the sea, fifty miles away. Walking through orchards and cleared avenues of aged oak, past lily ponds and the Hermit's Cave of unknown origin, the two reached the Temple of Mercury perched on a hilltop. Bea recounted the family legend. In the 1700s, Sir Edward had built the turret-shaped house. Surrounded by its luxurious furnishings, he watched over his racehorses in the fields below. At the Newmarket races one year, he bet the entire estate, castle and lands, on a horse named Mercury. In honor of its triumph, Sir Edward named the temple for the victor and buried it nearby.

Despite the pleasurable recollections of past O'Briens, these first days together may not have been that easy. Dromoland may have been a mistake. In speaking of them later, Lilah said:

> Much as she enjoyed going to her old house for their honeymoon and showing him all the old haunts, making him known to the old people, the change and the quiet was enormous. Previously the castle had never been empty. (FN 8)

Beatrice felt disappointed and let down. Dromoland was not what it had been in her youth. Its ambiance fell far short of what she had depicted to her new husband. On his part, although there was no particular crisis at MWT, he cut the honeymoon short after a week with the announcement that they must return to London so that he might attend to business.

CHAPTER 14

The Young Edwardians

Marconi was young, just married, good-looking, rich, famous, and very much in demand on the social circuit. On top of that, he was in Edwardian London in the spring of 1905. The United Kingdom was at the peak of its commercial success. The wealth production of the Industrial Revolution and the return on investments from throughout the British Empire swelled the coffers of the English business class. Edward set the tone of the day admirably. He loved to party, he traveled to Paris, he collected racehorses, yachts, and fast motorcars, he hobnobbed with the new money as well as the old, and he was promiscuous. Despite his notorious infidelities, his wife, Queen Alexandra, behaved impeccably, graciously performing her royal duties with no public indication she was aware of the affairs. In the United States, the prior decade had been called the Gay Nineties. In France, the current period was the Belle Époque. In England, it was simply the Edwardian Era. Beatrice and Guglielmo had to be exhilarated. They did not know, of course, with what nostalgia these golden days would later be looked upon.

Returning from Dromoland, the couple first stayed at Marconi's normal bachelor lodgings near MWT's office. They soon moved on to smarter quarters in the Carlton, one of the city's very best hotels. Beatrice had never stayed in a hotel before. They had just begun to unpack when, excited and eager to explore her new settings, she left their suite by herself without telling her husband. She lightheartedly sampled the public rooms and nearby shops. An agitated Marconi greeted her return. He announced in no uncertain terms that she was not to go out without telling him when she was leaving, where she was going, and how long she would be gone. She was flabbergasted. She quickly learned that Marky, her mother's nickname for her new son-in-law because her tongue tangled on Guglielmo, meant every word. If tardy in reappearing from some solitary outward venture, she became the subject of a frantic search and an emotional lecturing. At first surprised and then pleased, she soon felt hemmed in by his overbearing concern.

In May, the Marconis gathered up their bags for New York and Glace Bay. The directors had taken a giant step forward in response to Marconi's relentless prodding. Over the winter, they allowed Vyvyan, the engineer Marconi had assigned to be responsible for Canada, to relocate the Glace Bay station inland to a much larger tract to accommodate the more expansive aerial Marconi envisioned. The board had not yet determined which English or Irish coastal site would be best, but they had assiduously worked over the numbers that commercial transatlantic service might produce. According to the calculations, the UK-U.S. exchange could earn fifty-six thousand pounds annually, assuming the transmission of fifteen words per minute, ten hours a day, three hundred days a year. A pair of existing shore stations was experimentally attaining a twenty-four-word rate. Company engineers expected the huge new transmitters to be capable of thirty to thirty-five. A fifty-six-thousand-pound return would be very attractive considering that company gross profit the prior year from all activities totaled thirty-four thousand pounds.

The directors recognized that cable remained a potent competitor. Undersea transmission speeds had reached eighty words per minute, an amount that could be doubled if pressed. The cost of placing submarine cable on the ocean floor had risen to thirteen hundred dollars per mile. The latest technology, however, permitted a line to carry two messages simultaneously. In an extraordinary feat, a new link, fifteen thousand miles long, had been laid to Australia. Nonetheless, the contribution long-distance wireless might make to MWT's bottom line was too significant to pass up. In April, the board accepted Marconi's arguments and authorized him to build Glace Bay as he had recommended. Marconi was relieved to be back on track.

On board the *Campania*, Marky again surprised Bea as bride and groom settled into their cabin. From his meticulously organized trunk emerged a series of clocks that he carefully placed around the room.

He set each at a different time around the world. No scientific experiment required the collection. He just could not resist a store window displaying a clock. His impulse quickly extended to wristwatches for Bea. She deposited them in her jewel boxes, soon overflowing, unwound as she was unable to stand the simultaneous ticking. Not long after the clocks had been properly arranged, Beatrice noticed her husband, when he thought she wasn't looking, stuffing his socks out the porthole. As a bachelor it had been more convenient to buy new ones than to deal with laundry.

Topside, Marconi went to work in the wireless cabin. Bea stood outside in the fresh sea breezes, talking to other passengers, male and female. This displeased Marconi. Icily he returned her to their salon, where he admonished her against being overly friendly with men. Bea was gregarious. Laughter floated about her. She liked the opposite sex, and they responded to her. The sound of her chatter amidst male voices provoked jealousy and possessiveness in her Irish-Italian husband. He made no effort to control or conceal it. He spoke unpleasant words in the heat of the moment. In these early days of the marriage, Beatrice was too taken aback to defend herself against such unexpected emotional outbursts. During courtship, no signs had warned that her suitor might impose unwarranted restrictions on her behavior. But she too had an Irish temper and a will of her own.

In other, more relaxed moments, Marconi taught Beatrice Morse code and how to deal graciously with reporters without revealing anything.

A round of parties greeted their New York arrival. Lunches and dinners filled their days. At Oyster Bay, the happy couple lunched with Teddy Roosevelt and his daughter, Alice Roosevelt Longworth.

The few New York days flew by. The Guglielmo Marconis then proceeded to Glace Bay. No world-class hotel and no glamorous entertainment awaited. Instead, they crowded in with Vyvyan, the chief engineer, his wife Jane, and their first baby. Their small house contained two bedrooms, one tiny bath, a kitchen, dining room, and living room. Marconi and Vyvyan disappeared at once, absorbed by the construction of the relocated station and new antenna. Jane rebuffed every offer of help by the direct descendent of Brian Boru.

Beatrice had little to do. She took over answering Marconi's nontechnical correspondence. She darned his socks. At times he allowed her to visit the station, even to listen to signals from Poldhu. But she didn't know how to cook. She was not going to clean. Jane wouldn't let her near her infant. Bea took to walking the railroad tracks that ran past the minute residence to the village of Sydney, ten miles distant. One afternoon she tried to go all the way to the town. By the time its lights began to glimmer in the distance, she knew she could not reach it. She started back, stumbling in the quickly fading light, encumbered by her long skirts. An endless number of engines steamed back and forth on the single track, forcing her to walk in the ditch below the stone embankment. Wearily, she persisted in the dark, reaching the Vyvyans' at eight thirty. She faced an anxious, overwrought Marconi. He scolded her at length. The engines had been intended to rescue her. Everyone had been terrified. What might the mine laborers have done had they come upon her alone in the dark?

At last Bea told Marky of her troubles with Jane. He rose to her defense at once, threatening an immediate showdown with the Vyvyans. Instead, Bea decided to confront Jane directly herself. Both women broke down and wept. Jane, the daughter of a civil servant, confessed her fear that Beatrice would put her down. By her coldness, Jane had hoped to hold her own. The air cleared, Jane and Bea became friends.

The boredom persisted for Bea, however. The long, freezing, dark winter was far more severe than any Beatrice had ever encountered in England or Ireland.

Her misery intensified in March. Marconi sailed without her on the *Campania.* He wanted to test the Glace Bay signals from the redesigned aerial on the liner's voyage to Liverpool. Not knowing what the outcome might be and what the results might require him to do next, he believed it better for her to remain where she was. Living with the Vyvyans without her husband in frigid Nova Scotia within the confines of a house that in its entirety would have fit in the drawing room at Dromoland was hardly the life Beatrice had anticipated when contemplating marriage to Guglielmo. How could she not long for England and her family and friends?

Marconi's concern as to the uncertainty of what he might need to do was based in part on the unprecedented shape of the enormous antenna. Its four 200-foot-high towers formed a center, and 200 wires spread outward from these poles like an umbrella to two circles of 180-foot-tall masts. The inner ring had a diameter of 220 feet and the outer 290 feet. On the *Campania*, Marconi measured reception up to eighteen hundred miles in daylight, a 50 percent improvement, but to him still unsatisfactory. He wanted reception clear across the Atlantic. Instead of returning to Beatrice, he concluded he must go to Cornwall and attempt to raise its performance to Glace Bay's level.

At Poldhu, he discovered that a receiving antenna pointed away from the transmitting station, rather than towards it, yielded stronger reception. Further trial and error experiments demonstrated the same to be true of a transmitting aerial. It produced superior results if directed in the opposite direction from the receiver. Immediately Marconi instructed Glace Bay to dismantle three-quarters of its new umbrella antenna, leaving in circuit only that portion not on the side facing Poldhu. This configuration he called the bent aerial because first the wires climbed from the receiving shack straight up to the top of the towers, then they bent horizontally to be carried through the air to a quarter of a circle of masts. The directional, bent aerial, registered in the London Patent Office in July, increased antenna range and efficiency and represented a significant wireless advancement.

With Glace Bay transmitting on a 3,660-meter wavelength, Marconi in June 1906, achieved steady cross-Atlantic daylight transmission. It had taken four and a half years since receiving the first transatlantic signal at St. John's to achieve this vital result.

Yet Marconi did not race to Nova Scotia to be with his bride of scarcely more than a year, whom he had not seen since March. He did not hurry to her side to celebrate together this grand step forward. Instead, the board, fortified by his success, authorized him while still in England to select a UK site for the transatlantic commercial service. He was far too interested in at last having the Atlantic transmissions up and running on a regular basis to defer locating the eastern site just to join his wife. Not Glace Bay but Ireland became his destination. Its remote western shores, the closest to North America but so far from London headquarters, no longer posed a logistics problem for MWT. Now the company had a large staff. It had enough engineers to dedicate several solely to the new location. After consultations within MWT and numerous inspections and tests, Marconi chose Clifden on the southwestern tip of Ireland near Bantry Bay.

Marconi

The immediate business needs met, Marconi at last embarked for Cape Breton. He noted with satisfaction that unlike the outward passage to Liverpool, signals were received throughout the return.

The couple happily reunited. Beatrice, sick with jaundice and loneliness, was overjoyed to see him. She could not hide her desire to be home. He granted her wish without delay. On this leg of their voyage, Marconi relaxed, his most pressing scientific problem of the moment resolved. The couple enjoyed the intimacy and time together they had so completely lacked since landing at Glace Bay.

But they were not to live in London as Bea had hoped. After what seemed to her to be the briefest of stays in the capital city, with all of its amenities and pleasures, Marconi felt compelled to continue his research in Cornwall. He installed Beatrice at the Poldhu Hotel. The dreary, stark inn, solitary walks, and loneliness during the lengthy hours without him cast her back into the Nova Scotia unhappiness. She felt sick again and queasy. It did not feel like a return of the jaundice. A new cause accounted for Bea's summer discomfort, as her mother soon enlightened her. Her daughter was pregnant. Lady Inchiquin rescued Beatrice at once from her gloomy surroundings, declaring Cornwall facilities inadequate for a mother-in-waiting. The widow rented a house for the expectant couple at 34 Charles Street off Berkeley Square, a prestigious location at a prestigious price and not far from Marble Arch. Lilah came to stay. Poldhu and the long-distance commercial service held Marconi captive. He visited when he could, but the train trip required eleven hours. The pressure to render the Clifden-Glace Bay service operational never relented. Recurring vestiges of the Balkan malaria eroded his energy, flushing his highly charged, overheated body. Beatrice later confessed:

> I was almost too young to realize the strain he was under during the first year of our marriage. In view of my condition he kept his increasingly pressing financial difficulties from me. He was dreadfully overworked yet he couldn't allow himself to neglect his experiments.(FN 1)

No step along the path of wireless had been easy for the inventor/ entrepreneur. He poured his entire capital, everything he had saved from the beginning, back into the investment essential to finance the long-distance service, the dream he held from the beginning. The costs of the transatlantic service stations exploded by another forty-five thousand pounds, more than the total cash flow generated by the company's operations over the past three years. Berkeley Square only drained his resources more rapidly. At last he confessed his financial condition to Beatrice. Face-to-face, in the second year of their marriage, each of them had to confront the truth about the other's finances and their lack of wealth as a couple. Degna described her mother's reaction:

> She received the news in good heart—it could not alter her feelings towards Guglielmo, rather it bound them closer. She took it upon herself to make what economies she could and to give her time and help.(FN 2)

Nor were Telefunken and Germany making life easier for Marconi. They succeeded in convening a second international conference and this one on their home grounds. It met in Berlin in October 1906 and threatened the financial heart of the company. Overcoming Italian and British objections, the delegates overwhelmingly accepted the 1903 conference recommendation that "all coastal wireless stations should receive from, and transmit to, all shipping regardless of the type of apparatus which the vessels were using."(FN 3) MWT, at its own expense, had built its series of shore stations, by far the most extensive in the business. They would now be obligated to accept messages from any manufacturer's equipment, something they had refused to do except in emergencies. Recognizing the losses this would impose on the company, the delegates from the UK and Italy proposed international subsidies to reimburse MWT. The proposition failed. Every government approved the 1903 conclusion. When a House of Commons subcommittee considered the measure, MWT argued vehemently in opposition. It passed by one vote.

The universal adoption of the convention's mandate prohibited the strategy upon which the company had founded its attempt, begun in 1899 with the terms it provided to the U.S. Navy, to establish a monopoly in ocean ship-to-shore traffic, similar to the telephone and telegraph monopolies. The board had gambled. It had constructed its comprehensive station network along the North Atlantic shipping lanes and allowed only its equipment to contact these installations. There were few opportunities for passenger and commercial lines to exchange signals with the Italian, English, Scottish, Welsh, Irish, Newfoundland, Labrador, St. Lawrence, and eastern North American seacoasts other than through the company. Shippers who wished to communicate with land were forced to purchase MWT transmitters and receivers on terms dictated by the board. It set prices at a level high enough to earn a significant profit and simultaneously recover its huge investment in the system. Now at the moment when the company's position had become sufficiently dominant to reap the benefit from its six years' commitment, its right to refuse messages from other equipment, the essential underpinning of its program, was outlawed. Its tactics were at risk. MWT's profit margins and its ability to recoup the vast amounts raised from its shareholders to construct its shore positions were in jeopardy.

In February 1907, the Marconis had their first child—a daughter. They called her Lucia, the female equivalent of the historical O'Brien male line—Lucius. But before she could be christened, after she had lived only a few weeks, Lucia died suddenly. Grief-stricken, Marconi wrote Annie:

> My own darling Mama, our darling little baby was taken away from us suddenly on Friday morning. (I was at Poldhu at the time and only got here when it was all over.) She had been very well all the time before and the doctor said she was a more than usually healthy baby. On Thursday night she had what was thought to be a slight attack of indigestion and at about 3:00 a.m. on Friday morning an attack of convulsion and all was over in a few minutes. Bea got a most awful shock and she is now very weak.(FN 4)

Distraught, Marconi drove about London in a taxi, in search of a cemetery for his baby daughter. None wanted to inter an unbaptised child. Finally a burial ground at Ealing accepted Lucia. The clergyman who had married the thirteenth baron's daughter and the world-famous inventor less than two years before read the graveside service.

Mentally and physically, Beatrice recovered only slowly. Marconi, at the same time, increasingly suffered bouts of malaria and high fevers until he collapsed, bedridden at Charles Street for three months. Perhaps miraculously, Beatrice survived the ordeal of caring for herself and her patient. Fuming at what he considered to be insipid British diagnoses and sugarcoated pills, as opposed to the more open analysis of Italian doctors, Marconi, the *salutista* who always carefully watched over his body, exploded at Bea, asking if the English took him for an idiot. He sent nurses packing, content only in Beatrice's care. In the end, Dr. Tallarico from the Italian Hospital in London to which Marconi had donated his cadet-in-training salary took charge of the ailing inventor.

As a favorite bedtime pastime, Marconi cut out newspaper ads for funeral homes, prominently displaying the lugubrious clippings on the bedside table. Beatrice, while uncertain as to his demise, could only be reminded of Lucia. Once she had to run to the chemist for a prescription. On reentering the bedroom, she was stunned to see Marconi standing on his head. His face, flushed with blood, had turned beet red. Nothing had prepared her to diagnose this malady. It could be mental. Her husband voluntarily resumed an upright position. He had bitten off the end of the thermometer and swallowed the quick silver. He tried to assure her that he could think of no other way to rid himself of the mercury.

While Marconi suffered and recuperated, he could devote little attention to MWT affairs. Nonetheless, Clifden construction progressed. It incorporated every new device he and MWT's scientists had developed. Workers aligned the Irish directional antenna away from Canada. Housed in a specially constructed building, a huge capacitor utilized air rather than glass as the dielectric between its metal plates. MWT built its own railroad, christened the Marconi Light Railway, to deliver fuel to the generating plant from bogs one and a half miles away. The peat-fired boilers provided steam to drive the generator's turbines that created three hundred kilowatts direct current up to twenty thousand volts. With the current, the innovative engineers charged secondary storage cells. The station could run for sixteen hours from the cells without recourse to the generator, or alternatively the backup units and generator could work in tandem to boost the voltage. The assemblage when finally operational produced a prodigious electromagnetic wave 6,666 meters or almost four miles long.

Edison and his associates, in creating electricity distribution systems for city streets, invented a host of by-products. Similarly, MWT conceived other significant devices in designing long-distance wireless. Marconi's earlier syntonic or tuned system had reduced the spectrum or band of frequencies of radiation generated by the spark. More stations crowding the air demanded more precise bands. In response, Marconi fitted the middles of three rotating discs with copper studs and produced an oscillating continuous wave with a narrower band. He called the device a rotating disc charger. Bell had come tantalizingly close to the concept of the telephone by experimenting with "harmonic" telegraphy. Marconi's continuous wave bordered on radio telephony. Its frequency, higher than the frequency he used in sending wireless messages, had the capacity to send sound. But Marconi was not interested in a wave that was continuous. He created wireless messages by breaking off the electromagnetic wave. The interruptions formed the dots and dashes of Morse code. Radio telephony might have intrigued Marconi, but he would not allow himself to be diverted from his concentration on long-distance communication.

Dr. J. A. Fleming, the company consultant, developed a portable wavemeter, or cymometer, to read a transmitter's wavelength or frequency. This instrument would have facilitated Marconi's initial transmission to St. John's when he could only guess at the length of the waves they were transmitting. C. S. Franklin, while on duty for MWT in Russia, sent home notes for a disc or variable capacitor, a greatly simplified method of adjusting tuned circuits. The company patented it as the multiple tuner. H. J. Round joined the company after obtaining first class honors at the Royal College of Science. He came up with an arc telephony transmitter that, like Marconi's three discs, produced continuous waves. Unlike Marconi, however, Round pursued his concept. Several years later, his waves carried intelligible speech a distance of fifty miles.

Telefunken continued to press the company on all fronts. From its research came a quenched spark gap, a notable improvement in increasing the strength and efficiency of the spark transmitter. The German corporation persisted relentlessly in its efforts to make sure that the convention's recommendations were enforced.

De Forest Wireless Telegraph Co. remained the leading U.S. competitor, continuing to open sites on the eastern coast and in the interior. De Forest unwittingly lost control of the company to White. The inventor was bitterly disappointed, but the loss freed him to return to his research on telephony. He had developed a receiver that he called the audion.

Inside its vacuum tube he added an unusual third electrode, a tiny grid, between its filament and its plate, and succeeded in transmitting speech across his lab. The patents he subsequently received for the audion as a telephone repeater, relay, and amplifier were as important as Bell's and Marconi's most important patents.

MWT was gaining new clients, particularly two it had long sought. Trinity House contracted for installations at a number of lighthouses and lightships, including East Goodwin, where Marconi had demonstrated on Christmas Eve of 1898 in a then vain attempt to win Trinity House business. The GPO at last ordered sets for two remote Scottish islands to replace unreliable submarine cables. This was the purpose for which Preece had invited Marconi to first demonstrate to the GPO when Marconi landed in England eight years earlier.

The company established wireless between Tasmania and the mainland for the Australian government and demonstrated for the New Zealand authorities. The number of stations on Canadian shores and along the St. Lawrence swelled to twenty. Newfoundland granted the company exclusive wireless rights. Labrador had five locations. MWT formed an Argentine subsidiary as the Italian government considered upgrading the Coltano superstation to link Italy to Buenos Aires. Twenty-two installations dotted Italy's coast. Fourteen Italian mercantile ships carried Marconi equipment. Excluding warships, the company's ocean business, the world's largest, had prospered as follows:

	Steamers Equipped	Words Sent	Net Receipts
1905	80	643,000	£13,000
1906	92	1,354,000	£27,000

The year 1907 was running at an explosive rate. If it continued for the entire year, it would shatter 1906's record, earning revenue of thirty-seven thousand pounds based on a volume of more than 1.8 million words. Considering contracts on hand, the year would end with as many as 118 ships with Marconi wireless. The 1903 convention did not threaten MWT's receipts from messages. The company's stations were everywhere. There were few sites operated by others. Ocean vessels had no choice but to communicate with MWT, no matter whose equipment they carried. The directors were holding their breath, however, to see if they could hold the line on equipment pricing or whether they would be severely undercut by their competitors, none of which had significant shore system expenditures to recapture.

The company presented a bold plan to the British Colonial Office to build a British Imperial Wireless Network. It would tie the dominions together with thousand-mile wireless links. Despite MWT's successes, the Colonial Office declined to consider the idea. Cable and telegraph already connected the overseas empire.

By late spring with the Marconis just barely back on their feet and the transatlantic preparations in the final stages, Marconi found it imperative to return to Canada. Beatrice refused to be left behind. She did not want to endure another indefinite session of endless waiting, but she also insisted that her first Nova Scotia experience not be repeated. Marconi agreed. The couple invited Bea's older sister Eileen to join them. Brother Barney, now a company engineer, also came along. The sea air invigorated Marconi. The captain of the RMS *Empress of Ireland*, however, upset the inventor's still-frayed nerves. For three days and nights, the shipmaster, intent on his schedule, maintained full speed through the fogs of the iceberg zone. In the night, Marconi woke to tell Bea the speed constituted utter stupidity. All of their lives were being put in jeopardy. On landing he suffered another fever, delaying the party several days.

At Glace Bay, they stayed in a Victorian house with a veranda set between bay windows. White birch lined the walkway to the house. Among potted palms, the family group posed merrily on the porch. A horse and carriage excursion carried them all to a picnic at Father Point. Marconi, however, decreed it inappropriate in North America for women to join the few shooting and fishing expeditions the party undertook. His decision disappointed Bea. She enjoyed blood sports because of the opportunity it gave her to be with the men. On the rare occasions Marconi came home from the station in the early evening, he played the parlor piano. The others gathered around to sing. He could not stay up late as he rose at three o'clock every morning. Predawn seemed to offer the best conditions under which to exchange signals with Clifden and Poldhu.

In August 1907, the group returned to London. Marconi went at once to Clifden. By September all appeared ready, and he departed once more for Glace Bay, this time without Bea, hoping to inaugurate transatlantic commercial service. Once more the company reached the end of its cash. Forty thousand pounds had been invested in Clifden and the new Glace Bay station. The new plant and equipment at Dalston, which had replaced Chelmsford, cost seventy thousand pounds, of which only twenty thousand pounds had been financed by a mortgage. In the past two years, company debt to bankers, directors, and large shareholders had risen from sixty-nine thousand pounds to ninety-four thousand pounds. Another 130,000 shares had been sold, increasing outstanding shares by 50 percent, from 251,000 to 384,000, and the board had under consideration a request to shareholders to create a new class of preferred shares. At times cash on hand would cover only the next week's needs. Cuthbert Hall, the managing director, sought thirty thousand pounds for three month's breathing room. He expressed appreciation for thousand-pound sums received from various sources but asked the directors who had not already done so if they could not make some contribution. Hall dismissed a hundred and fifty factory employees at Dalston to save on wages, even though MWT had back orders.

On October 15, 1907, Marconi at Glace Bay reopened the transatlantic service, this time between Nova Scotia and Ireland. Not quite six years earlier he heard the fragile signals at St. John's. Four years had passed since the directors had closed MWT's struggling efforts between Glace Bay and Poldhu. Vyvyan said:

> Only those who worked with Marconi throughout these four years realize the wonderful courage he showed under frequent disappointments, the extraordinary fertility of his mind in inventing new methods to displace others found faulty and his willingness to work, often for sixteen hours at a time when any interesting development was being tested. At the same time, the Directors of the Marconi Company showed wonderful confidence in Marconi, and courage in continuing to vote the large sums necessary from year to year until success was finally achieved.(FN 5)

The board had been remarkably loyal. Of the original five directors, four still remained—James Fitzgerald Bannatyne, William Woodcock

Marconi

Goodbody, Henry Jameson-Davis, and Marconi. Henry Spearman Saunders had joined in 1899, Colonel Sir Charles Euan-Smith (chairman of the board), and Albert Lionel Ochs in 1900. Major Samuel Flood-Page had been added to the board when he became managing director, succeeding Jameson-Davis in 1899. Cuthbert Hall had similarly come on board upon his promotion to managing director.

On February 8, 1908, the company instituted ordinary commercial service between London and Montreal. But it had a serious problem with New York. Overbookings constantly clogged the eight-hundred-mile Glace Bay–New York telegraph landline. When the line cleared, a rare event, London–New York messages via wireless passed in ten minutes. The overloads delayed messages for as long as twelve hours. Cable, of course, running undersea directly into New York Harbor, avoided this saturated pipeline and suffered no comparable delay. With the principal source of commercial international business bogged down in uncompetitive delays beyond MWT's control, the low level of revenues from this highly costly investment highly frustrated and irritated the board.

The company again faced an immediate crisis, an unfortunately common quandary for MWT. It once more had no cash. The annual profits of the previous years had in the last two twelve-month periods returned to a loss. The transatlantic service, at last inaugurated, was delivering negative figures, not the profit flow long assured by Marconi. The enormous, four-story Dalston works, which produced automobile ignition coils as well as wireless equipment, had overnight become a disastrous white elephant. The promising, fledgling auto market had suddenly slumped. At the same time, the predicted impact of the 1903 convention hit MWT. Its wireless equipment unit volume sagged, and prices fell. Further, the board suspected widespread infringement of its patents, but Hall, fearing the impact of litigation costs on the company's precarious financial position and the likelihood of losing in foreign courts, had brought only the New York de Forest suit. The emergency required strong action. The board appealed to the shareholders to authorize 250,000 preference shares. It asserted that all the shares could be sold and MWT's future assured.

Someone had to bear the responsibility for MWT's return to such a dire predicament after several years of positive cash flow and profits. Hall relinquished his position as managing director and retired from the board. The directors, however, had no suitable successor within the company, nor had they located a replacement on the outside. The circumstances forced them to form a committee to act as managing director. Marconi accepted the interim assignment, to be assisted by Jameson-Davis and Flood-Page. Marconi could not have welcomed the diversion from research, but he did not shun the assignment.

In another personnel change, Marconi's longtime friend, Luigi Solari, resigned from the Italian navy and joined MWT as its representative in Italy. A skilled electrical engineer and wireless inventor in his own right, he was assigned responsibility for sales across the northern Mediterranean in Spain, Portugal, Greece, Rumania, and Turkey.

By this time, the Marconis had departed Charles Street, leaving behind as much as possible its memories of sickness and sadness. They moved to a beautiful house in the country, Sunborne in Hampshire, its rural setting reminiscent of their childhood surroundings. Here Bea was closer to Haven and Poldhu. Marconi could more easily be home for weekends. Sunborne belonged to Sir Frederick Harvey-Bathurst, husband of Bea's sister Moira. Marconi's duties as managing director required more of his presence in London. Beatrice frequently joined him. At last, between the greater convenience of Sunborne and leisurely nights in London, they spent more time together. In town in the evenings they often went to dinner and the theater. It did not escape Bea's notice that in the darkness of their box her husband either dozed contentedly or happily daydreamed, contemplating further advances in long-distance wireless. Under these pleasant circumstances, an event soon occurred that surprised no one. Bea was pregnant again.

Marconi received the news of his second child's birth on September 11, 1908, while traveling in the United States. Immediately he returned home. On the voyage back, in an old Venetian book he was reading he came across a name that he chose for his daughter. At St. George's, Hanover Square, the child was christened Degna.

While Marconi enjoyed this new start to his family, an event occurred that demonstrated the value of wireless. In January 1909, in thick fog twenty-six miles southwest of Nantucket, the *Florida*, carrying 1,230 passengers, rammed the *Republic*, carrying 460 passengers. The blow stove in the *Florida*'s bow, ripped open the *Republic*'s engine room, and smashed its wireless room. The *Florida* carried no wireless. The *Republic*'s sole operator, off-duty, struggled into the wrecked cabin. He discovered the power cut off but found the Marconi equipment miraculously intact. Switching to battery power, he transmitted the distress signal CQD: dash, dot, dash, dot–dash, dash, dot, dash–dash, dot, dot. The Siasconset, Nantucket, coast guard station picked up the distress signal and rebroadcast it. The liner *Baltic* and seven other vessels responded, altering course and increasing speed. Unable to stop the inflow of water, the *Republic* transferred its passengers to the *Florida*, overcrowding it. Averaging twenty-two knots an hour and guided by the bearings broadcast by the *Republic*, the *Baltic* reached the scene in twelve hours. It took aboard both ships' passengers in a rising wind. Under escort, the *Florida* reached port, but the *Republic* sank. The world followed the rescue. The *Baltic's* Marconi transmitter flashed out reports that newspapers picked up and published in special editions. Marconi received thanks. Cheering crowds greeted the *Republic's* operator upon his arrival in New York, Liverpool, and his hometown, Peterborough. Marconi presented him a gold watch. From the beginning, Preece and Marconi had been convinced wireless could save lives. No example to date had been so dramatic and so convincing.

The board in June 1909 reported to the shareholders with relief that in 1908 the company had overcome the initial adverse impact of the feared 1903 edict. Maritime installations had exploded and reached 185, and 38 more orders were in hand. MWT had actually increased its rate of sales and restored its pricing. At least two factors accounted for the recovery. First, Marconi equipment outperformed the competition in terms of distance and reliability to such an extent that even a much lower price offered by a rival did not justify the purchase of an inferior set. Second, prudent buyers could realistically assume that the most effective communication would be between a shore station and a ship each utilizing wireless made by the same corporation, particularly when that manufacturer also operated the station. The company ran most of the seaboard sites. MWT's clear technical superiority and unique comprehensive land system combined to achieve market domination in the sale of its transmitters and receivers without having to require that only its sets be permitted to connect to its network. The company could accept messages from others' products without adversely affecting its ability to boost its pricing. The German-sponsored mandate had no teeth. It had taken the directors a decade of fortitude to establish ship-to-shore primacy. They had persisted despite international regulation and the nearly fatal effort to finance simultaneously both its investment in that business and the development of long-distance transmission.

The directors also advised MWT's owners that the sale of preferred stock had been disappointing. Nonetheless, 125,000 shares had been sold. The number produced sufficient funds to meet current commitments and also operate Clifden and Glace Bay. The Dalston losses had been halted by leasing the entire works to Siemens Electrical Company. The company quit auto ignition coil production altogether and transferred its wireless assembly back to Chelmsford. The cash position remained precarious, but the bleeding had been stopped.

Marconi departed to review American operations. Beatrice remained behind to be with baby Degna. It soon became happily apparent she was pregnant once more. Thrilled, she decided to surprise Guglielmo with her good news. She knew he was en route on his return home. She crossed over to Ireland. On reaching the southern coastal port at Cork, she gaily booked passage on a tug that was delivering mail to his liner inbound from New York to Liverpool. Hoisted aboard at dusk, unannounced to Marconi, she set out to find him. On the long evenings of cross-ocean passages, ship passengers had little to do but entertain each other over dinner and drinks and tobacco. Marconi would have to have been a hermit, which he was not, to be shut up in his cabin. Under the tutelage of Thomas Lipton, then Inez Milholland, and even now his prominent wife, he had become well experienced in the manners and ways of the soiree. He and Bea had been introduced to many actors and actresses by her sister and brother-in-law, Moira and Frederick Harvey-Bathurst. Moira was a set designer. She and her husband circulated socially in Drury Lane circles. The theater world crowd, whose morals were not Victorian, frequently traveled between New York and London. Marconi was very much in demand by Edwardian women. Degna reported what happened when Bea found her spouse in the ship salon:

> His welcome, which Mother had been sure would be ecstatic, was like a pail of icy water poured over her head. Returning to his bachelor habits, he was having a gay time with the ship's passengers, who included not only Enrico Caruso but also more than one enchantress from the theater world. The last thing he expected or wanted

to see, popping out of the sea like a mermaid, was his wife's face. Mother realized that she was intruding and retired to Father's cabin where she spent a miserable night dissolved in tears.

The next morning, covered with shame, he apologized and implored her to join the party. By then she was disheveled and distraught. She would have none of it and she stayed in the stateroom until the ship docked at Liverpool.(FN 6)

The episode had to damage Beatrice's and Guglielmo's marital relationship. Whatever rumors she may have heard before, here with her own eyes she saw how he conducted himself on these cruises. Worse, instead of welcoming her and introducing her to his companions, his cold reception told her he did not want her there. This attitude carried a host of implications about his regard for her and her standing relative to these shipboard creatures. On top of it all, his too obvious rejection of her in front of these strangers humiliated her. Over and above the emotional scarring she suffered, how now could she trust him when he was away from her overnight, which was a majority of the time? Even under the double standards of the time, could he still lecture her against flirting and expect to be taken seriously?

Several other incidents marred 1909 as well. Fire destroyed the Glace Bay station. Looking always for silver linings for its shareholders, the board professed the destruction an opportunity to rebuild Nova Scotia with all the efficiencies incorporated in Clifden. These might lower Canadian operating expenses enough to offset the reconstruction costs and revenue loss while out of operation. The GPO indicated its desire to buy MWT's nine UK ship-to-shore coastal stations. The General Post Office, fortunately, was not interested in acquiring the Poldhu and Clifden superstations. MWT had no desire to sell until it came to understand that its licenses to operate the stations, granted by the GPO and expiring in four years, would not be renewed. On September 29, the GPO for seventy-five thousand pounds consummated the purchase and obtained a license to use all future patents bearing on ship-to-shore operations. The board was upset to lose control of these sites located on such a vital part of the North Atlantic sea lanes and on the precedent it set for other countries, but at least the seventy-five thousand pounds improved MWT's cash position.

Still, the year ended well. Despite any lingering effects of the 1903 rule, the Glace Bay disaster, and the GPO appropriation of important revenue-generating assets, MWT operations had returned to the black. And Marconi in December journeyed to Sweden to receive the newly established Nobel Prize for Physics. Edison had never received the award. The first prize committee in 1901 had nominated the preeminent American to share the honor with Tesla. Tesla could have used the prize money for his World Tower, but he refused the grant, nonetheless. He believed that he was entitled to be recognized before Edison. Further, he (a scientist) would not share the physics award with an inventor (Edison). As a result, the committee withdrew both Tesla's and Edison's names and replaced them with a Swede.

Fleming had first written to Marconi about the prize in 1901:

> I do not know whether you have ever heard of the Nobel Prizes of the Swedish Academy. Mr. Nobel was the inventor of dynamite and he left an enormous fortune to the Swedish Academy for founding Institutes and awarding prizes to inventors...One of these is for physics or inventions in physics. I am one of six people in England who have been appointed to nominate someone for a prize... It occurs to me that your name should be put forward as a candidate if you have no objection and I shall be very pleased to nominate you.(FN 7)

Marconi had made up with Beatrice by the end of the year. The pregnancy did not interfere with her ability to travel. They invited Lilah to join them. Throughout the train trip to Stockholm, an unusually solicitous Marconi looked after Bea, tucking her in at night and fetching her tea from the dining car in the morning.

To Marconi's surprise, the committee asked him to share the prize with Braun. A cartoon in a Swedish paper had Marconi say, "I can't seem to place him," and Braun, bowing and protesting, say, "I am well known." Actually, Marconi knew who Braun was. He had been a member of the Braun-Slaby-Arco wireless team and had contributed to Telefunken as well. For the first few days in the Scandinavian capital, however, they refused to meet each other. When they did, Braun said he was sorry to be there. Marconi alone should have been recognized. In the end, they parted friends.

As a last treat, Beatrice and Guglielmo had tea at the royal palace with the crown prince and princess. The royals' little boys cleared the tea, and Beatrice at once recognized their nursemaid. She had been at Dromoland for years and in fact kept pictures of the O'Brien children everywhere in the palace nursery.

CHAPTER 15

Dominance at Last, but in a World Fast Souring

Never before had there been, nor would there ever again be, such a royal gathering. Nine kings, three queens, five heirs apparent, three dowager queens, forty princes, joined by prime ministers and special envoys, representing altogether seventy sovereign countries, rode on horseback or in magnificent carriages in the extraordinary funeral procession marking Edward's death.

He would have enjoyed it.

The parade began at Buckingham Palace, led by the kings. In front and slightly ahead came the most recently crowned of all, George V, Edward's eldest son and successor. Disrespectfully close to the new King of England, only two paces behind on his right, followed Edward's first cousin and Marconi's nemesis, Kaiser Wilhelm of Germany. Hopeful successors-in-waiting followed their monarchs, among them the Balkan crown princes of Montenegro and Serbia and Austrian Archduke Francis Ferdinand, who expected soon to sit on the throne of the Austro-Hungarian emperor, octogenarian Franz Joseph. As the Westminster service ended, His Majesty's sailors carried Edward's coffin to a waiting gun carriage. So began the march through the stilled masses to Paddington Station and entrainment to Windsor Castle. Mourning aides-de-camp walked solemnly beside the body. Close on came field marshals, admirals, and regiments in full dress. Foreign cavalry riding highly groomed chargers preceded Edward's favorite horse. The stirrups of its empty saddle bore his boots sadly mounted in reverse. Legions of loyal yeomen and archers marched in doleful cadence. Finally the royal parade concluded the moving tribute.

In the view of an English lord, "There never was such a break-up. All the old buoys which have marked the channel of our lives seem to have been swept away."

The decade during which Edward reigned had not been kind to the kaiser or his country. What Bismarck feared had come to pass. Germany, not France, faced isolation. In 1905, the Liberals came to power in the United Kingdom with a great majority. Under Foreign Minister Sir Earl Grey, they continued Britain's diplomatic realignment in opposition to the recently consolidated nation. The Liberal Party also took up as a primary goal the realization of Irish home rule in response to the large Irish parliamentary bloc within its ranks.

The directors found little benefit from Liberal government. It had neither adopted MWT's position on the 1903 wireless convention nor prevented the GPO from acquiring the Marconi shore stations. Nor had the Colonial Office responded affirmatively to the board's proposal to build an Imperial Wireless Network.

In the world of wireless, three subdivisions were emerging. Data communication in the form of signals generally sent over water for maritime and government users opened the way and spawned the others. Competition in this first sector was fierce. Telefunken fought MWT, the largest worldwide, with substantial government subsidies and nationalistic bank backing. De Forest's former company, taken over by Abraham White, its promoter, had been renamed United Wireless. It was by far the most extensive operation in the U.S. Despite glowing publicity, it was not profitable. It required constant cash infusions. It gained customers by undercharging for services and equipment and building additional transmission sites simultaneously on all three saltwater coasts, the Atlantic, the Gulf of Mexico, and the Pacific, and on the Great Lakes. Without resources to keep up in the battle between White's forces and second-place American Marconi, Reginald Fessenden's smaller National Electric Signaling suffered. In California, Cyril F. Ewell's Federal Wireless Telephone & Telegraph Company held the U.S. rights to the arc transmitter of a Danish engineer, Valdemar Poulsen. It had stations at Stockton and Sacramento.

De Forest had abandoned the first category to experiment with wireless radiation of sound. In its embryonic stage, this second division was called radiotelephony. De Forest also utilized an arc transmitter. His receiver incorporated crystal detectors and his audion tube. Principles embodied in the audion tube had provoked MWT's suit against de Forest in New York. In 1908, de Forest aired music from phonograph records from the top of the Eiffel Tower in Paris. The songs were heard in Marseilles, five hundred miles to the south. His De Forest Radio Co. received an order from the Italian navy for four aerophones, or radiophones. The U.S. Navy installed twenty-six aerophones on a squadron of warships embarking on a world cruise. In 1910, de Forest broadcast two operas sung by Enrico Caruso live from the Metropolitan Opera House.

This second segment was itself giving birth to a new concept. Fessenden, with a number of others as well as de Forest, was also experimenting with sound. He superimposed it on electromagnetic waves and called the result a continuous wave. He wanted to send his product out as far as possible and to as many people as he could. His target, unlike wireless's, was not a single intended recipient but multiple listeners. He asked General Electric in Schenectady, New York, to design and build an unusually powerful, one-hundred-kilohertz high-frequency generator. The task, considered impossible by the GE experts, was handed off to a young immigrant, Swedish-born Ernest F. W. Alexanderson. He delivered his unprecedented machine to Fessenden's coastal station at Brant Rock, Massachusetts. On Christmas Eve of 1906, ship wireless operators in the Atlantic hundreds of miles off Cape Cod listening on telephone earphones for the dots and dashes of Morse code were astonished to hear Fessenden's broadcast of words and music.

A third division rose spontaneously, generated by the fun and excitement of plucking invisible messages out of the atmosphere. Newspapers and magazines had covered wireless for a decade. From numerous articles, an interested person could learn the mechanics of its workings. With ingenuity and knowledge of electricity, an amateur could build a crude transmitter and receiver. In 1906, the *Scientific American* published an ad detailing a do-it-yourself kit. It included a one-inch spark coil, balls, telegraph key, coherer with automatic decipherer and sounder, fifty-ohm relay, four-cell dry battery, send and catch wires, connections, instructions, and diagrams. The text asserted the assembly would send signals as far as a mile. Hugo Gernsback, a migrant from Luxembourg, supplied components through his Electro Importing Company located under the "El" at Fulton Street in New York City. In 1908, he began a magazine, *Modern Electrics.*

Its circulation exploded from two thousand to thirty thousand in two years. In 1909, he formed the first national amateur organization. By 1911, it had ten thousand members, suggesting the swelling number of ham operators in the United States. The first wireless manufacturers were the Marconi, Telefunken, United Wireless, and Fessenden corporations. They focused on commercial purchasers that bought sophisticated, complete, heavy-duty units in limited numbers. The amateurs, called hams, a popular nickname for nonprofessionals, wanted inexpensive parts to assemble themselves. Many of their pieces, like crystals and electrolytic detectors, were not covered by the established companies' patents. MWT and United Wireless moved in quickly to supply the novel demand, but the door had opened to new producers of nonpatented components.

Amateur signals were broadcast on the same wavelengths as commercial and military messages. As the number of hams multiplied, their transmissions more and more often interfered with professional traffic, garbling messages on the same frequency. This soon led to calls for legislation to regulate wireless. In 1909, American Marconi and the amateurs defeated a U.S. bill to limit the hobbyists. In 1910, awakened by the life-saving role of wireless in the *Republic-Florida* collision, Congress passed the Wireless Ship Act. It required any ship with fifty or more aboard to have a transmitter, receiver, and operator. In 1911, the nonprofessionals again defeated efforts to restrict their activities. The combination of Congressional action and inaction compelled the one well-established market to buy more sets and allowed the fast-growing use by individuals to remain unfettered. The outcome delighted the manufacturing corporations.

In the popular vernacular in the early 1900s, each of the various aspects of airborne signaling, whether data or sound, were sometimes called radio or radiotelephone. This recognized their common characteristic of being borne by electromagnetic waves radiated outward into space. The two terms were used interchangeably with one other and with wireless. The word "radiotelephone" arose from the use of telephone earpieces to assist operators straining to hear the clicking noises of incoming signals arriving at their wireless receivers.

Before the Marconis' expedition to Stockholm, Bea's brother, Donough, had introduced the Nobel Prize winner to a businessman, Godfrey C. Isaacs, as someone to consider for the role of managing director. Isaacs, one of nine children, together with a brother, Harry, ran the Isaacs' family business. Its extensive activities, ranging from fruit to publishing, were also heavily involved in city and continental money matters. Another brother, Rufus, had run successfully for Parliament and was in his sixth year as a Liberal MP. Godfrey Isaacs had neither experience in the industry nor a technical background. MWT, however, was no longer solely a research company. It engaged in highly complex, fiercely competitive international sales and marketing and skilled manufacturing. It had enormous financial needs. The breadth of the job required many talents, including commercial business sophistication, keen intelligence, and aggressiveness. Godfrey's vigor particularly impressed Marconi. In January, the directors named Isaacs managing director on a six-month probationary basis. He quickly fulfilled everyone's expectations. Marconi could be relieved of his unwanted duties. Jameson-Davis felt sufficiently confident in the newly acquired chief executive officer to step down from the board.

Beatrice had become pregnant again. Marconi knew this child would be a boy. He deeply wanted his son to be born in Italy and be an Italian citizen. He asked Bea if she would move to Villa Grifone for the balance of her term. She readily agreed. The prospect of a late winter and early spring in the relatively sunny Apennine foothills appeared to her a welcome counterpoint to the freezing cold winter she had endured in Nova Scotia. Beatrice departed happily for Italy. Marconi boarded the *Majestic* for Glace Bay.

When the *Majestic* stopped to take on passengers at Dublin, Marconi dispatched a thankful note to Solari. His friend and colleague had on short notice arranged a twenty-thousand-pound loan for MWT from the Bank of Rome. Once more out of cash, the company had for the moment exhausted its English resources.

Bea persuaded Lilah to join her. No one had lived at Villa Grifone since Giuseppe's death in 1905. The caretaker and his wife swept and aired the house for the sisters' arrival with Degna and Degna's governess who found Villa Grifone primitive. She couldn't imagine how the baby's nurse would manage without a bathroom in the house. Not unaware of the need, Marconi had had all the proper fixtures installed. They connected to no pipes, however, and hence had no water. He had been forced to dedicate his plumbing moneys to MWT payroll as its acute cash crisis continued. The lack of fish and tea in the shops surprised Bea and Lilah, and in the beginning they had trouble making themselves understood. Nor did they appreciate Bolognese cooking. They went through "one weird cook after another." Nonetheless, they laughed and irrepressibly chattered their way through their muddles. They were as delighted as Annie had once been to enjoy the warm Italian days, free of fog and cold rain. They sent for a domestic English couple to run the house, including shopping and cooking. The pair, knowing no Italian, boarded the wrong train. It was headed for Florence, not Venice. Before it pulled out from the station, they realized their mistake. They walked through the cars saying "Marconi, Marconi" until a passenger redirected them to the Bologna-bound train.

On May 21, 1910, Beatrice gave birth to a boy. Marconi was at sea, returning from Glace Bay. His cablegram advising as to which liner he had boarded had not yet made its way through the provincial postal system to Villa Grifone. Bea, however, knowing how excited he would be, could not wait for its delivery to tell him the news. She sent him a wireless addressed to "Marconi-Atlantic." While a ship had to be within several hundred miles of a shore station to receive a land message, so many transatlantic vessels now carried the company's equipment that a boat throughout its voyage, even in mid-ocean, was likely to be within range of another MWT set. Bea's airborne message, relayed from operator to operator, most whom knew each other and Marconi, quickly found the extremely pleased father.

On landing in England, he proceeded at once to Italy. It was a joyous time. Beatrice and Guglielmo named their son Giulio Giovanni Vittorio Marconi after Giulio Camperio. He had been Marconi's close boyhood friend in Leghorn. He had subsequently died at a young age from "galloping consumption." They asked his sister, Sita, and Beatrice's friend, Lady Marjorie Coke, to be godmothers. Both Marconi and his brother Alfonso as teenagers had had crushes on Sita. William Waldorf Astor, who had moved to England after failing to become the arbitrator of who were New York's one hundred top social figures, agreed to be a godfather. Sita and Marjorie came for the christening, a splendid occasion. Spring passed gaily into summer on the villa's warm terraces. Guglielmo was glad to be home. He and Beatrice had patched over their differences. Marconi did little traveling other than to Pisa to overview the upgrading at the Coltano superstation. Bea did not entertain. With few visitors and social engagements, the jealousy, suspicion, and bickering abated. They relaxed and enjoyed each other and their two very young children.

While the stress in Marconi's life subsided somewhat as the relationship with his wife became more congenial, he also benefited from MWT having taken onboard such a competent managing director. Isaacs wasted no time in seizing hold of the company. On March 10, 1910, he had formally reinstated the application to the Colonial Office for the Imperial Wireless Network. The Colonial Office referred the request to the Cable Landing Rights Committee.

Hall as managing director had resisted patent actions. He feared their expense and uncertain outcome. Isaacs believed MWT's competitors significantly enhanced their technical performance by incorporating in their devices concepts belonging exclusively to MWT. They gained sales at the expense of the company that they would not have won had they limited themselves to what was legally open to them. The company, for its own future, could not allow this to continue. Isaacs carefully chose where he would make his first mark. He brought an action on MWT's home ground. He sued the British Radio Telegraph and Telephone Company in England for infringing Marconi's tuning patent, No. 7777.

Isaacs also realized that Telefunken had to be confronted. The German competitor, with strong government and bank backing, was gaining ground on MWT. The directors felt that such institutional support, not available to the company, constituted unfair competition. Every time the board sought a new customer, it seemed to find Germans already there. The managing director's fellow officers constantly grumbled about the "Telefunken Wall." Spain was a case in point. With assistance from the German embassy in Madrid, Telefunken had just won an order to outfit the Spanish army and navy. Isaacs cast about for help.

Godfrey's brother, Rufus, had just become the Liberal government's solicitor general. Not hesitating to use the connection, Isaacs arranged a meeting for himself with the foreign minister, Sir Edward Grey. He persuaded the influential cabinet member to agree that in the future MWT would receive all possible support from British officials abroad, just as Telefunken did from the German foreign offices. The managing director immediately capitalized on the promise. Assisted by Great Britain, he convinced Spain to adopt a strategic, overall communication program. Powerful transmitters would be built at Madrid, Barcelona, Cadiz, Tenerife, Las Palmas, and Vigo. They would reach the entire Iberian Peninsula, the armed services, the Canary Island possessions, England at Poldhu, Italy at Coltano, and shipping to the two American continents. In other words, Spain would have its own, private long-distance network. To realize the most effective operation between the superstations and governmental and military receivers, a contract for the transmission construction and receiving equipment, including the military's, would be awarded to a single supplier. The government took bids from MWT, Telefunken, and consortiums from other countries. It appointed a technical commission to pass on the bidders' qualifications. The commission, as Isaacs expected, found MWT to be superior to all the competitors, including the Germans. Telefunken lost its contract to supply the Spanish army and navy. Spain did not wish to pay for the cost of its new system. Instead, it accepted Isaacs' proposal that the company arrange private financing in exchange for a broad, long-term concession to run the facilities and charge the government for the service.

Telefunken retaliated immediately. It announced that its shore stations would no longer accept communications from Marconi equipment. Its government supported the action by prohibiting foreign apparatus aboard German vessels. MWT had been the sole outfitter of two large German lines, Hapag and Bremer Lloyd. Austria-Hungary enacted a measure excluding every nondomestic supplier except Telefunken. Up to this point, exchanges with Marconi apparatus had been permitted by all seashore installations, even though MWT had had a policy of refusing messages from other manufacturers' sets. Isaacs thought it critical to the company's long-term dominance that its signals continue to be universally received, particularly on the heavily traveled North Sea and Baltic Sea routes. He initiated discussions with Telefunken, seeking a compromise to benefit both corporations. The archrivals agreed to pool their German and Austro-Hungarian ship-to-shore businesses in a single entity, owned one-third each by Telefunken, MWT, and a Belgian banking consortium.

Signals from the venture's products would be acknowledged at MWT's and Telefunken's coastal sites.

By summer's end, MWT completed the Coltano refitting. In September 1910, Marconi with H. J. Round sailed for Buenos Aires on the Italian liner *Principessa Mafalda* to test Coltano and the long-range Clifden transmitter. Clifden particularly delighted them. Raising antenna by kites, Marconi and Round received Clifden daylight signals at a range of 4,000 miles and at night 6,735 miles. In his unrelenting drive for distance, Marconi could now send an intelligible message one-quarter of the way around the earth.

The accomplishment put the inventor in a marvelous mood. Lifting kites from the ship's stern was not the easiest task to accomplish. He was particularly adept at it. One afternoon when the direction of the vessel relative to that of the wind made it unusually difficult, no one succeeded. Marconi, at last, with a wry smile, volunteered to try. To everyone's amazement, the kite rose without hesitation. It was not until dinner that, much amused, he confessed the captain had altered course to favor Marconi's attempt.

When asked how far a signal might ultimately go, Marconi answered philosophically and prophetically:

> The messages wirelessed ten years ago have not reached some of the nearest stars. When they arrive there, why should they stop? It is like the attempt to express one-third as a decimal fraction; you can go on forever without coming to any sign of an end.
>
> What is jolly about science is this: It encourages one to go on dreaming. Science demands a flexible mind. It's no use interrogating the universe with a formula. You've got to observe it, take what it gives you and then reflect upon it with the aid of reason and experience.
>
> Science keeps one young. I cannot understand the savant who grows bowed and yellow in a workroom. I like to be out in the open looking at the universe, asking it questions, letting the mystery of it soak right into the mind, admiring the wonderful beauty of it all, and then think my way to the truth of things.(FN 1)

Marconi

It was a remarkable statement. It articulated Marconi's joy in discovery and learning. It revealed his appreciation for the universe. He was not blinded from its truths by preoccupation with a micro portion immediately before him. Instead, his specialty led him to observe its immensity. He sensed that electromagnetic waves constituted an elemental part of its composition. They could travel perhaps infinitely within it. He was constantly outdoors engaged in his experiments. He was forced to deal constantly with the mysteries of weather and atmosphere surrounding the earth. Above him was the great canopy of the sky, where electromagnetic waves soared without restraint. He may well have thought that these waves gave him an insight into the essence of life. Perhaps his waves, which seemingly could go on forever, represented infinity.

Marconi's departure from Villa Grifone for the South Atlantic voyage marked the end of a blissful marital period. The couple did not return to Sunborne in Hampshire. Instead, they found a new home, the Old Palace, in London in Richmond Park. Beatrice particularly wanted to be back in town. It was the debutante year for two of her younger sisters. She intended to throw proper entertainments for them and to attend their functions. Back in the days of Charles Street when she and Guglielmo confronted their lack of capital, she had tried to economize. She no longer stinted. She loved the parties. She adored the clothes. As she later recalled:

> We wore suits of ribbed material with embroidered peek-a-boo muslin blouses with lace jabots and stiffly boned collars. Waists were tiny. At Ascot, we all went to Ascot, gowns trailed on the ground and hats, Gainsborough style, were heavy with flowers and feathers and were secured to our heads with huge pins...In the evening we wore diamond dog-collars and sheath-like lame or brocade gowns with long trains.(FN 2)

Her level of spending drove her husband to his banker, seeking permission for overdrafts. He cancelled his standing order with his broker to buy MWT shares whenever the price fell below a certain level. He replaced it with instructions to sell whenever the stock exceeded a higher amount. He resumed his travels. He seldom came home, even when working at headquarters. Sometimes he even sought the company of Beatrice's sister and brother-in-law and stayed with the Harvey-Bathursts in their London flat. The nasty suspicions and jealousies once more flooded to the forefront. The couple's super-sensitivity to their partner's imagined or real infidelities led to quarrels over inconsequential matters. Both were headstrong. Neither would rein their self in. They would not sit down together to acknowledge that they did love each other and to seek ways to moderate the behavior that upset their mate.

MWT continued its success under Isaacs. His efforts combined with Marconi's and Solari's landed contracts in Turkey and Rumania. Greece equipped its navy with Marconi wireless. Portugal was persuaded to consider a strategic system similar to Spain's. It would link Lisbon, Oporto, the Azores, Madeira, and the Cape Verde Islands. It would be a second extension of Marconi service deep into the South Atlantic.

The first step in Isaacs' campaign to enforce Marconi patent rights paid off. In March 1911, the company prevailed against British Radio Telegraph and Telephone Company. This favorable precedent emboldened the managing director to proceed simultaneously against MWT's two most formidable opponents, United Wireless and Telefunken. The managing director attacked the Americans on their own ground. In a proceeding based on the winning British arguments, United and a customer, the Clyde Steamship Company, were sued in the United States. Isaacs pursued Telefunken on two fronts. However, he did not venture into the German judicial system. Instead, staying within England, he chose as his first target Telefunken's agent in the United Kingdom, the Siemens Company, the same corporation on whom the company had earlier unloaded the Dalston works. A victory here would be a shot across the German bow. The second stroke was bolder and potentially more significant. Australia was about to instruct Telefunken to build a continental system of superstations modeled on the Spanish network. A suit in Australia would still be within British common law. Its courts should not be predisposed to a German corporation over a UK company. However, an Australian judge might not be inclined to MWT if it sought to enjoin the Australian government. Nonetheless, the directors felt the risk worth taking. In an effort to stop the down under grand scheme from going forward, the board authorized Isaacs to proceed in Australia against Telefunken's subsidiary there and against the government.

Marconi

Marconi's efforts were also paying off. The *Principessa Mafalda* results had impressed the British. On May 19, 1911, the Cable Landing Rights Committee agreed to MWT's Imperial Wireless Network proposal. It required, however, that it belong to the administration. The committee directed the GPO to negotiate with the company to build the long-wave, high-power stations. Herbert Samuel, the postmaster general, opened talks. The committee also forwarded its report to the Committee of Imperial Defense for further study.

Coltano, when first built, had been the world's most powerful station. Italy wanted to regain that status. It authorized Marconi and Solari to make improvements to surpass Clifden. To possess the earth's greatest transmitter fit the Italian quest to act as a superpower. Since its defeat by Ethiopians at Aduwa, the government had sought another opportunity for imperialistic overseas growth. It watched Austria, Turkey, and the Balkans like a hawk, ready to seize upon any opening to recover land once belonging to it or currently inhabited by Italians. For years, the cabinet had at each chance assiduously collected promises from the great powers not to interfere with Italian ambitions to Turkey's Libya. It had extracted such a commitment from Austria and Germany when it renewed its membership in 1887 in the Triple Alliance. In 1901, France and Italy exchanged reciprocal guarantees not to interfere with each other in Morocco and Libya. The United Kingdom came into line as the price for Italy not protesting Great Britain's Egyptian occupation. Finally, in 1909, Italy made a deal with Russia by supporting the Kremlin's pleas for access to the Bosporus Straits.

The Marconis' marriage was rapidly deteriorating. The unhappy couple saw less and less of each other. Rather than mend their relationship, they considered formal separation. Friends and family dissuaded them. Everyone thought a trip together would be salutary. In August 1911, Bea accompanied Marconi for a third time to Nova Scotia. Nothing went right. Terrible weather ruined the crossing and any chance of a relaxed, good time. Seasickness plagued Bea. Once landed, a throbbing toothache made her feel miserable. They had just reached Cape Breton when Italy, without warning or pretext, delivered Turkey an ultimatum to hand over Libya.

The unprovoked act was triggered by the success of the French in Morocco. The sultan invited France to occupy Fez to defend it against tribal incursions. Germany protested and dispatched a battleship to Agadir. It withdrew when offered a Central African territory by France. With that little effort, Morocco fell under French control. Without waiting for a response to its demand, Italy sent troops storming ashore in Libya. The Turks acknowledged they could not stop the invasion and surrendered Tripoli and Benghazi. The Arab population, however, vigorously defended the country outside the two cities. A protracted war began.

Marconi's deep feeling of patriotism for his country of birth asserted itself at once. He told Bea he should contribute his wireless expertise to the battlefront. He packed his bags and volunteered for duty. This abruptly ended the Nova Scotia experiment. The couple, however, still wanted to save the marriage. Bea and the children moved to Pisa to be near Guglielmo while he readied the superstation at Coltano to communicate directly to the war front. He then shipped aboard the RN *Pisa* for Libya. The gunship operated just off the hostile coast, often bombarding Telefunken shore stations. The navy landed the inventor on the beach to inspect captured and destroyed sites. The army provided a mule on which he rode into the desert. There he conducted experiments with mobile wireless units mounted on camels. He made a militarily important discovery. It obviated the need to raise aerials and expose the set's position to enemy fire. He found that if he laid an antenna in the sand where it could not be easily observed and ran it away from the direction of the signal, messages could still be exchanged.

The campaign symbolized a shriller atmosphere permeating Europe. General von Berhardi, a German, authored *Germany and the Next War*. War, he argued, is a biological necessity. Germany must choose world power or downfall. What Germany wished to attain must be fought for. Plans for a two-front war in the event France and Russia both turned on Germany were drawn up by the German chief of staff, General Alfred von Schliefflen. They were anonymously published. They called for a swift, preemptive strike through Belgium's poorly protected flatlands to knock out France. That would be followed by an assault on Russia, which was not expected to be as prepared as the French.

Labor unrest riled factories and streets. Work stoppages and strikes became commonplace in England and France. A host of militant and revolutionary splinter parties, Bulkanites, nihilists, Marxists, and Leninists, threatened political stability in Italy and Russia. A young Herzegovinian trained by a Serbian army officer tried to assassinate the Austrian governor of Bosnia. At rallies and public places, female suffragists raised strident voices. One of them in England fatally threw herself before the king's horse in a steeplechase.

The company's belligerent program to enforce its intellectual property rights suffered a momentary setback in October 1911. Oliver Lodge, Preece's and Marconi's critic when the GPO and the inventor collaborated following Marconi's arrival in England, had been operating a wireless venture with Muirhead in India and several other locations. The professor successfully sued MWT. A court ruled his 1897 patent complementary to Marconi's major tuning patent No. 7777. The directors immediately negotiated with Lodge to acquire his rights. In addition, the board retained the scientist as an advisor for a thousand pounds per year on the condition he disband the Lodge-Muirhead syndicate. Lodge's claims and verbal attacks over the past decade had cast a shadow over No. 7777. The acquisition strengthened it and MWT's pending cases against Siemens in England, United Wireless in the U.S., and Telefunken in Australia.

Upon the loyal citizen's return from duty in Libya, Sita and Giulio Camperio's older brother, Filippo, whom everyone called Pippo, sat the patriot down for a heart-to-heart marital conversation. Pippo, a naval cadet at the time Annie wintered in Leghorn with her two sons, had been Guglielmo's hero. The friend pointed out that living in London imposed stresses and temptations on the couple. Once before, they had left town and discovered a better life in the country. Hampshire and Sunborne had helped relieve the unhappiness of Lucia's death and Guglielmo's malaria. Pippo urged them to reflect on how close they became at Villa Grifone. For their own sake and their children's, leave Richmond Park.

Marconi and Beatrice genuinely wanted to remain a family unit. In January 1912, she found Eaglehurst in Fawley. It was a marvelous, ornate Victorian Gothic. It sprawled above a stony beach on the Southampton Waterway's western shore looking over the Solent out to the Isle of Wight. An observation tower, a folly complete with battlements and smugglers' underground passages, guarded the mansion. Fawley lay conveniently between Marconi's research at Haven and MWT's London headquarters. What principally excited the sophisticated couple about Eaglehurst were its boathouse and motor launch and just offshore a mooring for a small sailboat. Marconi promised Bea a sloop.

The four Marconis moved at once from Richmond Park. Bea and Guglielmo looked forward to racing about over the water in the warmer spring weather and to the fun they had had while courting at Brownsea Island. They anticipated April with particular pleasure. The White Star had invited the famous couple to what would undoubtedly be the year's premier social event. They were to be the passenger line's guests aboard the maiden voyage of its newest, most luxurious liner, the *Titanic*. Together with many other prominent people, they would sail from Southampton to New York. There would be cocktail parties, dinners, and dancing, a nonstop week-long party.

In February, the company submitted a formal tender to the British government to build the Imperial Wireless Network. The government accepted on March 7, subject to execution of a detailed formal contract and then parliamentary ratification. The board also authorized Isaacs to replace the Chelmsford factory on Hall Street with a modern facility. In March, MWT headquarters in Watergate House and Durham House were consolidated in new quarters, Marconi House on the Strand.

In March 1912, United Wireless collapsed. Two dramatic blows hit American Marconi's principal nemesis almost simultaneously. They struck at the heart of the way it functioned. First, the United States judge found its equipment infringed Marconi's tuning patent. This immediately raised the question whether the de Forest transmitters and receivers when reconstituted without poaching on MWT's exclusive rights could function effectively. Second, a U.S. grand jury indicted two United stock salesmen, de Forest, and his lawyer. They were charged with using the mail to defraud United shareholders. The indictments claimed that out of $1,507,505 in capital raised from investors, only $345,694 went to corporate purposes. The balance was alleged to have been siphoned off to benefit the defendants and their agents.(FN 3) United Wireless had no cash on hand. Its operations ran at a loss. It had been kept afloat by the portion it received of the stream of stock offerings. Once the particulars became known, the stockholders and public refused to pour any more money into the corporation. It had no choice but to file for bankruptcy.

The petition delighted MWT's directors. This was an incredibly good opportunity. They immediately ordered American Marconi to purchase

United Wireless's assets out of bankruptcy. The board proposed to raise the sums to finance the acquisition by offering the subsidiary's shareholders the right to buy additional American Marconi stock.

The financing would be patterned on MWT's method of raising money for itself. After the board determined the amount needed, it authorized the sale of as many new shares at the current market price as was required to raise the capital. Because the company's business was risky and its ability to sell enough stock uncertain, a few directors and investors who themselves had deep financial resources would offer to underwrite the sale. They would commit to buy a minimum number of shares to assure that at least that figure would be sold. They would then hold the stock for themselves or resell it to others.

Isaacs and Marconi went to New York in early March to arrange the American Marconi financing. The timing seemed propitious. MWT's own stock had doubled from two pounds per share in August 1911 to a current price of four pounds.

On March 16, Marconi attended a dinner in the Tower Hall of the New York Times building. The occasion celebrated the first three months of daily foreign news provided by MWT wireless and published by the *Times*. It was a personally satisfying moment for the inventor. The service fulfilled his inspiration eighteen years earlier at Biellese. It dramatically confirmed his mountain retreat instinct that electromagnetic waves could be harnessed to send useful messages and information through the air.

Isaacs, Marconi, American Marconi officers, and Wall Street bankers developed a plan to purchase United Wireless's assets out of bankruptcy. The U.S. subsidiary would seek ten million dollars with which to buy and improve the defunct corporation's properties. American Marconi would ask its stockholders at a meeting to be held on April 18 to authorize the sale of one million of its shares at ten dollars each. They would be offered first to the shareholders. The financial advisers estimated that the holders, other than MWT itself that owned the most American Marconi stock, would purchase three hundred thousand shares. Therefore, MWT and its subsidiary must find buyers for seven hundred thousand shares. Isaacs volunteered to take care of five hundred thousand. Trading in the new shares would commence April 19, the day after stockholder approval.

Isaacs stayed in New York for the balance of March to finalize arrangements there. He would be back in London from the beginning of

April to try to dispose of his five-hundred-thousand-share commitment. Marconi returned to London at the end of March to supervise details of the deal in London. More important to Bea, he arrived in time to make their April 10 sailing date on the *Titanic*. Her excitement mounted as she heard more and more about who would be aboard. She couldn't stand her husband's fretting. Guglielmo increasingly worried about landing in New York sufficiently in advance of the American Marconi shareholder meeting on April 18. The *Titanic* was not due until the seventeenth. That did not allow him time to make sure all was in order for the stock sale. If the ship were late, it could be a disaster. Beatrice no doubt assured him that the captain would never allow himself to be delayed on such an important voyage. Checking schedules, Marconi found the *Lusitania* departing April 7 for arrival Monday April 15. That allowed several days' preparation. He knew the *Lusitania* to have a competent public stenographer. Marconi had an enormous amount of work to complete during the crossing. If he took the *Titanic,* he would have to bring his own stenographer. Unfortunately, the gentleman would be useless most of the trip. He became seasick very easily. Chagrined at disappointing Beatrice, he nonetheless put business first. She, however, would not miss this event. She insisted on going, without him if need be. He too well understood her desire. He could not stop her. The passenger list glittered. To make up for not accompanying her, he promised her a week's holiday in New York after he concluded the shareholder business.

Marconi sailed on Sunday, April 7. On Monday, Isaacs landed in London. He had already sold 250,000 shares to the broker Crofts and had them approved for trading on the New York, Toronto, and London stock exchanges. Marconi said he would take 10,000 and other directors and employees another 31,500. On Tuesday, Godfrey had luncheon with brothers Harry and Rufus at the Savoy. He intended to keep 100,000 shares for himself, but Harry wanted half of the 100,000 and the next day asked for another 6,000 shares for his wife's family. Rufus, the solicitor general, declined to purchase any shares. Several days later, however, Harry persuaded him to take 10,000 of Harry's 50,000. That same evening Rufus called upon Lord Murray, Liberal Chief Whip, and Lloyd George, Liberal Chancellor of the Exchequer, at Lloyd George's home. Each took 1,000 of Rufus's shares. Murray subsequently bought 9,000 more shares from his broker for the Liberal Party fund.

Marconi

On the Tuesday Godfrey, Harry, and Rufus lunched, Beatrice finished her packing at Eaglehurst and readied herself to travel the short distance to Southampton to board the *Titanic*. She was terribly excited. Giulio, however, felt feverish. She consulted with the nanny. Neither could be certain if it was only a light fever young children sometimes run or the precursor of something more serious. Beatrice could not forget their heartbreaking, fatal experience with Lucia. She did not dare risk being so far away for so long. Crushed with disappointment, she cabled ahead to Marconi's hotel in New York. She would not be able to join him for the New York holiday. She must be with Giulio.

Wednesday morning, April 10, 1912, the $7.5 million, 46,328-ton *Titanic*, the world's largest vessel, equipped with the latest model Marconi wireless, pulled away from her Southampton berth with 2,340 people aboard. If stood on end, her four-city-block, 882-foot length would have topped New York's tallest building, the Metropolitan Tower, by 181 feet. Its suction as it got underway pulled the steamer *New York* from its mooring, almost causing the two passenger ships to collide.

The *Titanic* steamed down the Southampton Waterway past Eaglehurst. Two figures waved it good-bye from the folly tower. Beatrice held three-and-a-half-year-old Degna tightly by the hand, trying to hide her unhappiness.

On Sunday, the four-funneled *Titanic*, sailing through the warmer waters of the Gulf Stream, approached Newfoundland's Grand Banks and the southward flow of icebergs coming down from the Labrador coast. At noon, the *Baltic* warned the *Titanic* by wireless that ice floated within five miles of the *Titanic*'s sea-lane. Some of the ice stood two hundred feet above the ocean, with seven-eighths of its bulk hidden below the water. The *Titanic* never lessened her speed of 24.5 miles per hour. The *Baltic* issued a second warning at 5:00 p.m., and similar warnings followed from the *Coronian, Parisian,* and *New Amsterdam*. After sunset, the temperature of the star-studded, clear night dropped to bitter cold. At 6:30 p.m., the *Titanic* approached the *California*, who had cautiously stopped her forward motion. At 7:15 p.m., she wired the *Titanic* that she had passed one iceberg and observed two to the south. At 8:00 p.m., *Titanic*'s steersman saw thick-ribbed ice when he came up on the bridge. At 10:20 p.m., *California* reported that ice surrounded her.

In the *Titanic* wireless room, John George Phillips, the senior operator due to be on duty until 2:00 a.m., had had a long day. Across the room, behind a green curtain, Harold Bride, the second operator, slept. Phillips had been interrupted by messages that made it difficult for him to complete receiving the wireless news from Cape Race, Newfoundland. He knew the lookout had been alerted for ice. At 10:30 p.m., Phillips answered the *California*: "Shut up, shut up I am busy; I am working Cape Race." When he finished with Cape Race, he went to bed.

At 11:30 p.m., the crow's nest signaled large icebergs looming ahead. At 11:40 p.m., the first officer ordered, "Hard astarboard, full speed astern." The bow swung, but insufficiently. There was a lightly felt jolt. The ship grazed the iceberg. The ice slashed the hull below the waterline. It opened a gash three hundred feet long, almost a third of the boat's length. The impact of the hit had been hard enough to throw the watertight doors between the major compartments below deck out of working order. Water poured into the forward compartments and the boiler room.

The *California* lay ten miles from the *Titanic*, within sight and within an hour's reach. The sole *California* wireless operator, after a sixteen-hour tour, had gone to bed. *California* crew members on deck saw the *Titanic* but because of the relative angles of the two ships did not identify it as a liner. Nor did they recognize the *Titanic*'s green rockets as distress signals. An attempt by the *California* to signal with a Morse lamp went unanswered. At 2:20 a.m. when the *Titanic* went nose down and end up before diving into the depths with funnels emitting smoke and sparks, the *California*'s observers misread the motions of the *Titanic*'s lights. They believed the unidentified vessel had gotten steam up and moved away from the *California*, receding into the darkness and over the horizon. As soon as the *California*'s captain determined that the ice about him had sufficiently cleared, he resumed his course and, unaware of the disaster, left the scene of the sunken ship.

Had there been no wireless, the *Titanic* might have disappeared, its fate unknown. Before wireless, sinkings at sea without survivors left no trace of where they had last been on the surface or why they never arrived in port, leaving those who gathered to greet them only to worry and wonder.

Marconi

About 11:45 p.m. on the *Titanic*, Bride awoke and put on the earphones. At 11:50 p.m., Captain Smith entered the wireless room. He advised the operators that the ship had struck an iceberg. He asked them to stand by while the crew inspected the ship and not to send any message until told to do so. Ten minutes later, he returned and ordered the call for assistance.

Aboard the *Carpathia*, fifty-eight miles from the *Titanic* and headed for Gibraltar, the sole operator, off duty and half-undressed on his way to bed, by a whim returned to his wireless set to send a few more routine traffic calls before falling asleep. At 12:20 a.m., he tuned into the *Titanic*'s distress calls. At 12:36 a.m., Captain Smith ordered Phillips and Bride to abandon ship, every man for himself. Nonetheless, the two operators remained at their station. The brave, devoted men transmitted signals until the wireless spark expired at 1:27 a.m. They then ran up to the deck and jumped into the ocean. They made it to the lifeboats, but Phillips died immediately from the cold.

Racing to the scene, the *Carpathia* first spotted lifeboat flares at 4:10 a.m., almost two hours after the *Titanic* sank. The boats were thirty-four miles from the liner's reported position. The rescuers lifted survivors aboard from the boats and icy water, whose temperature lay below freezing. Both Bride's feet were frostbitten. After ten hours in sickbay, he relieved the *Carpathia*'s operator in the wireless room. By 9:00 a.m. that Monday morning, the *Carpathia* had all 712 survivors aboard; 1,595 people perished.

The *Lusitania* docked early that same morning in New York. Marconi learned at once that Cape Race had received a message indicating a possible catastrophe at sea. The *New York Times* shortly reported: "The *Titanic* called CQD to the Marconi wireless station here and reported having struck an iceberg. The steamship said that immediate assistance was needed."

Total confusion prevailed about the *Titanic*'s condition. The afternoon edition of the *New York Evening Sun*'s headline proclaimed, "ALL SAVED FROM TITANIC AFTER COLLISION." The story followed:

RESCUE BY CARPATHIA AND PARISIAN; LINER IS BEING
TOWED TO HALIFAX AFTER SMASHING INTO AN ICEBERG.
And it began: Canso, N.S. The White Star liner *Titanic*,

having transferred her passengers to the *Parisian* and *Carpathia* at 2 o'clock this afternoon, being towed to Halifax by the *Virginian* of the Allan Line.

The *Virginian* passed a line to the *Titanic* as soon as the passengers had been transferred and the latest word received by wireless said that there was no doubt that the new White Star liner would reach port.

Agents of the White Star at Halifax had been ordered to have working tugs sent out to aid the *Virginian* with her tow.

By evening, however, New York understood that the *Titanic* had sunk. Terrible confusion arose over who might have survived. At least Marconi by this time had been able to reach his hotel and read Bea's cable that she was unable to make the voyage on the *Titanic* In Britain, even greater uncertainty prevailed as false news continued to circulate. The chaos stemmed in part from the sketchy reports from the *Carpathia* but more so from the hams. The amateurs flooded the air with inquiries to ships in the North Atlantic. They relayed what they intercepted, sometimes accurately and sometimes not. In no time, the number of operators broadcasting created so much interference that almost no wireless communication could be understood.

The stock market reacted wildly to wireless's prominent role in the tragedy. Company stock rose from $55 to $225. Charges followed that Marconi intentionally blocked out other wireless companies to obtain exclusive news and to rig the stock price. Others criticized wireless for inadequately or inaccurately providing news. Marconi answered the accusations:

> Good gracious, hasn't the wireless done enough in this instance to free it from complaints? If you can prove that one of our operators either sent or gave out that message, I'll take off my hat to you. It is you journalists who are responsible for the confused and unreliable rumors about the *Titanic*, not the wireless.
> This sort of thing happened before there was any wireless. Look at the confused and false reports circulated about

the Spanish-American war. Yet there was no wireless in operation then. Here is John Smith, who happens to have a wireless outfit of his own. He gets what he thinks is a flash from the *Titanic* or some other ship, and he reads it best he can. Then he sends word to the newspapers that he has word from the disaster. He gives it out and the papers print it. It may be entirely wrong or it may be only partly correct; but how is anyone to know?

Now it is perfectly simple to understand why there should have been the long wait between the first wireless message telling of the collision and the dispatch telling of the *Titanic*'s sinking. What happened was this: The *Titanic* struck the iceberg. Immediately the ship's wireless sent out the word and it reached land. The wireless kept working until it could not operate any longer; the ship had gone down.

Then came the long silence. The *Carpathia* reached the scene, but could send no word to shore. Her wireless was too weak. All she could do was to keep on flashing until the *Olympic*, which had also caught the *Titanic*'s call, got within range. Then the *Olympic*, with her more powerful apparatus, relayed to land what the *Carpathia* sent. Hence, until the *Olympic* got near enough to receive the *Carpathia*'s waves, there was no means of communicating with land after the *Titanic* sank. Whatever messages came during that interval certainly would not have been very reliable.

Why, I myself sent a long message to the *Carpathia* and was unable to get a reply. As for the action of the wireless operator who sold his story that had nothing to do with us. After he went ashore the marketable value of what he knew was his own property.(FN 4)

In the American Marconi wireless station at the top of John Wanamaker's new Manhattan department store, the subsidiary's twenty-one-year-old operator, David Sarnoff, heard the first news of the *Titanic* flashed from Cape Race. The station became the clearing point for *Titanic* information. For the next seventy-two hours, Sarnoff stayed at his seat. When interference threatened the listening post, President Howard Taft ordered all other east coast wireless to cease broadcasting.

On Wednesday evening, April 17, 1912, the New York Electrical Society invited Marconi to lecture at the Engineering Societies' auditorium. The hall overflowed. The moment he stepped on the platform, the crowd rose in roaring, prolonged ovation. Marconi bowed and bowed and bowed. Wild cheers greeted the reading of a telegram from Edison:

> I regret my inability to be present at your lecture, but hasten to congratulate you upon the success of your beautiful invention—the wireless telegraph—and in the splendid work your system has done in saving human life in disasters at sea.(FN 5)

Marconi delivered a technical lecture, illustrated by slide pictures of wireless stations around the world. Pupin followed Marconi to the lectern:

> Marconi is the most modest man that I know. Tonight we heard him give credit to his predecessors, Henry, Faraday, Maxwell and Hertz; and yet the invention of wireless telegraphy belongs solely and absolutely to him. The others had nothing whatever to do with it, and yet Marconi would give them credit. They were all experimenting in other lines.
>
> When Marconi grounded the transmitter and then grounded the receiver and let the spark go, then the world had wireless telegraphy, and no one had ever done that before.
>
> If we must call our aerial waves by some name let us not call them Hertzian waves but Marconi waves. They are his.
>
> The only fault I find with Dr. Marconi is that he worries his brain with the troubles of the investors in his patent. That is a foolish thing for any inventor to do.(FN 6)

Marconi

The next day, Thursday, April 18, American Marconi shareholders approved the sale of its shares to raise money to acquire United Wireless's assets. The *Times* reported significant price advances in American, British, and Canadian Marconi stock in an otherwise depressed market.

That evening the *Carpathia* landed the *Titanic* survivors at Hudson River Pier 54. It was jammed with relatives and spectators. Marconi and a *Times* reporter arrived by "El." With a police escort, they pressed past tearful reunions full of joy and sorrow. On board, Marconi interviewed Bride and the *Carpathia* operator on their experiences. The arrival of an ambulance stretcher crew to carry Bride to the hospital cut the interview short. As Marconi debarked down the gangplank, the reporter quoted him as saying:

> It is worth while to have lived to have made it possible for these people to have been saved. Just now all the world is thinking of this greatest sea disasters, I feel that I must speak of it, but I do it reluctantly. I know you will understand me if I say that all those who have been working with me, entertain a true feeling of gratitude that wireless telegraphy has again helped to save human lives. I also want to express my thanks to the press for the hearty approval it has given my invention.
>
> I am proud, but I see many things that will have to be done if wireless is to be of the fullest utility. It will be necessary to compel all ships to carry two operators, so that one may be on duty at all times.
>
> Some of the ships failed to hear the Titanic's call for help because they were receiving news bulletins from Cape Cod. With two operators, one could be working the news, the other—on any ship equipped properly—could be listening for distress signals, which would not interfere with the long distance news messages.(FN 7)

On Friday, trading opened in the new American Marconi shares. Lloyd George, Rufus Isaacs, and Lord Murray, the three Liberal ministers, each sold half their personal shares, at prices sufficiently above their purchase price, to recoup most of the cost of all their shares. On the New

York Stock Exchange, the shares opened at sixteen dollars and rose to twenty dollars by the time trading closed. Monday the market broke and the shares fell, eventually reaching five dollars.

Titanic survivors marched en bloc to Holland House, Marconi's hotel, to express their appreciation personally to the inventor for the device so instrumental to their rescue from further suffering and possible death. They presented him a gold medal. In the words of one:

> In the midst of our thankfulness for deliverance, one name mentioned with deepest feeling of gratitude was that of Marconi. I wish that he had been there to hear the chorus of gratitude that went out to him for the wonderful invention that spared us many hours, and perhaps days of wandering about the sea in hunger, storm and cold. (FN 8)

Marconi returned to England full of ideas to avoid further maritime disasters, among them wireless triangular navigational guides and alarm bells to ring automatically on receipt of distress signals.

Because in the aftermath of the sinking of the *Titanic*, radio hams had flooded the airwaves with messages that interfered with more official communications, and sometimes reported events erroneously, authorities quickly acted against hams. A previously called London international radio conference allocated specific frequencies to specific functions, such as maritime services and transmitting radio beacons. The conference granted none of the longer wave, lower frequencies where wireless operated to amateur operators. On May 7, 1912, the United States Radio Act required all operators to be licensed (but contained no provision to deny an applicant a license). Over vigorous ham protests, the act assigned specific ranges to government, maritime, and amateur operators. It limited nonprofessionals to wavelengths below two hundred meters (frequencies above 1.5 MHz). By this restriction, the act attempted to kill amateur radio. All available evidence indicated frequencies above 1.5 MHz to be useless for wireless.

On May 12, 1912, only eighteen months after signing the Spanish contracts, Isaacs and Marconi traveled to Madrid for the official inauguration of Spain's wireless network. In recognition of the importance of the communication system to the country, King Alfonso awarded Marconi the Grand Cross of the Order of King Alfonso XII.

American Marconi successfully completed its shareholders' rights offering. The subsidiary acquired United Wireless's seventy land stations and five hundred ship installations. The results de Forest bitterly described:

> Only by this forced receivership and sale was the American Marconi Company enabled to survive commercially. But by this strategic move and dominating stratagem the latter company acquired overnight almost a total monopoly of wireless telegraphy in the United States, a thing which they never could have accomplished by dint of their incomplete and sadly shattered patent position, or by virtue of any superiority of their system or methods. Until after World War I and the subsequent gradual substitution of the three-electrode tube transmitter and Audion (as detector, oscillator, and amplifier), the bulk of the ship-to-shore equipment in America was still the remains of United Wireless built upon American De Forest Wireless Company's designs and manufacture. At the time of the receiver's sale, United owned over 600 ship-to-shore installations, six times those of the Marconi Company.(FN 9)

By this acquisition the company, including its controlled, partially owned subsidiaries, had become the dominant wireless power.

In ship-to-shore, the vast majority of shore stations were controlled by MWT, other than the British Isles stations held by the GPO and those in Germany and Austria where the company shared a joint interest with Telefunken. Most ships carried company transmitting and receiving equipment. The Marconi sets still far outperformed the competition.

In long-distance communication, MWT owned and/or operated almost every one of the superstations. In terms of the distance the company could send a signal, it had no peer.

The crown to Marconi's efforts fell into place on July 9, 1912. The GPO and MWT signed a detailed work contract for the Imperial Wireless Network. Only a vote by Parliament scheduled for later in the summer was required before the agreement went into full effect. Its committees had already finished their examination of the project. Ratification was expected to be perfunctory.

Once the network was constructed and operational, Marconi would realize his dearest ambition. Information would be sent around the earth through the air on a regular basis.

In wireless no corporation, not even Telefunken, nor any government, including the British Empire, came close to matching the worldwide operations of Marconi's company. In messaging, manufacturing, research, patent position, and control of assets, it dominated wireless.

No other communication organization matched MWT's worldwide position. There were powerful telephone companies and potent telegraph corporations that had local monopolies, but their operations were almost all limited to their countries of origin. Cable entities were international but competed with other cable groups.

The challenge for MWT was to realize economic gain from its position.

Nor had the company's problems disappeared. The landlines from Clifden to London and particularly from Glace Bay to New York still slowed the transatlantic service. To avoid the roadblocks and speed service, the directors authorized two new super-powerstations, one at Belmar, New Jersey, near New York City, and one in Wales at Carnarvon, Preece's hometown. Once American Marconi acquired United Wireless, it discovered that many more than anticipated of United's commitments for wireless service were uneconomic. In its eagerness to acquire customers, the bankrupt corporation had promised rates that fell far below costs. The American subsidiary undertook the daunting task of renegotiating the sales contracts.

Most disturbing, stories began to circulate that the GPO had granted MWT overly generous payments in the Imperial Wireless Network agreement. Suspicions rose because the directors, while disclosing few details, circulated a glowing report to the shareholders, boasting about the contract. At the same time, PostMaster General Samuel refused to discuss the arrangement or any of its terms. Tory critics were quick to point out the relationship between the company's managing director and the Liberal government's solicitor general. The *Eye Witness* published the allegations: "Isaacs' brother is chairman of the Marconi Company.

It has therefore been secretly arranged between Isaacs and Samuel that the British people shall give the Marconi Company a very large sum of money through the agency of the said Samuel and for the benefit of the said Isaacs."(FN 10) Rufus Isaacs and Samuel considered a libel action, but the prime minister, on the premise that the action would only bring notoriety to the attention-seeking publication, dissuaded them. A second set of accusations arose from angry stockholders hurt by the rise and subsequent fall in the price of company stock. Their whispers hinted at a stock ring with implications that Marconi and Godfrey Isaacs manipulated prices of the stocks of various Marconi companies.

The rumors soon affected MWT adversely. Liberals and Tories were engaged in increasingly contentious arguments over a number of issues that divided them, including the question of Irish home rule. The propriety of the Imperial Wireless Network contract fell into the swirl of controversies. It became a hot political issue for conservatives trying to undermine the government. Instead of a vote in the House in August to ratify the agreement, a motion was introduced to establish a Select Committee of Inquiry to investigate all aspects of the agreement. Debate on the issue was not scheduled until October.

The political dispute depressed Marconi. He and the board knew of no GPO corruption or stock ring. All the construction details had been spelled out by the General Post Office. The directors had to decide whether or not to risk building the stations while awaiting ratification. They remained confident of approval and were eager to be underway. Time assumed additional significance because of growing expectations of war with Germany. In such an event, a network all on Empire soil would have immense importance.

Marconi was particularly upset because the affair was publicly referred to as the "Marconi Scandal." The phrase implicitly smeared MWT and the inventor personally in each utterance and publication of the two words. It did not matter that there had been no formal charges, only unsubstantiated rumors, against Marconi or the company. As an MP said to Marconi, "Unfortunately your name is the name of the company. I hear no suggestion made against you, Mr. Marconi, at all."(FN 11)

The unpleasantness of the adverse publicity and Marconi's resulting bad humor did nothing to enhance the restoration of Bea's and Guglielmo's relationship. Even Eaglehurst had not provided the hoped-for balm to their quarrels. Marconi rarely visited. When he did, someone from MWT usually accompanied him in his magnificent Rolls Royce. If it were Kemp, they would quickly head for the folly, where they had installed a research laboratory. If the guest were an engineer, they would disappear on a walk to the Fawley town pier, where they would talk for hours about current projects. On one occasion, Guglielmo arrived in the midst of Beatrice's French lesson given by a handsome young teacher. Marconi's jealously arose at once. The tutor never returned. The children's pet Pekinese thought Marconi a stranger. When he went to the nursery to see Degna and Giulio, the dog leapt to their defense and nipped their father. The dog, too, was soon gone.

The couple's relationship became acrimonious. Again they talked of separation. Annie stepped in to dissuade Beatrice. Pippo once more intervened with Guglielmo. The four-way negotiation resulted in another vacation where the pair would once more try to save their marriage, this time in Italy. Marconi loved to drive. He rented a brand-new Fiat open touring car with a chauffeur. The driver most often found himself in the rear seat while Marconi drove with Bea at his side. Despite the purpose of the trip, Marconi could not resist visiting Coltano. The royal Italian family, on tour itself, was at its residence in nearby San Rossore. Marconi invited the king to the superstation. Victor Emmanuel, a principal supporter of the station, readily accepted. He reciprocated by asking the Marconis to San Rossore. Beatrice was thrilled. Hoping for such an occasion, she had given up her French studies for Italian. She wanted to be able to converse with the family in their own language. Marconi insisted that he drive them to San Rossore in the topless car. By their arrival, Beatrice was furious at her husband. She was mortified by what the swirling, dusty air had done to her hair and clothes. Her embarrassment increased when she discovered that the Italians thought it much more socially acceptable to chat away volubly in French. She could not keep up with the conversation. Despite these setbacks, Queen Elena invited Beatrice to come to Rome and join her court as a lady-in-waiting. It was a rare honor. Foreigners were seldom asked to become a member of the court. The queen graciously overcame this objection. She said, quite rightly, that Bea's family was as old as theirs.

On September 25, 1912, several days after the San Rossore dinner, the Marconis left Pisa. Guglielmo was driving, Bea beside him and the chauffeur in back. No matter how well the deeply patriotic inventor could hold his scientific emotions in check, and despite the uneasy relationship with Bea and the contretemps over the Imperial Wireless Network contract, overall he must have been immensely pleased. He was on holiday, in Italy, on a beautiful September morning. He was driving. His wireless was on top of the world. He had spent the weekend with his king. His wife had been asked to become a member of the queen's court. Fortuitously, he and Beatrice had each avoided being on the *Titanic*.

At long last, Marconi's stubbornly held conviction that long-distance wireless would lead to a highly profitable company was bearing significant results. The transatlantic business and national systems like Spain's and Australia's laid an excellent foundation. A worldwide system initiated with the Imperial Wireless Network, a monopoly whose only competition was cable, would bring his vision to full fruit. The icing on the cake was that with the acquisition of United Wireless, the company had achieved overwhelming pricing power in ship-to-shore as well. Within a few years, when United Wireless was properly structured and the global system was up and running, the combination would be awesome. It would exceed anything Marconi could have dreamt of.

Just after noon, the Marconi party sped through Spezia and zoomed onto the road to Genoa. A car coming in the opposite direction spun out of a hairpin curve. It tore into the open touring vehicle. The Fiat crashed into the roadside ditch. The errant driver and his companion climbed out of their automobile, bruised but not hurt. Marconi sat quietly at the Fiat's wheel. Bea and the chauffeur seemed more seriously shaken. Bea turned to her husband to ask how he felt. Shocked, she saw blood covering his face. Self-analytical and composed as ever, he calmly answered, "I believe I've lost my eye."

The king's uncle, the Duke of Abruzzi, was the first advised of the accident. He immediately dispatched his car to the scene. Within an hour, Marconi lay in the military hospital in Spezia, his right eye visionless, the right side of his face badly bruised, and the pain steadily increasing. The attendant doctor discovered that Marconi's optic nerve had been damaged. In addition to the loss of sight in the right eye, sight in the left eye was fading rapidly. Dr. Baiardi, a well-known eye specialist, was summoned from Turin. He consulted with Dr. Fuchs, a leading surgeon in Venice. They concluded that to save the left eye the right eye must be removed.

Marconi agreed to the operation. He insisted on walking without assistance to the operating room. Bea, bruised from the waist down, accompanied him on one side and Solari, who had come at once, on the other. Dr. Baiardi administered no anesthesia during the operation and removal of Marconi's right eye. Marconi groaned, but never cried out.

For nine days, the patient lay in his bed with no sight. Doctors, family, and supporters waited anxiously for the bandages to be removed and the predicted restoration of vision in the left eye to be confirmed. On the tenth day, Dr. Baiardi snipped away the wrappings. To Marconi's great dismay, he saw nothing. He was totally blind.

CHAPTER 16

A Dicadumus Era Ends

Marconi lay in his seaside bed in Spezia. As if it were a scientific matter to be dealt with, he coldly came to grips with his terrible new condition. He determined to return to his roots. He would remain in Italy. Villa Grifone once more would be his home. The company would assign an engineering staff there to assist him.

Sympathetic messages poured in. Victor Emmanuel and Elena sailed to Spezia aboard the royal yacht, *Yela*, and came ashore to visit him. Beatrice stayed by Guglielmo's side. She read to him most of the day and into the night. He would not let her stop. Together they went through the London *Times* from beginning to end. Other newspapers and magazine articles were devoured aloud as well. Of course he must hear each of the messages. Their affection for each other grew once more. It followed a pattern. When alone with each other, when the tempting, external social world was removed from their presence, as it had been in the halcyon days following Giulio's birth, their love for each other flourished.

The king assigned the court's master of ceremonies to assure that the hospital do everything possible for Marconi. Commendatore Beltrami, the driver of the other car, said, "I would have preferred to die or to have both legs cut off rather than even without blame to have caused an accident whereof the victim was Mr. Marconi whom I fervently admire."(FN 1)

The surgeon's prognosis was that Marconi's left eye would improve. It did, but scarcely. After several weeks, he could distinguish only between light and dark.

Marconi

While Marconi waited anxiously, hoping to recover the sight in his left eye, the time for the October parliamentary debate on the appointment of a committee to review the Imperial Wireless Network contract approached. Rumors and criticism increased. Word spread that Liberal ministers had been dealing in some kind of Marconi stock. Newspapers questioned the contract terms. A critic suggested that "Mother Marconi has been a prolific parent and her chickens are spread all over the globe; they have assumed a half-dozen nationalities...The Marconi ring apparently hoped to make as much out of wireless as Andrew Carnegie got out of the steel tariff."(FN 2) A Tory MP who owned stock in the company sued Isaacs, his brother Harry, the directors, and MWT's brokers for an accounting on the five hundred thousand shares handled by Isaacs. Other investors claimed losses exceeding five million dollars. They demanded the board reimburse them an amount equal to the spread between the stock's highest and current market value. In the course of the October debate, Chancellor of the Exchequer Lloyd George, Attorney General Rufus Isaacs, and Postmaster General Samuel denied all charges made. They asserted that they were not MWT shareholders. Many construed their answers to imply that they owned no stock in any Marconi company. They were not specifically asked if they held any American Marconi shares, nor did they volunteer the information.

The agreement became increasingly embroiled in the politics swirling through Parliament in the bitter struggle between the minority Tories or Unionists against the Liberals. Their battle now focused sharply on the disagreement over Irish home rule. But the hope to uncover a scandal that might help unseat the governing party fed the Conservative Party's appetite to attack the contract. MWT's competitors, particularly cable, joined in the frenzy. The clamor for an investigation, based on rampant speculation as to possible wrongdoing, grew too great to ignore. The government, giving in to the opposition, allowed the appointment of a Select Committee, but loaded its members with Liberals. Parliament directed that all aspects of the relationship between the GPO and MWT be looked into, including government malfeasance. The Select Committee created a technical subcommittee, named the Parker Committee, to evaluate the scientific competence of the company and each of its competitors to build and operate the proposed network. In the view of some, the Select Committee had been charged to solve "The Great Marconi

Mystery, which would tax the pen of Conan Doyle, assisted by the brains of Sherlock Holmes to do anything approaching justice to it."(FN 3)

While Marconi stoically suffered in bed, trying not to allow the parliamentary intrigue and delay and hostile public comment as well as the loss of his sight to upset him, headquarters forward some very good news. MWT had routed Telefunken in the courts.

In Australia, the High Court found the equipment the German corporation proposed for the Aussie network infringed Marconi patents. In settlement, the parties agreed to form a joint venture to hold and operate all wireless on the continent. The company received one half of the new venture, Telefunken 5.7 percent, and Australians the balance. Before Isaacs initiated the action, MWT was excluded from Australia. Now the company effectively controlled the country's airborne transmission.

At the same time in London, Telefunken's agent, Siemens, concluded it would lose the English action. Before an adverse verdict could be entered, it conceded the validity of the Marconi tuning patent. Once more Isaacs negotiated a compromise. The directors authorized a global intellectual property agreement with Telefunken. MWT gained access to the German patents and licensed its rival to use the company's.

These were huge victories. They prevented MWT's principal rival from using Marconi concepts in competition against MWT. Together with the spring victory over de Forest and the prior fall's acquisition of Lodge's right, the supremacy and enforceability of Marconi's patents had been clearly established. No doubt credit was due Isaacs for acumen in initiating and managing the litigations and settlements. But underneath the triumphs lay Marconi's brilliance. In the beginning he was attacked for simply picking up on others' ideas, although no one else had his insights into the practical application of these concepts. For the last ten years, he had been running in an open field where wireless's significance was notorious. Courts and parliaments scrutinized his work. Governments and corporations, Americans, Germans, French, English, and Russians, competed against him. The constant challenges and attempts to best him underscored the magnitude of his accomplishment.

November was passing. Marconi had been in hospital for close to two months. He turned to look towards the light of the window. To his surprise and delight, he unexpectedly detected white sails on the sea. From that moment, his left eye improved rapidly. Its sight recovered completely. Marconi regained enough strength to travel to Dr. Fuchs in Venice for reconstructive surgery. The highly regarded specialist fitted Marconi with an artificial right eye. Only close observers could detect the difference between his eyes or noticed that when he occasionally dabbed a tear from an eye, it was always the left one. Dr. Fuchs refused payment for his services. He was honored to have assisted Italian science. Marconi expressed his gratitude by a donation to the hospital.

In December, the inventor was sufficiently recovered physically and in appearance to return to Eaglehurst and his work. His arrival delighted Kemp. In honor of the occasion, the former sailor had erected a 180-foot-high mast in front of the mansion. As Bea and Guglielmo stepped from their Rolls Royce, not driven by Marconi, and embraced Degna and Giulio, Kemp hoisted aloft the flag of the *Carlo Alberto* that had been given to the scientist by its captain in fond memory of Gibraltar. The devoted engineer then flew the Italian ensign from the height of the folly's tower.

Internal scars from the consequences of the accident remained, however. In the view of one who knew him well:

> Marconi always took great care over his personal appearance, and consciousness of the missing eye, and perhaps too the shock of having come near permanent blindness, possibly added to his natural reserve, indeed coldness, which so many acquaintances remarked upon.(FN 4)

The Parker Committee studied the company's long-distance apparatus meticulously. Just as the Admiralty in 1900 compared Marconi's fledgling wireless to Captain Jackson's and Professor Lodge's, the parliamentary technical experts now contrasted MWT's equipment to Telefunken, Poulsen, and de Forest. The six-month-long exam irritated anxious company engineers. Marconi, recuperating at Eaglehurst, expressed annoyance at the time wasted and the indignity of the review. When called to testify, he bridled at opinions offered by others. He corrected the record. "It has often been stated that the Marconi system was first and always a spark system. This is not so."(FN 5) He was quick to point out that Clifden currently utilized continuous waves and no spark. The board decided it could no longer defer construction of the network. Nothing reported to the directors from any of the hearings upset their confidence that in the end the company and its system would be vindicated and the GPO contract upheld.

The Select Committee proceedings dragged into spring, 1913. At the hearings, Marconi, in exasperation, addressed the innuendos that connected him personally to the scandalous rumors:

> I wish to state most emphatically that I have never at any time speculated in any of the shares of my companies. I have always supported them with whatever money has been required, and frequently to very large sums. I have occasionally sold shares, not in consequence of markets or circumstances connected with the company's business, but only when I have required moneys for business in which I am interested other than that of the Marconi companies. During the whole of the period of the boom in shares in the parent company or the American company, or any other of the companies with which I am associated, I have never bought or sold a share.
>
> I have never taken part in any syndicate, nor have I ever heard of any syndicate, nor do I believe any syndicate ever existed, in connection with any of the shares of any of the Marconi companies. Neither I nor my company has in any way been responsible for the fluctuations of the prices in the market, but I believe that these prices have varied entirely according to the natural supply and demand, in the same way as prices of any security upon the Stock Exchange will fluctuate.
>
> I do not wish to conclude without expressing my resentment at the reflections which have been made upon my company and upon me for having innocently entered into a contract with His Majesty's Government. I resent the inquiry into and publication given to the affairs of my company, which have no relation whatsoever to the contract entered into with His Majesty's Government, and I would in this respect particularly express my regret that the services which my company and I have for so many

years rendered to the Post Office, the Admiralty, the merchant marine, and in fact the whole nation, should not have been deemed worthy of higher consideration. (FN 6)

The chancellor, attorney general, and whip had to unwillingly publicly correct the false impression they had perhaps intentionally created. *Le Matin*, a Paris journal, misquoted a witness before the committee to say that the postmaster general and the attorney general bought MWT shares before the Imperial Wireless Network negotiations began and sold them at a considerable profit after the GPO signed. This time Samuel and Rufus Isaacs could not be dissuaded from initiating a libel suit. The defendant paper, however, in the judicial proceeding asked them to describe all interests they had had in any Marconi company. The postmaster general had never had any such holdings, but the question compelled Rufus Isaacs to disclose the American Marconi share transactions. He acknowledged that he had purchased ten thousand shares in the subsidiary and resold a thousand each to the chancellor and the whip.

In less contentious times, this confession might have dispelled the controversy. American Marconi received no benefit from its parent's contract. Instead of removing suspicions of corruption, however, the revelation raised cries of outrage. The three Liberal ministers had deceived Parliament. The officials' prior blanket denial that they owned MWT stock was a deliberate attempt to mislead the legislative body. Lord Murray did nothing for appearances by resigning as whip and removing himself to South America. All the old rumors resurfaced.

Despite the salacious sideshows, the Parker Committee at the end of April completed its technical review. It concluded without doubt that only MWT had the capacity to fulfill the demands of the Imperial Wireless Network.

On May 28, 1913, the Select Committee issued majority and minority draft reports. The majority Liberal report could see no corruption touching the Imperial Wireless Network contract. It struck out at those who levied accusations without foundation as committing "a slander of a particularly vile character, which could not be too strongly condemned." The minority found the Liberal ministers guilty of serious impropriety in speculating in American Marconi shares while its parent negotiated with the government and in misleading Parliament about their share ownership—"a grave error of judgment and wanting in frankness and respect for the House of Commons." Debate on the two committee reports opened in the full House in June. At the outset, Lloyd George and Rufus Isaacs apologized while maintaining they had done no wrong. The Liberal Party majority upheld the majority report by 346 to 268 and ratified the contract.

On July 31, the government and MWT signed the Imperial Wireless Network agreement.

The London *Chronicle* commented on the result:

> Some of the meaner critics attacked Mr. Marconi as a "foreigner," and more belittled his genius or derided his invention. That his mother is an Irish lady, that he loves British institutions, speaks English like a native, and is married to an Irish lady are facts which do not count with malicious critics who emphasize the "Guglielmo" in his name. And yet Marconi has been a purer British patriot than all his critics combined.
>
> It is time that this country wiped away the stain that has been put upon him and gave to the discoverer of an invention that has not only revolutionized the fabric of society, established a new and cheaper means of communication, saved much valuable property and hundreds of lives, the honor that is due him. It would be only just that the nation should do so, even if his inventions were superseded tomorrow.(FN 7)

Marconi and the company had been vindicated. The board paid no price for the risk it took in initiating construction before the signing. Instead, its acting upon its convictions avoided a year's delay. The personal anger and internal anguish from the slurs and adverse publicity abated, but scars remained. In the view of Marconi's oldest child and biographer, "To the end of his life Father was racked with anger at the abuse of his name. It seemed a denial of everything he had accomplished, an intolerable injustice."(FN 8) There was, however, at least some public understanding of the injustice.

Marconi

American Marconi reported its financial condition for its fiscal year that ended January 31, 1913. It had exploded in size to become a $10 million corporation. Its $9,866,443 in assets included $6 million cash and liquid investments. Indebtedness and reserves together were a relatively miniscule $250,000. Operation of land and shore stations and sale of apparatus produced profit of $170,694. The investment portfolio earned another $161,548. The unusually strong balance sheet and income statement resulted from the stock sale the prior April 1912 and the first nine months' combined operation of the subsidiary and United Wireless.

American Marconi had an exciting future before it. As the corporation eagerly pointed out in its annual report, it dominated the North American continental wireless market. It controlled "all the coast stations of importance on the Atlantic and Pacific coasts, besides practically the whole of the American Mercantile Marine at present fitted with wireless installations." Two splendid opportunities promised increased profits. Its officers were already deeply immersed in the first. Hard-nosed negotiations, taking full advantage of American Marconi's monopoly position, were attempting to reconstitute the "inequitable terms" of United Wireless's contracts. The myriad of unprofitable commitments to which the acquired competitor had agreed to win new customers was being re-priced to make money. The second, even more dramatic prospect appeared in an American Marconi announcement. Like its parent, it too intended to build an international wireless network. In the initial stage, the long-distance transmission would leap from California to Hawaii, then to Japan. The two systems, the parent's and the subsidiary's, would tie into each other, complementing and strengthening each other. The Americans had two advantages not possessed by the British. No overarching governmental approval was required, and the project could be funded out of internal funds already on hand.

The world knew and acknowledged Marconi as a preeminent scientist, inventor, and businessman. He had led the world—not alone, of course—into a new technology. It advanced communication among continents and islands and between ships and ship and shore. Through the company, he organized and effected the first of the multitude of vast, revolutionary, electronic wireless advances that have followed. He and MWT unleashed and controlled the power of electromagnetic transmission through the air. What he started continues today in ever-widening circles with profound significance for mankind.(FN 9)

Marconi companies girdled the globe, without governmental or private peer. They monopolized the shorelines and ships of Europe and the United States, through which flowed the bulk of the world's maritime activity. Except in limited geographical markets, no rival bridled MWT's maritime ship and shore power. With the North Atlantic, Italian, and Spanish long-distance systems in operation, and with the construction of similar programs in Australia, Norway, and Portugal and the building of the British Imperial Network and the U.S. international long-distance stations just a question of time, Marconi airborne messaging would be the sole comprehensive worldwide wireless service. Only underwater cable, with its enormous capital and maintenance costs and rigid route structures, exerted any competitive restraint on the company. Had the company and its subsidiaries been left on their own as an independent, privately owned organization, to develop the new technology in its many parts, MWT could have been not only the world's largest communication enterprise, but perhaps one of the world's largest corporations.

Marconi himself enjoyed enormous stature. His reputation and integrity were untarnished. They remained unblemished even after the relentless, hostile focus of press, Parliament, and commercial and scientific foes during the course of the "Marconi Scandal." Guglielmo and Beatrice moved in the highest social circles. He had a driving ego, but he did not hold grandiose illusions of himself. He did not lose sight of his lifetime goal to develop long-distance wireless communication. He was loyal to his native government, but he did not abandon his company or his service to Great Britain. He did not exploit his reputation and MWT's position to branch out into other industries or to aggrandize himself or his family or his favorites.

At age thirty-nine, Marconi had covered incredible ground in the nearly twenty years following the nineteen-year-old's inspiration at Biellese and in the decade plus since the bitter, cold days in which the twenty-seven-year-old at St. John's clung desperately to his dreams.

The death of Lady Inchiquin in 1913 upset both her daughter and Guglielmo, who had grown very fond of his mother-in-law. Humor too rarely graced the couple's life. The culminating pressures of the Select Committee coupled with the loss of his eye, compounded by years of relentless scientific and business activity and anxiety, evoked in Marconi periods of bitterness and irritability. His jealousy never lessened, separating and dividing the couple, depriving Bea of her friends who one by one dropped by the wayside. It affected his relationship with his own close acquaintances. Solari, Pippo, Marchese Imperiali, Italian ambassador to London, Prince Gino Potenziaru, and Godfrey and Rufus Isaacs were all fond of Bea. She was attractive. They enjoyed being in her presence and were animated by her high spirits and responsiveness to their attentiveness. They too distanced themselves from the couple in reaction to Marconi's displeasure with the attention they paid to Bea.

In the fall, Bea could stand it no longer. She needed a change and announced she would assume her duties as lady-in-waiting for Queen Elena of Italy. In October 1913, Bea, Degna, and Giulio moved into the Hotel Regina in Rome across the street from Palazzo Margherita, the queen mother's palace. Lilah went as well. She lived in a family pension recommended by Solari at 42 Via Sicilia and studied painting under Onirato Carlandi. Degna and Giulio attended the Montessori school. Marconi remained in London. The couple had separated.

Degna described the sad condition into which Beatrice and Guglielmo had allowed their marriage to fall:

> If jealousy were justified, it was Mother who had every right to be jealous. This theatre world was no part of her world, neither as to its morals, which she knew were deplorable, nor its manners, which could hardly conform with her upper-class conventions. At a time when a single standard of behavior for men and women was inconceivable, her flirtations were limited to come-hither glances from behind a fan. His affairs were doubtless outrageous, but she was bound to accept them as long as she remained married.
>
> Undoubtedly Mother found Father's friends bizarre but her small circle of intimates did not appeal to him, either. As Aunt Lilah described them, they "had not much brains and were not worth a rap." One reason why Father enjoyed his theatrical friendships was that they were so frankly superficial they did not impinge on his inner

heart. At the same time he longed for the warm, human love of which he believed his wife capable but which he never wholly won from her. In her way she failed him because she was incapable of expressing her feelings. The gap between them widened.(FN 10)

On his fortieth birthday in April 1914, Marconi became eligible to be appointed a *senatore*, a life member of the Italian Upper Legislative Chamber. The Chamber itself had the authority to confer the position in recognition of accomplishments of a high order in the arts, literature, or science. Although it normally awarded membership at a much older age, it acted at its earliest opportunity to recognize the world-famous innovator. Marconi came to Rome to receive the honor. He thereafter could be called Senatore Marconi. The Senate had legislative powers. Marconi had earned the position for scientific achievement. Through no desire of his own, he had become a legislator and a politician. He thought of himself as neither.

After the ceremony, he visited Bea. They had not seen each other for six months. For the sake of the children, they decided to end their separation. Together, the family of four returned to Eaglehurst.

On Sunday, June 28, 1914, Archduke Francis Ferdinand, heir to the emperor of Austria-Hungary, in connection with Austrian military reviews, rode with his wife in an open car into Sarajevo, Bosnia's provincial capital. The archduke had responded to Serbian threats to Austria by advocating that Slavs be absorbed into the Austro-Hungarian Empire. Unwittingly, the day selected for his appearance fell on the Serbian national holiday. A vague warning delivered by the Serbian ambassador to the Austro-Hungarian minister of finance had not been forwarded to the archduke's party. In fact, along the parade route to the city hall, three armed youths, trained by the Black Hand, waited. As the car drove slowly by, one threw a bomb. It missed the royal couple, wounding an aide instead. The procession sped off. The failed killers escaped in the confusion. At city hall, the archduke conducted scheduled formalities. The previously determined departure route was altered to avoid any further planned attempts on his life, but he remained in the open car and insisted on visiting his wounded aide in the hospital. The chauffer misunderstood the new direction. He started off on a street that led away from the hospital. The archduke ordered the automobile turned around. With incredible bad luck, the driver pulled up to reverse direction in front of the tavern where one of the would-be assassins, Gavrilo Princep, a nineteen-year-old Bosnian, had sought refuge. Princep was despondent over the miss. He did not know when he would have another chance at Ferdinand. At the moment the car stopped, Princep decided to leave the pub. As he walked out the door, there before his eyes sat the archduke. The young Slav reached for his pistol and shot Francis Ferdinand and his wife to death.

The world reacted with shock and distress. The general consensus held the Serbs responsible. Many Austrians felt their empire could no longer act indecisively in the Balkans. The assassination presented an excuse to deal definitively with Serbia.

In July, George V invited Marconi to Buckingham Palace. The king personally presented the Irish-Italian the GCVO, the Victorian Order. It was an extraordinary acknowledgment of what he had contributed to Britain. It recognized his role in saving British lives on the *Titanic*. Perhaps it was intended to atone for what the inventor/industrialist had suffered in the course of the "Marconi Scandal." Certainly it could not have been a greater affirmation of his good standing in the United Kingdom. The honor entitled him to be called "Sir Marconi." Consistent with his deep Italian patriotism, however, he asked that if he were to be addressed by a title in the future, that it be "Senatore Marconi."

Tuesday, July 28, 1918, a month after the assassination of Francis Ferdinand, Austria-Hungary declared war on Serbia. Government officials throughout Europe worried about Russia's reaction. It had promised to come to Serbia's defense in the event of an attack.

That night, Senatore and Mrs. Marconi in their small launch motored from Eaglehurst out of the Southampton Waterway into the Solent to HMS *Lion*. The fleet had anchored off Spithead after concluding the annual summer maneuvers in which in earlier years Marconi had participated. They dined aboard the flagship with Admiral Beatty.

The next morning, Wednesday, July 29, when the Marconis, back home at Eaglehurst, awoke and looked out to sea, there was no sign of the fleet. It had been ordered to battle positions. In the afternoon, Great Britain warned it would not be neutral if war began.

The German chief of staff observed that realistically Austria, with which Germany was allied, could not mobilize only against Serbia. Russia would most likely honor its commitment to the Serbs and intervene. Therefore, Austria must prepare for Russia as well as Serbia. Russia would strike both Germany and Austria-Hungary because of their alliance. Therefore, Germany should mobilize at once before Russia won a head start. Knowledgeable politicians predicted that if the Germans and Russians fought, France would attempt to recapture the provinces of Alsace and Lorraine that it had lost earlier to Germany. Italy's intentions were unclear. It itched for territorial gains. Italy had previously formed a triple alliance with Austria and Germany, but it had not yet renewed its membership. It was negotiating with both sides to secure the maximum advantage for itself.

Russia declared a "Period Preparatory to War," a state of readiness short of full mobilization. The step set off a cataclysmic chain reaction. It forced all the European countries to consider whether to implement their war strategies. For a generation, England and the continental nations had negotiated their way through crisis after crisis. They had settled animosities and ambitions with threats of force followed by territorial settlements. But the possibility of localizing and buying off this Austrian-Serbian conflict faded with incredible rapidity.

The German chief of staff believed a multi-country, two-front war unavoidable. He urged Germany to implement the strategy he had outlined: Roll through Belgium and knock out France. Then turn on Russia. The monstrous country was expected to require more time than France to mobilize. Speed became paramount.

A delegation of MWT senior engineers was visiting Berlin. They had been invited to discuss wireless communication and observe Telefunken's research and manufacturing facilities. They were generously entertained. Relationships were courteous and friendly. At the end of the tour, their hosts took them to Nauen. The party inspected the two-hundred-kilowatt, high-frequency alternators and enormous antennas that had just been installed. The English suspected these machines generated the greatest range of any station in the world. The moment the visitors left for the night boat back to England, the German military closed down all commercial operation and took over the station.

Marconi

On Thursday, July 30, Russian generals recommended full mobilization against Austria and Germany to protect their country in the event of war. The government agreed and ordered the top level of preparation for war.

The French manned their frontier defenses, particularly in Alsace and Lorraine.

The British Admiralty by wireless ordered the full Guard Fleet to battle stations and alerted its ships worldwide.

Friday, July 31, Austria-Hungary, responded to Russia's new status. It mobilized against Russia as well as Serbia. Germany declared a "State of Danger of War." It delivered two ultimatums: It threatened Moscow that Germany would mobilize unless Russia suspended every war measure against Austria-Hungary by Saturday afternoon. The Germans also demanded of Paris whether France would remain neutral in a German-Russian war.

The Paris Bourse and the St. Petersburg stock exchanges closed. The New York Stock Exchange followed.

Saturday, August 1, 1914, at 3:45 p.m., France ordered general mobilization. At 5:00 p.m., Germany ordered mobilization. At 6:00 p.m., the German ambassador in Moscow asked the Russians three times if they would meet Germany's demands. Each time the answer was no. The ambassador thereupon delivered to the Russian government Germany's declaration of war.

On Sunday, August 2, the United Kingdom forbade the use of wireless to all ships other than British vessels while in its waters. The government assumed control of all wireless messages in its territory. At 7:00 p.m., the German ambassador in Belgium delivered a demand that German troops be permitted to pass through Belgium.

Monday, August 3, Belgium rejected Germany's demand. Germany declared war on France.

Britain shut down all amateur wireless stations and announced its intention to impound their equipment. The Admiralty prohibited wireless on all merchant ships. Nauen warned German shipping to head immediately for German ports.

Tuesday, August 4, Germany invaded Belgium. Great Britain declared war on Germany.

Poldhu broadcast the declaration of war and carried messages to the fleet to commence hostilities against Germany.

Wednesday, August 5, the British placed Marconi, who had just received the GCVO from the king of England, under house arrest at Eaglehurst.

CHAPTER 17

World War I

Immediately upon the outbreak of hostilities, Great Britain, well aware of wireless's military significance, commandeered key company operations. The seizures dramatically illustrated the past twelve years' developments. Not until long after fighting commenced in the Boer War did the British army and navy utilize airborne signaling. The services then engaged only a few dozen sets and deployed them in a manner MWT felt failed to maximize their usefulness.

With wartime powers, the GPO took control of Carnarvon. The Admiralty shut down Clifden–Glace Bay commercial traffic. It changed the Irish station's wavelength to one better suited to transmit naval messages. At Hall Street's research center, operations were swiftly redirected to intercept German transmissions. The War Office assigned H. J. Round to Intelligence to develop directional finding stations for the French front lines. The entire Brooklands, Surrey, experimental station and staff were seconded to the Royal Flying Corps. Marconi factory works fell under military jurisdiction. A field site was designated as a separate department dedicated to army battlefield requirements. Orders for naval transmitters and receivers flooded the company.

The Royal Navy summoned Marconi merchant ship operators to duty. Arriving in port, they found themselves immediately put onto naval ships. The government requested MWT to increase its training facilities for military and cargo fleet operators and sent the head of its training school at Broomfield near Chelmsford to the War Office. There he was to establish a major school at the Crystal Palace for officers and engineers of all the allies, with emphasis on work in the field.

The conflict removed any doubts about the importance of the Imperial Wireless Network. Completion of the high-power facility at Abu Zaabal in Egypt became a top priority. Detailed construction drawings for the power plant and transmitting floor were converted into telegraphic messages to accelerate delivery of the plans to the site. The company collected parts throughout England for the steam generator to support the hundred-kilowatt transmitter. Plans to upgrade shorter range shore installations were authorized to proceed at once.

The UK raced to destroy the enemy's underwater cable system and in little time had severed critical overseas lines. Only the long-distance wireless radiated by Nauen's extraordinary power provided rapid communication to Germany's foreign colonies. Britain attacked the far-flung network of receivers. The Dar-es-Salaam site fell on August 9. Three days later, halfway across the world in the South Pacific, the station at Yap in the Carolinas was destroyed. British invaders from the Gold Coast and French forces from Dahomey marched into Togo. The Germans blew up the installation at Kamina to avoid its surrender. New Zealanders supported by Australian, British, and French warships captured Western Samoa. The Samoan operators succumbed to the Royal Australian Navy on August 29. In September, German New Guinea surrendered to the Australians, giving up the Herbertshire facility on the island of New Pommern. During the fall, Cameroon was knocked out, and the Japanese seized Kiauchau. The last principal site at Windhock, German East Africa, held out until May 1915.

The United Kingdom began the war with twenty-nine capital ships and thirteen more under construction. Its opponent had eighteen major vessels and nine in the yards. Initially, neither wanted a full face-to-face confrontation. The ocean empire needed to preserve its fleet to protect its trade routes. With submarines and mines, the continental force hoped to whittle away at the superior numbers. In September, a lone U-boat in one hour destroyed three cruisers. In October, a torpedo sent down a fourth cruiser, the *Hawke,* and a mine laid off the Irish coast sank a battleship, *Audacious,* killing the first of 348 Marconi wireless operators to die during the war.

Marconi was astonished by his house arrest at Eaglehurst. The king had just personally awarded him one of Britain's most prestigious awards. He had never been disloyal to England. Italy had remained neutral. Under mandate of the Aliens Restriction Act, Home Office refused Marconi a pass to travel about the country, even on government-related business. The office claimed that none of the act's exemptions applied to the Irish-Italian.

Not until January 1915 was Marconi free to leave Fawley. He was then permitted to go to Rome. He left at once, while Bea stayed behind at Eaglehurst. On his arrival, he took his seat in the Italian Senate for the first time since his selection the prior April. One of his first tasks was to rescue Lilah. She had been in Rome and unable to return to England. He arranged through the British ambassador for her to travel with a diplomatic courier. With a touch of his former dry humor, he admonished her as she parted not to blame him if she were held up in Paris and had to eat rats in the deserted city. He had done all he could for her.

In the six months since August, Italy had not joined the struggle. A growing minority of Italians, led by Prime Minister Antonio Salandra and his foreign minister and supported by the king, favored entering the war. They considered it undignified for a great nation to be absent from the struggle raging around the world. More practically, they worried that once one side achieved a clear superiority, the Italian bargaining opportunity would pass. Rejoining the Triple Alliance, Italy could wrest Tunis from France and Corsica, Malta, and Nice as well. With the Triple Entente, however, Italy could restore its natural alpine boundary and broaden its Adriatic position.

Salandra was a Nationalist. A flame of idealism inspired him. It burned with ambition for Italy. The fire was born out of patriotism and love of country. He succeeded Giovanni Giolitti, a Liberal, who had been prime minister for most of the period from 1900 to 1914. Giolitti had been a master at bringing diverse parties into his tent and absorbing assertive political groups by including them in the government.

In February 1915, a secret courier delivered to Britain's Prime Minister Grey a memorandum indicating Italy's willingness to consider joining the Entente. The price included cash compensation, a share of redistributed German colonies, enough of the Dalmatian Islands to assure control over the Adriatic, pieces of Turkey's foreign holdings, and expansion of the peninsula's borders to the Alps and Trieste.

That same month Germany proclaimed the waters around Great Britain and Ireland a war zone. It warned the seas would be mined and disclaimed all responsibility for what might happen to neutral vessels that ventured into the area. To demonstrate its meaning, the German navy immediately sank two American ships and torpedoed a Norwegian vessel.

In March, Russian victories in the Carpathians weakened Salandra's negotiating position with the Entente. Under pressure from the Russians acting on behalf of the Slavs, he yielded to Croatian/Serbian demands for an outlet on the Adriatic Croatian coast held by Hungary, namely the port city of Fiume (Rijeka) just south of Trieste, even though it contained an Italian population.

Throughout this period, Italy had continued to bargain with the Triple Alliance. In April, it consented to giving up its neutrality in favor of the Alliance in exchange for Tyrol, Trieste, and Isteria.

Britain lifted all travel restrictions on Marconi. The Italian Parliament adjourned. Despite the German threat, Marconi returned to England. In London, on April 13, he received the Albert Medal of the Royal Society of Arts in recognition of his contributions to England. The award served as an apology for the imposition of the Alien Restrictions Act on his movements. Perhaps it also had a diplomatic purpose, to help attract Italy to the Entente.

Lilah had become engaged to Coulson Fellowes, eldest son of Lord de Ramsay. Bea and Guglielmo attended the small war-time wedding. Coly, as Coulson was affectionately called by Lilah, left for France and the front line trenches immediately afterwards.

Again ignoring the danger, Marconi embarked on the *Lusitania* for New York to conduct company business. Off the Fastnet Rock by Cape Clear, the crew sighted a U-boat periscope. No torpedo, however, was spotted, and no attack followed. The captain speculated to Marconi that the *Lusitania*'s twenty-two-knot speed might have discouraged the submarine.

While Marconi sailed, Salandra, despite the pact just made with the Alliance, agreed to terms with the Entente. On April 26, he signed the secret Treaty of London. It provided the Italians would begin fighting in one month. Marconi's native land was now simultaneously committed to both the Triple Alliance and the Triple Entente.

The purpose of Marconi's visit that merited the risk taken in crossing the Atlantic was to testify in a suit brought against American Marconi by the Atlantic Communication Company, Telefunken's U.S. subsidiary. The suit challenged the validity of Marconi's first patent.

Wireless rights in the United States were immersed in a bog of lawsuits, cross licenses, and vitriolic claims. Under Isaacs' aggressive program to protect the company's intellectual property, which included Professor Fleming's developments and the patent acquired from Edison, American Marconi had initiated actions against de Forest and the U.S. Navy as well as United Wireless. De Forest had licensed AT&T and American Marconi to use his audion, but he insisted he had retained rights of use. Edwin Armstrong asserted that he had patented improvements to the audion. The conflicts slowed product advancement.

Tesla had at last abandoned any hope of finding financing to salvage his World Communication Tower at Wardenclyffe. Instead, he decided to make money off his wireless ideas by bringing lawsuits for infringement and by becoming a consultant to others. Telefunken, through Atlantic Communication, was operating a transatlantic transmitter at Sayville near Wardenclyffe. Because the British had destroyed Germany's undersea cables, Telefunken wanted to increase Sayville's power to reach Germany directly. Slaby, one of Telefunken's founders, had a very high regard for Tesla and recommended him to Atlantic Communication. Tesla agreed to help using his Wardenclyffe ideas.

Atlantic Communication and Tesla also decided to sue American Marconi on the grounds that Tesla and Telefunken had priority over Marconi's patents. Tesla had already succeeded in establishing priority in France. The board and Marconi took the proceedings very seriously.

While in New York, Marconi visited Ernst F. V. Alexanderson at General Electric. Alexanderson had continued to enhance his huge, high-frequency alternator that had broadcast Fessenden's Christmas Eve music from Brant Rock far out into the ocean. Marconi was convinced that the machine's power and reliability vastly exceeded any other development in its field. If he were to obtain exclusive rights to the Scandinavian's creation for MWT, the company could preclude everyone else from competing meaningfully with the Marconi organizations in long-distance transmission. The scientist/inventor/businessman opened negotiations with GE's general counsel, Owen D. Young. The lawyer wanted full control of manufacturing. Marconi insisted on sole rights of use in exchange for a large order.

American Marconi's profit from operations in 1914 fell to $121,000 from $170,000 in 1913. North Atlantic mercantile and passenger traffic, fearing German submarines, declined. The conversion of United Wireless service and equipment rental agreements to more profitable terms slowed as customers insisted the legally binding contracts be honored. The ambitious long-distance network, despite successes, suffered from consequences of the European war. The transpacific link opened between San Francisco and Honolulu on September 24. Alaskan prospects looked bright. But construction of high-power duplex receiving and transmitting installations at Belmar and New Brunswick, New Jersey, for transatlantic exchanges with Carnarvon and Towyn in Wales was stalled when Great Britain took over the Welsh sites. Similarly, uncertainties caused by the conflict halted completion of a potent transmitter and receiver at Marion and Chatham, Massachusetts, intended for communication with Norway.

David Sarnoff, the wireless operator at the Wanamaker listening post following the *Titanic* catastrophe, had risen steadily in American Marconi ranks. He arrived in the United States in 1900 at age nine from Minsk, Russia. As a teenager, he worked hard to help support his family. In 1906, he left school to become a telegraph messenger boy. He then hired on as office boy in American Marconi's Manhattan office. He met Marconi and could hardly contain his excitement. He had become a highly proficient wireless operator by the time of his Wanamaker assignment. At the end of 1912, American Marconi named him radio inspector for all Marconi-equipped ships in New York Harbor and a few months later chief inspector for the whole country.

When Isaacs joined MWT, he concluded New York required local rather than British management. He hired Edward J. Nally, general manager of the Postal Telegraph Company, to run the U.S. operation. Nally also had experience with international messaging and submarine cables. In 1914, Nally appointed Sarnoff to the position of contract manager. Sarnoff became deeply involved in upgrading United Wireless's arrangements and negotiating new relationships. He interacted between

Frederick M. Sammis, chief engineer, whose department built and maintained the wireless sets, and George de Sousa, traffic manager, responsible for message operations. Sarnoff's ceaseless efforts and exposure to all facets of the business, both technical and commercial, made him highly knowledgeable. He asserted ideas about development and direction of airborne communication within the company and in industry circles. On his own initiative, he sent his memoranda to Nally and even Isaacs and Marconi. He advocated equipment improvement and acquisition of licenses to use other manufacturers' more advanced apparatus. In one document he asked fifteen pointed questions of the technical committee created by Nally to assess the state of Marconi hardware and technology. In the fall of 1914, Sarnoff, now twenty-three, presented a paper to the Institute of Radio Engineers. The paper analyzed all the rules, procedures, and problems involved in routing international and national messages between ship and shore, including division of tolls, rate structures per word or message, and the effect of different equipment on rates of transmission.

While Marconi remained in New York attending to business and preparing for the Atlantic Communication litigation, the *Lusitania* returned to England from New York, this time with Marconi not on board. On May 7, at 2:00 p.m., only ten miles off the Irish coast, the thirty-thousand-ton ship carrying 1,251 passengers and 650 crew crossed the path of a U-boat. The enemy fired twice. Despite the liner's speed, one torpedo struck it forward and the other aft. The *Lusitania* listed immediately. The launching mechanics for half of the lifeboats jammed. The ship sank quickly. Close to 1,200 people died, including 124 Americans. The Germans claimed the *Lusitania* carried munitions for England. In fact she did.

Marconi and Pupin testified on behalf of American Marconi in the Atlantic Communication litigation. Pupin said it was Marconi's genius that gave the idea to the world, and he taught the world how to build a telegraphic practice based on this idea. Tesla and John Stone Stone, one of America's earliest wireless inventors, took the stand for the German subsidiary. Stone said that Marconi stressed electric radiation through the air, but Tesla's earlier concept of radiation through the earth was more serviceable.

On May 20, Marconi was advised that Italy had joined the Triple Entente and was about to enter the war. He announced that he must withdraw from the lawsuit and return to Europe to serve his country. He addressed presiding Judge Van Vechten Veeder:

> Your Honor, after consultation with the Italian authorities here, I have decided to return to Italy at once. While war between Italy and her foes has not yet been declared, it seems to be only a matter of a few hours. I shall leave for Italy tomorrow and I am therefore impelled to cease my attendance here.(FN 1)

Judge Veeder stepped down from the bench to shake the inventor's hand. A German expert who had come from Belgium to testify said that he and Marconi could part as friends as the Triple Alliance had not yet been formally dissolved. The trial adjourned.

On May 22, 1915, Marconi's native land ordered general mobilization and declared war on Austria but not Germany. Although the southern nation initiated the new relationship, its northern neighbor struck first. Austria bombed arsenals at Venice. It seized Trieste and Fiume on the eastern Adriatic coast. Its troops swarmed across Italy's northeast border.

Marconi left New York for London on the *St. Paul*. Rumors circulated among the passengers that a German sub might try to halt the ship and send sailors aboard to capture Marconi. The *New York Tribune* printed a dispatch from London about the voyage:

> As we approached the war zone rather elaborate precautions were taken to safeguard Mr. Marconi. His name was not on either the regular passenger list or the purser's list. There was a general tacit agreement among the passengers that if the *St. Paul* was stopped by a submarine and Mr. Marconi's person demanded we would "lie like gentlemen."
>
> Meanwhile Mr. Marconi removed all labels from his luggage, gave his private papers into my care and got into clothes suitable for slipping into a hiding place somewhere down in the bowels of the ship next to the keel, where the chief engineer said the captain himself would be unable to find him.

We had a concert that night at which Mr. Marconi was to preside. The programs were inadvertently printed with his name as chairman. The captain ordered all programs destroyed. When the concert began the historian, Mr. Trevelyan, took the chair saying, "We were to have had the pleasure of having Mr. Marconi preside, but unfortunately he is not on board.(FN 2)

After arriving safely in London, Marconi went on to Italy, where he was appointed to the Army General Staff as a lieutenant in the engineers in charge of the organization of the army's wireless service. One of his duties was to inspect mobile sets at the front. The government also appointed the former naval cadet to the Naval Electrical Equipment Committee to assure that the navy received the latest technology. Marconi consulted on the Coltano to St. Petersburg wireless service being established. No telegraph connection existed between the two new allies.

The Italians were ill prepared for war.

In July, Marconi traveled to England on behalf of Italy to procure wireless equipment and war stores. In addition, the government asked him to seek lower shipping charges on coal. Ninety percent of Italy's coal came from Britain. Freight charges for the passage through submarine infested waters had escalated.

In December, Marconi, accompanying General Cordona of Italy, attended a meeting of the allied commanders at Marshall Joffre's headquarters in France. Wireless application to battle needs had become increasingly sophisticated. The British Expeditionary Force had landed in France with one lorry equipped with a receiver and transmitter. By the Battle of the Marne, they had ten mobile units. A relay system began with a power buzzer at the front line that fed to a 50-watt mobile spark that transmitted to a 120-watt spark. Each one was set further behind the trenches. The 120 transmitted to a light 1.5 KW motor set that could send messages the rest of the way to headquarters. Ultimately, the British Army organized wireless into a separate unit, the Wireless Signal Company.

The first Royal Flying Corp unit flown to France had one airborne spark transmitter and one ground receiver. Within a month came the first success. A pilot sent the coordinates of a German target to a British artillery battery. The Brooklands experimental station coupled a telephone set to a continuous wave transmitter mounted in an airplane trailing a 250-foot antenna and achieved voice air-to-ground communication.

The Admiralty, as well as the land forces, recognized how to apply the directional finding equipment that Round had developed just before the war's outbreak. It installed a network along the British coasts to eavesdrop on enemy submarine, Zeppelin, and battleship exchanges. The foe was unaware that Round's valve amplifiers were far more sophisticated than its own. It used very short range wireless in its own water to avoid interception. It had no idea that Round's finders on the English Channel regularly picked up its signals. Throughout the war, his invention provided British intelligence a steady flow of information. For his contribution, he was awarded the Military Cross. He refused to accept it because the medal was created to recognize gallantry in battle. The government persisted and delivered the honor by mail.

In the United States, which at the time of Marconi's return to London and Italy had not entered the war, Sarnoff at American Marconi closely studied radiotelephony developments. His employer experimentally refitted the Wanamaker transmitter for phonograph music. The young immigrant sailed out of Manhattan's harbor with receiving equipment aboard the SS *Antilles*. Sixty miles from the store, he put on earphones and could listen to the recorded sound. He shared his hearing pieces with other passengers and saw they were as excited as he. With great interest, he noted that programs broadcast in New York City by Dr. Alfred Goldsmith, an electrical engineering professor, were avidly received on crystal sets by an audience of hams situated on every side of the transmitter and some as far as 750 miles away.

Wireless, if not beamed or directed towards a particular point, spread out in all directions. Experiments in radio telephony, like Dr. Goldsmith's that attempted to reach as many people as possible, were nondirected. The sound was allowed to radiate freely. The words broadcasting and radio, while still often used interchangeably with the word wireless, more and more frequently meant specifically sound transmissions intended for multiple listeners.

Mulling over his observations, Sarnoff devised a brilliant and novel business plan unlike anything in existence at the time. Late in 1915, he wrote a memorandum to Nally:

I have in mind a plan of development which would make radio a "household utility" in the same sense as the piano or phonograph. The idea is to bring music into the home by wireless.

While this has been tried in the past by wires, it has been a failure because wires do not lend themselves to this scheme. With radio, however, it would be entirely feasible.

For example, a radio telephone transmitter having a range of 25 to 50 miles can be installed at a fixed point where the instrumental or vocal music or both are produced. The problem of transmitting music has already been solved in principle and therefore all the receivers attuned to the transmitting wavelength should be capable of receiving such music. The receiver can be designed in the form of a simple "Radio Music Box" and arranged for several different wave lengths, which should be changeable with the throwing of a single switch or pressing of a single button.

The "Radio Music Box" can be supplied with amplifying tubes and a loudspeaking telephone, all of which can be neatly mounted in one box. The box can be placed on a table in the parlor or living room, the switch set accordingly and the music received. There should be no difficulty in receiving music perfectly when transmitted within a radius of 25 miles.

Within such a radius there reside hundreds of thousands of families; and as all can simultaneously receive from a single transmitter, there should be no question of obtaining sufficiently loud signals to make the performance enjoyable. The power of the transmitter can be made 5 K.W., if necessary, to cover even a short radius of 25 to 50 miles; thereby giving extra loud signals in the home if desired. The use of head telephones would be obviated by this method. The development of a small loop antenna to go with each "Radio Music Box" would likewise solve the antennae problem.

The same principle can be extended to numerous other fields as, for example, receiving lectures at home which can be made perfectly audible; also events of national importance can be simultaneously announced and received. Baseball scores can be transmitted in the air by the use of one set installed at the Polo Grounds. The same would be true of other cities. This proposition would be especially interesting to farmers and others in outlying districts removed from cities. By the purchase of a "Radio Music Box" they could enjoy concerts, lectures, music, recital, etc. which may be going on in the nearest city within their radius.

While I have indicated a few of the most probable fields of usefulness for such a device, yet there are numerous other fields to which the principle can be extended.

The manufacture of the "Radio Music Box" including antenna, in large quantities, would make possible their sale at a moderate figure of perhaps $75 per outfit. The main revenue would be derived from the sale of "Radio Music Boxes" which if manufactured in quantities of 100,000 or so could yield a handsome profit when sold at the price mentioned above.

Secondary sources of revenue would be from the sale of transmitters and from increased advertising and circulation of the *Wireless Age*.

The company would have to undertake the arrangements, I am sure, for music recitals, lectures, etc. which arrangements can be satisfactorily worked out.

It is not possible to estimate the total amount of business obtainable with this plan until it has been developed and actually tried out; but there are about 15,000,000 families in the United States alone, and if only one million or seven percent of the total families thought well of the idea it would, at the figure mentioned, mean a gross business of about $75,000,000 which should yield considerable revenue.

Aside from the profit to be derived from this proposition the possibilities for advertising for the company are tremendous, for its name would ultimately receive national and universal attention.(FN 3)

American Marconi suffered only a small net decrease in message traffic receipts in 1915. The heavy drop caused by reduced European shipping was almost completely offset by increased Alaskan activity, replacement of expiring United Wireless contracts with agreements with more favorable terms, and new customers. Standard Oil of New Jersey equipped thirty ships, while Inland Navigation Company began installations on thirty-six Mississippi River barges. Ambitious cost-cutting resulted in increased profit for the year.

But a specter overhung the results. American Marconi worried that it was controlled by MWT, a foreign corporation. The strategic significance to the United States of possessing long-distance wireless was attracting growing attention. To minimize the company's position as majority stockowner, the subsidiary in its annual report stressed that of its 23,027 shareholders, 21,664 were U.S. residents. In an effort to generate good will for Marconi and the dominant Brits, a fifteen-page attachment listed all the marine accidents since SSRF *Matthews* rammed the East Goodwin Lightship in March 1899 in which wireless helped save lives.

U.S. officials were not persuaded. The navy was preparing for combat. Secretary of the Navy Josephus Daniels proposed that it acquire and operate all coastal stations. The postmaster general, in a recommendation dangerous for wireless, advocated nationalization of telephone and telegraph. American Marconi did not question the administration's need to be in charge of airborne communication in wartime, but argued strenuously against its permanent ownership of the industry.

Daniels was the most zealous advocate of government control. He was a Progressive and outspoken owner and editor of an influential North Carolina newspaper. He had served in the Interior Department. As a member of the Executive Committee of the Democratic Party, he had supported Woodrow Wilson to be the party's presidential candidate in 1912. After winning the election, Wilson appointed William Jennings Bryan, a long-standing Progressive leader, as secretary of state and Daniels to the naval post in recognition of their party's importance to the Democratic victory. Progressives were suspicious of big business and favored federal intervention to accomplish desired goals.

Daniels, an astute political in-fighter, appointed Franklin Delano Roosevelt assistant secretary of the navy. Roosevelt, a Democratic New York State senator, had also favored Wilson's nomination. Franklin carried with him the aura of the Roosevelt name. Theodore, although he had been a Republican president, was deeply involved with the Progressive Party and was still hugely popular. Roosevelt became involved in the litigation brought by American Marconi against the navy. Roosevelt hoped that communications in its files from Tesla at the turn of the century would establish Tesla's priority of invention that could be useful in defeating Marconi's claims.

Upon taking office, Daniels had immediately understood the importance of long-distance wireless to the navy and the United States. He promoted the development of an enormous transmitter, call letters NAA, under navy auspices at Arlington, Virginia. Included in the 1912 Radio Act adopted by Congress in response to the *Titanic* was authority to commandeer wireless facilities in war-time conditions. In 1914 after hostilities broke out in Europe and Britain severed Germany's undersea cables, including its American links, Daniels acted swiftly. The navy seized American Marconi's Siasconset station on Nantucket and wireless at Tuckerton, New Jersey. Tuckerton was equipped with Telefunken apparatus. Daniels had it transferred to Arlington. Siasconset and Tuckerton could be used to reach Germany. Daniels had two purposes. The first was to prevent the transmission of spy information, particularly ship movements. Second, the United States was neutral in the conflict. It continued to maintain diplomatic relations with Germany. Navy operation of the stations permitted Washington to communicate with Germany.

Daniels thought it would be useful to have a naval radio advisory board. He turned the project over to Roosevelt. Edison agreed to act as chair. Fessenden and Pupin were appointed members, but not de Forest, Stone, or Tesla.

In Italy, where Marconi had remained after returning from New York via London, a septic throat forced Marconi into a Genoa hospital in March, 1916. Beginning in late 1914, he, Solari, and the Italian air service had been working on messaging from airplanes. Marconi flew over the Italian front to observe the operation of long guns. Solari in a two-seater biplane transmitted Morse code to a ground receiver. When Solari visited the hospital, he found Marconi's thinking had jumped ahead another step. The scientist was preoccupied with a fundamental decision. Should he shift his research from long waves requiring aerials stretched out in Libyan sand or dangled behind airplanes to short waves that needed only small antenna or metal reflectors? The MWT works in Genoa provided experimental equipment. The recuperating patient and his Italian collaborator conducted their first trials before startled nurses in the hospital's long corridors.

Since Marconi's release from house arrest, he and Bea had seen little of each other. She had remained in England while he executed his military and political duties in Italy and fulfilled company obligations in the United States. When they were together, however, they put their differences aside under the duress of war and managed to be on more amicable terms. One by-product of their closer relationship was Bea's fourth pregnancy. At the start of April 1916, despite German air raids focused on the city, Beatrice left the relative security of Eaglehurst for London to be closer to her doctor and hospital. On April 10, 1916, their third daughter was born, Gioia Jolanda Marconi. As soon as mother and daughter could be safely moved, they were taken back to Fawley.

Sorrow accompanied the time of birth. Eight-year-old Degna was particularly upset by the death of her uncle Desmond, Bea's youngest brother. He had often visited Eaglehurst while in flight training at nearby Calshot and played with his young niece and nephew. He was lost in one of England's first bombing runs, above Zeebrugge. Coly, Lilah's husband, came home to a soldiers' invalid home. He survived only a short time. He was fatally ill from poison gas and overexposure in the trenches.

On the morning of May 30, 1916, Rounds' directional finders on the English side of the Channel noticed prolific signals from a warship tucked away in the German inland harbor of Wilhelmshaven, three hundred miles to the northeast. That afternoon the vessel's bearing changed by a degree. UK intelligence interpolated. The craft had moved seven miles downstream on the Jade River, in all likelihood readying to put to sea. The Admiralty had changed strategy. It had failed to protect its capital ships from devastating mines and submarines. Nor had it succeeded in stopping unpredictable, sudden forays of the enemy into the North Sea. Seemingly at will, the lethal rival destroyed defenseless allied and neutral shipping and slipped back unharmed into secure ports. The British wanted a major encounter to halt and annihilate its opponent. Henry Jackson, once Marconi's competitor and colleague, had risen to the top of his service. As Admiral Sir Henry Jackson, First Sea Lord and professional head of the Royal Navy, he described the events leading to the Battle of Jutland, the main maritime engagement of the war:

> We have heard much about the use of direction finding for minor tactical movements of all arms, but this is a case of a major strategical operation which brought about the historical meeting of the British and German fleets at the Battle of Jutland on 31 May 1916. I was First Sea Lord at the time, and so was responsible for the disposition of the Grand Fleet.
>
> Our wireless direction-finding stations, under Captain Round, kept careful and very intelligent watch on the positions of German ships using wireless, and on 30 May 1916 heard an unusual amount of wireless signals from one of the enemy ships which they located at Wilhelmshaven. This was reported to me, the time was a critical and anxious one in the War, and I also had some reasons for expecting the German fleet might put out to sea during the week. Our fleet was ready at short notice, and had arranged, unless otherwise prevented, to put to sea on the following day for a sweep of the North Sea. But if the German Fleet got to sea first, the chance of our meeting in waters not unfavourable to us was remote; our object was to try to get to sea before or shortly after the Germans, and hitherto we had not succeeded in doing so. Later on in the afternoon it was reported to me that the German ship conducting the wireless traffic had changed her position a few miles to the northward. Evidently she and her consorts had left the basins at Wilhelmshaven and taken up a position in the Jade River, ready to put to sea. This movement decided me to send our Grand Fleet to sea and move towards the German Bight at once and try to meet the German Fleet and bring it to action.(FN 4)

Jackson's decision paid off. His fleet caught its adversary off the Danish coast. The results were hugely disappointing to the Sea Lord and his colleagues. The Royal Navy lost more armament—a battleship, a battlecruiser, four light cruisers, and five destroyers—and twice as many men—6,907. Due to poor British tactics, the Germans escaped encirclement. The British squandered twenty-two precious minutes realigning to advance in formation. Once more the elusive foe made it into Wilhelmshaven. The battle had a salutary effect, however. Mindful of how narrowly they had avoided entrapment, the enemy thereafter rarely ventured out again in force.

At the time of Jutland, Marconi and C. S. Franklin, assisted by the Regia Marina, were at sea conducting short-wave experiments. Franklin had created a spark transmitter that radiated a minute, two-meter wavelength. No other valve generated such a brief wave. Together the collaborators were able to communicate between two battleships six miles apart. The short, high frequency had several advantages in shielding communication from detection. It operated effectively with relatively minor antenna. Its beam path was slender. Radiating less broadly, it reduced the chance of interception. In addition, its messages could be aimed more precisely at the intended receiver.

During these experiments, Marconi noticed that sometimes the wave he transmitted bounced off the other war vessel and came back to his ship. Few others had noted this phenomena. Heinrich Hertz in 1888 recorded his observation that electromagnetic waves were subject to reflection. In 1904, a German engineer, Christian Hulsmeyer, patented in Germany and Great Britain a radio-echo ship collision prevention device he called a "Telemobiloskop." He demonstrated to technical experts for transatlantic shipping companies in Rotterdam Harbor, but nothing came of it. In 1910, Gotthelf Leimbach and Heinrich Lowy filed a patent to use reflecting waves for geological discovery. The patents attracted little attention.

Marconi returned to England in July for MWT's annual meeting. While there, Gioia was christened in a small church in Fawley near Eaglehurst. With the war's duration unclear, Guglielmo and Beatrice decided that to be together they must give up their waterfront property and move to Rome. They booked almost the entire fifth floor of the Hotel Excelsior overlooking Via Veneto. In typical fashion, Marconi carved a laboratory out of the living quarters. They ate in the hotel restaurant. The elder Marconis deplored the lack of privacy. Each mealtime they had to pass through a crush of people in the lobby. The Excelsior was one of the city's major meeting points. Guglielmo did not want to be waylaid by the milling clusters of businessmen and politicians who might want to engage him in conversation or by strangers who might claim to know him. He led his family party of four as rapidly as he could through the throng, navigating or forcing openings in the crowd, looking neither left nor right and doing his best to recognize no one. The two older children and Bea scrambled behind, trying to keep pace. When at last they were seated at their table, Bea would wring her hands in despair at all the people they must have insulted and who must consider her and her husband rude for refusing to say hello.

Otherwise, Beatrice was glad for the change of venue. She was back in an urban center. She had many acquaintances from her time as lady-in-waiting. Rome had the buzz of excitement of a wartime capital, but it was far from the front. Unlike London, it was free of aerial attack. Close by the hotel, Lilia Patami, a friend of Guglielmo, held a salon where many of the country's elite gathered. Guglielmo and Beatrice became friends of novelist, poet, and military activist Gabriele D'Annunzio, Enrico de Nicolia, president of the Chamber of Deputies, Paulo Michetti, the artist under whom Lilah had studied, and Francesco Saverio Nitti, a professor of economics at the University of Naples who had first entered parliament in 1904. Nitti had favored entering the war on the side of the Entente. He was close to the prime minister.

The Italians had contained the Austrians' initial advance. The action settled into trench warfare along an established front with little movement except for the flamboyant D'Annunzio. His literary themes were erotic and dealt with virile conflict, vendettas, incest, and death. His own love affairs were notorious. He was an outspoken Nationalist. He had longed for a war to give Italy an opportunity to change its status as a second-rate power. One of his slogans, "Arm the prow and sail towards the world," became the rallying cry for his fellow patriots. Given authority in all three military services, he engaged in random, freelance raids where and as he pleased by land, sea, and air. He loved the spotlight of publicity. In one of his more daring flying attacks, he like Marconi lost an eye. He regretted only that the Italian government could award no more than three gallantry medals to any one individual. He felt he deserved six.

Benito Mussolini was another well-known Nationalist. In 1912, at age twenty-nine, he had become the editor of *Avanti*, the Italian Socialists' official paper. Two years later, he announced he favored entering the war. The PSI, Partito Socialist Italiano, avowed neutralists, threw him out of their party. Mussolini became editor of his own paper, *Popolo d'Italia,* where he advocated intervention.

In August 1916, the French and British prepared to partition the Turkish Empire. They intended to exclude Italy from a share because Italy had not fought Germany, Turkey's protector. Anxious to protect its aspirations to Turkish territory, Italy declared war on the Germans.

Marconi wireless applications spread. Belgian paratroopers, the war's first, jumped behind German lines with MWT equipment strapped to their backs. Seventy-five Royal Navy ships carried Marconi valve units. Seaplanes utilized company transmitters to report U-boat sightings.

On November 15, 1916, the Japanese Marconi station at Funabashi near Yokohama initiated transpacific service with a transmission to Koko Head, Hawaii. Emperor Yoshihito and President Wilson exchanged greetings. Marconi's dream of sending wireless messages around the world was a step closer. Airborne communications could now be relayed two-thirds of the way around the globe. The U.S. subsidiary priced Pacific messages 33 percent below cable. Volume leapt at the expense of its underwater competition.

American Marconi reorganized a number of its activities into a commercial department and named Sarnoff, not yet twenty-six years old, to its head; 725 employees reported to him. His responsibilities included radio installations on 528 ships, providing operators, negotiating all service contracts, supervising sales to private and governmental customers, and regulating radio and telegraph traffic. The Institute of Radio Engineers elected him secretary, and newspapers began to quote him.

The American corporation was struggling with the United States government. Under a 1910 statute, industrialists making products useful for war preparation were permitted to use patented concepts without license from the owner. Roosevelt cleared the way through the legal thicket of claims and counterclaims that stymied improvements in radio technology. He directed the navy to order whatever it needed without regard to who held rights to apparatus. He authorized contractors to use any invention necessary and indemnified them against consequent claims. Marconi patents were infringed by other manufacturers. In order to recover damages, American Marconi had to go to court and include the administration as a defendant.

Worse, the threat of federal ownership of wireless had come closer. A bill proposed by an inter-department committee on radio legislation, supported by Daniels, had been introduced in Congress. It would authorize the navy to operate wireless stations in competition with private firms even in peacetime. The secretary of commerce would set rates and regulate traffic. With these powers, government would effectively control the industry. Inasmuch as American Marconi dominated the continent, there was no question as to the law's target. Transoceanic airborne communication was critical to security. It should not be solely in foreign hands.

To counter the growing political menace, Isaacs had John W. Griggs, former governor of New Jersey and former attorney general of the United States under President McKinley, appointed president of American Marconi. Nally gave up his title of president but retained his role as general manager. In the last week of January 1917, Griggs addressed a House of Representatives committee considering the legislation:

> What danger is there to this country because Mr. Marconi is the vice-president of the company I represent? Will anybody suggest to me what danger there is to this country because one-third of the stock is owned by aliens either in Great Britain or Italy?
>
> The company is amenable to the laws of the United States. And with what face can the American Government, through its telegraph companies, go to foreign countries and ask for a concession to land its cable on their shores. The concession for the Western Union cable to Great Britain will expire in two or three years.(FN 5)

Sarnoff testified in his corporate capacity and as the new secretary of the Institute of Radio Engineers. He asserted that government competition or confiscation by government would stifle inventive efforts. Further, private enterprise operators were superior:

> It is known by all radio men—and I think if they will speak frankly and sincerely they will bear me out—that the Navy operators are not anywhere near as efficient as the commercial operators. The men in the Navy Department receive their positions by assignment. They have to take an electrical course, and I am not deprecating the value of electrical knowledge, but when a man is a wireless operator, I say he must be a good wireless operator and not primarily a good electrician. Most of the Navy operators are electricians rather than telegraph men.(FN 6)

The corporate representatives had scarcely spoken when Germany, which had restrained its submarines in response to the international outcry over the *Lusitania*, let them loose again. On January 31, it declared it would resume attacks on all neutral ships in the war zone. The United States answered on February 3. It severed diplomatic ties. Griggs patriotically sent a telegram to President Wilson:

> The Marconi Wireless Telegraph Company of America, in accordance with the Act to Regulate Radio Communication approved August 13, 1912, hereby places at the disposal of the Government for use in any emergency, its entire organization and personnel, including its high power and coastal stations wherever situated, its manufactories, workshops and trained staff. Myself, associate officials, and staff are subject to your orders or the orders of any particular department of the Government which may need our services. I shall be glad to proceed to Washington for conference if you so desire.(FN 7)

The president, the secretary of war, and Daniels expressed their appreciation for American Marconi's cooperative spirit.

In six weeks, the bellicose nation sent 134 non-belligerents ships to the bottom. On March 17, two British destroyers in the English Channel went down. The next day, the *City of Memphis, Vigilante,* and *Illinois,* all American, were sunk. The U.S. had had enough. On March 21, President Wilson called a special session of Congress. On April 2, he asked Congress to declare war. "The world," he said, "must be made safe for democracy." Two days later, the Senate voted 90–6 in favor. On April 6, 1917, the House passed the declaration of war 373–50. The United States had become an active participant.

Daniels saw his opportunity. With President Wilson's consent, the navy took over all the nation's amateur and commercial stations other than a handful operated by the U.S. Signal Corps. Immediately following the declaration, the U.S. placed all wireless facilities, commercial and amateur, under the navy's jurisdiction. The order included American Marconi's long-distance stations at South Wellfleet on Cape Cod, Sagaponack on Long Island, Sea Gate at Coney Island, and New Brunswick, New Jersey.(FN 8) Only manufacturing and a limited number of installations on ships remained under private management.

Daniels directed that the fifty-kilowatt Alexanderson alternator, the prize Marconi had sought from GE for American Marconi's global network, be delivered to the navy and installed at New Brunswick. It became the world's most powerful transmitter, stronger even than Nauen. With its call letters NFF, it reached European battlefields and behind enemy lines.

As soon as America joined the war, Italy organized a mission to New York and Washington for goodwill purposes and to discuss war aims, economic assistance, and the spoils of war. Prince Udine, nephew to the king, headed the delegation. Marconi, under consideration to be ambassador to the United States, and Nitti were members of the party. Every night Marconi was gone, his two older children knelt by their beds and in their prayers asked for his safe return. Degna said:

> When he got back he made light of the dangers of mines and submarines but complained of having to make too many speeches. The delegates had agreed to alternate but none of the others was known in America and audiences began shouting, "We want Marconi!" when anyone else got to his feet.(FN 9)

As the group prepared to depart to reenter the Atlantic war zone, Marconi spoke of his feelings about the country:

> I have been in the United States forty times in twenty years. Some of my best friends are here. I belong to many of America's great scientific bodies and I had encouragement and help from the United States in the early days of my work when I very sadly needed it.
>
> Applause after one has gained his victory is all very well and may be extremely pleasant, but what counts most is the cordial helping hand held out when one is struggling and cannot achieve without it. That was extended to me by America as heartily as it was from my own country at a time when there was much galling skepticism in all Europe except Italy.
>
> I shall never forget Mr. Edison's laconic comment when the first weak signal vibrated across the ocean—"If Marconi says it's true, it's true." Nothing ever pleased me as those words.(FN 10)

On Guglielmo's return, he informed his wife he thought it best the family relocate from Rome to Villa Grifone. He could be closer to the front, where it continued to be his job to inspect wireless units in the field. The villa turned out to be impractical. No transport was available from Pontecchio to Bologna's center, where military carriers departed for the battle lines. Instead, the family accepted an invitation to house themselves with Count and Countess Ugo Gregorini. They and two daughters lived in a three-hundred-year-old villa in Casalecchio on Bologna's outskirts. The count and Marconi had been classmates. Marconi could walk to the suburb's tramline that ran into the city for his commute to war. The countess worked for the Red Cross. Beatrice visited the wounded and wrote letters for them. On one occasion, the Prince of Wales, who had been inspecting the Entente's forces, came to visit with his two aides-de-camp, Claud Hamilton and Piers Leigh. Beatrice had known the prince at Holkham Hall. His assistants were old London friends of hers. To the music of a gramophone, the prince spent the evening dancing with the Gregorini daughters.

Marconi

In July, Tesla gave up his New York endeavors. He surrendered his Waldorf Astoria quarters, leaving his voluminous files in its basement, and moved to Chicago. He took up residency in the Blackstone Hotel. In August, the Smiley Steel Company's explosive expert was ordered to Wardenclyffe. The federal government suspected the apparatus was being used by German spies. With press and military in attendance, Tesla's World Communication Tower was brought to the ground.

In October, the Austrians burst out of their trenches and routed the defenders at Caporetto in northeastern Italy. The overwhelmed army fled in disorder and disgrace. The troops finally held after crossing the Piave River, which provided a natural defensive line. The pro-war elements, including the Nationalists, were furious about the disaster. They formed a parliamentary group, or a fascio, called the fascio of national defense to overcome defeatism and promote patriotism. Local *fasci* of national defense sprang up to overcome neutralism.

The company continued its strides in air communication. Nighttime bombers with a hundred-mile range carried Marconi air-to-ground continuous wave sets. Air force land networks adopted the technology. Most important, telephony became operable between aircraft in flight. Assisted by an advance in modulation, choke control suggested initially by Round, production in quantity commenced of two-way airborne units. For the first time, pilots in combat could talk to each other. The ability to coordinate activities was a significant advantage against fliers who had no comparable device. By war's end, six hundred British airplanes could exchange information with each other and one thousand interconnected ground stations manned by eighteen thousand operators.

On January 18, 1918, President Wilson announced to the world on NFF his Fourteen Points peace proposal that he had just delivered to Congress. His words reached European battlefields and cities. The inventor of NFF's alternator, GE's Alexanderson, ran the transmitter for the broadcast at American Marconi's U.S. Navy–controlled New Brunswick station. The navy asked American Marconi to finance a new two-hundred-thousand-watt alternator being built for the site by General Electric. The British subsidiary refused. GE installed it at its expense. NFF was now the world's most powerful transmitter. It penetrated Germany. NFF pronouncements reached German soldiers and civilians.

The Russian Reds and their antagonists reached peace terms in March, permitting Germany to transfer troops to the Western front.

In April, the Italian government named Marconi the representative of the Italian Parliament at the Allied Parliamentary Conference in London. Nitti, who had become finance minister, was instrumental in the appointment. Marconi remained at the conference until July, pressing Italy's interests at Buckingham Palace, the House of Lords, Guildhall banquets, and conference sessions.

Marconi returned to Italy in July. He brought his family back from Bologna to Rome to the Villa Sforza Cesarini on Janiculum Hill, northwest of Rome where city and countryside merged. In this relatively isolated location, he thought there would be less contact with people who distracted him from his research. On the top floor he created another laboratory. He built a particularly sensitive radio receiver on which he often picked up signals and messages from London, Paris, and Berlin not received elsewhere in Rome. As a result, he frequently forwarded important news to the government. He was driven back and forth to his senatorial duties. Nitti was a frequent lunchtime guest. Women and children were banned from riding in cars in wartime Rome. Beatrice after her childbearing days never again mounted a bike. As result, she led a very country-centric life at the villa. She did not mind, however, as the children's governess, an excellent pianist, gave her lessons. Bea loved it. She often practiced six hours a day. The Vatican became interested in a radio station of its own. Cardinal Gasparri announced he would call on Marconi in the evening to discuss the project. The Protestant family had no idea how to greet such a high level Catholic dignitary. After much discussion, Beatrice and Guglielmo had each household servant line up at the door with a lighted taper to create a ceremonial entrance for their visitor.

In September, Marconi and Prince Colonna, the mayor of Rome, led a delegation to London for a festival of Anglo-Italian goodwill. Together with Italian government officials, representatives of Italian worker organizations, and a detachment of the Royal Regiment of Carabinieri, a joint demonstration was held in Hyde Park with British Trade Unionists. The celebrations lasted a week. King George invited Marconi and Prince Colonna to Buckingham Palace. The king awarded the prince with the newly created Order of the British Empire.

Marconi

An acquaintance who had met Marconi when he first came to London and now saw him again more than twenty years later observed:

> The pale youth now is tall and of that firm, high-headed carriage which is given by conviction of success of real importance; but his manner is as unobtrusive, almost shy, his voice is as gently modulated and his words are as modestly considered as they were when all the world was wondering whether he was maniac or genius, and when he was wondering about his various experiments.
> In the old days Marconi was unknown, or if known to any was regarded as a dreamer who possibly might have stumbled onto something big; but probably was merely in a mental mess. Then he was a supplicator at the doors of the powerful; now he is powerful in science and in the upper legislative house of one of the greatest nations fighting for the freedom of the world.(FN 11)

On October 24, the anniversary of Caporetto, the Italian army at last mounted an offensive and re-crossed the Piave. In two weeks, it retook all of its invaded land and entered Austria. The navy seized Trieste. The southern war was over.

President Wilson rejected German pleas for peace with honor based on his Fourteen Points speech. The U.S. president toughened the terms. Germany must evacuate all occupied territory. It must guarantee Allied military supremacy. It must indicate that it had reformed, and Kaiser Wilhelm must abdicate.

On November 5 in the evening, Marconi called Degna upstairs to his laboratory. When she arrived, he had his earphones on, and he motioned to her not to speak. After listening intently for several minutes, he took off his earphones and told her that the kaiser had abdicated. Marconi and Degna were the first in Rome to know it.

On November 11, 1918, the following message transmitted from the Eiffel Tower was picked up at the Marconi House in the Strand and at Villa Sforza Cesarini:

Les hostilities seront arretees sur toute le front a partir du onze Novembre onze herures (herure francaise).
Les troupes alliees ne dispasseront pas jusqu' a nouvelle ordre la ligne atteinte a cette date et a cette heure.

Marechal Foch

CHAPTER 18

The Radio Corporation of America (RCA)

The struggle was over.

Marconi's side had won.

During wartime, his corporations had prospered, not, however, as long-distance communications systems, which had been their *raison d'être* and their founder's source of inspiration. Rather, they had profited from radio equipment manufacture.

With the cessation of hostilities came exaltation, relief, expectation of reward for victory, and a belief that things going forward would be better. But as peace began, the company's entire UK communications system remained in the hands of the British government. American Marconi possessed only a portion of its network. The two entities' projects to build an interrelated, long-distance, worldwide scheme lay paralyzed in a state of partial construction. Nor did either the UK or the U.S. governments appear ready to return the appropriated assets.

To the contrary, no sooner had fighting ceased than a bill appeared in the House of Representatives. It would authorize the United States Navy to continue its control. Hearings lasted a full week in December 1918. Continuing his relentless push to take over American Marconi's long-distance wireless permanently, Daniels testified:

> The passage of this bill will secure for all time to the Navy Department the control of radio in the United States, and will enable the Navy to continue the splendid work it has carried on during the war...

> We would lose very much by dissipating it and open-
> ing the use of radio communication again to rival
> companies...
> It is my profound conviction and is the conviction of every
> person I have talked within this country and abroad who
> had studied this question that it must be a monopoly. It
> is up to the Congress to say whether it is a monopoly for
> the government or a monopoly for a company.(FN 1)

Daniels' close relationship with President Wilson implied that the
White House supported the measure. William Jennings Bryan had resigned as secretary of state. Daniels was the principal Progressive Party
representative in the administration. The State Department endorsed the
legislation in its entirety. The army complained, but only of the navy's
attempt through the act to gain control over army wireless.

Meanwhile, a state of calm had settled over the Marconi marriage.
The chaotic swings in Guglielmo's relations with Beatrice had abated
during the conflict. The peaceful interlude soon proved to have been only
a lull in the progressive deterioration of their ability to work out their
differences. As Degna observed:

> I can see now that the war years were a time of reprieve
> for my parents' marriage. It was nonetheless drifting to-
> ward catastrophe. For four years the Marconi family was
> drawn and held together by the immensity of the hor-
> ror which swept Europe. There was no place for pettiness
> against the background of death and destruction. After
> the nations found peace again, we lost ours.(FN 2)

With the war over, Marconi bought a large house near the Borghese
Gardens complete with gardens, lawns, and a tennis court. Their tran-
sient status had ended. Beatrice felt sufficiently at home in Rome to begin entertaining once more. Marconi had to travel. The atmosphere of
restraint had lifted. The conditions for discord had reappeared.

In the U.S., Daniels continued to push for navy operation of the U.S.
network. The Radio League, claiming that there were now a hundred
and fifty thousand hams in the United States and a hundred thousand

returning servicemen with wireless experience, spoke out in opposition. Griggs, the president of American Marconi, accused the government of stealing the fruit from someone else's tree:

> Just when the farmer has planted his seed, plowed his field, and harrowed it, and cultivated his crop, and the corn is ready to husk, the government comes in and says, "We want that crop."(FN 3)

Fundamentally, people opposed government ownership of private enterprise. Congressman William S. Greene of Massachusetts said it squarely: "Having just won a fight against autocracy, we would start an autocratic movement with this bill." The navy's chronicler concluded that the navy so believed in the beneficence of its guidance during the war that it could not comprehend the sudden and violent repudiation of things military in the weeks after November 11, 1918. In fact, a navy historian labeled the 1914–1918 period the Golden Years of Naval Radio. The congressional committee, however, recognized the return to peacetime values. It tabled the proposal.

The Paris conference to rebuild the shattered world commenced January 18, 1919. Prime Minister Orlando headed the Italian delegation. Marconi was once more drafted by Nitti, who was now the treasury minister. The inventor was designated a plenipotentiary delegate with full powers to sign a treaty on behalf of Italy. The real bargaining fell to four men: Wilson; Clemenceau, the French prime minister; Lloyd George, now the British prime minister; and Orlando.

Marconi had no taste for diplomatic maneuvering and bickering. The scientific idleness forced upon him increased moods of depression that swept over him. At home the pro-war interests, the democratic interventionists, and the Nationalists had high hopes for territorial gains. The prime minister was to demand Trent, Trieste, South Tyrol to the Brenner, Istria, and Northern Dalmatia. Claims to Fiume, the Croation port on the Adriatic south of Trieste, were added to the list. Its city center was populated by ex-patriots. The surrounding suburbs and countryside were not. Neither was Northern Dalmatia. President Wilson had made clear that the "principle of nationality" was to govern country realignment.

Marconi

Marconi expressed to Lilah his distress that Orlando was not making more progress to win all of Italy's demands to control Adriatic lands where large groups of Italians were concentrated. D'Annunzio made the award of Fiume a symbol of national pride. Lilah asked Marconi why he did not speak out. "I do," he replied. "Everyone turns down my ideas bluntly. They think of me as a mere scientist." Accustomed to respect for his views, Marconi found it a bitter blow to be disregarded on a mission to which he had been assigned.

In Degna's words, "As the months passed, Father's ups and downs grew more marked...He confessed to Mother that he had lost all desire to go on living, convinced that his creative faculties were failing. These bouts of melancholy were followed by violent rebounds into brilliantly creative phases. In his successive times of triumph and despair, all the old tensions latent in the days at Eaglehurst reasserted themselves."(FN 4)

There were bright moments. Marconi met President Wilson and had an opportunity to exchange views with him. Marconi favored the League of Nations.

On returns to Rome between conference sessions, Beatrice organized dinner entertainments or luncheon outings to their favorite country restaurant, Rustic La Villetta. D'Annunzio was a frequent guest. As the merry party motored along the hillsides past Villa Doria-Pamphili, he would make up poems and recite them to his delighted audience. The group would sit outdoors at the trattoria's long, wooden tables under the olive trees, chatting amicably into the late afternoon. On another occasion, D'Annunzio with some fellow guitarists serenaded Bea in the evening beneath her bedroom window, apparently without evoking a jealous response from Marconi. Perhaps the friendship between Marconi and D'Annunzio, two fellow patriots, or Marconi's calmer relationship with Beatrice during the war, tempered Marconi's reaction. Marconi and Beatrice were not so distracted by these divertissements that they ignored their children. Guglielmo gave Giulio a magnificent toy boat. The eight-year-old launched it in the nearby Paolina Fountain, but it slipped beyond his control in the bubbling water. When the tiny craft threatened to plunge over the fountain's waterfall to destruction. Bea jumped into the pool to save it.

Nothing frustrated Marconi more than Great Britain and the United States of America. After more than four years' dedicated participation in the war effort, the company required substantial effort and capital to return its activities to civilian competition. Its foreign affiliates were in a wide variety of disarray. The Imperial Wireless Network remained frozen in embryonic form, approved but unfunded. The tremendous military advances in technology that created exciting opportunities for commercial adaptation also required significant retooling. Engineers and technicians who had been seconded to the government and who flooded back to MWT, eager for useful employment, needed to be paid.

But the company was severely limited. Once again, it lacked money. Orders for army and navy equipment that had sustained the company during the struggle dried up immediately. Instead of facilitating the peacetime conversion, the British government crippled it. The superstations were not returned. Substantial money was owed. The authorities had not compensated MWT for commandeering its sites and for staff summoned to the multitude of posts. The GPO had not paid for the company's interception and translation from German, Russian, French, Italian, and Rumanian of eighty million words of enemy wireless communication. The General Post Office offered to reimburse the company at the rate of one and one-fifth pence per word, or £847,000. The directors turned the proposition down. It barely covered out-of-pocket expenses. The bureaucrats refused to arbitrate. Left with no alternative, the board filed against the government in the Courts of Petition of Right.

MWT eagerly reactivated one particular project. It resumed Marconi's conversations with U.S. General Electric for exclusive rights to the Alexanderson alternator. Many experts concurred with company judgment that whoever controlled the generator could gain an insurmountable advantage in long-distance messaging. Sarnoff, in evaluating principle methods of driving electromagnetic signaling, had long held the device paramount. He had a rising reputation in military and electronic circles. The American subsidiary had been the largest supplier of wartime radio equipment to the U.S. Navy and government. Its sales in 1917 exceeded five million dollars. Sarnoff had overseen this effort, dealing directly with top army and navy brass.

Although the threat of a permanent government takeover had subsided in the United States, aversion to "overseas" control of radio telegraphy and telephony grew. The struggle dramatically increased awareness of the

345

importance of international communication. Nationalism, stoked by the conflict, demanded U.S. autonomy in long-distance transmission free of "foreign influence." Patriotism called for a role of world leadership. The board and American Marconi knew that "overseas" meant English and Italian and that "foreign" meant MWT. British interests monopolized submarine cables serving the United States. MWT's dominance in wireless meant that U.S. interests were locked out of the burgeoning oceanic market.

Despite the defeat of the legislation, Daniels continued to lobby Congress. Within the Navy Department a new idea was growing. Commander Stanford C. Hooper, chief of the Navy Radio Bureau on whom Daniels had relied since becoming secretary of the navy, suggested that a powerful private U.S. corporation be formed, with the backing of the government, to take over the assets soon to be released to their respective owners. The concept immediately won the support of the director of naval communications, Rear Admiral W. H. G. Bullard. Roosevelt concurred. Daniels still favored direct government control.

The GE negotiations progressed rapidly with Young, GE general counsel, once more very much involved. The Marconi group agreed to buy twenty-four transmitters with generators, ten for MWT and fourteen for American Marconi. The $4,098,000 purchase price included the exclusive right to use the alternator. General Electric retained all manufacturing rights.

It was an awkward moment for American Marconi's officers. As one of Sarnoff's biographers said:

> This put the operating executives of American Marconi, Americans all, in something of a psychological dilemma. Basically they shared Washington's apprehensions over British ambitions. Some of them, indeed, saw even more sharply than did military men that Americans were about to be squeezed out of the world's major radio channels. Yet they were dependent, in the final analysis, upon majority stockholders in England. Theirs was an uncomfortable position and they were gratified when forces outside their company moved to extricate them.(FN 5)

As the talks proceeded to conclusion, it became generally known that Round at Ballybunion, Ireland, was testing an extremely powerful wireless radio telephony transmitter incorporating his valves. With a wavelength thirty-eight hundred meters long, he broadcast from the Irish coast the first British or European radio telephony to be heard in the United States. It was not the first transatlantic telephony. American Telephone & Telegraph, in experiments with the U.S. Navy at Arlington, had radiotelephoned from the Virginia site to the Eiffel Tower. Arlington employed three hundred valves. Ballybunion, however, had only two main valves and a modulator. Americans could only view this breakthrough as one more development securing British domination.

Young wrote Roosevelt. The navy had been unaware of the private negotiations. The general counsel of the major New York corporation advised the assistant secretary of the navy, an ambitious New York Democratic politician, that General Electric was about to enter into a contract giving the company exclusivity in the use of the alternator. He explained the significance of the agreement.

Roosevelt at once handed Young's letter to Hooper. Hooper had worked closely with Sarnoff on the navy's wartime purchases from American Marconi. Hooper was fully aware of MWT's overwhelming presence. He immediately cabled Daniels, who was in Paris with President Wilson. Daniels advised Bullard back in Washington that the Brits were about to acquire worldwide control of Alexanderson's machine.

On Friday, April 4, Roosevelt answered Young. He asked General Electric to confer with naval representatives before committing to any agreement with MWT or American Marconi. On Monday, April 7, Young received the response and agreed to a meeting. The next day, Hooper and Bullard arrived at the general counsel's office in the General Electric Building at 120 Broadway in New York City. The chairman of GE, Charles Coffin, joined Young.

Young believed Bullard acted under instructions from President Wilson. The rear admiral said it was a matter of the highest national priority that GE not proceed with the company. Bullard said that the president believed three dominating factors governed a country's influence over world affairs—transportation, petroleum, and communication. The UK held the lead in international transportation and the U.S. in petroleum. Britain monopolized cable. With GE's Alexanderson alternator, America could have the best radio and a standoff with the British in communication. The alternator should not come under MWT's control. General Electric patriotically deferred to its government.(FN 6)

The naval emissaries planted the seed of an idea. Over the years, the navy had acquired a number of valuable wireless licenses. Perhaps they could be combined with GE's to start an American corporation.(FN 7)

At the same time the GE discussions were underway, MWT also petitioned the British to implement the Imperial Wireless Network. The authorities created a committee to recommend a plan. Unfortunately, they appointed as its chairman Sir Henry Norman, who was considered to be unfriendly to the company. Isaacs, managing director for almost a decade, submitted a proposal utilizing spark transmitters called for by the prewar contract. The committee, whose members were generally predisposed to using valve transmitters, scheduled hearings on the relative merits of the two systems. The directors reacted badly. The network had been reviewed in all aspects, including its technology, and approved in 1914. The board did not want the agreement opened up for review and renegotiation. MWT refused to testify. In a discouraging replay of past disputes with the GPO, the two sides came to loggerheads. Norman rejected Isaacs' plan. The committee stated its preference for valves and criticized the managing director's scheme as financially impractical.

Beneath the squabbling, a fundamental problem affected the company's prospects. The war effort had resulted in significant technical advances developed by others. Arc, radio-frequency alternator, and thermal valve transmissions provided continuous waves systems. The company no longer held all the rights to build the most possibly up-to-date system. With patents held by several competitors, no one could legally operate a radio circuit that encompassed all advances.

In the midst of all the difficulties, one development particularly delighted Marconi. The success of his preliminary short wave experiments called for further tests over longer distances. He and MWT acquired a vessel for the research.

The Admiralty had pressed a wide variety of ships into its war service. They were now being decommissioned. The *Rovenska* had been confiscated from an Austrian nobleman as enemy property and converted into a minesweeper. The 220-foot steam yacht had been built by the

Scots for Empress Maria Theresa of Austria. Using all his and MWT's contacts with the Admiralty, Marconi was able to purchase *Rovenska*. He placed her in Kemp's charge to transform into a laboratory with amenities. Reconfigured, the ship had a major wireless room, two main state-rooms, and several smaller guest cabins. It carried a crew of thirty. Its range and seaworthiness were sufficient to cross the Atlantic or sail to most points in the world.

Of course, the boat had to be renamed. His daughter reported:

> Renaming the *Rovenska* became an immediate family project. While all offered various names, Marconi pre-ferred *Scintilla* but was so sure the English would mispro-nounce it that he chose *Elettra*. The yacht gave Marconi the independence he sought to conduct his experiments away from curious eyes as well as a mobile platform to test transmissions at different distances.(FN 8)

President Wilson, in a letter published in a leading Paris newspaper, publicly embarrassed Orlando by rebuffing his demands for Fiume and Dalmatia. Italy was awarded only Brenner, Trent, and Trieste. The British and French made sure that no North African spoils went to Italy. D'Annunzio, the most popular post-war Nationalist, called the war a "mutilated victory." The prime minister withdrew his delegation from France. His government fell.

The king of Italy named Nitti, Marconi's diplomatic patron, prime minister.

As a reward for Marconi's friendship and support on overseas missions, Nitti secured for the scientist/inventor/diplomat/businessman a prominent position. He was elected chairman of a major bank, the Banca di Sconto. Marconi had no experience with the institution or its industry, nor did he have any time to devote to either. The politician assured him that the office was an honor carrying only nominal responsibilities. Formed in 1905 by Germans, French, and Swiss, the bank had been purchased during the war by the Italian Perrone brothers. They owned Ansaldo, a huge steel empire. Like other conglomerates, it had exploded in size in order to meet the country's need for war equipment and materials. Fiat became the top European manufacturer of trucks and lorries.

It increased its production from forty-five hundred vehicles in 1914 to twenty-five thousand in 1918. Ansaldo bought up iron mines, installed hydroelectric plants, and acquired two shipping companies. All this cost money it did not have. It borrowed heavily from the government that itself was printing money to finance the struggle. The Perrones took over Banca di Sconto to gain access to credit. Their next target was Banca Commerciale. With the conflict over and military orders gone, Ansaldo had an insatiable thirst for working capital.

The new prime minister returned to the bargaining table in Paris, but he granted Marconi's request to be released from the mission. Nitti's ascension and the chairmanship pleased Marconi, but he devoted no energy to political tangles or bank matters. Nitti had his problems. The Nationalists still wanted the peace conference to hand over Fiume. Italy was desperately short of cash and coal and suffering from both internal inflation and currency deflation against sterling. Nitti had no desire to antagonize Britain and France with territorial demands when he really needed their economic help. D'Annunzio called Nitti an "abject coward." The Right was furious with Nitti. He reduced military spending and granted amnesty to deserters. The loyalty of some army posts was in doubt.

On May 12, Young invited Nally to lunch at the Bankers Club in the General Electric Building at 120 Broadway. He broke the news to American Marconi's general manager that GE was not going to sell Alexanderson's alternators to any of the Marconi companies. Nally was shocked. He was fully aware of the significance of this setback. Young intimated that American Marconi was in danger because of English control. The U.S. government could prevent the sale of the alternators, but it could not force GE to compete with American Marconi. Was this an invitation to join forces? Young and Nally quietly began to explore such a possibility.

The coterie of U.S. Navy communication officials were encouraged by their success in preventing the Alexanderson alternator from falling into foreign hands. They saw this moment as an opportunity to break United States dependency on British interests for its oceanic messaging. It was time to implement Hooper's proposal to establish a new U.S. long-distance wireless organization. No formal Congressional petition or authorization was necessary. An entity strong enough technically and financially to vie at the world leadership level should be created. A major U.S. corporation could support such an effort. American Telephone & Telegraph and General Electric qualified. Both were well known to the navy, particularly through AT&T's experimentation at Arlington and GE and Alexanderson's work at New Brunswick. American Marconi's assets were an inviting target. They still remained in the navy's possession, but President Wilson had ordered their return to the British subsidiary in 1920. They could be the foundation of an American powerhouse. AT&T held many telegraphy and telephony patents. It had acquired rights to de Forest's audion. It possessed sufficient monetary resources. Its own operations would be enhanced by airborne properties and technical expertise. Economically strong, General Electric would profit from becoming the manufacturer of American Marconi transmitter and receiver tubes. Combining control of Alexanderson's machine and American Marconi in one body would create the most formidable global long-distance competitor.

Authorized by his board of directors, Young went to Washington on May 23. He was directed to see if he could work out the details of the formation and operation of a U.S. company utilizing American Marconi's properties. He met with Daniels and, at the secretary of the navy's suggestion, Senator Henry Cabot Lodge of Massachusetts. Lodge was highly influential. He was a member of the Senate Foreign Relations Committee and had just been elected chairman of the Republican House and Senate Conference Committee. Young suggested to Daniels that Congress charter a new government organization with a monopoly in radio communication. Reacting to his experience on the Hill, Daniels rejected the concept. He doubted legislators would approve. While he still favored administrative control, his comments encouraged Young to implement a plan for a private corporation. Lodge concurred.

On June 2, Nally and Young met. They agreed a new company should hold as many patents as possible. Nally asked what his position would be in such an entity. Young answered that American Marconi would do the operating and GE the manufacturing. Inasmuch as GE knew nothing about operations, it should take advantage of Nally's experience. Nally was not fully pleased with his British overseers. Isaacs had ruffled Nally's ego when he placed Griggs over the general manager as president. Isaacs and Marconi constantly closely reviewed Nally's performance. They disagreed with many of his recommendations. Urged on by Sarnoff, Nally often proposed purchasing more advanced equipment from rivals or inventors like Armstrong. UK management seemed disinterested.(FN 9)

Young was ready to move forward. He called upon MWT and American Marconi to hold discussions to explore how the subsidiary's business might be the nucleus of a wireless corporation associated with General Electric.

The directors had no desire for such talks. They were painfully aware, however, of GE's close relationship with the federal government and the administration's immense power over American Marconi. With extreme reluctance, the board decided it had no choice but at least to enter into the talks.

As a first step in the discussions, American Marconi made its financial statements available to GE. Sarnoff presented the figures to Young. When Sarnoff began to explain the numbers, Young interrupted him. The black numbers didn't interest the general counsel. He only wanted to know about the red ones. In the words of Sarnoff's biographer, Sarnoff replied:

> "It is not always the figures that tell the story. In this case, I believe, the greatest of our assets doesn't even show up...Our great asset...is the vast ignorance about electronics..."
>
> Young lifted an eyebrow that asked for an explanation. "I mean it literally, Mr. Young. The ignorance is what remains to be explored and conquered—because that's where we have unlimited potential for an industry, in fact for many industries, that are still in their infancy or as yet unborn."
>
> He then went on to sketch the electronic future as he sensed it, a projection of things to come which held the lawyer spellbound. Sarnoff talked calmly, as if he were dealing with the obvious, of his Music Box, of information and entertainment flowing into millions of homes. He talked of the coming use of wavelengths as yet inaccessible, of worldwide wireless telephony, and other miracles. What were mere figures, black or red, against

the vision of daily life transformed and enriched by the limitless magic of the electron?(FN 10)

In July 1919, Albert G. Davis, representing General Electric and Nally, sailed for England to negotiate with the company. MWT held few cards with which to resist the proposed transfer. The U.S. shore stations remained in naval hands. The government could require licenses to operate on American soil. Approval might not be forthcoming. Without it, American Marconi long-distance and ship-to-shore facilities would have little value.

Marconi was in London for a double purpose. He could not refuse Nitti's request to participate in a trip from Rome to Whitehall to seek British loans for Italy. He was also involved in the Davis/Nally talks. Nitti insisted Bea come along.

The Marconis stayed at the Savoy. In the evenings, they strolled along the Embankment to Westminster. He was amused by two Scotland Yard operatives who trailed behind them. However, Bea's enjoyment was skindeep. Beatrice knew Marconi was enamored of a married woman. Her rival wanted Marconi to sell the house at Villa Borghese. Beatrice's situation was becoming desperate. Degna said, "Mother fought to save it, seeing with tragic clarity that it was a great deal more than just a building. So long as it provided a retreat for Marconi, it was home, and a hope for the survival of their marriage...she knew he was captivated by a woman, beautiful, Paris-chic, and cunning, who had deliberately set out to undermine his marriage. Understanding Beatrice's feelings about the house, this woman used all her considerable weapons to persuade Marconi to sell it. She played on the side of his nature that dreaded permanence, feared entrapment."(FN 11)

Company prospects appeared dim. Its UK and other international operations did not generate sufficient fiscal durability to see MWT through a protracted struggle with the United States. The first postwar year's difficulties had drained away its cash. The British continued to hold the UK shore sites and superstations. No reimbursement had been received for the company cryptology. The commercial market for transmitters, receivers, and tubes was only slowly recovering from the war.

The likely adverse effects of the discussion's outcome on MWT affected Marconi. He had struggled emotionally to perform his duty to his country at the peace conference during the first half of the year. He deeply wanted to lead the engineering and research effort to modernize company equipment and systems. Now that he had freed himself from France for the developmental work, the negotiations were a terrible distraction. The time required for the Nitti loan assignment added to his burden.

By September, D'Annunzio was disgusted with the Paris process. At the request of prominent industrial Nationalists and top army brass, he organized a force of 2,000 legionnaires. It was not hard to do. The army had released 120,000 officers. Most of them were still unemployed. The volunteers included Arditi. They had been shock troops and commandos. They were wartime heroes. Deserters were everywhere and available. D'Annunzio led his column into the new Yugoslavia and invaded Fiume. It was defenseless. He occupied the city as its *comandante* and proclaimed it an independent state.

By October, three months of exhausting talks among the U.S. and UK corporate officials convinced the board that American Marconi could not survive in the face of determined American private and governmental opposition. The federal administration offered no assurances that it would return the American Marconi assets it held, license the subsidiary to do business on American shores, or do business with it. Without these actions, the value of American Marconi shares in the hands of the public as well as the majority shares held by the company would be substantially impaired. Nally and Davis informed their New York offices that an agreement had been reached with the British.

On October 17, 1919, a new corporation was formed in the United States. It was called the Radio Corporation of America. Its articles of incorporation prescribed that not more than 20 percent of its stock could be held by foreigners. Only United States citizens could be directors and officers. The articles provided for a government representative to be present at board meetings to present federal views on matters before the directors.

American Marconi agreed to transfer its assets and operations to RCA. In exchange, the American shareholders of American Marconi would swap their shares for an equal number of RCA shares. MWT's 364,826 shares of American Marconi, which constituted a majority of its stock and control of the American subsidiary, would become the same number of shares in RCA and would be the controlling interest in RCA. MWT would sell these shares to General Electric. GE and RCA were to cross-license each other in all rights each owned in patents relating to wireless. GE was to acquire the right to manufacture RCA's products. RCA would retain the right to market its products and operate its communication services.

In the midst of MWT's negotiations with General Electric, Annie died of a heart attack in London. Marconi had been traveling back and forth between England and Italy, staying abreast of the General Electric developments and overseeing the outfitting of the *Elettra*. His children had not seen their grandmother since before the war, although Marconi had visited her from time to time. He did not attend her funeral, a failure reminiscent of his failure to attend his father's funeral. For years, Alfonso had taken care of his mother while she thought only of Guglielmo.

On December 1, 1919, MWT, American Marconi, General Electric, and the new Radio Corporation of America consummated the transactions creating RCA. American Marconi, twenty-one years after incorporation, became a shell. Its former assets and operations were owned by Americans and controlled by General Electric. GE and the American stockholders elected Young chairman of the RCA board of directors. The board elected Nally president and E. F. W. Alexanderson chief engineer. Sarnoff, not named to the board, continued as commercial manager. The United States government selected Admiral Bullard as its board representative without vote. The parties to the transaction perceived its purpose to control wireless services and manufacturing. No matter what Sarnoff may have discussed with Young, not a word appeared in the official reports about radio broadcasting.

MWT had been bludgeoned into a terrible transaction. The American Marconi to RCA transfer constituted a punishing blow to the company. No dollar valuation of the physical assets and patent rights held by American Marconi could compensate MWT for what it had lost. Before the transfer, the company had no peer in its knowledge, ownership, and control of the apparatus and techniques of long-distance wireless transmission. The company's shore stations and sets on ships dominated the world's ship-to-shore, ship-to-ship, and shore-to-shore wireless traffic. The forced sale did not just reduce the company's properties substantially. The action removed the company's presence from half the commercial world. It cut MWT's operating income and cash flow substantially.

Worst of all, the company had over two decades struggled to build a worldwide monopoly with no peer anywhere near its level. Overnight, it faced in the Radio Corporation of America a rival of its own magnitude. In many ways, RCA's strengths surpassed MWT. RCA gained access to all of GE's wireless-related patents, tube manufacturing facilities, know-how, and research laboratories. It acquired full access to the Alexanderson alternator to the exclusion of MWT, just the reverse of what MWT wanted and had successfully negotiated for. RCA operated in a supportive government atmosphere. Perhaps most importantly, the Radio Corporation of America had a motivated parent with resources far greater than MWT's.

CHAPTER 19

The British Broadcasting Corporation (BBC)

Following the forced divestiture of American Marconi, the company was no longer subject to Sarnoff's prodding to generate sales of radio tubes and music boxes by broadcasting entertainment programs. Nonetheless, in stages it backed into executing his strategy.

Round continued to develop radiotelephony. In January 1920, he built two transmitters at Chelmsford. Each was more powerful than Ballybunion. The first was rated six kilowatts and the second fifteen kilowatts. For live testing, he read railroad station names over the air. He soon abandoned the practice as too boring. In its place, he found three company employees who played musical instruments and two who sang. He asked them to perform before a microphone. A piano, oboe, coronet, tenor, and soprano joined in concert. It turned out to be Great Britain's first live entertainment broadcast. Experimenters and shipboard operators, the furthest 1,450 miles away, who happened to tune into the frequency responded enthusiastically.

The company did not perceive the reaction as a directive to provide amusement to stimulate purchases of receivers. Instead, preoccupied with long-distance communication, it interpreted the result as encouraging voice messaging. It initiated a news program.

Sarnoff had been waiting for the first appropriate moment after General Electric consummated its acquisition of RCA to resurrect his proposal to make radio a household utility. In January, he updated his November 1916 memorandum for Young. He added to the economic rewards advertising benefits to *Wireless Age*, the American Marconi periodical acquired in the takeover:

> Every purchaser of a "Radio Music Box" would become encouraged to become a subscriber of the *Wireless Age* which would announce in its columns an advance monthly schedule of all lectures, recitals to be given in various cities of the country. With this arrangement the owner of the "Radio Music Box" can learn from the columns of the *Wireless Age* what is going on in the air at any given time and throw the "Radio Music Box" to the point [wavelength] corresponding with the music or lecture desired to be heard.
>
> If this plan is carried out, paid advertising that can be obtained for the *Wireless Age* on the basis of such increased circulation would in itself be a profitable venture. In other words, the *Wireless Age* would perform the same mission as is now being performed by the various motion picture magazines which enjoy so wide a circulation.(FN 1)

Several weeks passed without reaction. Then a vice president requested more financial details. Sarnoff proposed that Radio Music Boxes be priced at seventy-five dollars. He predicted a hundred thousand boxes would be sold in the first year for $7.5 million, three hundred thousand in year two for $22.5 million and six hundred thousand in year three for $45 million. Despite the tempting projections, GE had a higher priority for its new corporation. It put the project on the back burner. Sarnoff was to be assuaged with a two-thousand-dollar budget to build a model Radio Music Box.

RCA dominance was clearly established in domestic wireless. GE focused on opening international service in direct competition with the company. The United States government cooperated. It released to RCA all the shore stations in its possession that it had withheld from American Marconi while it was under MWT's control.

In England, Marconi attended to the final preparations of *Elettra*. He selected Captain Raffaele Lauro from Sorrento near Naples, an officer in the Italian navy, to command the ship. Not surprisingly, the thirty-one-man crew was all Italian. Guglielmo telegraphed Bea in Italy. He invited her to join him in England for the maiden voyage. She happily accepted. She packed the children off to Villa Beatrice, a holiday mansion that they had rented on the Bay of Naples. She hoped it would be a quiet time. The sea would lift her husband's spirits and perhaps heal their marriage. With luck, Pippo Camperio would be on the guest list to share her company while Guglielmo experimented.

Pippo was there. But incredibly, to Beatrice's great surprise and dismay, she discovered on boarding that Guglielmo had also invited another couple. The wife was the woman who captivated Marconi and intended to destroy his marriage. Beatrice retreated to her stateroom across the companionway from Guglielmo's. She had no interest in competing for his attention. She appeared only for meals. Pippo commiserated with her.

Marconi had christened the first cruise of his luxury research vehicle by cruelly embarrassing his wife. Predictably, he retreated to the sanctuary of his radio shack and his work.

When the vessel reached Spain, Beatrice felt somewhat better. They were greeted in Seville by Queen Victoria Eugenia. Beatrice had known her as a playmate in childhood when she was less formally called Ena. Their friendship rekindled immediately. The queen personally escorted Beatrice on a tour of the reception rooms and the dungeon below, where an earlier queen had once been imprisoned. Victoria Eugenia had missed nothing. She noted to Beatrice that even queens of Spain had been unhappy. At a grand ball given by the Duke of Alba during their visit, Beatrice observed that the unwanted woman's décolletage was more appropriate for a Parisian occasion than a royal gathering in Spain.

The select committee chaired by Sir Henry Norman to review the plan to link Britain, South Africa, and India by long-distance wireless, with which MWT had been at odds since the previous year, at last issued its final recommendations in May 1920. No private company should be permitted even the appearance of a monopoly. Instead, a chain of installations two thousand miles apart should be owned and operated by the General Post Office. The initial sites would be Leafield, England, and Cairo, Egypt, which the GPO had commandeered from MWT in 1914 at the outbreak of the war. The GPO ordered Poulsen arc transmitters for both posts. The report concluded that the balance of the system be built and run either by the GPO or other Dominion postal and telegraph authorities. The Australians reacted adversely. They did not wish to be the last in a series of relays located in numerous countries. Any of the nations, even if a Commonwealth member, could disrupt communication to the remote continent. The Australians preferred a company proposal to build a high-power facility to communicate directly with England.

Westinghouse Electric and Manufacturing Company, a major producer of wartime radio equipment and a direct competitor of General Electric, witnessed in frustration GE's acquisition of control over RCA. While no new orders replaced Westinghouse's military contracts, General Electric in combination with American Marconi had a stranglehold on marine and transoceanic equipment manufacture and communication. Westinghouse first tried to respond by acquiring Reginald Fessenden's patents from the continental heir of a Fessenden backer. But when a representative traveled to Europe in the spring of 1920, he discovered that he had arrived too late. GE had already negotiated an exclusive arrangement.

U.S. restrictions on amateurs had lifted in 1919. The hams at once reentered the airwaves. Many experimenters in addition to de Forest initiated broadcasting attempts. Professor Earle M. Terry's weather and music from the University of Wisconsin at Madison sometimes reached Texas. *Detroit News* publisher William E. Scripps tested de Forest equipment under the call letters 8MK. Similar efforts began in Hollywood, California; Stevensville, Montana; and Charlotte, North Carolina. Frank Conrad, an executive at Westinghouse, resumed under his prewar call letters 8KX. On Thursday and Saturday evenings he produced airborne concerts with phonograph records. On May 2, 1920, a newspaper story described a piano solo by his son. Shortly after the story appeared, Joseph Horne, a Pittsburgh department store, ran a newspaper ad:

> AIR CONCERT PICKED UP BY RADIO HERE
> Victrola music, played into the air over a wireless telephone, was "picked up" by listeners on the wireless receiving station which was recently installed here for patrons interested in wireless experiments. The concert was heard Thursday night about 1 o'clock, and continued 20 minutes. Two orchestra numbers, a soprano solo— which rang particularly high and clear through the air— and a juvenile "talking piece" constituted the program.

> The music was from a victrola pulled up close to the transmitter of a wireless telephone in the home of Frank Conrad, Penn and Peebles avenues, Wilkinburg. Mr. Conrad is a wireless enthusiast and "puts on" the wireless concerts periodically for the entertainment of the many people in the district who have wireless sets.
>
> Amateur Wireless Sets, made by the maker of the set which is in operation in our store, and on sale here $10.00 up.(FN 2)

Harry P. Davis, Westinghouse vice president to whom Conrad reported, on reading the ad suddenly understood for the first time that the market for wireless receivers was far greater than the limited number of technically orientated experimenters who assembled their own sets. Davis came to Sarnoff's conclusion. He wasted no time. He convened a meeting the next day and asked Conrad to build a more powerful transmitter at the Westinghouse plant. Not only would Westinghouse broadcast daily, but it would publish its schedule in advance to assure potential purchasers that there would be broadcasts to listen to. Westinghouse would gain revenue and publicity for its name. If Conrad could be ready by the November presidential election, Westinghouse's program would draw national attention.

At the same time Davis made his dramatic decision, Young was responding to a letter he had received from an admiral in the U.S. Navy. The writer pointed out that a foreign corporation could still purchase rights to U.S. patents crucial to producing the best equipment. What for the good of the country could the chairman of RCA do about that? RCA and General Electric soon scored a major victory. Their solution both tied up available patents and reduced conflicting claims. GE and RCA entered into exclusive cross-licensing agreements with American Telephone & Telegraph and its subsidiary, Western Electric. The parties gained full access to each other's rights and carved out between themselves various activities relating to manufacture, sale, and use. AT&T also acquired a block of RCA stock.

While Young in the United States effectively solved his problem with the admiral by collaborating with a competitor to their mutual advantage, Nitti in Italy had been unable to deal with D'Annunzio's and the Nationalists' continued cries that Fiume be incorporated within Italy. The occupation was an enormous embarrassment for the prime minister. It had become a rallying point for bellicose patriots. It demonstrated what activists could do while the government failed at the bargaining table. The swashbuckling poet soldier hurled insults at the head of the Italian government from his Adriatic stronghold. England, France, and the United States were outraged at the *comandante*'s unilateral action. In no way would they consent to Italian appropriation of Fiume. At home, sentiment swelled that the Nationalists' action should not be tolerated. D'Annunzio should be ousted by force. Nitti was reluctant to try. The romantic adventurer was highly popular. Military elements supported him. The politician was not sure the army would follow orders. Instead, a diplomatic solution was called for. A distinguished emissary should negotiate D'Annunzio's voluntary withdrawal. Nitti had a well-suited ambassador in mind. He was fully aware of Marconi's friendship with the playwright and the scientist's enormous stature within his country. Not even Nationalists could doubt his patriotism in the event he asked D'Annunzio to surrender his city-state. Nitti called upon the inventor. Marconi was torn. He could not turn down his government and Nitti. But he had expressed his own frustration about Fiume to Lilah. He was not unsympathetic to D'Annunzio. It was time again away from his research. However, he knew where his duty lay. He accepted the assignment.

As awkward a problem as Fiume was, Nitti had far more serious concerns. The war had dramatically altered farm ownership expectations. Inflation quadrupled from 1914 to 1918 and lifted the prices of agrarian products. Suddenly, tenants and peasants had enough cash to pay off their debts to their landlords and other creditors and free themselves of their domination. Hope rose of acquiring their own land. The same inflation ravaged the fixed rates of return, frozen by government edict under war powers, of landlords' interest and rent. It impoverished many and increased their willingness to sell their holdings. The administration, to offset the low morale of peasants conscripted by the army, liberally promised them land on their return.

In December 1918, Salandra had enacted universal male suffrage to reward homecoming soldiers for their suffering. Nitti, as prime minister and a member of a small minority party, the Radicals, feared that the two largest organized parties, the Socialists and the Catholics, would benefit most from the new vote and sweep to power. In August 1919, he had introduced two changes. First, he provided for proportional representation. In each district parties would be awarded seats in accordance with the portion of the vote they received instead of all the seats going to the party with the most votes. Second, rather than each party running independently, the government and the opposition in advance of an election would make up a list of the parties they would include in their parliamentary coalition if they won. With these rules, Nitti expected minority parties could continue to win representation. By putting their parties together in a list, they could secure a majority of the votes. The first election under the Salandra and Nitti procedures had been in November 1919. It was a disaster for Nitti. The minority parties listed together failed to win a majority. The Radicals won 67 seats, the Reform Socialists 21, the Giolittians 91, and the Right-wing Liberals 23 for a total of 202. The Socialists won 156 seats and the Catholics 100 for a total of 256. Shockingly, 146 of the Socialists and 76 of the Catholics came from the industrialized cities and rich agrarian lands of the northern half of the country, the heart of the nation's wealth. If the Socialists and Catholics, who had many opposing interests, acted together, Nitti's government would fall. He had survived into the spring of 1920. He might last into autumn, but then he feared the local elections for municipal and county governments scheduled for October and November. How would the homecoming soldier peasants, with their high expectation of land ownership, wield their new voting power?

While Round and MWT may have misread the significance of the popular reaction to broadcasting music through the air, others did not. On April 29, a Hague experimental station, PCGG, outfitted with Marconi equipment, produced an enthusiastically received concert. The *Daily Mail* in London saw an opportunity to publicize itself. It offered to sponsor a broadcast featuring Dame Nellie Melba, a celebrated Australian prima donna, at the company's Chelmsford plant. MWT agreed to do it. The GPO had retained its wartime authority over all wireless transmissions. It granted MWT an experimental license.

Upon Dame Nellie's arrival at the Chelmsford Works, a local company official proudly showed her the carefully prepared microphone and circuits, the transmitter, and the tall antenna masts. He explained that her voice would be carried from the top of the towers. "Young man," she retorted, "if you think I am going to climb up there, you are greatly mistaken." Reassured and firmly on ground level, she sang into the telephone mouthpiece that served as a microphone "Home Sweet Home," "Nymphes and Sylvanis," and "Addio" from La Boheme and concluded with the national anthem. For weeks after, complimentary letters poured into Chelmsford from Europe, Persia, and St. John's, Newfoundland. Reception in Paris had been so strong that a gramophone record of Melba's voice had been made at the Eiffel Tower.

MWT now understand what Westinghouse had grasped. Chelmsford initiated on its own a musical event with Lauritz Melchoir, a Danish tenor. His voice carried across the North Sea. A receiver connected to Danish telephone exchanges made the program available to their telephone subscribers. Another enthusiastic response followed.

Nitti lost control of his coalition. His government failed. Marconi, while disappointed for his friend, was relieved to be off the Fiume hot seat. The king searched for a conservatively reliable and strong prime minister. Orlando, Salandra, and Nitti had all failed. He saw no up-and-coming stars. He reached into the past and reappointed Giolitti, who had dominated prewar politics. The experienced politician, master of diplomatic compromise, brought the Catholics into his coalition. He immediately reinstated Marconi's mission. Again Marconi assented, but he remained uncertain how best to approach D'Annunzio. He refused to take instructions from Giolitti. Unaccompanied by any government officials, family, friends, or guests, Marconi in *Elettra* sailed down into the Mediterranean, around the bottom of Italy, and up the Adriatic. He would advise D'Annunzio in accordance with his own conscience on the matter.

Unescorted, Marconi steamed into Fiume's harbor. D'Annunzio waited on the dock, accompanied by a large crowd that greeted Marconi uproariously. In the public squares, anarchists, military fugitives, and flotsam from all over Italy swaggered about, wearing capes and knives and bullying the local Italian population they had come to integrate into their country. D'Annunzio ruled over a constant fiesta. There were processions and ceremonies and dancing in the street. He made long speeches from balconies. He issued a constitution calling for elections by guilds. He adopted the Roman salute. His out-of-control irregulars forced dissidents to purge themselves with castor oil.

The situation was worse in Trieste. It had been awarded to Italy by the peace conference. Former officers, Arditi, thugs, and drifters had taken over the port city. They were armed and organized into local *fasci*. They were patriots who wanted past glories restored.

For two days, D'Annunzio and Marconi, both so dedicated to Italy but dissimilar in most other ways, talked. The fiery writer-poet-romantic legislator, the self-made, self-proclaimed war hero, the orator was animated. The aloof, social, cosmopolitan, urbane scientist-inventor-businessman-diplomat-internationalist, the senator, was calm and collected. When at last the two men emerged from the Palazzo della Reggenza, their conversation unrecorded, Marconi stood silently at D'Annunzio's side. The fiery activist announced to his unruly, milling crowd of supporters that Fiume wished to remain Italian. The statement could not offend ex-patriots or Nationalists. It appeared to resolve nothing. The ambassador left, and the *comandante* remained. As a parting gift, D'Annunzio personally supervised the mounting of a machine gun on the bow of Marconi's great white ship. So armed with this vestige of defiance but otherwise empty-handed, Marconi sailed out of Fiume.

Giolitti was nonetheless satisfied. From the prime minister's viewpoint, an attempt had been made to talk. A figure respected by all sides had tried to end the dispute peacefully. Now other means could be pursued.

In its efforts to restore its international network after the war, the company secured licenses to operate wireless telegraph service between Britain, France, Spain, and Switzerland. In Essex, the company purchased a site at Ongar on which to build a centralized transmitting station for the service and a second site at Brentwood for a receiving station. In the fall, the British government, anticipating a high volume of traffic to be generated by the League of Nations' first assembly, to be held at Geneva's Hotel Victoria, issued the company an expedited order to provide a second, high-speed, Geneva-London channel. This request the company accommodated by establishing a London terminal at Fenchwich that remotely controlled the high-power transmitter at Carnarvon and the receiver at Towyn.

But the company found no British government support for its new entertainment efforts. The British General Post Office cancelled the company's temporary license in September on the ground it interfered with legitimate services. The amateurs reacted with outrage. The GPO persisted. It maintained that if it granted the company a license, it would have no basis on which to refuse applications by other manufacturers of tubes, transmitters, and receivers who also wished to broadcast. There would be chaos in the air.

Westinghouse continued to press its efforts to acquire patent rights in the tangled wireless areas where GE, RCA, and AT&T by their exchange of rights had gained a serious advantage. Edwin Howard Armstrong, an electrical engineering student of Professor Pupin at Columbia University before the war, had discovered the principle of regeneration for radio tubes. If some of the output of an amplifier, that is a triode metal configuration mounted in a vacuum in a glass jar such as de Forest's audion tube, were fed back into the tube's input, the instrument became a stable and powerful oscillator. It could both drive radio transmitters and be a sensitive receiver. Soon after returning from the U.S. Signal Corp, Armstrong found himself tied up in a patent dispute with de Forest. It prevented the ex-serviceman from earning any income from his invention. Armstrong had also developed a second brilliant innovation. He built a super-heterodyne circuit whose amplification exceeded that of his feedback circuit. It also faced origination claims. In debt to his lawyers and hoping only for a faculty appointment at Columbia, he considered offers for his patents from General Electric and Westinghouse. Westinghouse prevailed. On October 5, 1920, Westinghouse acquired Armstrong's feedback and super-heterodyne patents for $335,000, payable over ten years. If the courts sustained the patents, Armstrong received additional payments. At the same time, Westinghouse purchased Pupin's related patents.

Westinghouse scored another major strategic advance on election night, November 2, 1920. Conrad had succeeded in building a more powerful transmitter. From eight o'clock to midnight, on KDKA, Westinghouse broadcast election results pouring in as Ohio senator Warren G. Harding triumphed over Ohio governor James M. Cox. Although Westinghouse did not yet have its wireless receiving sets on the market, the KDKA broadcast, according to a wireless historian, "set off a national mania."

In Italy, the Socialists and Catholics swept the local fall elections. The Socialists were frightening. They preached revolution and dictatorship of the proletariat. They sent delegations to the Communist International Congresses in Moscow. They were not amenable to compromise and serving in government coalitions with established parties. The two parties won control of almost half the country's municipal council and rural "*co-muni*." That meant local government jobs would go to the union and peasant leaders and their friends. Public works would be awarded only to peasant leagues and Socialist and Catholic cooperatives. As a result of Giolitti's efforts to absorb his adversaries, the government, in the eyes of industrialists and large landowners, was befriending their enemies. Union "labor-exchanges" could dictate wages. Peasant co-ops usually composed of returning servicemen could permanently occupy uncultivated land. Giolitti's new Catholic Minister of Agriculture by decree guaranteed all agricultural jobs to the end of 1922. The number of peasant-owners doubled from 1911 to 1921 to 3.5 million.

In central Italy, in the bountiful provinces of Emila and Tuscany, the major owners and tenants were particularly adversely affected and distressed. They reacted by appealing to the *fasci* in the cities and towns. Since the creation of the Fascio of National Defense in 1917, many local *fasci* had been formed. The organizers were diverse elements of Nationalists, interventionists, patriots, and pro-war enthusiasts. They included Filippo Marinetti, who organized the "Futurists" political party and was the acknowledged leader of the Arditi. The groups were often modeled on the Trieste *fascio*. They were urban and paramilitary, relied on aggressive, patriotic myths, attracted pugnacious students and former military officers, and relentlessly and harshly raked over parliament, government, Nitti, Giolitti, Socialists, and Catholics. Squads of Fascist men responded to the pleas for help. Loaded into lorries, they descended on rural villages in the night and beat up the new local officials and burned down their party offices. The police stood by. The *squadrismo* in short order transformed the Po Valley from being the center of Europe's most powerful peasant leagues into the home of a belligerent Fascism.

Giolitti negotiated a settlement with the Yugoslavs for Fiume and other disputed lands claimed by Italy but which the peace conference intended to be united with Yugoslavia. Fiume would remain independent. On Christmas Day 1920, the navy shelled the town and D'Annunzio surrendered the city-state. At least Fiume had not gone to Croatia. The failure to win it for Italy, however, and the success of the *squadrismo* further weakened the credibility of Giolitti and the central administration. D'Annunzio remained a hero. His supporters formed the National Federation of Fiume Legionnaires.

Marconi

In the spring of 1921, the advocates of British wireless and broadcasting development organized to protest the GPO's denial of a broadcast license to MWT. The Wireless Society of London, the provincial societies, and amateurs convened under the chairmanship of Dr. J. Erskine Murray. Together they drew up and endorsed a petition to the General Post Office, requesting the company's license be renewed.

In the United States, the publicity generated by Westinghouse's KDKA broadcasts created a swelling demand at electric shops, department stores, and new radio shops across the country for wireless receivers or radio sets. Newspapers everywhere reported plans of amateurs and manufacturers to begin broadcast stations. Applications flooded the Commerce Department. To cope with the demand, the bureau created a new category called the broadcast license.

In May 1921, Giolitti attempted to pacify the Socialists by making concessions to their trade unions. In the process, he antagonized his Catholic partners. They withdrew from his government. Forced to call an election, he cast about for new supporters. He thought he could simultaneously strengthen his numbers and absorb the rampaging Fascists into the establishment. He offered to put them on the list of parties that would make up the new government. In the voting he succeeded in reducing the combined strength of the Socialists, Communists, and Catholics from 63 percent to 52 percent. But his own coalition included 64 Radical deputies, 24 Reform Socialists, and 35 Fascists. He could not form a stable government with such a group. Giolitti resigned. His successor was an eighty-two-year-old, Bonimi, never known for either energy or diplomatic skill. Public order was collapsing.

Armed with its increasing position in radio receiver sales and its Fessenden, Armstrong, and Pupin patents, Westinghouse opened negotiations with General Electric, RCA, and American Telephone & Telegraph. Young, still mindful of the admiral's warning, was receptive. United Fruit, holder of crystal detector patents and a loop antenna, joined the discussion. This powerful group in possession of two thousand patents agreed in June 1921 to cross-license each other in all their rights. The only potentially worthwhile U.S. wireless patent rights the group did not control were experimental and amateur rights that Armstrong and de Forest had reserved for themselves when they had disposed of their creations.

Westinghouse and United Fruit became RCA shareholders. Westinghouse was the second largest, holding 20.6 percent of the stock. GE had the most, 30.1 percent. AT&T held 10.3 percent. The group also divided various activities among themselves. RCA would market and sell receivers and parts under its RCA trademark. GE would manufacture 60 percent of these receivers and parts and Westinghouse 40 percent. AT&T would sell transmitters. All telephony, wires or wireless, belonged to AT&T, except that RCA had limited domestic rights in wireless telephony and the principal rights in international communication. The availability of the patent pool, the KDKA publicity, and the growing demand for wireless sets jarred AT&T, GE, and RCA into an interest in becoming broadcasters. The group from its preeminent patent and operating positions appeared ready to dominate the emerging radio broadcast and manufacturing field.

The United States, led by the navy, had succeeded in eliminating foreign ownership in its domestic wireless market. In its place it tolerated or perhaps even encouraged a massive manufacturing monopoly created by a cartel of three major American companies.

In the summer of 1921, Marconi and *Elettra* departed her winter port of Southampton and arrived in the Bay of Naples, where they anchored off Villa Beatrice. In England, Marconi had established short-wave stations for experimental signaling to *Elettra*. She had been equipped with a radiobeam aerial designed by Charles Samuel Franklin. With Marconi came Beatrice's youngest sister, Dorrien, now Mrs. Richard Coke. At Villa Beatrice, Beatrice, the children, and Lilah and her painting gear joined the party. No lady friend marred this idyllic trip. Down the coast the cozy family steamed to Amalfi and Taormina and Messina in Sicily. Around the heel of Italy the luxurious craft slipped through the inviting Mediterranean waters and then up the Adriatic to Venice. Marconi, as usual, spent most of his time in the wireless cabin. "I used to have to pretend," he said, "that I liked fishing in order to get off by myself and think. Now I don't have to pretend anymore."

Beatrice too responded to the warmer man. Degna recalled the following:

> [She was] happier than she had been for a long time. Though it was built on shifting sands, the illusion of

family solidarity surrounded us all for a few golden weeks. Certainly she never looked lovelier. Even I convinced at all times that she was perfect, saw her shine as I never had before. I made it a point to race through changing from the cottons I wore all day to the silk dress required for dinner so I could go into her cabin and watch her. Sitting at her dressing-table, powdering her fair face and neck and arms with little leaves of faintly perfumed rice paper, and brushing her gleaming thick hair she was, I felt lovingly, a fairy queen.(FN 3)

The *Elettra* put in at remote little bays where the party swam in coves and picnicked among Roman ruins overlooking the sea. Marconi often told stories about the histories of the places where they stopped. They anchored in the Tremiti Islands for two days. Captain Lauro hunted wild pigeons, on which they feasted at night. At Francaville Michetti, the painter, dashed out in his speedboat through the foaming breakers to greet them and return them to his garden. After Michetti showed the party his paintings, he could wait no longer to lead Marconi about the house to point out each electrical gadget he had rigged up himself. The house had been fully wired. Beside each bed Michetti had built a box to control the lights and ring distant bells. "Look at Michetti," Marconi said. "A genius of a painter, who wastes his time with contraptions." They happily dined together as the sun set, looking out from under the vine-covered trellises at *Elettra*, eating cannelloni and fresh fish from the local waters and drinking white wine from the countryside.

The idyllic trip ended in disillusionment. After the pleasant visit with Michetti, Beatrice, Lilah, and the children left the boat at Francaville and were driven across Italy in a Rolls Royce back to Villa Beatrice. Dorrien continued to Venice with Marconi. Nothing could have shocked her more than to find a strange lady, Marconi's married lady-friend, waiting at the dock in Venice to greet Marconi. Dorrien had had no idea of Marconi's affair. She abandoned *Elettra* at once and in a rented car made her way hastily to Beatrice in Naples. She demanded an explanation from Beatrice, wanting to know what was happening and why she had never been told.

Sadly, Beatrice explained her theory. Let Marconi roam. Let him act as a bachelor. The less she said and the less she restrained him, the greater she felt her chances of his returning home and to her. She knew she was at risk. She knew no other way to try to hold him. That might be a very continental point of view, Dorrien concluded, but certainly not one that she could have put up with for herself.

Turmoil also continued to roil Italian politics. Mussolini had been waiting for a window of opportunity. He had founded a political movement, the Fasci di Combattimento, on March 23, 1919, but it had gone nowhere. At the end of the year it had 870 members. Fascists, Futurists, and Arditi stood together in the Milan parliamentary elections and received 4,657 votes out of 270,000. Mussolini kept his name alive through his paper, *Popolo d'Italia.* Through it he claimed to be the voice of the *fascio.* He appealed to the industrialists and landowners by claiming he could control the Fascists and keep them within bounds. The Fascists were attracted to him because he egged them on. The *squadrismo* of violent men and their leaders, the ras in Cremona, Ferrera, and Bologna, as a result of their sweeping successes in Emilio and Tuscany dominated the northern and central *fasci.* In his role of self-proclaimed leader, Mussolini attempted to broker a peace between the Fascists and Socialist unions. The ras revolted. No one was to restrict their barn-burning ways. Wanting no peace, they abandoned Mussolini. Instead, the militants turned to D'Annunzio and his legionnaires for leadership. D'Annunzio was not interested. He refused to act on their behalf. He called the *squadrismo* agrarian slavery. Like Mussolini, he posed as a national peacemaker. Mussolini saw the error of his strategy. He dropped his "pact of pacification." He urged the ras to increase their armed takeovers. The squads spread into new northern provinces. Through the lack of an alternative choice, they once more tolerated his posture as spokesman. Mussolini had found his opening.

The Marconis' marital difficulties had not gone unnoticed in their circle of acquaintances. One very good friend from Rome, Princess Elsie Torlonia, felt such great concern that after Beatrice's return from Francaville, the princess invited Bea with the children to Holgate on the Normandy coast near Deauville. She hoped that Marconi would come over from Southampton and that the couple could repair their strained relationship. Marconi did drop down twice but with little beneficial effect. He stayed but briefly. Without him, even at the Deauville dinners and dances at the season's height, Beatrice could not cheer up. To the family, the Channel weather appeared dull and overcast compared to the bright Italian beaches.

Marconi returned a third time to take the family back to Naples on the *Elettra*. The voyage brought little respite to their difficulties. A storm caught *Elettra* in the Bay of Biscay and stayed with them until Gibraltar. Marconi deposited the family at Villa Beatrice and left immediately. A friend of Lilah's described Beatrice's conduct:

> I was for three years in the same hotel with her and her children. All that time I admired her reserve and constraint, the way she kept to herself and sheltered her small family. She allowed none of the corruption of Rome to touch her or her small family, and indeed Italy, for a young woman alone, offered many temptations. Not many women withstood them as she did.(FN 4)

Beatrice frequently took the children to swim at the nearby beach in front of Villa Roseberry where the British ambassador stayed and the mayor of Rome with his nephews often enjoyed the water. Marconi's affair had become public knowledge, Dorrien's ignorance notwithstanding. Even the newspapers made oblique references to Marconi's extramarital relationship. One warm afternoon in September 1921, when the lonely mother had taken her children to play in the sand, Beatrice met her neighbor, Marchese Liborio Marignoli. He fell in love with her at once. Knowing the difficulties of her marriage, he soon proposed. Beatrice declined. Her rejection, however, did not discourage the marchese.

One evening while Beatrice was still at Villa Beatrice and Marconi was working in Rome, he took Lilah to a concert at the Augusto. He noticed her strained silence that arose from her unhappiness at his treatment of her sister. When he asked what bothered her, she told him frankly that she could no longer excuse the scandal he had created. "My father," Degna said, "still in the grip of the passion of the woman he thought he could not live without, did not answer. But Lilah says that drips of perspiration ran down from his brow. Just moments before he had complained of the cold. I see now that he was a man tormented, and, what was always terrible to him, trapped in this relationship, when all he wanted was freedom to be himself and to be alone."(FN 5)

In October 1921, Mussolini organized a formal political party, the Nationalist Fascist Party (*Partito Nazionale Fascista,* PNF). It immediately attracted two hundred thousand dues-paying members. For the first time, he had a sizeable organization with money and offices. It gave him a third power base in addition to his newspaper and leadership of the unreliable ras.

The adverse effect of the Norman Commission's recommendations excluding the company's participation in the Imperial Wireless Network dissipated. South Africa had been no more impressed by the report than Australia. Winston Churchill, colonial secretary, refused to deal with it. The company's long-distance transmissions had continued to strengthen. In 1918, a signal from Carnarvon two-hundred-kilowatt "timed spark" disc transmitter, operating on a fourteen-thousand-meter wavelength and using an antenna with directional radiation, had reached Australia. In 1920, MWT acquired a two-hundred-kilowatt Alexanderson high-frequency alternator. Round designed and built a hundred-kilowatt transmitter employing fifty-four thermionic valves. In November 1921, this transmitter coupled with the alternator established regular communication directly between Carnarvon and Australia. At the company's invitation, on December 4, 1921, the *Daily Mail* in London sent its first press message directly to its Sydney correspondent.

For three years, the company around the world had been measuring the field strengths of all the high-power stations. With the Caernarvon-Australian demonstration in hand, MWT knew that no other organization, public or private, matched its long-distance transmission in distance or reliability. In his usual direct and expeditious style, Godfrey Isaacs wasted no time. Negotiations opened with Australia to establish a direct link with England. The remote continent would not have to be the last in a series of relay stations. Isaacs wired the government of South Africa:

> [MWT will] at our own expense erect within eighteen months in South Africa on a suitable site by mutual consent, a wireless station capable of maintaining wireless communication with England and elsewhere, if necessary and run such a station efficiently...As an alternative we offer to erect stations and to maintain wireless telegraphic

connection with the Union Government on the same basis as that approved by the Australian Government.

Isaacs later amplified the offer:

We wish to state that we do not ask for a monopoly but we shall need all inland telegraphic facilities and we shall give the Government rights to take over such a station on reasonable terms.(FN 6)

At the end of 1921, Ansaldo went bankrupt. Its fate reflected Italy's perilous economy and the consequent difficulties faced by its industries. The northern giants that had expanded rapidly to meet war needs were under particular duress. On cessation of hostilities, their military revenues vanished, but their mammoth borrowings remained. Inflation had soared four times over from 1913 to 1918. It rose half again from 1918 to 1920. The buying power of middle-class consumers, renters, and government employees was severely crippled. Imported raw materials became dear as the lira fell from thirty to the pound sterling in March 1919 to one hundred to the pound in December 1920. A recession hit Italy in 1920, and an international recession struck in 1921. Ansaldo had failed to acquire the Banca Commerciale. The steel conglomerate was excessively indebted to Banca di Sconto, its subsidiary, where Marconi was chairman. The bank's reserves were overwhelmed by the write-offs necessitated when Ansaldo defaulted on its loans. Sconto went down as well.

The institution's failure sent shockwaves through Marconi's life. MWT in its struggles to develop wireless had on several occasions been close to insolvency. But it had never failed. Now Marconi, one of Italy's most famous and celebrated persons, known throughout the world, named by the head of government as titular head of one of Italy's major banks, was associated with bankruptcy. The failure cost him enormous public and personal embarrassment. As Degna reported:

When in December, 1921, the bank collapsed, Father was emotionally incapable of taking its failure impersonally and it inflicted a deep blow to his faith in himself and

in Italy. For the first time he wanted to quit his country,
so deep was his depression.(FN 7)

There was an immediate and terrible consequence for Bea. After the Banca di Sconto disaster, Guglielmo announced to Beatrice what she had dreaded. He had decided to dispose of the house in Borghese Gardens. He was compelled to do so. His economic position had been adversely affected by the bank's demise and his investment in *Elettra*. She had long feared the sale would be the death knell of their marriage. During the years she had endured sharing her husband with other women, she had comforted herself with the thought that at least she would be with him when he returned home. Marconi found a buyer. The Dutch minister in Rome paid Marconi double his cost. Guglielmo did not replace the villa with another. He announced to his wife he would no longer be living with her. They would go to different residences. Beatrice and the children moved to the Hotel de Russie. Marconi went to the Grand.

This second separation came sixteen years after their wedding. The girls were thirteen and five and their son eleven. No doubt their relationship had to withstand great stress. They had moved more than eight times and lived in London, Rome, Bologna, Villa Grifone, Sunbeam, Eaglehurst, and Glace Bay. He had traveled constantly and for long periods, with all the attendant strains and dangers of being apart. His worldwide notoriety, celebrity status, and accomplishments in science and business exposed him to temptations. Her appetite to participate in social events was bound to create occasions that aroused his excessive jealousy. The expectations of the world, their business and social friends, and themselves as to the manner in which they would live caused financial pressure.

Nonetheless, it was not clear that the marriage had to dissolve. Despite the problems, each genuinely loved the other. They were friends and liked being together. There was mutual respect. Certainly Beatrice did not want to part.

Guglielmo at various times desired different things. It could be solitude or independence or both. The appeal of women made him susceptible to infatuations. Could Bea, who strained to love him in the beginning and suffered so in the first years after their honeymoon, have given enough affection to contain his flights of longing for something else? Perhaps it was not possible. The man who was deeply conscientious in his work ethic and devoted to the progress of long-distance wireless communication could also exhibit a cold indifference to his personal obligations to his father, mother, and wife. He did not reciprocate the love he received and turned an indifferent shoulder to those who loved him most.

As 1922 opened, the Socialists overthrew Bonimi's government. A crisis ensued. The king summoned to the palace all party leaders representing thirteen diverse parliamentary elements, including Mussolini and the Fascists. None would form a government. No coalition appeared workable. After close to four weeks without a government, the king in February appointed Luigi Facta prime minister. Facta had fewer credentials than Bonimi. The minister of the interior reported that Fascist violence against people and property occurred daily without a single person being punished. The control of the Fascists continued to spread through its violent tactics.

On January 13, 1922, the British General Post Office responded to the pressures of the wireless societies and amateurs. It allowed the company a single site operating on only 250-watt power. The broadcast was limited to one half hour per week. It had to shut down for three minutes in every ten to permit its engineer to listen for instructions to cease altogether in the event the program was interfering with other services. Within a month, MWT opened 2-MT at Writtle near Chelmsford. The entertainment aired from eight o'clock to eight thirty on Tuesday evenings. Two-Emma-Tock, as the broadcaster called the station, produced the first radio play (*Cyrano de Bergerac*). The microphone was handed from player to player.

Shortly after 2-MT commenced, MWT received a second license, 2 LO. This permitted speech for one hour daily at 1.5 KV from Marconi House in London. Later the company also secured permission to broadcast music.

By 1922, many types of U.S. radio sets, including the Grebe, Aeriola, and Radiola, and parts had come onto the market. The boom in receivers set off a boom in broadcasters. The Commerce Department under its new category, in contrast to the GPO, issued four licenses by the end of November 1921, twenty-three in December, eight in January, and twenty-four in February. Waiting applications far outnumbered the grants. All were issued on the same 360-meter wavelength that had been allocated to news, lectures, and entertainment. The only other available wavelength, 485 meters, could only cover government matters such as weather and crop reports.

On February 27, 1922, Secretary of Commerce Herbert Hoover called a meeting in Washington. His opening remarks to the booming start-up industry representatives addressed the growing interference and chaos from the increasing number of broadcasts on the same wavelength:

> It is the purpose of this conference to inquire into the critical situation that has now arisen through the astonishing development of the wireless telephone; to advise the Department of Commerce as to the application of its present powers of regulation and further to formulate such recommendation to Congress as to the legislation necessary.(FN 8)

The conference agreed that the industry needed more regulation. It could not agree on what the substance should be. Westinghouse already held four licenses. It argued that fifteen licenses would be adequate for the whole country as a whole. Others wanted to delegate full power of regulation to the secretary of commerce. Those who feared Hoover's presidential ambitions and the power such delegation would give him preferred an independent commission. The meeting ended without resolution.

In Britain, MWT opened its second station, 2 LO. Each broadcast was technically a demonstration that required its own special permit from the GPO and a specific audience, other than members of the general public who might happen to tune in, to whom the exhibition was being provided. MWT carefully designed each program not to offend anyone. It did not want to jeopardize permission for its next program. On May 11, a contemporaneous oral account of the Lewis-Carpenter fight was presented. Subsequent broadcasts included the King's Cup air race and a speech by the Prince of Wales to the Boy Scouts.

The success of Two-Emma-Tock and 2 LO immediately brought the consequences feared by the British General Post Office. Twenty-three other manufacturers filed applications. To grant them all, the postmaster general said, would create confusion. On May 18, 1922, he proposed to a meeting of the corporate representatives that they form a single group open to all interested parties. This consortium would constitute a broadcasting authority with which the GPO would deal. The response was the formation of a seven-member committee headed by the president of the Institution of Electrical Engineers.

On May 27, 1922, Marconi and Captain Lauro, confident that despite *Elettra*'s relatively small size her seaworthiness could sustain an Atlantic crossing, sailed from Southampton for New York. The captain estimated that it was a two-week voyage. *Elettra*'s bunkers held a fifteen-day supply of coal. In the mid-Atlantic, however, an enormous storm arose. Lauro turned south for Bermuda. He cut the speed in half and rationed the water. To the scientist, the storm was a delight. The danger appeared to be an adventure, and he would be at sea an extra two weeks. *Elettra* was the largest Italian yacht to cross the Atlantic.

On her arrival in New York Harbor, tugboats with their sirens whistling greeted her. Small boats full of newsmen followed her to anchor at the Columbia Yacht Club at Eighty-sixth Street. They bombarded the inventor with questions, beginning with any efforts to contact Mars, a favorite subject. He answered, "I am not trying to communicate with Mars or any such distant point in the universe. Moreover I have no plans to do so."Asked if he liked New York, he explained that on a previous trip he had returned from a meeting "by way of the subway and experienced the rather curious sensation of seeing people reading newspapers and looking at pictures of me. Also I could hear them discussing Marconi." When asked what that felt like, he answered, "Well, the only way I can describe it is by saying that it made me hope that they didn't recognize me." When asked to comment on Sir Arthur Conan Doyle's suggestion that radio be used to communicate with the spirit world, he replied with a laugh, "I think it would take too long a wavelength." The reporters returned with fascination to Mars, asking if the queer sounds sometimes heard on radio could come from Mars or some other planet. Marconi did not scoff at the idea. "Of course the signals may come from space outside the earth. They may come from the upper reaches of the atmosphere. They may be caused by magnetic disturbances on the sun; they may come from Mars or Venus. It may someday be practical to communicate with other planets."(FN 9)

A week later, *Elettra* steamed up the Hudson to visit General Electric at Schenectady. Along the banks, people gathered to wave Italian flags. At

Albany, a boatload of monks in cassocks ventured out to mark Marconi's passage. With difficulty, Marconi's friends persuaded him to come on deck to acknowledge the monks. One of Marconi's friends commented, "He just doesn't care for that sort of thing."

At General Electric, Marconi had a reunion with Charles Steinmetz, who twenty-one years earlier held the dinner in New York City honoring Marconi's receipt at St. John's of the first transatlantic wireless signal. Organizing the dinner had required courage on Steinmetz's part. So many experts had doubted that signals could carry such a distance. How the science had progressed. Now Steinmetz and Marconi discussed alternating current and loss of power due to magnetism. Marconi also met with Irving Langmuir, who had done important work on improving the radio tube by making it a vacuum tube. The visit was bittersweet. It was pleasant and useful to talk to eminent scientists in his field after arriving in upstate New York on his own research yacht after crossing the Atlantic. Still, he could not forget that his host, General Electric, had forcibly wrested half of his company from him against his will. It now controlled his principal rival in the form of the corporation he had created.

On June 20, 1922, in New York City it must have seemed to Marconi that he had stepped backwards in time. He addressed the American Institute of Electrical Engineers as he had after his early triumphs. He had aged in appearance as well as chronologically. The hairline receded. Wrinkles emerged. But he was still a dapper dresser.

Of course the mind had only expanded and continued to engender startling advances.

Hams had continued to be barred from using long waves allocated exclusively to commerce and government. Undaunted, they experimented with the short waves that fascinated and currently preoccupied Marconi. The past December, U.S. amateurs had emitted call letters picked up in Great Britain. One night a Greenwich, Connecticut, station sent an entire message to England. Interest lagged when no transmission crossed the ocean in daylight. One of the individual experimenters later said that Marconi "appeared to have been the only man in the commercial field whose imagination was fired with the spanning of the Atlantic by amateurs."

In his June 20 remarks, Marconi described their efforts. "I have brought these results to your notice," he said, "as I feel—and perhaps you will agree with me—that the study of short waves, although sadly neglected practically all through the history of wireless, is still likely to develop in many unexpected directions, and open up new fields of profitable research."

Indeed only a few nights earlier, at an address before the New York Institute of Radio Engineers, he had amazed his audience. With a miniature transmitter focused by a reflector, he shot waves of only one meter length along the stage lights to a receiver twenty feet away. It instantly sounded a clear note. When he turned the reflector's cuplike opening so that it no longer faced the receiver, the note was almost inaudible.

Marconi explained to the Institute of Electrical Engineers:

> Some years ago, during the war, I could not help feeling we had perhaps got rather in a rut by confining all our researches and tests to long waves. I remember that during my very early experiments so far back as 1895 and 1896, I had obtained some promising results with waves not more than a few inches long.
>
> The study of short waves dates from the discovery of electric waves, that is from the time of the classical experiments of Hertz...
>
> Progress made with long waves was so rapid, so comparatively easy, and so spectacular, that it distracted practically all attention and research from short waves...
>
> Since these early tests [by Marconi] of more than twenty years ago, practically no research was carried out... Research along these lines did not appear easy or promising. The use of reflectors of reasonable dimensions implied the use of waves only a few meters in length, which were difficult to produce. The power that could be utilized in them was small. The investigation of the subject was again taken up by me in 1916 in Italy for certain war purposes.
>
> As a result of the success of a series of experiments with fifteen-meter wave, tests were conducted between Henden and Birmingham, ninety seven miles apart. With reflectors at both ends clear speech was exchanged between

the two places. A receiver on a ship in Kingston Harbor picked up a beam from Carnarvon, seventy-eight miles distant. This important fact was also noted—there was no rapid diminution of signal strength after the ship had passed the horizon line from Carnarvon.(FN 10)

Marconi also described a concept that would soon attract increasing and then urgent attention. He enunciated the principles of what later came to be called radar. Before Marconi's appearance at the Institute of Electrical Engineers, no one had ever publicly addressed this phenomenon. Since Marconi's observations of electromagnetic wave reflection in 1916, very little had been done other than by Telefunken. Following on the earlier geological efforts of Leimbach and Lowy, it received a patent to detect subsurface minerals and water. On June 20 Marconi said:

> Before I conclude I should like to refer to another possible application of these waves which, if successful, would be of great value to navigators. As was first shown by Hertz, electric waves can be completely reflected by conducting bodies. In some of my tests I have noticed the effects of reflection and deflection of these waves by metallic objects miles away.
>
> It seems to me that it should be possible to design apparatus by means of which a ship could radiate or project a divergent beam of these rays in any desired direction, which rays, if coming across a metallic obstacle, such as another steamer or ship, would be reflected back to a receiver screened from the local transmitter on the sending ship, and thereby reveal the presence and bearing of the other ship in fog or thick weather. One further advantage of such an arrangement would be that it would be able to give warning of the presence and bearing of ships, even should these ships be unprovided with any kind of radio. (FN 11)

Marconi at this time did divert his attention to developing radar. As always, he was focused on long-distance messaging. His excitement over the potential for short waves would not allow him to be sidetracked from their pursuit.

The speeches characterized Marconi's scientific life. He never stopped dreaming, exploring, creating. When he fulfilled one set of goals, another beckoned. He lived on a long-distance continuum. The end was never achieved. Each accomplishment revealed more to be done.

Beatrice had come to the United States at the same time as Marconi to visit friends in Boston. She had planned to travel tourist class as she was afraid to ask her estranged husband for better accommodation. When he heard of her trip, however, he provided her a first-class stateroom. Although they had lived apart for past five months with no talk of re-uniting, he invited her to join him in New York. On the return voyage, pressing business prevented his leisurely return on *Elettra*. The couple traveled together to England on the *Mauretania* and separated once more on landing. He still loved her. He could be with her. He just didn't want to live with her.

Beatrice and the three children, Degna, just fourteen, Giulio, twelve, and Gioia, six, had become as nomadic as Marconi. After the trip, she returned to the Baveno on Lake Maggiore. The family was well treated there because the owner was a friend of Guglielmo. In September, the foursome would move on to Viareggio and then to the Pensione Gonnelli in Florence that was their most frequent residence. For Beatrice, the separation held no charm. Degna later thought that her father must have been achingly lonely, a lost, unhappy man. But of course he lived that way by his own choice.

Nine months had passed since MWT had offered to build a wireless station to enable South Africa to communicate directly with England. On September 6, after extended debate in the Union Parliament, the South African government authorized the company to erect a high-power station on terms that permitted the benefits of private enterprise while retaining for the government control over sales and profits. The company agreed that the station would be used as part of the Empire Wireless System with priority given to communication to other stations within the system.

Australia and South Africa had now both committed to Marconi equipment for long-distance wireless communication. Canada favored private enterprise, while India remained doubtful. The GPO for two years had unsuccessfully proposed a Cairo halfway station. Now it changed direction. In direct competition with the company, it advocated a master station be built in Lincolnshire under GPO control and capable of direct communication with India, Australia, and South Africa.

In early October, the Facta government fell for the second time. Throughout the year, the Fascists had continued to seize provincial towns. Their murdering members were not caught and held accountable. Mussolini continued his strategy of stimulating Fascist activities while offering compromise and control to the politicians. It was clear he would be in the next government. The question was on what terms. At the beginning of the month, he asked for four Fascist cabinet positions. After Facta's second resignation, Mussolini demanded to be prime minister.

On October 18, 1922, at a meeting of representatives of two hundred corporations that in May had formed the broadcasting consortium to work with the GPO on the question of how broadcast licenses should be issued, the seven-member committee appointed by the consortium announced the results of the committee's negotiations with the GPO. There was to be a single broadcasting entity. Six manufacturers would establish the British Broadcasting Company Ltd. (the BBC). The six were MWT, Metropolitan Vickers, Western Electric, British Thomson-Houston, Radio Communication, and British General Electric. The GPO granted BBC an exclusive license for four years to December 1926. No one else could broadcast.

BBC would be capitalized with a hundred thousand shares. Any qualified manufacturer could buy one or more shares at fifty pounds per share. BBC would earn revenue from two sources. It would receive half of the ten-shilling license fee the GPO would charge owners of wireless receivers who wanted to listen to the broadcasts. Manufacturers would be obligated to pay BBC 10 percent of revenues from the sale of wireless sets and accessories.

On October 24, forty thousand Fascists held a mass rally in Naples. On October 27, they marched on Rome. On October 28, Facta, still acting as prime minister, asked the king to decree martial law so that he might call out the army to defend the capital. The king first agreed, but then he changed his mind. His military advisers may have been uncertain if the troops would fire on the Fascist. One top officer reportedly told him that of course the army would do its duty. However, it would be well not to put it to the test. The monarch may have concluded it was not worth risking a civil war when the only issue was the number of cabinet positions. The Fascists already held most of the country. The king had been negotiating with Salandra to head the government and put together a parliamentary majority. Salandra thought it unrealistic. He refused. On October 29, the king summoned Mussolini from Milan. He asked the Fascist leader to be the next prime minister and form a government.

In the year 1922, RCA sold three hundred thousand radio music boxes for $22.5 million. It was only RCA's second year of production. The amount was almost exactly what Sarnoff predicted in January 1920 even before a decision had been made to build any sets. By the mid-1920s, the Commerce Department had granted more than five hundred broadcast licenses. It had run out of three-letter station designations. The department authorized another wavelength of four hundred meters, but limited this frequency to five hundred to a thousand watts and prohibited phonograph recordings. In 1922, sales of radio sets and parts reached $60 million. RCA radio set revenue far exceeded its marine and transoceanic receipts. Competitors complained that the RCA-GE-Westinghouse group unfairly dominated the industry.

The market exploded in Great Britain as well. Applicants for receiver licenses swamped the GPO, exceeding its processing capacity. Within the first several months after creating BBC, the GPO had issued eighty-seven thousand receiver licenses and thirty-five thousand experimental licenses. Thirty-three thousand applicants waited. The General Post Office estimated that more than two hundred thousand people listened in illegally without a license.

BBC promptly opened stations in Birmingham and Manchester. Newcastle, Cardiff, Glasgow, Aberdeen, and Bournemouth followed. Marconi apparatus, Q-type transmitters and Sykes-Round microphones, dominated the outfitting of the new stations.

Despite MWT's success in equipment sales, BBC's formation and its exclusive license to broadcast entertainment and news constituted the second major blow to the company since the end of the war.

On November 14, 1922, BBC assumed the operation and control of the company's London station 2-L0. On January 17, 1923, Two-Emma-Tock at Writtle went permanently off the air.

The British General Post Office avoided the confusion in the airwaves experienced in the United States. It sacrificed private ownership and innovation. It turned an entire nascent industry over to a single consortium. Operation and development were subject to government authorization and favor. The monopoly lacked competitive pressure to be creative.

Up to the moment of the government action, MWT had occupied the undisputed leadership position in UK broadcasting. It had the only two broadcasting stations in the UK. Now it had a one-sixth interest in an organization whose existence depended entirely upon the decisions of the government.

Any realistic opportunity to participate in the U.S. had already disappeared with the forced divestiture of American Marconi.

In less than four years, action by the world's two major capitalist governments had knocked the company out of U.S. wireless and the principal exploding markets for radio broadcasting.

Chapter 20

Short Waves and the Long Wave Crisis

The company and Marconi entered 1923 badly shaken. The world's two most powerful governments had dealt MWT successive blows. The company had been reduced to a peripheral role in the exploding radio broadcasting field. Its own assets were turned against it in the largest of the commercial wireless communication and equipment manufacturing markets.

MWT was once more struggling with Britain over the core of Marconi's dream in the one area where the company remained dominant. The GPO continued to seek maximum control over long-distance, airborne messaging. The company had contractually committed to build enormous, expensive stations for Australia and South Africa incorporating huge power plants and extremely high, multiple-tower aerials. Parliament, however, was unwilling to allow the Norman Committee's failure to leave transoceanic transmission from English shores unregulated. It authorized another study and fresh recommendations. MWT again faced the risk that new proposals would jeopardize its program.

Marconi had not fared well in the past four years, business-wise, politically, or in his marriage. With short waves, he was at least once more engaged in absorbing, state-of-the-art research. But his success in attaining ranges approaching those of long waves had disturbing implications. His results did not require massive generators. Antennae were less complex. If his progress persisted, Marconi could obsolete the principal creation of his efforts for the past thirty years.

Marconi

In the late 1890s, long waves had carried Marconi's transmissions over increasing lengths. His waves upset conventional physical theory. Their signals were received further and further over the horizon from the transmitter. Scientists asserted that these electromagnetic waves, like optical waves, traveled in a straight line. They could not be picked up beyond the horizon. In 1901, Maroni stunned the scientific world. Waves estimated to be between 366 to 3,000 meters long transported a message more than 2,100 miles from England to Newfoundland. The accomplishment apparently rested upon a combination of really long waves, increased transmitting power, and higher antennae. He had replaced conventional battery power with a twenty-five-kilowatt alternator that drove the signals to St. John's on twelve kilowatts. The top of the Poldhu antenna reached two hundred feet above sea level. The kite carrying the receiving aerial swirling wildly five hundred feet above Signal Hill, itself a six-hundred-foot promontory, was eleven hundred feet over the ocean.

St. John's forced the rethinking of the straight line concept. Applied literally, the signals would have had to pass through a massive portion of the earth. No one but Tesla would suggest that. If they traveled above the ocean, they would be too far over Newfoundland to be received. If they followed the contour of the surface, perhaps held there by the earth's magnetism, their direction would not have been lineal. Oliver Heaviside and Arthur E. Kennelley each independently theorized that assuming line-of-sight governed electromagnetic waves like optical waves, Marconi's signals might have shot straight up into the sky beyond the horizon and then been reflected or refracted in a straight line back to earth. An electric blanket or layer in the atmosphere, the ionosphere, might have caused the reflection. They had no proof for their theory.

In 1911, Marconi stated before the Royal Institute of Great Britain that although knowledge existed to produce and receive electric waves, no one could clearly explain the principles governing their transmission through space. Over the next three years, de Forest, working with continuous wave arc transmitters at the Federal Telegraph Company in San Francisco, noted that signals might fade at one frequency and increase at a nearby frequency. He suggested that a wave along the earth's surface might be alternately combining in and out of phase with a wave reflecting from the sky. In his comments published in the first issue of the Institute of Radio Engineers' *Proceedings*, de Forest guessed that the reflecting layer might be sixty-two miles high.

These ideas, however, were speculations. Marconi, competitors, customers, and government regulators all relied for long-distance achievement on Marconi's formula of long waves, power, and tall antennas. MWT's mammoth projects to Australia and South Africa were to be built on this premise.

In 1916, the Italian navy had requested short-range communication between elements of the fleet. In response, Marconi and Franklin developed experimental equipment utilizing a short wave only two meters long. Franklin continued the experiment at Carnarvon, Inchkeith, and Portsmouth. At the end of 1917, he felt sufficiently confident to ask Marconi's consent to a ninety-seven-mile test between London and Birmingham on a fifteen-meter wave. Marconi doubted it could be done. He bet Franklin five pounds that he would not succeed. In very good humor, Marconi parted with his pounds when Franklin spanned the distance using less than one kilowatt of power. Round during this period conducted successful wireless telephony experiments on one-hundred-meter wavelengths between Southwold and Holland. Marconi had also noted on his 1922 trip to the United States that English and American amateurs were at nighttime exchanging short-wave signals across the Atlantic powered by very few watts. Short wave had passed the St. John's milestone employing far less power and minor antennae.

In January 1923, Marconi authorized Franklin to build a short-wave transmitter at Poldhu for further experiments. Only twelve kilowatts of power would be applied. A parabolic reflector would focus and concentrate the beam of electromagnetic waves in the direction of the receiver.

Marconi remained apart from his family, immersed in his lifelong preoccupation with long-distance communication. What he wanted was to be alone, unfettered, and completely free to do his research. He had even broken up with the woman who had intended to destroy his marriage. He indicated no desire to return to Bea.

In Florence, she and the children completed a full, unhappy year apart from Guglielmo. The separation was now far longer than the first one. In February, Queen Elena requested Beatrice to attend court as a lady-in-waiting for King George and Queen Mary's visit. When Bea returned to Florence, she found Marchese Marignoli there to resume his patient courtship. This time she did not ask him to withdraw his attentions. Rather, in Degna's words:

> She was touched by his persistence, as she had been at Father more than twenty years before. Her Irish nature, hungry for love and sympathy, began to respond to this ardent, handsome man. Quite humanly she longed for affection that had been denied her, for home life that for her had ceased to exist, and for the close ties of companionship she had grown up to believe essential to a good existence. She had been drifting for a long time and now here was the promise of recapturing the security she craved. As the months passed Beatrice Marconi allowed herself to fall in love.(FN 1)

In March, the new Parliament committee made its recommendations. The General Post Office should own and operate all stations in Great Britain interacting with countries of the British Empire, including Australia and South Africa. Nongovernment enterprise would be encouraged for all other countries. Prime Minister Bonar Law, however, installed a more liberal policy. The GPO would license private interests to communicate with the dominions, colonies, and foreign countries. To protect British national security, Britain would build, own, and operate a station capable of reaching all parts of the empire. This facility could carry commercial as well as official messages. The General Post Office announced its intention to construct a high-power, very long wave installation at Rugby.

At last, the directors had a green light to proceed with its contracts with Australia and South Africa. The GPO might compete, but it could not block. The massive, long-wave super site for Australia, to be built by a MWT subsidiary, Amalgamated Wireless (Australia) Ltd., called for a thousand-kilowatt power plant. Twenty steel masts eight hundred feet high would carry the antenna system. In South Africa, the company organized the Wireless Company of South Africa to commence construction at Klipheuval near Cape Town.

By spring, Franklin had completed the twelve-kilowatt transmitter. He designed it to send a ninety-seven-meter wave from a half-wave antenna. Marconi fit *Elettra* with short-wave receiving equipment and an aerial created by G. A. Mathieu, another longtime company engineer. *Elettra*'s space limitations prevented the addition of a reflector to assist in picking up waves.

On April 11, *Elettra* steamed out of Falmouth. Franklin pointed the Poldhu parabolic reflector southwesterly. *Elettra* proceeded past France, Portugal, Gibraltar, and Tangiers. Signals weakened as the great white vessel moved south. After several hundred miles, they held and then strengthened. *Elettra* docked at St. Vincent in the Cape Verde Islands, 2,230 nautical miles from Poldhu. Marconi noted that at night the short waves radiated from Poldhu with only one kilowatt of power had greater strength than signals simultaneously received from the GPO's high-power, long-wave station at Leafield.

With regret, the inventor headed *Elettra* north. A meeting in London required his attendance. He reported to Solari:

> The results of these experiments have convinced me that I am at the beginning of a revolution in our ideas about the validity of the theory upon which long distance telegraphy depends.
>
> I believe that with short wave stations of only moderate power it will be possible to obtain an excellent commercial service between Italy and the Argentina.(FN 2)

MWT had relied on Bonar Law's policy and proceeded with Australia and South Africa. By summer, however, his mandate evaporated. Two successive postmasters general inconsistently interpreted his words. The second insisted that GPO officials had exclusive authority to run all international service. MWT would have no say. The directors were furious. By September 1923, the GPO and MWT had reached an impasse. The board was forced to defer construction. The Imperial and Economic Conference of the Empire Countries meeting in London failed to find a resolution.

In frustration, the administration appointed a third parliamentary committee. It reaffirmed Bonar Law. The board restarted the projects.

Beatrice made a fateful decision. She asked Marconi for a divorce. She would marry Marchese Marignoli. Degna had the following view:

> [Beatrice] was deeply troubled at what she was doing. She kept her courage up by telling herself that we children, whom she loved unreservedly, would have stability in our new environment, a proper home that would be better for us all. As for us—I was nearing sixteen, and Giulio was close to fourteen—it was already too late. We were too old to feel at home in another man's house.(FN 3)

Degna believed that it had never occurred to her father that his wife might wish a divorce. In his mind, he could leave her as long as he wished and return when he pleased. In Bea's effort to hold onto him, she had never drawn a line in the sand on this practice. Nonetheless, he must have been aware of the pain it caused her. Degna wrote:

> [Bea's request was] the last thing he wanted…Yet he was, alas, too proud to come to her now, hat in hand, and ask her to stay with him. The tragedy is that he was sorry for ever after that he did not, and told Solari so years later. (FN 4)

Degna was right. It was a tragedy. Marconi thought he wanted to be alone. He constantly hungered for time to himself to conduct his research. He longed to be free of the impositions of his family. While Degna may have thought pride prevented him from asking her mother to refrain from divorce, he may not have been that disturbed by the prospect. The insatiable drive that led him to separate may have persuaded him to allow Bea the freedom to remarry. Only in retrospect did it become apparent that Guglielmo did not understand himself.

Perhaps Annie had unwittingly contributed to ruining Marconi for a genuine marriage. Since childhood, she had looked after him, run his household, and supported and encouraged him. She was always there when he wanted or needed her. She never in his bachelorhood imposed any restrictions or demands upon him. He could ignore her or be off on his business. When he returned on his own time, she was there waiting, ready to serve him. It was a different role than that of a wife who could reasonably expect that he be loving and faithful and home whenever possible.

On Bea's part, Guglielmo's rabid jealousy had led him to attempt to severely limit her social activity while he behaved badly and promiscuously. It is hard to believe her flirtations were anything but innocuous. She certainly tried to keep him.

Beatrice returned to Rome to resign as a lady-in-waiting. The queen was sympathetic. A man like Marconi, she told Beatrice, should never marry. Pippo acted as go-between to establish the terms of the divorce. The children would divide their time equally between Beatrice and Guglielmo. He was never to remove them permanently from her.

Italian civil law offered no basis for divorce. Marconi refused to act under the jurisdiction of another nation. He feared it might jeopardize his Italian citizenship. In Fiume, the Marconis would have adequate grounds if they were residents. Fiume's status was about to change. Under Mussolini, the patriotic demand to which he and Nationalists subscribed that the city-state be part of Italy had risen to the forefront of the government's agenda. Negotiations with Yugoslavia were opened. This time Yugoslavia assented. On January 27, 1924, Italy began the annexation. Beatrice and Guglielmo, traveling separately and secretively to avoid attracting attention to their actions, each "moved" to Fiume. As soon as they established residency, the Tribulane di Fiume granted their divorce. In March, Yugoslavia formally acknowledged the acquisition. Fiume citizens and residents became Italian. Marconi's Italian credentials could not be challenged.

In April, Beatrice married Marchese Liborio Marignoli. In Degna's view:

> While outwardly accepting the divorce and the remarriage of his "B," Marconi seems to have erased this inconvenient fact from his mind. Everything was as usual. His letters continued. He was in all ways considerate. Our allowances were generous. Our problems, if any, were discussed in frequent meetings between our parents. Father went right on consulting his ex-wife about anything that bothered him, perfectly un-self-consciously."(FN 5)

Degna was fifteen, Giulio thirteen, and Gioia had just turned eight; they remained in Florence with Beatrice. Once Degna and Giulio completed spring exams, they departed for England. The parents agreed that until Gioia was older, she should stay with Beatrice. Considering her age, that was easier for Marconi. The two older siblings stayed at the Savoy in London with Marconi. In the mornings, they were sent off on long sightseeing tours. In the evening, Marconi treated them to the theater. As soon as he could, Marconi stuffed his charges into his two-seater Rolls and made for the coast. At Southampton they boarded *Elettra.* To the children, their father appeared to have arranged an idle cruise for them along the coasts of Devonshire, Cornwall, and Spain.

In fact, Marconi was pursuing his short wave research and wrestling with a looming, climactic decision. The incoming signals were strengthening. He was convinced that had he been able to continue south from Cape Verdes the prior summer, he would have received messages well beyond 2,230 nautical miles. He now believed he was well into the enormous breakthrough whose beginnings he had described to Solari. He realized it threatened the foundations of his life's work in long waves and the premises of the gigantic Australian and South African installations. He did not hesitate. He continued to push the envelope. He had the Poldhu short-wave transmitter upgraded from twelve kilowatts to seventeen kilowatts. He adjusted the wavelength down from ninety-seven to ninety-two meters. No reflector would be used to bolster the next experiment or limit where it might be received. He ordered a short-wave receiver installed on the *Cedric* that was about to cross the Atlantic from England to New York.

Cedric pulled in daylight signals up to fourteen hundred nautical miles. It received strong nighttime signals throughout the voyage and in New York Harbor. Canadian listeners heard signals sixteen out of twenty-four hours.

Amalgamated Wireless in Australia had been ordered to maintain a watch on the odd chance it might pick up a signal. To everyone's surprise and delight, Sydney regularly heard clear signals from 5:00 p.m. to 9:00 p.m. Greenwich Mean Time and from 6:30 a.m. to 8:30 a.m..

On May 30, 1924, still on the ninety-two-meter wavelength and with no reflector, the company attempted to radiotelephone Australia. Sydney received good quality speech direct from Poldhu.

Marconi and the company faced an immediate crisis. The contracts with Australia and South Africa required the two countries to make huge capital payments for thousand-kilowatt super-powerstations and enormous antenna systems. Negotiations to build superstations for the GPO had been dragging on for five years. They were all based on long waves and huge generators. The short wave experiments suggested that it might be possible to create these communication systems with only 10 percent of the power needed for long waves. This would result in significant cost savings.

But the tests were only in the preliminary stage. Marconi had signaled halfway around the globe for only a month. MWT had absolutely no operating experience with short waves.

One course would be to continue with the three governments on the proven basis of long waves. Two to three years of experimentation would determine the merit and reliability of short waves. If the latter then proved out and rendered the prior long wave investment obsolete, could the company be faulted or held liable for not previously adequately disclosing or recommending an unproven system? What effect would it have on future customer relationships, government regulation, or the company's and Marconi's reputation?

If instead the inventor and MWT immediately recommended short wave and had to guarantee performance, then failure to achieve satisfactory performance, a very real possibility, could bankrupt the company. Marconi could lose the value of twenty-five years of effort. Damage to his reputation would far exceed the unfortunate Banca di Sconto experience.

The middle position would be to describe the development but not yet recommend it. The likely result would be deferral of all major long wave projects until the choice was clear. The competition would be alerted to the significance of the breakthrough and would undoubtedly try to develop the new techniques ahead of the company.

The risks posed by the decision came at a time when MWT's operations and asset values were adversely affected by economic and political turmoil. Inflation and currency devaluations eroded historical values at which the company reported overseas reserves and ownership interests in foreign subsidiaries and affiliates. Conversion of international assets into pounds resulted in less and less sterling. The German mark collapsed beyond comprehension. Russian operations had no translatable value. As a protest against Britain, not the company, Irish revolutionaries burned the Clifden superstation down to the ground. Governments refused to meet their obligations. Compounding these difficulties, the company concluded it must recognize obsolescence in plant and equipment resulting from new inventions and designs, including its own. As a result, MWT provided reserves for its German and Russian investments and overdue debts of foreign governments, converted foreign security holdings into pound sterling, wrote off Clifden, losses on foreign currency holdings and plant and stock obsolescence, and recognized its share of losses in affiliates. The total charge against the company's assets, £2,335,000, was four times greater than revenues for 1923 and fourteen times greater than net profits. It reduced MWT's net worth by an enormous 25 percent.

The 1923 profit of £172,000 had already been reduced by currency devaluation and loss of Clifden revenue. It was a third below the average postwar income that from 1920 through 1922 ranged between £275,000 and £300,000.

There were bright spots. The company's claims against the British government for wartime services appeared near resolution. Operations in the second half of 1923 recovered materially and continued to recover in the first half of 1924.

To Marconi, the decision over disclosure of the short wave research became a matter of principle. The answer was clear. The company had represented to Australia and South Africa that a super-power, long-wave system was the only way to achieve long-distance communication. That no longer seemed to be true. The cost savings of the new method appeared to be significant. He could not stand by while others attempted to emulate his research.

MWT advised all three governments as to the tests and recommended proceeding with short waves.

Australia and South Africa, after the shock of the advice, agreed to short wave stations. Canada, who was considering a long-distance installation, concurred. The decision of all three, however, depended upon Great Britain's assent at the center of the network.

For Britain, the decision posed complex questions. It preferred to own and operate its communication system, but it had no experience with the new method. The technique was untried. In an emergency, the government wanted to be able to simultaneously reach Royal Navy vessels wherever in the world they might be located. Even if the new system worked, it beamed its waves in a single direction whereas long waves literally broadcast in all directions at once. Short waves had achieved only limited distances in daylight, a theoretically unexplained phenomena.

But the British government did not want to be left behind. It fully understood short waves' significance. It was sensitive to costs. On July 2, 1924, it accepted the concept. To protect the Royal Navy, the GPO would proceed with the super-power, long-wave station at Rugby. The administration authorized MWT to build first a short wave station for transmission to Canada, and if that proved satisfactory, subsequent transmitters to Australia, South Africa, and India.

The risk and opportunity were breathtaking.

The GPO insisted upon harsh terms. It required completion and satisfactory performance before it would pay for any of the construction costs for transmitting to Canada. It limited MWT to a 5 percent overhead charge and a 10 percent profit. The total could not exceed £35,120.

The company had to construct the installation within twenty-eight weeks of the date that GPO made the station site available.

Only if MWT met the deadline and then demonstrated over a seven-day period that transmissions satisfied contractual performance standards would the government be obligated to pay half of the company's costs. After a third period, this one six months long, and the satisfaction of further tests, the company would be entitled to another 25 percent of costs. A final payment covering the remaining costs, overhead, and profit would not be due for another six months and satisfaction of final standards.

If the station failed to pass any of the standards in the prescribed time, MWT must return all payments and clear the station from the site.

In exchange for the all-or-nothing risk on the Canadian station, the GPO agreed to pay a 6.25 percent royalty on the station's gross receipts as long as the site utilized company patents. In addition, MWT would be entitled to build the Australian, Indian, and South African stations and to be licensee for non-Commonwealth stations.

By disclosure and recommendation of its short wave development, the company had rendered its own superstation and long wave system obsolete. Failure to meet the strictures of the Canadian contract or commitments it may have to make in subsequent agreements could seriously jeopardize MWT's financial and long-distance positions.

But if it succeeded, the company would have given itself an opportunity to reestablish its worldwide, long-distance domination.

Marconi

No competitor at the moment had significant experience or patents in short waves. MWT would again threaten the foundation of the cable companies. If it constructed and operated short wave stations at a fraction of the cost of its long wave stations that currently competed equally with the underwater carriers, short wave would have a predatory economic advantage over cable.

Once more Marconi stood at the brink of collapse or unprecedented success. Thirty years earlier, a young man, twenty years old, uncertain of himself and his future, trembled in excitement on the slopes of the Italian Alps at Biellese and contemplated for the first time the nascent prospect of long-distance, wireless telegraphy. Now an adult of world stature as a scientist, inventor, and businessman, still obsessed with his dream, he had forged a chance of achievement to a degree he could never have imagined.

CHAPTER 21

Crippling Short Wave Dominance

Once more the company was at risk. In Vyvyan's words:

> The Marconi Company found itself in a position where it was essential to take enormous risks and give guarantees of performance for the effective working of a new system that had as yet never been used on any commercial circuit.(FN 1)

The occasions on which MWT's continued existence had depended upon Marconi's ingenuity and vitality had been endless. Perhaps the most dramatic had been in at St. John's in 1901 with Kemp and Paget. A year later, he and Vyvyan struggled to a second critical victory at Glace Bay.

In this 1924 crisis, the fifty-year-old inventor was supported by two veterans. Vyvyan was to construct the transmitting and receiving stations and antenna systems. Franklin had design responsibility. Three primary problems had to be resolved at once. He needed to convert the experimental short wave into a commercially reliable transmitter. Sending and receiving aerials had to be conceived for a wave whose length had not yet been determined. The transmitter's energy must be efficiently conveyed to the sending antenna and thence to a receptor a continent away without debilitating loss. The GPO contract required the cumulative result meet exacting operating standards and time schedules.

Following St. John's, Franklin had sailed with Marconi on the *Philadelphian* to confirm Marconi's claim that he heard signals in Newfoundland. Two years later, the engineer became a personal assistant to the scientist. By 1924, Franklin headed the Research Department, one of two company research divisions. The other was the Independent Research Department led by H. J. Round. Franklin had six engineers, twelve technical assistants, and laboratories at seven locations. He also looked after BBC's 2 LO broadcasting transmitter. Round had fourteen engineers, fourteen technical assistants, and five research sites. Franklin and Round were good friends, keen rivals, and very independent researchers. The board regarded both highly. Recognizing that neither would report to the other, the directors allowed them each their own organization. Franklin ultimately received sixty-five patents.

Marconi had become a regular at Cowes Regatta race week. Not even Imperial Network demands could keep him away. He had been elected to the Royal Yacht Squadron. In fact, arranging the membership had been his first order of business after acquiring *Elettra*. It was a matter of great pride to him. He wrote Godfrey Isaacs:

> The king came on board my yacht yesterday afternoon and remained over an hour looking over the wireless apparatus and the yacht generally. I was able to show him my good signals arriving from America and discuss more matters of interest. Last night I dined with the King and Queen on the Royal Yacht. Tomorrow I am expecting the Prince of Piedmont...I have met more people here who may be of use to us...As you probably know I have been elected a member of the Royal Yacht Squadron.(FN 2)

At Cowes, only *Elettra* flew both the white ensign of the Royal Navy and the tricolour bearing the Crown of Savoy. Its guest log included newspaper magnates Lord Camrose and Lord Kemsley. Diana Theodoli, Cristina Casati, Poppy Baring, Constance Bennett, and Mary Pickford, a bevy of beauties, had also been on board.

One particularly attractive woman who had joined a party on *Elettra* when it was anchored off Viareggio was Countessa Cristina Bezzi-Scali. She was a reigning belle in Roman society, a blonde with a fair complexion and blue eyes. That evening she wore a long, red velvet evening dress with a red rose pinned to one shoulder. She made an impression on the new divorcé.

Following the races at Cowes, Marconi and *Elettra* set out to return Degna and Giulio to the Italian coast. En route the inventor pressed his efforts to find the most effective wavelength. The clock was running. The experiments concentrated on ninety-two, sixty, forty-seven, and thirty-two meters. Test data pointed to an important principle. For daylight, distance increased as wavelength decreased.

After relieving himself of his children, Marconi sailed eastward the length of the Mediterranean. As Vyvyan noted:

> The employment of the *Elettra* for this important experiment, which demonstrated the practicality of short waves working over long distances, reduced the period of preliminary research very substantially. A moving station for purpose of observation and measurement, possesses great advantages over a fixed station where problems of range, directional effects, and other propagation questions required solutions. The *Elettra* was able to sail across the path of the beam to ascertain if the signals from Poldhu still traveled in the form of a beam at great distances, and also to measure the intensity of the signals both day and night over varying distances and with different wave lengths. Many months investigation were undoubtedly saved by the use of Marconi's yacht for this purpose.(FN 3)

In September, anchored at Beirut, twenty-four hundred miles from Poldhu, Marconi received signals on the thirty-two-meter wavelength throughout the day. He rushed back to England to conduct a final test to confirm thirty-two meters as the choice.

Stunning verification occurred in October. Marconi picked an hour when the electromagnetic waves would be in daylight over their entire route from Poldhu. He applied only twelve kilowatts of power. Signals arrived clearly in Montreal, New York, Rio de Janeiro, and Buenos Aires. Sydney, Australia, had constant reception for twenty-three and a half out of twenty-four hours. There was jubilation at MWT.

Sydney was a milestone. It affirmed the decision to break with long wave and rely on short wave for great distances. The success allowed the engineers to proceed with the design and construction of the transmitters, receivers, and antenna.

Godfrey Isaacs resigned as managing director. It had been fifteen years since Donough O'Brien introduced Isaacs to Marconi and the rest of the board. The managing director had contributed magnificently. From the outset, his forcefulness had sharpened executive direction, focus, and aggressiveness. With financial and marketing acumen, he opened important European countries to MWT previously monopolized by Telefunken. MWT patents were enforced and enhanced. He played a primary role in the United Wireless acquisition that established American Marconi's U.S. preeminence. In times of financial duress, Isaacs raised essential capital. He directed the company's wartime wireless intelligence service that benefited the Allies.

The Right Honourable F. G. Kellaway succeeded Isaacs. Formerly postmaster general in Prime Minister Asquith's postwar government, he had joined the board in 1922. This was an astute move by the company considering the historically troubled relationship with the GPO and its importance to the Imperial Wireless Network. With him Kellaway brought the experience of government chairmanships and large organization management, the qualities of a diplomat and conciliator, and a reputation of being a firm decision-maker. He was, however, bureaucratic and establishment-minded rather than entrepreneurial or dedicated to scientific advancement. The prior June as MWT suffered through the painful write-off of assets, the board named Kellaway chairman of a special finance committee to establish control over the company's financial policies. The committee halted investment in non-core businesses. It reorganized profit centers. It heightened attention on manufacturing sound broadcasting equipment, obtaining a worldwide license for wireless telegraphic services from the British government, and short wave.

Profits for 1924 improved marginally to £225,000. Asset valuation deterioration continued, albeit at a slower pace. MWT wrote off another £677,000. That lowered its general reserves to £1 million. Retooling and the short wave project had consumed the company's capital. MWT was forced to issue five hundred thousand shares to raise £633,000.

Despite the enormous demands the short wave crisis imposed upon him and his long-stated desire to end all relationships that took him away from research, Marconi found time to see Cristina again. The occasion was an afternoon party in Rome in the palace of their mutual friends, Prince and Princess del Drago, on Via Quattro Fontane. Cristina was half Marconi's age and fourteen years younger than Bea. Like Beatrice, she was very pretty. She appeared to be serious, quiet, and unsophisticated in comparison to the women normally swirling about Marconi. The family appealed to him as well. Her father, Count Francesco Bezzi-Scali, was a member of papal nobility. He held the rank of brigadier general in the Papal Guarda Nobile. Her mother was the daughter of Princess Beatrice Orsini and Marchese Urbano Sacchetti. He headed a venerable Roman family.

Cristina was not the youngest of Marconi's interests. The cruises along the Cornish coast had served more purposes than wireless research and summer holidays for the children. A local newspaper noted:

> Marconi's Love Romance: Engagement to a Cornish Girl Expected.
> It is understood that an announcement of the engagement of Senatore Marconi, the world famous wireless genius, to Miss Elisabeth Narcissa Paynter, only daughter of Lt. Col. Camborne H. Paynter and Mrs. Paynter, is likely to be made in the course of the next few days.
> Senatore Marconi is at present on his yacht *Elettra* at Gibraltar, and but for illness would have been with Col. Paynter and his family for the celebration of Miss Paynter's eighteenth birthday on Tuesday.
> Senatore Marconi and Col. and Mrs. Paynter have been the closest friends for many years. Miss Paynter has known Senatore Marconi since she was a child of fourteen. He was a visitor at Christmas and with Miss Paynter attended a ball in Penzance.(FN 4)

Marconi, twice Cristina's age, was almost three times Betty's age. But from his point of view, fifty-one years old when he celebrated his birthday in April, was there that much difference between a twenty-six-year-old and an eighteen-year-old? From the vantage point of the unhappy father of the eighteen-year-old, there certainly was.

Marconi

While Marconi struggled with the practical consequences of his discoveries about short waves, new theories emerged as to what caused waves, short or long, to be received at such great distances from their transmission point. In the April 1925 issue of *QST*, American amateur John Reinartz speculated that reflection of radio waves by the Kennelly-Heaviside layer related to their frequency. K. M. Jansly postulated that the distance waves attenuated to the earth must also be affected by frequency. The greater the repetition per second, the more they clung to the surface. Under this perception, if signals traveled further than expected, they must be both moving along the ground and bouncing off the layer.

MWT had no theoretical or practical way to pretest the performance of its proposed installations until they were erected. To have any chance to meet the Canadian deadline, the entire system had to be put up at once on both sides of the Atlantic. As a result, without any assurance of success, the company began construction of a transmitter at Bodmin in Cornwall, a receiving antenna at Bridgwater in Somerset, and Canadian counterparts at Montreal and Yamachiche. It was a huge risk, but the board saw no way to avoid it. To maximize the efficiency of its ultimate hoped-for network, MWT also selected Bodmin for South Africa transmission and Bridgwater for South African receiving. Sending sites were chosen near Grimsby for India and Australia and in Dorchester for New York, Buenos Aires, and Rio. To receive, Skegness was designated for India and Australia and Somerset for New York, Buenos Aires, and Rio.

Antenna constructions constituted major projects. To permit the transmitter to use two wavelengths, a safety precaution in the event one did not perform satisfactorily and an effort to increase capacity if both worked, Franklin designed a dual receiving antenna. For support, it required five 287-foot masts. It was a significant undertaking. Still, the design presented major cost savings compared to the previously planned Australian long wave receiver. It consisted of twenty 800-foot masts. Marconi called for the antenna to be placed at right angles to the direction of the shortest great circle route from transmitter to receiver. He also used a reflector to focus the wave in the narrowest beam possible. This concentrated the use of the available energy but required the sender and reflector be precisely aimed to hit such a faraway target. For direction, the engineers took fixes on the sun and stars. For elevation, trial and error experiments were run to select the best angle above the horizon at which to loft the signal. The consensus was ten to fifteen degrees.

None of this had been done before. Together, the tight band of company men by experience, calculation, experimentation, and intuition forged ahead. MWT's future depended upon how right they turned out to be.

Franklin arranged an elaborate transmitting antenna. Aerials were lined up behind each other to reinforce the signal. They were also stacked one above another to narrow the beam width. The structure's complexity threatened to absorb all the energy being transferred from transmitter to individual antenna. Under fierce pressure, Franklin overcame the danger by conceiving a concentric feeder. The waves generated by the transmitter were carried to the exact center of the antenna system. Then in precisely symmetric pairs he divided and re-divided the line until each aerial had been simultaneously fed. To serve as carrier, Franklin devised concentric copper tubes, one air-insulated from the other by a space created by porcelain conduit. The inner tube acted as the conductor and the outer as the earth. The design became the coaxial cable.

The extraordinary oscillation of short waves also presented novel demands. A wave 333 meters long repeated itself one hundred thousand times per second. Its frequency would be one hundred kilohertz. The 32-meter wave would be reiterated one hundred million times each second. Its frequency would be one hundred megahertz, or a thousand times greater than that to which MWT was accustomed. Typical of the consequent problems, the seals of thermionic valves used for long waves broke down when transmitting short waves. Excessive grid and anode currents were released. To meet this challenge, the engineering team worked out a copper anode envelope cooled by oil circulation named CAT valve for cooled anode transmitting. As soon as he dared, Vyvyan incorporated each new idea into his construction program.

Time was not in MWT's favor. In addition to building the apparatus without assurance it would work, the board had faced a second dilemma where again it had been forced to make a decision. The Imperial Wireless Network contract terms authorized the GPO to select the UK site from which messages would be sent to Canada. Within twenty-eight weeks of formal selection, the agreement required the system be on-line and operating at prescribed levels. If it failed to meet this deadline, the company lost all rights to build and run the network and be reimbursed for its costs. MWT had desperately needed to start construction, but obviously it must be at the spot GPO ultimately chose. Before spending money on Bodmin, the board had had to reach an informal understanding with the bureaucrats that that station would be their choice. Many weeks, certainly more than twenty-eight, were still needed to construct, test, and adjust the unique concepts. Having informally concluded that Bodmin was the site, the General Post Office, Marconi's competitor in many regards, could whenever it wished officially start the period running. If GPO pulled the trigger now, the company could not complete its work in the allotted period.

Despite this exigency and fevered activity by all hands to reduce the estimated time to attain satisfactory results in less than twenty-eight weeks, Marconi in early August 1925 anchored at Cowes. Race week had become an essence of life.

Elettra rewarded him psychically for his success. Its very presence, his command of the yacht, and his life aboard it embodied the recognition he craved. He did not have an ego that drove him to flaunt his success. He did not require third-party adulation, although he received an incredible amount. He did not attempt to leverage his recognition into personal aggrandizement. But from his earliest boyhood, he yearned to be someone in a role he savored. *Elettra*'s possession was a self-evident statement of wealth, success, and importance.

Housed in the great white yacht at the annual regatta, he was anyone's equal. Society's leaders came to him. They boarded his ship. They were his guests in his domain. He was at ease there. Even to the King of England, titular head of the world's greatest empires, he could be host.

Elettra, not the Savoy, was home. Thirty crewmen, nearly all his countrymen, not English, established its Italian atmosphere. It was a science center. It was freedom. He ruled it entirely, without distraction or interruption, except those he permitted or indulged in. He had refuges in his personal quarters, wireless cabin, and smoking room. The last also served as study and held the piano. Occasionally he played for those on board. More frequently he lingered at the keys when he was alone. Perhaps he sensed the romance he hungered for. His fingers may have softly tapped out tunes Annie sang to which Giuseppe's heart had responded. The dining room often sat a dozen at race week. Neighboring yachts complained that in late evening the lilting dance notes of the Savoy Orpheans borne by radio wave from London wafted too clearly across the waters from that unique ship that bore ensigns of both Italy and England.

Following Cowes, Marconi dropped a bombshell on Bea. He wrote her August 13:

> Don't be surprised, he said, or upset if you hear I have become engaged to Betty Paynter. I care for the girl an awful lot, more than I ever thought I could, and she for me. I have been fighting against myself over this for a long time, but I am afraid it's no use. After all even you know how lonely I am. She is an only child. There would of course, be no question of settlements from me or anything of that kind if I married her.(FN 5)

Beatrice exploded. Livid, she did not attempt to conceal her reaction. It was absolutely galling that he reached out to her for sympathy and to justify remarriage on the grounds that he was lonely. "After all even you know how lonely I am." He had left her to be alone! Beatrice wasted no words in response:

> I am surprised to hear you have decided to take the step you write me of in your last letter and create new ties and most probably a new family. I would like to wish you every happiness but this news distresses me for I wonder after all the years we were together when your own desire expressed continually was for freedom to concentrate on your work as your family impeded and oppressed you, why you should suddenly feel this great loneliness and need of a home—this craving for fresh ties!! These ties were eventually what broke up your home and ended in our divorce. I fail to understand.(FN 6)

Incredible as Marconi's announcement was, more unbelievably her response upset him. By telegraph, he requested they meet in Florence. Once together, he did not placate her or answer her question. It was not her anger that bothered him. He was surprised she thought he should not marry Betty. He sought her opinion and asked what people were saying. She could not have but looked at him in amazement. Why, she demanded, did he seek her advice, of all people. Again, his words must have stunned her. "Because you are the only person in the world who will tell me the truth."

What relationship did Marconi think he had with this woman? Apparently, his inquiries of her were sincere. How naïve then could he be. After years of faithless conduct and absence and a separation for reasons absolutely contradictory to his rationale for a new alliance, he expected her empathy. His insensitivity was monstrous. How could he ask Bea about another woman in her place? What might possibly this teenage innocent have that Beatrice had not? How well did he know himself? After unhappily struggling for aloneness, he in no time longed for permanent companionship.

Marconi could be emotional about others. He experienced overwhelming infatuations. He engaged in dalliances. He was loyal to Kemp and had a warm, lifetime friendship with Solari. But Marconi had a frigid spot. Often with regard to people who should be dear to him no expression of feeling appeared beyond superficial engagement. On many occasions important to him, he exhibited no evidence of an internal sensation. Perhaps responding to boyhood estrangements and embarrassments and fatherly disapproval he so steeled himself to obliterate hurts and disappointments that from part of his being he excised sentiment. Paget noted that after an early disaster Marconi had evinced nothing:

> He was never unduly elated and never unduly depressed. When the twenty masts erected at Poldhu for the transatlantic transmission collapsed in a gale Marconi looked at the wreckage and said quietly to me: "Well, they will be built again." That was all.(FN 7)

But if scientifically engrossed, he could find satisfaction and elation. He once confided to Solari: "When I am allowed to work in my own technical field, I am the happiest man in the world." The clinical, person-less world of physics, mechanics, numbers, and formulas yielded desirable outcomes without personal price tags. The results were most important. Here Marconi felt most comfortable. Human relationships came second.

Wife, children, mother, and father were afforded less recognition and sentiment than invention.

But his detachment should not be overstated. During this period of unending crisis, Guglielmo corresponded with Beatrice as if she were the closest and best of friends. He was solicitous and caring for his children, although on occasion in a somewhat domineering fashion.

Giulio advised Marconi that he did not feel attracted to sea life. Consequently, he preferred not to try for the naval academy. The former cadet and officer made a special trip from London to Italy to talk with his son. The father who at a similar age had been unable to gain admission to that institution to his own sire's disappointment and disgust pointed out the merits of the Accademia Navale. The boy came around all of his own, Guglielmo insisted in a letter to Bea. He expressed relief as he felt much more in harmony with navy officers than university professors. This was hardly surprising considering his acrimonious disagreements with Professor Lodge.

Finding Degna unnecessarily shy and studious, Marconi determined she should attend school in London or Paris. He wrote Bea that it would be a great pity if their daughter did not attend Ozanne School in the French capital and he "will be glad if you will come to the same conclusion." Bea did. Guglielmo visited his oldest child there. He took her to the theater and dinner and personally brought her the fun he thought she was so badly missing. He saw to it that she had an operation on her teeth. Degna was amazed. This man, in her opinion, had no understanding of women. He was totally ignorant that her life was in shambles. How could he prescribe what was best for her? At the end of the year she confessed to herself it may have been just what she needed.

Not surprisingly, the affair with Betty Paynter could not survive the thirty-four years age difference. Its failure did not affect the distinguished-looking scientist's social schedule. Lady Cunard, Cynthia Nosley, Constance Bennett, and many other women filled his calendar. There were even suggestions that he simultaneously carried on with more than one. One arrangement was so notorious that London tradesmen routinely forwarded the lady's bills to Marconi.

Even while he considered marriage to Betty Paynter, Marconi became increasingly preoccupied with Cristina. At Via Reggio, he posted himself near her on the beach or at a table in the Savoia, a small restaurant where she ate with her mother and father. He invited the parents to visit or travel on *Elettra*. Their daughter was welcome as well. Years earlier Beatrice had driven Marconi wild by spurning his marriage proposal. Now Cristina seemed equally out of reach. Even if the Catholic Church recognized Marconi's Fiume divorce, it would not permit Cristina, a Catholic, to marry a divorced person.

The year ended well. On the last day of 1925, the General Post Office granted the company a general license to establish wireless telegraph services with thirteen European countries and all foreign countries outside of Europe.

In February 1926, Beatrice, forty-two-years-old, had a baby girl. Giulio advised his father of the birth. Guglielmo wrote his former wife that he had been very anxious about her. He was really relieved to know that it was over. He ended the letter with congratulations and best wishes and best love. "Ever yours affectionately."

On March 29, 1926, Spain conferred on Maroni the Plus Ultra Order Gold Medal for "extraordinary service on behalf of mankind."

At the end of April, the GPO officially declared Bodmin the UK site for the Canadian system. That started the clock. MWT had twenty-eight weeks to meet the contractual standards. Otherwise, the GPO owed the company nothing for all its expenditures and effort. The Marconi interests would have no rights to the Imperial Wireless Network.

Despite Vyvyan's best efforts, construction had not advanced sufficiently to conduct preliminary field tests. Marconi and the engineers could not tell if they were on the right track.

Adverse, unsettled foreign economic conditions continued unmercifully. A review of the company's properties disclosed that the asset value hemorrhaging had not ceased despite write-offs in excess of two and a half million pounds over the past two years.

Marconi's fascination with the unattainable Cristina grew unchecked. Sensitive to his age and deeply desirous of her, he dyed his few grey hairs black. Obstinately, he determined he would have her. He obsessed over clearing the obstacles imposed by the Church. Solicitors expert in Catholic ecclesiastical law and mores were retained. They advised that to marry Cristina, the marriage to Beatrice must be annulled. Three grounds were recognized. First, the union had been entered into under moral or physical pressure. Second, after two non-Catholics united, one converted to Catholicism and the other then refused to remain in the relationship. Third, the vows had been entered into with lack of consent. That is, a condition existed at the time of the wedding that the bonds might be subsequently cancelled other than death. Only this reason appeared even remotely available to Marconi. He recalled that Beatrice had rejected his first proposal. Furthermore, her family had resisted his courtship because he was a foreigner. The lawyers thought these objections might be sufficient to establish lack of consent. But to prove his case, Marconi needed witnesses who would swear under oath as to their awareness of the reservation. Most of all, he needed Beatrice's agreement that indeed they had entered into their contract with the understanding if they could not make it work they would divorce.

Marconi restated his vows in the Catholic Church. Under Cristina's guidance, he wanted to make a thorough study of its teachings. She advised him to read the New Testament with the commentaries of great scholars and gave him a well-known ascetic book, *The Imitation of Christ*, that he found particularly interesting. He told Cristina that he felt like a ship that has found a safe harbor. The Sacrament of Confirmation was administered by a Bishop in the Bezzi-Scali palace in Rome at 11 Via Condotti, where Cristina was born and lived with her parents. Her father stood godfather to Guglielmo.(FN 8)

Vyvyan announced the transmitter, reflector, and antenna at Bodmin ready for an initial effort. It had been less than two years since execution of the GPO contract and one and a half from selection of the thirty-two meter wavelength. The trial and annulment preparations competed for Marconi's attention. But he gathered with Vyvyan, Franklin, company engineers, and anxious MWT officers in Cornwall. The system was turned on. Franklin shot the signals across the ocean. In Canada, there was only sickening silence. Engineers there donning earphones heard no noise of any sort. Nancarrow, senior engineer in charge at Bodmin, recounted what he called a true test of Marconi's nature and spirit:

> From the first period of shock when it was found that the expected communication to Canada did not materialise...I never saw Marconi other than calm, quiet spoken, and apparently unaffected by the setback which had

411

overtaken this quite new venture in long distance radio communication.(FN 9)

Obviously, much remained to be done. The veteran staff resolutely set about to discover what modifications would make the new technology operational.

Marconi returned to London to pursue clearing the path to Cristina. He contacted Beatrice and asked to meet in Rome. He won her consent to his plan. She felt she must allow him a chance to find the same happiness in marriage she now had. Next, he needed relatives or friends who could from twenty-one years earlier recall events that favored his case. He hastened back to the UK capital, where he worked feverishly readying for his own appearance. He hoped his experience appearing in MWT's patent cases would stand him in good stead.

On July 7, 1926, Marconi testified before the Roman Catholic Ecclesiastical Commission at Archbishops House, Westminster Cathedral. He told the panel he and Beatrice had determined in the unfortunate event their marriage not be a happy one they might later try to obtain divorce. He was asked the meaning of the conditionless phrase in the couple's Church of England wedding "till death do us part." He answered that despite those words traditionally repeated in its ceremonies, the Church of England recognized divorce. He, therefore, did not believe their literal recitation obviated the exception to which he and his bride had agreed. They were no more binding than her promise to obey.

Marconi left England again, this time for Bologna to celebrate the thirtieth anniversary of his initial experiments at Villa Grifone. On July 12, he stepped off the train at the railway station to be welcomed by his nephews Giovanni and Pietro Marconi and in their estimation half the citizens of Bologna. The next day, rector and faculty in full silk and ermine academic regalia greeted Marconi at the University of Bologna and paraded him through the Renaissance courtyard into the Aula Magna ringing with cheers. Putting away his notes, Marconi spontaneously delivered a long speech. He recounted his life in ten-year cycles. He began in 1896 when he received his first patent. Now at the end of the third decade, he had arrived once more at a high point. The long waves had led down a blind alley. That would soon be rectified. Despite the lack of success at Bodmin, he expressed only optimism about short wave. He proclaimed his scientific faith:

> The more a man bends the phenomena of nature to his will the more he discovers and the more he will continue to discover. Because of this he will increasingly realize the infinity of the Infinite.(FN 10)

From Bologna Marconi traveled to Rome. In what may have been one of the proudest moments of his life, and in retrospect one of the most bittersweet, he walked into the Senate accompanied by Mussolini. Cheers greeted Il Duce. The prime minister directed the applause to Marconi, whom he had just appointed president of the Italian Royal Academy.

Mussolini established the academy to coordinate Italian culture and enhance the Fascist government's reputation. He personally selected as members Italy's leading intellectuals, including Maruretti the poet, Mascagni the composer, the dramatist Pirandello, and physicist Enrico Fermi. Marconi topped this august, cerebral, elite body. Mussolini purposely attracted non-Fascists. With the academy's entitlements, he bribed support for his regime. The luminaries received a salary without duties, helmets with plumes, and ceremonial recognition. The prestige was enormous. In return, each appointee swore a loyalty oath to Fascism, and every meeting opened with a formal salute to Il Duce.

Marconi's views about Mussolini from his ascension in 1924 to the prime ministership at the request of the king until the scientist's death are not well documented. His daughter Degna in her biography of her father thought he had serious reservations and contemplated giving up Rome for London. His second wife, who was with him to his dying days, denies he considered such a move.

Mussolini had not included Marconi in the academy until the third list because of the inventor's British ties. Degna said Marconi hesitated for three years before going along with the Fascists. Once designated, however, he was elevated to the premier position of leadership. He accepted the role.

Marconi deeply loved Italy. He was an Italian citizen by deep commitment and choice as well as by birth. He was loyal to king and government.

Marconi

He answered every official summons to duty. In many cases, he volunteered before he was called. Mussolini came to power on the back of the *squadrismo*. Marconi, as an Italian leader and hero and senator, could have spoken out. He did not. Some people of his magnitude did. Some went into exile. Marconi said the Fascist loyalty oath. To his end, Marconi met and consulted with Mussolini and never rejected his emoluments.

Was Marconi an active believer in Fascism? It is doubtful. He was politically disinterested. He regarded himself a scientist and inventor. From age twenty, he primarily thought of long-distance wireless. But did he allow himself to be used by Il Duce? The answer is yes.

Marconi, in courting Cristina, restated his Catholic vows. Was he a proactive participant? It is not likely. His observation of electromagnetic waves led to his frequently stated appreciation of the infinite. Did he also to the last see the pope and assist the worldwide dissemination of his Holy Word through the use of Marconi apparatus? The answer is yes.

Back in London, Marconi's frenetic pace continued without relief. It was a highly tense and nervous time for him.

Twelve of the twenty-eight weeks to meet the Bodmin deadline had passed without results. Vyvyan's first tests had failed. The board wanted evidence of progress. Adjustments were being made at a furious pace, but Marconi was not sufficiently confident in their effect to allow another try to reach Canada.

The annulment gnawed at him. The proceedings had moved rapidly, but he feared the outcome would turn on Bea's testimony at Spoleto. Could she convincingly explain why the officially stated reason for divorce in their Fiume divorce papers differed from the lack of consent grounds he had presented the Ecclesiastical Commission? He found time to write her two long, anxious letters instructing her on her responses.

The directors were also up in arms over the continuing decline in the company's asset value. The preliminary review for the 1925 year identified another £1 million deterioration. That wiped out MWT's entire remaining reserves. In addition, profits plunged one-third from £225,000 to £150,000, the lowest since 1913. Alarmed, the board deferred the annual stockholder meeting. It called in Cooper Brothers & Co., its outside auditors, for a special investigation of the company's principal operations. Marconi's vast short wave expenditures without results were to be scrutinized.

Not even this myriad of extreme difficulties, however, prevented Marconi from being at Cowes in the beginning of August.

There was little Marconi could do for the annulment process now except worry. He could not rest easy at the Regatta. After only two days, he left for Cornwall.

The intractable problems began to give way. At the deferred shareholder gathering, the board reported that it would deal with the financial difficulties assisted by the auditors' special study. Marconi told the assembled owners he saw short wave progress. He expected the deadline to be met.

Beatrice, however, had still not been called to Spoleto.

It was mid-October. Twenty-one days were left until the all-or-nothing date. MWT had still not conducted a full test, but there were encouraging moments. Marconi, Franklin, and Vyvyan decided they must allow the post office officials an attempt to communicate with Canada while several weeks remained. The engineers would then have one last opportunity to make adjustments in a last-ditch attempt to try to meet the contractual standards by the November deadline.

On October 18, 1926, GPO operators sat at the controls at Bodmin and Bridgewater and the corresponding North American stations at Montreal and Yamachiche.

Sixteen faultless transmitting hours at a very high signaling rate had to be produced every twenty-four hours.

The General Post Office transmissions surpassed all contractual requirements.

The performance exceeded that of every other wireless system in the world. Global acclaim greeted the triumph.

On October 24, 1926, Canada opened for public traffic.

In December 1901, Marconi had doubtfully received a weak transatlantic signal. He awakened the world to a coming telecommunication revolution. In 1926, he rendered obsolete what had taken him a quarter century to create. In its place he delivered a far more powerful and efficient fully operational system. He predicted the balance of the British short wave imperial network would be in service shortly.

In November, very good personal news arrived. The Court of Westminster Cathedral granted the religious invalidation of his marriage to Beatrice. Rome must still approve. In a favorable sign, the Catholic

Court in Rome approved the cancellation of bonds between the Duke of Marlborough and Consuelo Vanderbilt.

At the very moment of the Canadian triumph, Marconi's standing with members of the board suddenly soured. Cooper Brothers' investigation into the decline of MWT's assets and cash position spotlighted Marconi. He had spent a huge sum. More dramatically, the degree of his success forced a new and enormous write-down. Short wave obsolesced the long wave stations. The prodigious amounts MWT had poured into these installations since 1902 and carried on its books had to be significantly reduced. The accountants were about to recommend the largest write-off in company history. Its surplus accounts would be wiped out and in a significant deficit position. Short wave earning power could not be written up to offset the negative actions. Marconi was the only operating and scientific board member. Some of the others, all financial men, could not see the future beyond the immediate number crisis. Marconi sorely missed Isaacs, who had been respected by the directors for his understanding of the balance between pounds and progress. Fingers thoughtlessly or intentionally were pointed at the inventor. He was furious and hurt. He wrote Bea:

> I have been rushed to death with things and I now have another lecture coming on in Rome. I am very likely to have a row with the Company here and tell them to go hell in which case I would come to live in Italy for a time. How could I arrange for a house here under the circumstances? My work has gone splendidly, and I have got lots of new inventions, that I may be able to sell in America, if I split with the Company, but it is nevertheless probable that things will be arranged.(FN 11)

It was an amazing split between the man who continued to be the genius behind the company and the financial directors who now dominated the board. On their part, they were frustrated and fearful for MWT. The write-offs from a variety of causes threatened to destroy the value of the enterprise.

The lecture and Rome went well as Marconi advised Bea on November 26, his last night there:

As you may have seen in the papers on Wednesday evening, I was received by the Pope. He was quite charming and I found him quite broad-minded. Of course I never mentioned anything about our case. He told me he had listened to the whole of my lecture at the Augusteo on the wireless.

On my leaving he made me a present of a beautiful gold medal as a remembrance of my visit. I had asked to see him on the suggestion of Cardinal Gasparri...I am in a most awful hurry and not feeling very well from overwork.(FN 12)

While Pius XI may not have mentioned the annulment proceeding, it was a well-timed meeting. It would be surprising if he was unaware of Marconi's petition. Cardinal Gasparri was secretary of state to the pope. Cristina's spiritual adviser was Bishop Eugenio Pacelli, an undersecretary of state and a former student of Gasparri. Marconi had first met the secretary of state at the end of the War when Guglielmo and Bea had the servants line up at the front door to greet the cardinal. Cristina reintroduced her suitor to the powerful priest.(FN 13)

The tension from MWT's financial condition, the contractual deadlines for Australia, South Africa, and India, and the annulment continued to wear on Marconi. As Christmas approached, he struggled to leave London for Rome. On Christmas Eve, still in London, he wrote Cristina: "Whatever happens, you have been the Angel of my conversion, of my redemption, an Angel like the one that stopped St. Paul on the road to Damascus."(FN 14)

At last, six months after he had opened his campaign, the Roman authorities called Beatrice. She went to Spoleto and testified. The months of high anxiety continued, however, as Marconi awaited the outcome.

The license of the British Broadcasting Corporation, run by the seven manufacturers, expired on December 31, 1926. The GPO did not renew it. Instead, the organization was reorganized under a royal charter. The government took the place of the seven companies. Radio broadcasting had been nationalized. Private ownership had been eliminated. MWT had lost its last vestige of participation.

Marconi

On March 27, 1927, with Marconi in the chair, the company held its annual meeting of shareholders to review the results of 1926. The restive board, quietly confident that it had weathered the worst, had patched over matters with Marconi. Canada assured everyone of short wave's technical success. Profit in 1926 had rebounded to £198,000, helped in part by the two months of transatlantic operation. The board had manfully responded to the Cooper Brothers report. A £2,766,000 asset charge left a net £1,625,000 deficit in the surplus account and substantially impaired the capital account. Dividends could not be paid. Kellaway proposed, and the stockholders approved, the reduction of the nominal value of the 4 million one-pound ordinary shares to ten shillings. That restored the surplus account to a positive number and the ability to make distributions. The assembly then authorized the sale of 3.6 million new shares to generate cash. Marconi could only protect against another substantial reduction in his percentage ownership of the company by purchasing additional shares. With the financial problems sorted, the directors looked forward. They could now foresee substantial profit once the full network was in place.

MWT submitted to Australian officials on April 8, 1927. An average daily capacity of words had been guaranteed in either direction, to or from Australia, equal to twenty thousand words. The requirement was immediately exceeded. In short order, three times the standard, or sixty thousand words per day, was produced. Relatively little additional labor and electric expense were required to reach this level. Consequently, cost per word fell drastically. Profit margin climbed steeply with volume.

Suddenly and significantly, MWT could compete with cable in the amount of traffic it could carry and at a price well below cable.

South Africa opened July 5, 1927 and India September 5, 1927. Performance with both countries far surpassed contract terms.

In the thirty-nine months from May 1924, when it disclosed its short wave experiments and risked its future, the company had achieved its goals brilliantly. Commercial communication links between Great Britain and Canada, Australia, South Africa, and India had been designed, engineered, built, and rendered operational in compliance with all commitments.

On April 27, 1927, Marconi could at last be relieved and privately content. The Tribunal of the Sacco Rota in Rome confirmed the annulment of Beatrice and Guglielmo's marriage on the grounds of defective intent. Although for Marconi the process took forever, considering the reluctance of the Catholic Church to abrogate contracts, it had gone off quite quickly.

Marconi and Cristina let no time go by. On June 12, 1927, they exchanged civil vows at Campidoglio. Three days later, the wedding ceremony followed in the stunning church of Santa Maria degli Angeli. Cristina's wedding dress was white satin with a long train. She wore an antique Irish lace veil that had been Annie's and a diamond tiara that Guglielmo designed for her himself. He did not think that any of the jewelers' offerings were sufficiently beautiful for Cristina.(FN 15). His witnesses were Prince del Drago and Prince Ludovico Spada Potenziani. Mussolini was his best man. Alfonso came from London. Cardinal Evaristo Lucidi blessed the marriage. Cristina's witnesses were her uncles Prince Domenico Orsini and the Marquis Guglielmo Guglielmi d'Antognolla. The reception, which was attended by Roman aristocracy, representatives of the Vatican, and ambassadors of a number of countries, was held in the Bezzi-Scali castle.

In July, the short wave system assured, Marconi retired as chairman of the board of directors. He remained a director and technical adviser. At age fifty-three, after thirty-three years of prodigious effort and achievement, he was free to devote himself full time to the company's scientific and engineering aspects and the research he loved.

Cristina and Marconi remained in Italy and England until India went online. He was ready for a long vacation. He had not enjoyed one since short wave testing intensified five years earlier. It had been an exhausting period. In October, they sailed for New York on the *Biancamano*. Cristina had not sailed the Atlantic before. It was his eighty-fifth crossing in twenty-eight years. They were greeted with open arms. Mayor James J. Walker had just returned from Italy, where he had visited Mussolini and the pope. He invited the newlyweds to City Hall and "to the biggest Italian City in the world." He confided he was called him Jimmy in Rome. While he did not wish to be familiar, he said to Marconi, "What we feel like doing is to take you by the arm and say 'Bill, you're welcome.'" Marconi beamed in response.

The trip had all the trappings of a Marconi New York festival. There were receptions, reporters, interviews, lectures, attendance at professional societies, luncheons, dinners, and social events. As much as Cristina may have been impressed by his stature and importance in Italy and England, the outpouring of attention paid her husband in New York must have been overwhelming and satisfying.

Pupin introduced Marconi once more to the Institute of Radio Engineers. With warm words he said, "Marconi, we love you. We have come to see your boyish smile as much as to hear what you have to say."(FN 16) Marconi, at the height of his career as a scientist, inventor, and businessman, continued to credit the efforts of others. He looked forward to wireless's ever-expanding future.

This trip may have been the most climactic and happiest moment of his life. He was flushed with the realization of his dream to create global wireless. The public and leading Italian, English, and North American figures recognized and respected him. His attractive young wife loved him. Taking nothing from Cristina, it is only sad to note it was a victory lap that Beatrice deserved as well.

The triumph of short wave was symbolized by its achievement in December, 1927. In one week, it carried 670,000 words. The annualized rate would equal 34,840,000. It averaged 95,000 words per day.

The company had arrived at crippling dominance. No competitor's apparatus approached MWT's. Wireless rivals would have to acquire new equipment from the company or attempt to build their own in the face of MWT's superior experience and patents. Marconi pricing undercut everyone.

Cable felt short wave immediately. Even before its impact, submarine systems servicing the British Empire were receiving UK and Dominion subsidies to meet cash requirements and avoid rate increases. They had little or no leeway to lower capital or operating costs. The values at which they carried their capitalized building investments faced the same issues that had forced the write-down of MWT's long wave installations.

British authorities were not pleased. They had poured money into cable. The underwater systems that linked the empire needed their support and accepted their influence. Ministers saw in the company a private corporation independent of Westminster. MWT had constantly fought with the GPO. Marconi's new invention might well bankrupt both cable and wireless industries. With such a great competitive advantage, MWT would require no financial aid. It would need only to be licensed. If the company's technology and costs were so dramatically superior, how could Great Britain afford to be without its services?

UK officials saw the same issues that had earlier upset President Wilson and Daniels. They feared control of vital, long-distance communication would be out of their hands.

Chapter 22

The Last Merger

Marconi lived at a level of elegance rarely achieved. Scientists infrequently break to the forefront at the young age he did. He was twenty-seven at St. John's. For the past quarter century, he had been setting the pace. Not many play such a preeminent role for so long. Even fewer create a global, industry-dominating enterprise in which they remain one of the principal executives. Neither Thomas Edison nor Alexander Graham Bell did. It would be difficult to find a handful of examples in other fields. On top of this close to unique dual distinction, Marconi attracted star-like notoriety on two continents. He was feted and recognized with nations' honors. He led his country's elite royal academy. With a noble, young wife at his side, he was acquaintance, friend, host, or guest of kings and queens, the pope, state heads, movie stars, and society figures. Life and research on *Elettra* were frosting on his cake.

Short wave cut at once into the underwater companies. Submarine lines had one advantage. Along a route such as London-Singapore, messages could be picked up and delivered between intermediate points where cable came ashore. Wireless traveled point to point with no in-between stops. As a result, the underwater system serviced markets where MWT had no installation. But, depending upon conditions, airborne transmitters spit out 100–250 words per minute against cable's 35–100 words. Where the two types of carriers went head-to-head, MWT had speed, volume capacity, and lower per-unit invested and operating costs. If cable matched price, it lost money. If it charged more, customers abandoned it. By the end of 1927, submarine corporations experienced 50 percent volume losses in competitive markets. Their business went to MWT. With lower tariffs, MWT also attracted new users. Revenue exploded. Even without the network in place for the full year, MWT's leaping profits doubled in 1927 to £430,000.

The British and Dominion authorities became concerned. They believed the underwater systems important to the Commonwealth, both commercially and politically. As long as their countries controlled the oceans, the network in wartime was vital to national security. The subsidies regarded as investments in the network now suddenly were at risk. The UK government had had close ties to the industry's owners ever since it provided Royal Navy ships to support the effort to lay the first transatlantic submarine line.

In January 1928, bureaucrats convened an Empire Government Conference, the Imperial Wireless and Cable Conference. Corporations whose undersea communications were connected to the member countries and the company were asked to present their viewpoints to assembled representatives of Home Government, Dominions, and India. The threat of government ownership to which the GPO continued to be predisposed surfaced again. The convention offered the private parties an opportunity to work out a solution among themselves. The unveiled hint was that the massive, subsidized organizations and the high-flyer, independent, self-financed, new technology challenger should explore merger. MWT depended upon these officials for permission to operate from their territories.

Both sides agreed to talk. The Associated Cable Companies appointed Sir William Plender, and MWT picked Sir Culbert Garnsey as their respective representatives. The two men were instructed to explore basis for merger and report back with a joint proposal.

These events required Marconi to return from New York. He must have sorely missed Jameson-Davis and Isaacs. Those managing directors knew the company roots and Marconi. They appreciated research and reinvestment in the never-ending drive for better long-distance communication. For them, the goal had not been comfortable monetary returns. Capital funded advances. Neither Garnsey nor the board, all but the inventor financial men, understood MWT tradition. Kellaway, company chairman, steeped in government service and his role as a former postmaster general, placed before MWT's historical ambition the country's interest in its overall communication system.

In midwinter of 1928, the newlyweds crossed the Atlantic again. Marconi walked the cold, windy decks in his customary fashion. No doubt he was preoccupied with the negotiations. He supposed the sometimes sharp chest pain meant he had caught a chill from the raw air. On arriving at the Savoy in London, the spasms continued and grew more severe. Cristina anxiously called on Dr. Prince, a heart specialist. The doctor visited Marconi at the hotel and diagnosed a severe case of angina pectoris.

This shocked Marconi. Only a few years before, he had passed a life insurance medical without any difficulties. Cristina, a bride for less than a year, moved her husband to a nursing home. After two weeks, he emerged apparently recovered.

Back in the Savoy, he suffered another attack. It was far more violent than the earlier ones. Rumors immediately spread. A London newspaper reported his death. Dr. Tallarico from the Italian Hospital and other specialists joined Dr. Prince. The immediate threat to the inventor's life receded. But he was still too ill to travel to Rome for treatment, which Cristina would have preferred, or to participate in the cable discussions. His recovery proceeded slowly.

On March 16, 1928, Sir Plender and Sir Garnsey issued a joint report. They recommended that all the submarine corporations and MWT merge into a single organization. Despite MWT's superior technical and commercial strength and that in open competition absent government intervention or subsidies it might well bring the underwater mammoths to their knees, both representatives agreed cable interests should receive a controlling 56.25 percent of the resulting enterprise. The MWT share would be a minority position of 43.75 percent.

Marconi was incapable of raising an effective protest among the directors. His energies were focused on recovering sufficiently to be allowed to go home where Italian doctors could care for him. He progressed slowly to the point where he was released to travel. By careful, easy stages, Cristina brought him to Rome. Professors Bastianelli and Frugoni were chosen to be responsible for his further recuperation. Several more months were required before he could resume the basic routine of his life.

He could not exert his normal effort. The seriousness and length of the illness precluded exercising leadership in board deliberations. He could not persuade the directors to resist Sir Garnsey's conclusion, nor could he participate in determining how multiple aspects of the transaction would be handled. The process acquired a momentum of its own. On behalf of the Empire Government Conference, administrative and submarine interests pushed and shaped the merger's details in preparation for submission to Parliament and the Dominion governments.

On July 27, 1928, the conference presented its report to Parliament. After debate, the House of Commons on August 2 adopted the document's recommendations. The undersea organizations and MWT would all merge into a new corporation. It would create a communication subsidiary to own and manage all the undersea and over the air installations in one combined operation. Other subsidiaries would run non-traffic assets and activities such as manufacturing and research.

Over the next months, Canada, Australia, India, and South Africa approved the consolidation. In December 1928, Parliament passed the Imperial Telegraphs Bill. The merger became law. On April 8, 1929, a new merged entity, Cable and Wireless (Holding) Ltd., and a communication subsidiary, Cable and Wireless Ltd., were registered. Messrs. J. C. Denison-Pender and Kellaway were appointed joint managing directors of both. Lord Inverforth became president of the parent and Sir Basil P. Blackett chairman of the communication corporation.

Marconi was assigned to a subsidiary organized for wireless equipment manufacture and research.

In April 1927, Marconi and MWT had opened commercial wireless service to Australia. They celebrated the realization of the inventor's 1894 inspiration and his aspiration to establish worldwide long-distance communication.

In less than two years, as a result of the magnitude of his short wave success, he lost any semblance of control of his dream. It was tragic.

He now worked for a division in which he had no leadership role. He did not participate in the affairs of the holding organization or the communication operation.

Since 1919, the American assets had been stripped from the company. It was denied the opportunity to pursue British radio broadcasting. In 1929, it was in effect acquired and broken up.

The consolation prize for the ill and deposed founder/inventor/leader was he could still engage in research and work aboard *Elettra* to the extent his health permitted.

Some small solace was offered Marconi by his native country. On June 18, 1929, Italy recognized his many contributions. Vittorio Emanuele conferred upon him the title of marquis. The monarchy had staunchly supported Marconi since providing him transport in *Carlo Alberto* to Glace Bay in the early days of its development.

Cristina and Marconi commemorated their second anniversary. After the excitement of their first seven months together, the next year and a half had been extremely difficult.

That summer Beatrice and the children awaited Marconi's annual request to join him on *Elettra*. They had not seen him since the prior outing. No telegram came nor did any explanation as to why there was no invitation. The frequent consultations between former husband and wife ceased. Without warning, Marconi reduced Degna's, Giulio's, and Gioia's allowances. Beatrice became concerned that he had made no long-term provision for his children.

Cristina exercised growing influence over Marconi. The grip of his first family and the old guard that surrounded him was loosened. Solari, despite being Marconi's compatriot throughout his career and a witness at his second wedding, found himself less welcome. Marconi dismissed both Captain Lauro, the only captain he had had for *Elettra,* and Mr. Magrini, his personal secretary for twenty years. Civita Veechia, on the coast an hour's drive from Rome, replaced Villa Grifone and Viareggio as his summer home. At the initiation of the procedure to annul his marriage to Beatrice, his new love's faith, the religion of his baptism, had recalled him. It had overcome his Church of England upraising by Annie, his confirmation as a Waldensian, an Italian Presbyterian, and his baptism of his own son a Waldensian.

Cristina was formally presented to George V and Queen Mary and members of the British royal family. She appeared in a light-colored evening dress with a long train, three ostrich feathers pinned to her hair just behind Marconi's tiara, jewels, and her decoration of a Dame of Honour and Devotion of the Sovereign Military Order of Malta. Guglielmo accompanied her in the dress uniform of a captain of the Italian navy and wore the Knight's Grand Cross of the Royal Victorian Order George V had awarded him in 1914. Three times Cristina curtseyed before the monarch and his wife and the Prince of Wales and Dukes of York, Gloucester, and Kent. Of those in attendance, the papal noblewoman was most impressed with the Scottish lords in kilts, black velvet jackets, and lace jabots and the Maharaja of Patiala in light blue embroidered silk and a sky blue turban with a plume of feathers affixed by an enormous diamond.

In September when *Elettra* was anchored off Viareggio, Vittorio Emanuele came for a visit. He arrived at the quay at eight in the morning and was personally picked up by the new marquis in *Elettra's* open launch. At the head of the gangplank, Cristina extended cordial greetings. Marconi invited his royal guest to the wireless cabinet. He donned earphones and listened to signals from South Africa. It was part of a longstanding dialogue between the two men. The king annually asked the Italian patriot to the Quirinale Palace in Rome in order to be apprised firsthand of the latest wireless developments.(FN 1)

In November 1929, enormous disturbances on the ocean floor broke ten of the twenty-one cables crossing the Atlantic. The new Cable & Wireless communication subsidiary shifted traffic from the severed submarine lines to wireless. Had the merger not occurred, the natural catastrophe itself might have severely crippled and bankrupted the North Atlantic undersea carriers. The company might have acquired them as it had United Wireless in 1912.

As Marconi grew stronger, he returned to research on *Elettra*. Having mastered long and short waves, he focused on ultra short waves. Their length measured from under ten meters to less than one. Scientific theory called them semi-optical. They could go no further than the eye could see.

Cristina was not going to let her husband go to sea without her. The two had become inseparable. To their delight, she became pregnant. She did not feel well. Out on the open water, rough seas and vibrations and noise from the generators worsened her condition. Marconi decided to give up his work on the ship and move to the land. Cristina would not hear of it.

They arrived in Genoa in late January to begin two months' preparation for a public demonstration of the wonders of short wave wireless. Marconi planned at the end of March to press a switch in *Elettra* docked in Genoa's Duca D'Abruzzi harbor and turn on thousands of lights in the

Town Hall of Sydney, Australia. In addition to the joy of a stable boat, Cristina was pleased by the round of evening and weekend parties ashore and on board that they enjoyed with local acquaintances.

In the beginning of March, Marconi had to attend a session of the Senate in Rome. *Elettra* steamed down the west coast of Italy and anchored off Fiumicino near the capital. Mussolini came to call on very short notice. He arrived in a naval vessel wearing yachting attire, Marconi's customary uniform while on the ship. The two men paused for a moment for a picture before entering the wireless cabin. They were identically dressed in white cap with dark brim, blue blazer and tie, a white shirt, white pants, and brown and white shoes.

His political duties concluded, Marconi returned his party to the northern port. On March 26, a host of dignitaries boarded the great white ship. More stood in formally organized ranks on the dock. Small vessels crammed with people crowded around *Elettra*. Marconi spoke by short-wave radio telephone to Sydney, saying it was a great honor to illuminate the symbol of the new project of the Association for the Radioelectric Development of New South Wales. He pressed a wireless key. It released a radiowave from England to Rockbank in the State of Victoria that automatically retransmitted 550 miles to Sydney. Immediately, innumerable light bulbs lit up Town Hall.

Nothing signified Marconi's return to health that summer more aptly than the birth of his fifth child and fourth daughter. She was born July 20, 1930, at the seaside villa of Prince Odelscalchi near Civita Veechia. Marconi was fifty-six years old. Cristina was thirty. Queen Elena consented to stand godmother. Bishop Pacelli, who was in the process of being elevated to cardinal and appointed secretary of state upon Cardinal Gasparri's retirement, christened the baby Maria Elettra Elena Anna Marconi. The appellation was for her mother, the yacht, the queen, and her two grandmothers, who fortunately both had the same name. After the ceremony, the guests took refreshments in the villa's park of pine, cypress, and eucalyptus. *Elettra* could be seen in the distance riding at anchor in the bay. Congratulations poured in to the couple from around the world.

Cardinal Gasparri, who was seventy-eight, had the prior year led the negotiations culminating in the Lateran Treaty. It established a concordat between the kingdom of Italy and the Holy See. Vatican City was recognized as a new and fully sovereign independent state. Cardinal Pacelli, in one of his first acts as secretary of state, determined to modernize the Vatican infrastructure. In addition to acquiring typewriters and updating the telephones, the religious hierarchy authorized the construction of the church's own powerful shortwave radio station. It would allow the pope to broadcast to the world without depending upon Italian government facilities.

The pope personally asked the Irish-Italian scientist to undertake the project. Cristina had introduced Pius XI and Marconi to each other. The pontiff was very interested in science. Cristina often attended long sessions in his study while he and her husband intensely discussed the inventor's discoveries. Marconi and Cristina frequently traveled from London to Rome so that he could oversee the installation in the Vatican garden.

The inauguration ceremony took place in the garden on February 12, 1931. Cristina and Guglielmo greeted the pope upon his arrival at 4:20 p.m., accompanied by Cardinal Pacelli. Cristina's uncle Luigi Barberini was there as was her cousin Marquis Giovanni Battatista Sacchetti. Marconi expressed his happiness as an Italian and researcher that his important discovery was being carried through the skies and land of Italy. (FN 2)

In recognition of his services to the papacy, Pius made Marconi a member of the Pontifical Academy of Science and conferred upon him the Grand Cross of the Order of Pius XI.

While in London, the Marconis were frequently invited to the great houses of Mayfair and joined groups of as many as ten to fifteen couples at country mansion weekends. They mingled with royalty, aristocracy, and politicians. Among their favorites were the Duke and Duchess of Marlborough and their Blenheim Palace. There they enjoyed the first of many dinners with Winston Churchill and Lady Clementine.

Marconi returned to his new ultra short wave focus. He had Mathieu design and G. A. Isted, another veteran company engineer, construct a special transmitter and receiver for *Elettra*. The three men were ready to open a third frontier in long-distance wireless communication.

The first tests they conducted in Santa Margherita Ligure south of Genoa. Signals were sent from a transmitter mounted on the roof of the Hotel Miramar to *Elettra*, steaming out into the Ligurean Sea. In October

1931, the trio felt sufficiently confident to invite Italian officials on board. They successfully demonstrated receipt of the ultra high frequency waves at a range of eleven miles out to sea from the hotel.

At month's end, Fleming, who had been scientific advisor to the company since December 1900, resigned. Architect of the original Poldhu station, inventor of the wave meter, and patentee of the thermionic diode, he wrote the *Principles of Electric Wave Telegraph*, the standard reference work for years. In November, Andrew Grey stepped down. He had been chief engineer from the company's earliest days. Under him had worked the brilliant MWT researchers, Franklin and Round, for whom the company had created separate but equal research arms. In the reorganization following Grey's retirement, Dowsett filled his place and was given the title research manager. Round and Franklin were both upset. Round left to become a consultant. He had joined the company in 1902 and became a personal assistant to Marconi. He worked on dust-core inductance, direction finding, the thermionic triode, and countless inventions in sound broadcast. Franklin, assigned to a research department at Poldhu supervised by Vyvyan, withdrew into a reclusive shell.

At year's end 1931, fourteen nations on four continents celebrated the thirtieth anniversary of Marconi's first transatlantic signal. Kemp, Paget, and Marconi, St. John's pioneers, reunited in London at Elettra House and participated in a program recounting the event. The broadcast was the greatest radio hook-up the world had seen. It reached the American continents, Europe, Asia, and the world's great capitol cities. Marconi recalled that news of the signal had been greeted with doubt in England and Europe:

> All but a few of the great American scientists believed in me, and the American Institute of Electrical Engineers was the first scientific body to endorse my statement. Naturally at this time my thoughts go back to the moment thirty years ago when, instead of sitting in a comfortable room in London sending signals I know will be received and understood on the other side of the Atlantic, I was standing in a bitter cold room on top of a hill in Newfoundland, wondering if I should ever be able to hear the letter S transmitted from England.(FN 3)

Marconi

From New York, Pupin paid tribute to Marconi:

> Few of us understood the full meaning of Galileo's simple experiments, three hundred years ago, when from the leaning tower of Pisa he dropped little weights and from their motions derived the laws which guide the motions of the planets.
> Few of us understand the full meaning of Marconi's vision. But just as all of us now know and admire the sublime courage with which Galileo defended his new science, so we admire Marconi's sublime courage which enabled him to transform his vision of thirty years ago into the beautiful reality of our present radio. Italy can be justly proud of her two great sons, Galileo and Marconi.(FN 4)

The year 1932 opened with another recognition from the King of Italy. On January 15, he decorated Marconi with the Knight of the Grand Cross of the Order of Saints Maurice and Lazarus. The distinction was second only to the Order of Annunziata. Two months later, the city of Philadelphia awarded Marconi the John Scot medal. In May came a coveted award from England. The Kelvin medal was one of the most highly prized by the engineering profession. It was awarded only triannually and memorialized Lord Kelvin. Lord Kelvin had been the first to pay Marconi for a wireless telegram.

Apart from these pleasant distractions, Marconi pursued ultra short waves. He replaced the Santa Margherita transmitter with the most powerful microwave transmitter yet. Transmitting on a fifty-seven-centimeter wavelength to a receiver on *Elettra*'s rear deck, the signals began to fade at 11 miles, but they were still distinguishable at 28 miles. Most important, the height of the transmitter and receiver set the optical limit at 14.6 miles. The microwaves transcended the theoretical optical-line-of-sight. Marconi concluded they reflected off the sky like longer waves. This attracted the attention of the Propagation Section in Chelmsford. Taking up the idea, the group developed telephone microwave.

The Vatican asked Marconi to create an ultra short wave telephone service between the Vatican and Castel Gandolfo the papal summer residence, fifteen miles away. In November, the fifty-eight-year-old built the world's first commercial telephone system to operate on a wave of less than one meter. It was sixty-eight centimeters long.

On January 2, 1933, Kemp died at age seventy-six. He first met Marconi thirty-seven years earlier in Preece's office. Of all of Marconi's personal assistants, he was probably the most devoted.

On February 11, 1933, the Vatican radiotelephone service officially opened. Marconi stood at microphones with Pope Pius XI, who graciously said:

> Our first word shall be for you, Marchese Marconi, and it will be a word of congratulation for the continuous success that Divine Providence and divine goodness have reserved for your researches and applications in this field.

To which Marconi answered:

> This first application of microwaves fills my heart both as an Italian and a scientist with pride and hope for the future. May my modest work contribute to the achievement of true Christian peace throughout the world.(FN 5)

Once the system was in regular service, the Vatican transmitter operator heard an irregular noise at the same time each day. The disturbance sounded like a sizzle produced by someone walking across slushy ground. It coincided with a gardener pushing a cart across the path of the wave beam. Marconi was advised and determined to research the phenomena at his next opportunity. He recognized it. It was what he had observed doing short wave research during the War and then described in 1922. It was another example of radar. He intended to explore the concept as soon as he could free time from his microwave research.

Little had been done on the subject since Marconi's address to the New York Institute of Electrical Engineers. In 1926 in the United States, Gregory Breit and Merle Antony Tuve had bounced radio beams off the ionosphere to prove its existence and measure its height. Four years later, the U.S. Naval Research Laboratory at Anacostia in the District of Columbia used a radio system to detect an airplane. In Great Britain, the Signals

Experimental Establishment at Woolwich proposed pulsed transmission as a means of providing echoes from a target. Neither the War Office nor the Admiralty were interested. The GPO's engineering department working with BBC published a paper in 1932. It noted beats in signals received by a transmitting station when an airplane was in the vicinity of the propagation path. On June 13, 1933, Albert Hoyt Taylor, Leo C. Young, and Lawrence A. Hyland at the Anacostia lab filed a patent application for detecting moving objects in the air or on the ground by means of radio transmitting and receiving equipment.

Encouraged by the Santa Margherita tests the prior fall and with the Vatican project completed, Marconi returned to his efforts to increase the range of the ultra short waves. He moved the transmitter to Rocca di Papa, 12 miles southeast of Rome, 15 miles from the sea, and 750 meters high. With Italian officials aboard again, *Elettra* sailed from Civita Vecchia on August 6 and headed towards Sardinia. The transmitter height established the optical range at 52 miles. *Elettra* received good radiotelegraphy at 58 miles. At 80 the signals fell off but revived from 87 to 100 before fading once more and disappearing altogether at 110. On August 12 signals reappeared at 125 miles.

On August 14, 1933, Marconi formally announced from the podium at the Royal Academy in Rome that ultra short wave telegraphic and radiophone signals had been received at a distance of 94 miles, clearly beyond optical range.

For the next experiment, engineers at Sardinia's Cape Figari installed the receiver on a tower 340 meters above sea level; 168 miles separated receiver and transmitter. Optical range was 72 miles. Cape Figari picked up Rocca di Pappa's signals sporadically. To Marconi, it confirmed his judgment. Microwaves could exceed the theoretical optical limitation.

In the fall of 1933, Marconi put research aside to enjoy a trip with all expenses paid including Cristina's. It was sponsored by Chicago and its World Fair entitled a "Century of Progress Exhibition."

On September 21, Guglielmo and Cristina left *Elettra* anchored in Genoa's Duca degli Abruzzi harbor and embarked on the Lloyd line *Conte di Savoia.* From the bridge where they had been invited by the captain they waved good-bye to the crowd that had come to see them off. They left three-year-old Elettra behind with Cristina's parents.

In New York the couple was again greeted with interviews, speeches, tours, and meetings. With motorcycle outriders' sirens blaring, they crossed the city on their way to City Hall between two lines of cheering people. Reporters invaded their suite at the Ritz. Sarnoff welcomed them. They toured the new Radio City Music Hall and RCA broadcast studios.

In response to a reporter's question about the future, Marconi said, "We might arrive at person-to-person communication, that is to say each person will go around with his own little pocket apparatus on which to fix appointments, give orders to his broker, and make dates with his girl friend."(FN 6)

In Washington they stayed at the Mayflower Hotel. Franklin Delano Roosevelt, now president, greeted them in the Oval Office. A reception and dinner were held in their honor in the private quarters upstairs. Cristina enjoyed a long chat with Eleanor Roosevelt. The former assistant secretary of the navy remembered with pleasure meeting Marconi in 1917. Marconi, perhaps with the forced 1919 divestiture of American Marconi to RCA, foremost in his mind had perhaps no such pleasant recollection. A joint session of Congress was held to hear Marconi speak.

The couple traveled to Chicago on an overnight sleeper train, the *Twentieth Century*. They stayed at the Drake Hotel. October 2, Marconi Day at the fair, featured the inventor sending the letter S around the globe via Rome, Bombay, and Manila in less than three and a half minutes. Northwestern University honored him with a doctor of science degree. Cristina was delighted that the Catholic University of Notre Dame awarded her husband an honorary doctor of law.

The couple went west. Roosevelt had put at their disposal a Pullman car with a large bedroom and bathroom for each of them and compartments for her maid, his secretary, and their detective, a dining car with lounge, and an observation car with a well-stocked library. The Grand Canyon was followed by a Hollywood visit to Pickfair with Mary Pickford. Charlie Chaplin and Paulette Goddard joined the stunning actress in entertaining the touring couple. Robert Millikan took them for a nighttime visit up to the Mount Wilson Observatory. They did not return to their hotel until four in the morning. Samuel Goldwyn told her that he would be very happy to use her as an actress in a decent and important part.

Marconi

Ten thousand people welcomed the Marconis to San Francisco. They visited Yosemite. The mayor, in an open car, took them across the just constructed Golden Gate Bridge that was not yet open for traffic.

While in California, the Japanese Foreign Ministry invited them to visit Japan. The couple hesitated. They called Rome to see how their daughter was. Cristina's parents encouraged them to come home via the Far East. Cristina and Guglielmo could not resist making their journey a trip around the world.

They boarded the *Chichibu Mara* at San Francisco for Yokahama. In Japan, Marconi, always on a businessman's holiday, visited radio stations. The couple continued on to China, India, and Ceylon. Not until January 1934 did Cristina and Marconi return home.

Home was an apartment in her parents' residence, the Bezzi-Scali Palace on 11 Via Condotti. The narrow street, in parts an English-American center with elegant shops, ran through the heart of Rome from Corso Umberto I to the Spanish Steps. Keats had lived a block away. No matter how grand his in-laws, Marconi had come a long way from his living arrangements with Bea.

In April the three Marconis and *Elettra* returned to Santa Margherita. They anchored offshore to protect their privacy. In the garden of the Villa Repellini, high above the sea and overlooking the research vessel, the tireless inventor designed a new receiver. It was in the shape of a parabola and was the forerunner of satellite dishes. He said it would be very useful for universal communication.(FN 7)

In July, Marconi demonstrated another navigational use for wireless. With experts on board from Britain and the United States, the great white yacht proceeded to the mouth of the narrow but straight passage into the port of Sistri Levante just below Santa Margherita. Two radio transmitters had been placed at the channel's far end. *Elettra* carried two receivers. The windows on the bridge were covered with canvas. The helm had no visibility. Marconi ordered his new captain, who could not see water, buoys, or shore, to steam into the harbor at normal speed as if he had full vision. The transmitters' beams converged on a straight line the length of the entrance. Whenever the helmsman went off that line, one set of signals being received on *Elettra* became stronger than the other. Marconi, observing the difference, advised the captain each time to correct course until the vessel had safely entered the marina.

In September, Cristina and Guglielmo traveled to Gardone to visit d'Annunzio at Vittoriale, his residence on Lake Garda. The poet affectionately embraced the scientist, calling him "my dear brother" and took them to his writing sanctuary where he improvised some lines. At lunch they were joined by Luisa Baccara, a pianist who had given up her music to be with d'Annunzio. They ate fish that the military hero said he had been specially delivered from Fiume for Marconi.

From Gardone, the Marconis went to Venice, where he delivered a speech on microwaves and radiotherapy to the International Congress on Electrobiology. Although Marconi had felt well during the summer, he suffered a severe heart attack following his address. Dr. Frugoni came from Rome. This time Marconi recovered rapidly.

Marconi requested a meeting with Mussolini at Palazzo Venezia in Rome. He was received in the Map Room. The president of the Royal Academy and president/founder of the National Council of Scientific Research wanted to warn the head of his government against allying with Hitler in a war against England. The United States would surely intervene. As a physicist, Marconi was aware of the destruction that could result from increasingly powerful armaments. He feared Italy would lose. The dictator dismissed his plea. "You say these things because your mother was English," Mussolini said.(FN 8)

In November, Guglielmo and Cristina could not resist an invitation to England to attend the wedding of the Duke of Kent to Princess Marina. He was the youngest son of George V and she the daughter of Prince Nicholas of Greece and Denmark and Princess Olga of Russia. The ceremony was in St. Margaret's, Westminster. It may have been the last major gathering of European royalty. The entire British royal family and almost all the crowned heads were there.

If that were not enough exertion, the couple traveled to Scotland where the University of St. Andrews in Fifeshire named Marconi "Lord Rector of the University." Afterward, he watched a soccer match, sitting outside in the wet, cold fog. Not surprisingly, he fell ill again. He spent Christmas at the Empire Nursing Home in Vincent Square, Westminster. Cristina, not wanting to sit alone in her hotel room, sent for her mother and daughter to join her in London.

By the end of 1934, interest in radar increased dramatically. At the request of the German navy, Paul Ebersloh and Hans-Karl von Willisen radiated off vessels twelve kilometers away. Their patent application was rejected because of the 1904 Hulsmeyer patent. In the U.S., however, the Taylor/Young/Hyland petition was granted. In December, under Taylor's direction, a small plane was detected over the Potomac River.

England had suffered over a hundred air raids in the Great War. With Hitler's rapidly growing menace, the Air Ministry canvassed the country's plans for air defense. They found fifty-seven proposals, none promising. In desperation, Robert Alexander Watson Watt, superintendent of the Radio Department of the National Physical Laboratory, was asked if damaging radiation, a death ray, could be developed. Arnold F. "Skip" Wilson, a junior lab scientist, answered that it could not, but he calculated that a fifty-meter electromagnetic wave with fifteen amperes of current should produce a detectable echo from a plane ten miles away at twenty thousand feet. On February 26, 1935, Wilson and Watson Watt using a BBC pulse transmitter at Daventry detected a Heyford bomber sent overhead by the Royal Air Force. The reflection system came to be called radar.(FN 9)

Spurred on by his poor health, Marconi wrote a new will. He left Cristina and Elettra everything. Under Italian law, Degna, Giulio, and Gioia were entitled only to *legittima*, an orphan's pittance. The relations between father and former family had steadily deteriorated. Beatrice had not seen Marconi since 1928. The children had not seen their new half-sister. Beatrice's attempts to reach some understanding as to Marconi's ultimate provision for their children alienated him. He resisted her efforts. He made appointments but never kept them. When she sent his friends as emissaries on her behalf, including even Cardinal Gasparri, he resented their intrusion. She asked the children to speak on their own behalf. They too became estranged from Marconi.

Beatrice's efforts reached an unfriendly climax. She consulted a lawyer to determine if she could undo the annulment by contradicting the testimony. This was going too far for the children, as Degna acknowledged:

> My mother, desperate at father's failure to honor his pledge that he would provide for us financially, was tempted to use any means she could to force a showdown. The means were hers. Father's letters to her at the time

of the annulment were so susceptible to being miscon-
strued that they might cause the Roman Catholic authorities to question the validity of his second marriage.
I have serious doubts that she would ever have used them
to hurt him publicly but she had every intention, I think,
of invoking them privately to get her way. Without the
knowledge of any of us children, she consulted a lawyer in
Rome who advised that she bring action against Father.
When, at the eleventh hour, we were told what was im-
pending, we were horrified. As Mother had no real wish
to be vindictive, she readily acceded when we begged her
to withdraw from her position.

Father, alas, did not know what role we had played and
allowed himself to be persuaded that it was not Mother
but we who were the real culprits in what he may well
have thought of as blackmail.(FN 10)

On March 16, 1935, in Rome, Marconi had another heart attack.
Dr. Frugoni ordered him to stay home and do no work. Marconi refused
to obey the edict. He was anxious for his research and to fulfill his responsibilities to the Italian Royal Academy and the National Council of
Scientific Research. Without telling anyone, he would leave the house to
do business. In frustration, Dr. Frugoni assigned a nurse equipped with a
hypodermic needle to trail the relentless scientist.

Marconi turned his attention to the sound heard by the microwave
operator at the Vatican and joined the radar hunt. He and Solari arranged
for the Italian navy to lend the National Council a small experimental
wireless station at Torre Chiaruccia between Civita Vecchia and Rome.
One month after his March heart attack, Marconi and Solari were chauffeur-
driven to the facility. The driver was directed to go slowly up and down
the road past the site while Marconi and Solari alternately manned its
transmitter and receiver. They made notes of the hissing each time waves
struck the vehicle and bounced back.

Marconi continued the experiments whenever he could. He arranged
for a military plane to circle for hours between Tivoli and Frascati while
he tried to catch reflections. Mussolini came to observe. Rumors spread
that Marconi was developing a military death ray.

Marconi

Italy watched Germany's bellicose threats to Austria. Protective of his northeastern border, Mussolini sent arms and money to support the Dollfuss Austrian government, and when Dollfuss was murdered, he mobilized troops at Brenner Pass. In May, Italy, France, and Britain met to discuss means to prevent Germany from rearming. Mussolini sought guarantees for Austria's security.

He also asked for recognition of his ambitions in Abyssinia, the last unoccupied territory in Africa and the scene of Italy's highly embarrassing defeat in 1896. Mussolini had completed the suppression of the Berbers. He boasted of Italy's right to empire and its will to propagate its race over the face of the earth.

In October 1935, tiring of diplomatic and economic efforts to establish hegemony over the unwilling Ethiopians, Mussolini unleashed his military forces.

The world reacted angrily. The League of Nations condemned Italy and moved to impose sanctions. Neither France nor Great Britain supported Mussolini. The British public particularly denounced the action. Germany encouraged Italy. It was delighted to see the country squander its resources far from home and the Austrian border and to split apart from England and France.

Marconi patriotically supported Italy. He spoke out against the League of Nations' sanctions. From Rome, he broadcast a speech of justification to the United States. As part of an effort to stem adverse global opinion, Mussolini enlisted Marconi to undertake a goodwill tour. Although he must have known the toll the mission might take on his health, Marconi, loyal as ever to his country's call, agreed to go. At the end of October, he and Cristina crossed the South Atlantic to Brazil. For a month, he visited Rio de Janeiro and Sao Paulo and attempted to rally their large Italian populations.

The couple next undertook the long sea voyage to England. Marconi met with King Edward VIII, who was deep in his own constitutional crisis. Marconi asked for airtime on BBC to explain Italy's position to the English people. He felt no one had completely clean hands in Abyssinia. It had been admitted to the League on condition it abolish slavery. No steps had been taken in that direction. England and France had planned to split up the country with Italy. The partition had been abandoned only because of premature publicity.

BBC refused Marconi use of its facilities. That deeply offended him. He was particularly upset because of his historic relationship with the radio broadcaster.

Marconi and Cristina continued on to Paris. He conferred with Laval, who had been a principal participant in the English-French-Italian discussions.

On December 16, 1935, after two ocean crossings and four city visits in a month and a half, the couple departed on the Paris-Rome Express to be home for Christmas. The scientist's new personal secretary, Umberto Marconi, accompanied them. He was not a relative. Everyone called him Mr. Di Marco to avoid confusion. He recalled that Marconi slept little that night as the train rumbled towards the Italian frontier. The next morning, pale but meticulously dressed, he joined Cristina for breakfast. He gave a journalist an interview and spent the balance of the morning working in his compartment. He returned to the diner to lunch alone.

Several minutes later, a waiter anxiously approached Di Marco, who was eating in a separate section of the car. Marconi was not well. Di Marco found him sitting upright, eyes closed, head lolling to one side. The secretary, Cristina, and a doctor, who fortunately passed by, carried Marconi, still unconscious, back to his berth. He suddenly came to. He asked what was wrong. For the rest of the journey, Marconi stayed in bed. When the train arrived in Rome, he walked down the platform without assistance and greeted the people who had come to welcome him home as if nothing had happened.

This time, however, Marconi did not make a speedy rehabilitation. His movement definitely slowed. On April 25, 1936, Marconi's birthday, Alfonso died in a London hotel, the Splendide. Marconi could not attend the funeral. As a result, Marconi did not go to the funerals of any of his family, father, mother, or sibling, except for his own daughter Lucia's. Degna and Giulio both living in London attended as did Dr. Corbett from the Italian Hospital. Henry Jameson-Davis, once more of service to the Marconis, handled the funeral arrangements. They buried Alfonso in Highgate Cemetery next to Annie. Mother and brother both died of the heart ailment afflicting Marconi.

During the year Marconi reconciled with Degna. She visited him at the Belli-Scalli's. She never once saw Cristina. She never met Elettra. Marconi had not seen Beatrice since 1928. Father and daughter reminisced and talked of many things. Degna thought doubts had entered his mind about Mussolini. At the end of 1936, she returned to London. She believed he seriously contemplated taking a house in London where he might live with her and Giulio.

Behind her she left a man in crisis. Marconi confronted serious personal decisions and fatal illness. Despite accomplishment and fame, at age sixty-two he saw no safe, snug harbor ahead. He had lost control of his company. Cable interests and financial men ran it. They threatened his research. Accountants complained of *Elettra*'s cost. The Italian government was far more supportive. But had he seen Mussolini in a harsh new light. On the trip to South America, England, and France Marconi sensed that his defense of the Abyssinian aggression tarnished his own reputation. Did he feel British abhorrence for the dictator? Did he fear the tyrant intended to use electromagnetic waves as a weapon? At the conclusion of his September 1934 St. Andrews' address, the honored scientist rhetorically asked if he had "done the world good, or have I added a menace?"(FN 11)

What were Marconi's options? Was the thought of a move to England realistic? Cristina was unlikely to leave Italy and her parent's family. Could he abandon his bride and new child? He had often lived apart from Beatrice while working out a scientific problem. If he took up residence in London, would it be interpreted as criticism of his native country? A lifelong patriot, he was deeply dedicated to its interests. In fact, though, he had lived much of his adult life elsewhere.

By early spring 1937, Marconi had recovered sufficiently to direct the radar experiments at Torre Chiaruccia. He was pleased by long-distance microwave progress. The BBC transmitter at Daventry sent clearly received fifty-five-centimeter waves to Rome. He renewed his commitment to high frequency research.

Health setbacks, however, soon followed. Three minor heart attacks retarded him again as he reached his sixty-third birthday in April. A severe attack shook him in May. Dauntless, he struggled to his feet in June. With Solari at his side, pale and moving slowly, he inspected a newly opened shortwave station not far from Rome at Santa Palomba.

Marconi longed to be back on his yacht. He worried about corporate support. The depression adversely affected revenue. Profits attributed to wireless operations by cable management dropped drastically. Research investment was cut. The managing director quarreled with Marconi. He demanded the founder personally pay Di Marco's salary and travel expenses. Mathieu was fired without advance consultation with Marconi. A rumor spread. *Elettra* was to be sold to a Genoa ship owner for six hundred thousand lire. In response, the Italian government considered purchasing the vessel for Marconi's work. Would it then direct what he did?

Marconi announced he must go to England. He needed to resolve his differences with the company. His doctors dissented. In their opinion, Marconi at best might establish a research site close to Rome. He searched in the Alban Hills but found nothing satisfactory. He talked again of the UK. Forced to a new compromise, the doctors allowed Marconi to go to Viareggio. He could stay at the Hotel Astor with *Elettra* anchored in view. Marconi saw the plan as a step in the right direction. It would be a short stay. Then he would continue to London.

Elettra's birthday fell on Tuesday, July 20. She was already at Viareggio with her grandmother, Countess Bezzi-Scali. Marconi had a meeting with Pius XI on Saturday, July 17, and Royal Academy business to conclude, including a Monday meeting with Mussolini, before he could leave. He and Cristina agreed. She would depart Rome on Monday to be with Elettra on her birthday. Marconi would follow on Wednesday.

On Saturday, Marconi, color drained from his face, traveled the short distance from Rome to Castel Gandolfo, the papal summer palace. He had written formally to the Pontifical Academy of Science to request the audience. "I must see the Holy Father by the nineteenth," he wrote, "because on the twentieth I am going away." The meeting was scheduled to discuss the latest developments in wireless. Marconi met privately with his friend. He asked for a special blessing. Degna believed her father advised the pope that despite Marconi's deep love of Italy he intended to move to London to reestablish his work. He had come to say good-bye.

On Monday the summer heat was scorching. At noon Marconi drove with Cristina from the Bezzi-Scali palace past the Piazzo della Republico and the Church of Santa Maria degli Angeli. He delivered her at the Stazione Termine in the Piazzo del Cinqucente. Tears welled in Marconi's eyes after they parted. "How silly we become when we grow old," he said. "Just like children."

From the train station the chauffer crossed ancient Rome to the Farnesina Villa. There, in his offices as president of the Italian Royal

Marconi

Academy and president of the Italian Council of Scientific Research, Marconi dictated several letters. He discussed last-minute matters with Carlo Formichi, who would be his deputy in his absence. Then he left with di Marco. The two did not speak except to instruct the chauffer to drop the scientist off at the Marconi Company Building. The car pressed through streets crowded with vehicles clattering on cobblestones and summer tourists swarming before a pending storm.

Marconi slowly climbed the stairs to his first-floor office. He slumped heavily into the couch across from his desk before greeting Solari. Their friendship had endured for fifty years since their days together as schoolboys in Florence. Now they discussed Marconi's latest microwave experiments that he expected to continue on the *Elettra*. They were also at work on ultra short waves for television and a new type of airplane radio transmitter. "There is a great deal yet to do in this field," Marconi said. "I wish I had the energy I used to have—the energy I no longer have." Solari accompanied Marconi to the landing. He watched his ashen-faced friend's deliberate progress down the stairs. Marconi turned and waved up a good-bye to Solari in fond farewell. At home at Via Condotti by four, not far from the legions of visitors basking on the Spanish Steps in the tropical sun, Marconi conferred with his lawyer Carlo d'Amelio.

By five, however, when di Marco arrived with more letters to sign, Marconi felt so weak and uncertain that he and Cristina's father, who had not gone to Viareggia, were on the telephone, searching for Professor Frugoni. Di Marco immediately cancelled Marconi's meeting with Mussolini scheduled for six o'clock. While they waited for the doctor, di Marco and the nurse who lived in the house to look after Marconi tried to make him comfortable. Professor Frugoni was out of town. He was due to return late that evening by train. Instead, his chief assistant, Dr. Arnaldo Pozzi, appeared. Mildly, with light humor, he chatted with Marconi. From the next room di Marco could hear the low murmur of their voices and laughter. Dr. Pozzi assured both men that Marconi's condition was nowhere as serious as in May. Reassured, di Marco, who had been through many of these crises with Marconi, departed with Dr. Pozzi.

But later in the evening, the trouble returned. Professor Frugoni was met at the station and brought directly to the house where Marconi quietly lay. The window of his room opened to the thick, still night air. From the top of the Spanish Steps, the ancient church of Trinita del Monti pealed the hour. In a letter to Degna, Frugoni later described what happened next:

> Perhaps you will remember that your father had an irregularity of the left cubital artery. By watching his pulse he could clearly see the pulsations of his artery and as he had been twice "in limite mortis" from occlusion of the heart, he had learned to watch his artery.
>
> Reclining and looking very pale he lifted his forearm and saw that the blood in the artery was not beating any more. Turning to me he said in a low voice, "How is it, Frugoni, that my heart has stopped beating and I am still alive?" To which I replied: "Don't ask such questions, it is only a matter of position, because your forearm is raised."
>
> With a little wry smile he said: "No my dear doctor, this would be correct for the veins but not for an artery," showing that, to him, as a scientist, one could not tell pitiful lies which broke the laws of physics. And in fact he was perfectly right in his conclusion.
>
> He then frowned slightly and said, "But I don't care" and again, while his forehead slowly relaxed, "I don't care at all."(FN 12)

At the entrance to Marconi's home, in accordance with Italian tradition, Cristina had the flag placed at half staff and one leaf of the front door closed. Lowered flags flew from every house on the street and shops shuttered. The next day his body, dressed in the gold-embroidered Royal Academy uniform, accompanied by the tri-cornered hat and straight sword of his office, was placed in state in Villa Farnesina's central hall beneath Raphael's painting. It portrayed Galatea, the nymph of the sea, born across the waves in a shell, an apt reminder of Marconi's wireless crossing the waters of the world. There were no floral arrangements or candles. His adornment was a blanket of flowers that soon covered his body. They were left by an endless file of grievers. Fifty thousand people of all nationalities and classes, from humble peasants to wealthy nobility, passed his bier.

Marconi

It was appropriate that this magnificent resting place, begun in 1514 and built of Coliseum stone with vast proportions, arched entranceway and multistoried reception rooms completed by Michelangelo and lavishly decorated in tapestries and frescos, served as the starting point for Marconi's funeral procession. From this setting, consonant with the spirit and genius of a man who first harnessed an unseeable force of nature, a building block fundamental to communications today, whose ramifications still unfold before us, the mourners somberly marched across the city's heart.

The cortege swung out from Piazza Farnese onto Corso Vittorio Emanuele. It moved down the broad boulevard commemorating Victor Emanuele II, King of Sardinia and Duke of Savoy, first King of Italy. He with other patriots—Mazzini, Garibaldi, and Cavour—united and created the modern Italian state at the time Giuseppe and Annie courted. Dense crowds lined the streets. Below the Pantheon into Piazza Venezia, then onto Via Nazionale the massive oak coffin pulled by six black horses rumbled through ancient Rome. A block away at the royal residence, the Quirinale, Emanuele III, Marconi's contemporary and friend, uneasily dwelt in passive allegiance with Mussolini. The palace flags drooped in sad salute. Mounted Carabineers led the procession ahead of a battalion representing Italy's fighting services and two long rows of monks bearing candles. Municipal employees in medieval costume flanked the hearse. They were followed by a procession a half mile long. Twenty-nine carriages and nine army trucks carried the wreaths sent by admirers.

All shops shut, closed for national bereavement. Rome stopped for this man who was so important to Italy and the world.

At last in the late afternoon sun, rich and full on the sandy stone of Rome, common people, nations' delegations, prime ministers and politicians, scientists and artists, men from the military, family and friends crowded behind the coffin. Across the Piazza Republica they slowly shuffled and into the colossal colonnaded Renaissance interior of the church where Cristina and Marconi married, the Church of Santa Maria degli Angeli. It was created by Michelangelo on commission from Pope Pius IV out of the Roman Baths of Diocletian. In the middle of Santa Maria's central nave atop the catafalque the coffin rested surrounded as its honor guard by *Elettra*'s white uniformed crew.

In the words of one observer close to the scene:

Those who saw the procession say they have never on any occasion in Rome seen anything to equal it. The dense crowds stood for hours and hours in the heat—the heart and soul of Rome and the whole nation seemed to go with him. It was the humble, loving thought that was so impressive.(FN 13)

After another day of public viewing, a special train bore Marconi's remains home to Bologna. A service was held at the Church of San Petronius close to where he was born. He was laid to rest in the family vault near the tomb of Luigi Galvani in the Apennine foothills at the fourteenth-century monastery, La Certosa.

How fitting that this loyal citizen of Italy who had realized so many of his accomplishments in London and New York, and whose travels had carried him across the oceans of the world, should die and be buried and honored at home, the home of his birth and the home of his heart.

A memorial service at the Cathedral in Chelmsford and a Requiem Mass at that city's Church of the Immaculate Conception celebrated the inventor's life. The *Marconi Review* found no words adequate. Instead, the company newsletter printed his portrait in an oak leaf wreath. Tributes flooded in, from French Professor Edouard Branley, whose early work Marconi had drawn upon, from de Forest, and from Sarnoff and Young. The *Times* editorialized:

> What other men have been content to prove impossible, he accomplished; and this is surely greatness. The history of wireless communication has been a history of miracles. (FN 14)
> It is difficult to imagine any diminution of the fame of Guglielmo Marconi. He may even be regarded as the supremely significant character of our epoch, the name by which the age is called.(FN 15)

In London at the post office, in Cornwall where the Lizard looks south and west out into the sea, in Crookhaven, County Cork, in Nova Scotia's Glace Bay, in Australia down under, post office and international

447

operators rose and stood with bowed heads behind their instruments. For two minutes around the wireless world of Italy and the vast British Empire, only silence occupied the air.

Cristina could only wonder if Marconi had lived longer how many more miracles might he have discovered for the world. In his last months he would say to her in words reminiscent of his excited whispers as a teenager to his cousin Daisy, "You can't imagine, Cristina, how many hidden forces there are in the atmosphere which we don't know about and which would be so necessary to humanity."(FN 16)

Thus ended the life of Guglielmo Marconi—inventor of wireless; father of long waves, short waves, and micro waves; grandfather of radio and radar; and great-grandfather of satellite signals and cell phones.

NOTES

Chapter 1

1. Degna Marconi, *My Father, Marconi* (New York: McGraw-Hill, 1962), 7.
2. W. P. Jolly, *Marconi* (London: Constable, 1972), 10.
3. Giancarlo Masini, *Marconi* (New York: Marsilio Publishers, 1976), 32.

Chapter 2

1. W. J. Baker, *A History of the Marconi Company* (London: Methuen, 1970), 25.
2. Masini, *Marconi*, 47.
3. Maria Cristina Marconi, *Marconi My Beloved* (Boston, MA: Dante University of America Press, 1999), 101.
4. E. C. Baker, *Sir William Preece, F. R. S.: Victorian Engineer Extraordinary* (London: Hutchinson, 1976), 257.
5. Marc J. Seifer, *Wizard: The Life and Times of Nikola Tesla: Biography of a Genius* (Secaucus, NJ: Carol Publishing Group, 1996), 89.
6. W. J. Baker, *A History of the Marconi Company*, 26.
7. Stanley Leinwoll, *From Spark to Satellite: A History of Radio Communication* (New York: Charles Scribner's Sons, 1979), 4.

Chapter 3

1. E. C. Baker, *Sir William Preece*, 266.
2. Seifer, *Wizard*, 172.
3. Jolly, *Marconi*, 37.

4. E. C. Baker, *Sir William Preece*, 268.
5. Masini, *Marconi*, 78.
6. W. J. Baker, *A History of the Marconi Company*, 53.
7. W. J. Baker, *Marconi* (London: Privately Published, circa 1970), 52.
8. Degna Marconi, *My Father, Marconi*, 40.
9. W. J. Baker, *Marconi*, 67
10. Masini, *Marconi*, 92
11. W. J. Baker, *Marconi*, 56.
12. Degna Marconi, *My Father, Marconi*, 38.
13. Seifer, *Wizard*, 183.

Chapter 4

1. Degna Marconi, *My Father, Marconi*, 53.
2. E. F. Geddes, *Marconi* (Ipswich: W.S.Cowell, 1974), 9.
3. At the end of the nineteenth century, the U.S. and the UK were both on the gold standard. The exchange fluctuated in a very narrow range around $4.87 to the pound. During World War I and most of the 1920s, the rate fluctuated, at one point being $3.66 to the pound. At the end of the 1920s, the gold standard was reinstated and the rate set at $4.87. *American Encyclopedia*, www.miketodd.net/encyc/dollhist.htm.
   From 1880 to World War I, a dollar would be approximately twenty dollars today. From the end of the War to the 1930s, a dollar would be approximately ten dollars today. Vittorio Grilli and Graciela Kaminsky, *NBER Working Paper No. W 3067*, Social Sciences Research Network,http://papers.ssrn.com/sol3/papers.cfm?abstract_id=463492.
4. E. C. Baker, *Sir William Preece*, 270.
5. Jolly, *Marconi*, 48.
6. Ibid.
7. E. C. Baker, *Sir William Preece*, 273.
8. Jolly, *Marconi*, 51.
9. Ibid.
10. R. F. Pocock and G. R. M. Garratt, *The Origins of Maritime Radio* (London: Her Majesty's Stationery Office, 1972), 12.
11. Degna Marconi, *My Father, Marconi*, 65.

Chapter 5

1. W. J. Baker, *Marconi*, 57.
2. Pocock and Garratt, *The Origins of Maritime Radio*, 19.
3. Ibid.
4. Jolly, *Marconi*, 60.
5. W. J. Baker, *Marconi*, 71.
6. Jolly, *Marconi*, 61.
7. Pocock and Garratt, *The Origins of Maritime Radio*, 33.
8. W. J. Baker, *Marconi*, 73.
9. Degna Marconi, *My Father, Marconi*, 71.
10. W. J. Baker, *Marconi*, 89.
11. W. J. Baker, *A History of the Marconi Company*, 46.

Chapter 6

1. W. J. Baker, *Marconi*, 77.
2. Masini, *Marconi*, 131–32.
3. Jolly, *Marconi*, 73.
4. W. J. Baker, *Marconi*, 79.
5. Degna Marconi, *My Father, Marconi*, 76.
6. W. J. Baker, *Marconi*, 80.
7. Seifer, *Wizard*, 237.
8. Masini, *Marconi*, 134.
9. Jolly, *Marconi*, 69.
10. Pocock and Garratt, *The Origins of Maritime Radio*, 35.
11. Ibid., 34.

Chapter 7

1. Bernard S. Finn, *Submarine Telegraphy: The Great Victorian Technology* (London: Thanet Press, 1973), 3.
2. Jolly, *Marconi*, 87.
3. W. J. Baker, *A History of the Marconi Company*, 55.
4. Ibid.

Chapter 8

1. Degna Marconi, *My Father, Marconi*, 93.
2. Pocock and Garratt, *The Origins of Maritime Radio*, 38.
3. Seifer, *Wizard*, 189.

4. Jolly, *Marconi*, 101.
5. Ibid.
6. Ibid. 92
7. Seifer, *Wizard*, 263.

Chapter 9
1. Degna Marconi, *My Father, Marconi*, 103.

Chapter 10
1. W. J. Baker, *Marconi*, 97.
2. Jolly, *Marconi*, 107.
3. W. J. Baker, *Marconi*, 99.
4. Leinwoll, *From Spark to Satellite*, 15.
5. W. J. Baker, *Marconi*, 104.
6. Masini, *Marconi*, 165.
7. Ibid., 162.
8. W. J. Baker, *Marconi*, 108.
9. Ibid., 111.
10. Ibid., 113.
11. Ibid., 114.
12. Ibid., 118.

Chapter 11
1. Degna Marconi, *My Father, Marconi*, 117.
2. Masini, *Marconi*, 172.
3. W. J. Baker, *Marconi*, 127.
4. Ibid., 130.
5. Masini, *Marconi*, 182 .
6. Degna Marconi, *My Father, Marconi*, 125.
7. Masini, *Marconi*, 190.
8. Ibid., 191.
9. Ibid., 197.
10. Degna Marconi, *My Father, Marconi*, 119.
11. Masini, *Marconi*, 209.
12. Jolly, *Marconi*, 130.
13. W. J. Baker, *Marconi*, 144.

Chapter 12

1. Degna Marconi, *My Father, Marconi*, 128.
2. Jolly, *Marconi*, 133.
3. Tom Lewis, *Empire of the Air: The Men Who Made Radio* (New York: Harper Collins, 1992), 42
4. Degna Marconi, *My Father, Marconi*, 129.

Chapter 13

1. Degna Marconi, *My Father, Marconi*, 140.
2. Ibid.
3. Masini, *Marconi*, 241.
4. Degna Marconi, *My Father, Marconi*, 142.
5. Ibid., 143.
6. Ibid., 146.
7. Ibid., 143.
8. Ibid., 145.

Chapter 14

1. Degna Marconi, *My Father, Marconi*, 152.
2. Ibid.
3. Jolly, *Marconi*, 140.
4. Ibid., 159.
5. Degna Marconi, *My Father, Marconi*, 155.
6. Ibid., 159.
7. Jolly, *Marconi*, 167.

Chapter 15

1. W. J. Baker, *Marconi*, 175.
2. Degna Marconi, *My Father, Marconi*, 162.
3. Lewis, *Empire of the Air*, 84. The two salesmen were convicted. De Forest and his attorney were acquitted.
4. W. J. Baker, *Marconi*, p. 194.
5. Ibid., 202.
6. Ibid.
7. Ibid., 193.
8. Ibid., 197.

9. Lee de Forest, *Father of Radio: The Autobiography of Lee de Forest* (Chicago: Wilcox and Follett, 1950), 38.
10. Jolly, *Marconi*, 197.
11. W. J. Baker, *Marconi*, 210.

Chapter 16

1. W. J. Baker, *Marconi*, 219.
2. Ibid., 207.
3. Ibid., 208.
4. Degna Marconi, *My Father, Marconi*, 164.
5. W. J. Baker, *Marconi*, 209.
6. Ibid.
7. Ibid., 213.
8. Jolly, *Marconi*, 212.
9. Radio, TV, radar, satellite communication, and cellular telephones are all derivatives of Marconi's wireless work.
10. Degna Marconi, *My Father, Marconi*, 178.

Chapter 17

1. W. J. Baker, *Marconi*, 239.
2. Ibid., 240.
3. Eugene Lyons, *David Sarnoff* (New York: Harper & Row, 1966), 88.
4. Jolly, *Marconi*, 228.
5. Lyons, *David Sarnoff*, 94.
6. Ibid.
7. Ibid.
8. Lewis, *Empire of the Air*, 122.
9. Degna Marconi, *My Father, Marconi*, 185.
10. W. J. Baker, *Marconi*, 248.
11. Degna Marconi, *My Father, Marconi*, 331.

Chapter 18

1. Erik Barnouw, *A Tower in Babel: A History of Broadcasting in the United States to 1933*, (New York: Oxford University Press, 1966), 53.
2. Degna Marconi, *My Father, Marconi*, 189.
3. Barnouw, *A Tower in Babel*, 54.
4. Degna Marconi, *My Father, Marconi*, 190.

5. Lyons, *David Sarnoff*, 100.
6. http://members.aol.com/gkb008/bullard/whg.htm citing Gleason L. Archer, *History of Radio*, 142.
7. Lewis, *Empire of the Air*, 142.
8. Marconi, *My Father, Marconi*, 231.
9. Lewis, *Empire of the Air*, 145.
10. Lyons, *David Sarnoff*, 106.
11. Degna Marconi, *My Father, Marconi*, 192.

Chapter 19

1. Lyons, *David Sarnoff*, 112.
2. Barnouw, *A Tower in Babel*, 68.
3. Degna Marconi, *My Father, Marconi*, 198.
4. Ibid., 201.
5. Ibid., 202.
6. W. J. Baker, *A History of the Marconi Company*, 209.
7. Degna Marconi, *My Father, Marconi*, 230.
8. Barnouw, *A Tower in Babel*, 94.
9. W. J. Baker, *Marconi*, 164.
10. Ibid., 171.
11. Degna Marconi, *My Father, Marconi*, 204.

Chapter 20

1. Degna Marconi, *My Father, Marconi*, 206.
2. Jolly, *Marconi*, 247.
3. Degna Marconi, *My Father, Marconi*, 208.
4. Ibid., 207.
5. Ibid., 208.

Chapter 21

1. Degna Marconi, *My Father, Marconi*, 207.
2. Jolly, *Marconi*, 235.
3. W. J. Baker, *Marconi*, 277
4. Jolly, *Marconi*, 255.
5. Ibid., 257.
6. Ibid.
7. Ibid., 253.

8. Maria Cristina Marconi, *Marconi My Beloved*, 21.
9. Jolly, *Marconi*, 250.
10. W. J. Baker, *Marconi*, 282.
11. Degna Marconi, *My Father, Marconi*, 225.
12. Ibid.
13. Maria Cristina Marconi, *Marconi My Beloved*, 22.
14. Ibid., 21.
15. Ibid., 23.
16. W. J. Baker, *Marconi*, 288.

Chapter 22
1. Maria Cristina Marconi, *Marconi My Beloved*, 197.
2. Ibid., 128.
3. W. J. Baker, *Marconi*, 305.
4. Ibid., 307.
5. Ibid., 321.
6. Maria Cristina Marconi, *Marconi My Beloved*, 210.
7. Ibid., 269.
8. Ibid., 194.
9. The British called the detection system radio direction finding (RDF). The Americans called it radio detection and ranging (radar).
10. Degna Marconi, *My Father, Marconi*, 232.
11. Masini, *Marconi*, 349.
12. Degna Marconi, *My Father, Marconi*, 255.
13. Ibid., 258.
14. Jolly, *Marconi*, 272.
15. W. J. Baker, *Marconi*, 353.
16. Maria Cristina Marconi, *Marconi My Beloved*, 301.

SELECTED BIBLIOGRAPHY

Aitken, Hugh G. J. *Syntony and Spark: The Origins of Radio*. Princeton, NJ: Princeton University Press, 1985.

Baker, E. C. *Sir William Preece, F. R. S: Victorian Engineer Extraordinary*. London: Hutchinson, 1976.

Baker, W. J. *A History of the Marconi Company*. London: Methuen, 1970.

———. *Marconi*. London: Privately Published, circa 1970.

Barnouw, Erik. *A Tower in Babel: A History of Broadcasting in the United States to 1933*. New York: Oxford University Press, 1966.

Black, R. M. *The History of Electric Wires and Cables*. London: Peter Peregrinus, 1983.

Bruce, R. V. *Bell: Alexander Graham Bell and the Conquest of Solitude*. Boston: Little Brown, 1973.

Buttrick, Jack (as told by Gail Lawson). *Brownsea Island*. Poole, Dorsetshire: Poole Historical Trust, 1978.

Carneal, Georgette *Conqueror of Space: The Authorized Biography of Lee de Forest*. New York: Horace Liveright, 1930.

Clark, Martin *Modern Italy, 1871–1982*. Essex, England: Longman Group, 1984.

Davies, Eryl. *Telecommunications: A Technology for Change*. London: Her Majesty's Stationery Office, 1983.

De Forest, Lee. *Father of Radio: The Autobiography of Lee de Forest*. Chicago: Wilcox and Follett, 1950.

Finn, Bernard S. *Submarine Telegraphy; The Grand Victorian Technology*. London: Thanet Press, 1973.

Geddes, Keith. *Guglielmo Marconi, 1874–1937*. Ipswich, England: W. S. Cowell, 1974.

Marconi

Howeth, Captain Linwood S., USN (Ret). *History of Communications Electronics in the United States*. Prepared under the auspices of the Bureau of Ships and Office of Naval History, 1963. www.earlyradio-history.us/1963

Jolly, W. P. *Marconi*. London: Constable, 1972.

———. *Electronics*. Seven Oaks, England: Hodder and Stoughton, 1972.

Josephson, Matthew. *Edison*. Norwalk, CT: Easton, 1959.

Kempner, Stanley. *Television Encyclopedia*. New York: Fairchild Publishing, 1948.

Lafore, Laurence. *The Long Fuse: An Interpretation of the Origins of World War I*. New York: J. B. Lippincott, 1971.

Leinwoll, Stanley. *From Spark to Satellite: A History of Radio Communication*. New York: Charles Scribner's Sons, 1979.

Lewis, Tom. *Empire of the Air: The Men Who Made Radio*. New York: Harper Collins, 1992.

Lyons, Eugene. *David Sarnoff*. New York: Harper & Row, 1966.

Mabee, Carleton. *American Leonardo: The Life of Samuel F. B Morse*. New York: Alfred Knopf, 1957.

Marconi, Degna *My Father, Marconi*. New York: McGraw-Hill, 1962.

Marconi, Maria Cristina. *Marconi My Beloved*. Boston, MA: Dante University of America Press, 1999.

Masini, Giancarlo. *Marconi*. New York: Marsilo Publishers, 1976.

McCarthy, Joe. *Dromoland Castle*. Newmarket-on-Ferfus, County Clare, Ireland: Dolmen Press, 1971.

Morgan, Nina. *Guglielmo Marconi*. New York: The Bookwright Press, 1991.

O'Brien, Ivar. *O'Brien of Thomond: The O'Briens in Irish History, 1500–1865*. Chichester, England: Phillimore, 1986.

Pocock, R. F. and G. R. M. Garratt. *The Origins of Maritime Radio*. London: Her Majesty's Stationery Office, 1972.

Seifer, Marc J. *Wizard: Nikola Tesla, the Biography of a Genius*. Secaucus, NJ: Carol Publishing Group, 1996.

Smith, Mack. *Italy*. Ann Arbor: University of Michigan Press, 1959.

Tames, Richard. *Guglielmo Marconi*. London: Franklin Watts, 1990.

Tesla, Nikola, and David Hatcher Childress. *The Fantastic Inventions of Nikola Tesla*, Stelle, IL: Adventures Unlimited, 1993.

Weightman, Gavin. *Senor Marconi's Magic Box*. London: Harper Collins, 2003.

INDEX

The Index has been subdivided into categories for ease of access to the subject matter. This arrangement will facilitate references for those interested in a particular subject and for students and teachers who may wish to use the material for case studies, particularly in the fields of business, government relations, science and telecommunication. The categories are Business Subjects; Corporations; Government; Marconi, Guglielmo; Maritime; People; Places; Ships, Lighthouses and Lightships; and Telecommunication and Science.

Business Subjects

Marconi

Corporations

Government

Marconi, Guglielmo

Maritime

People

Places

Ships, Lighthouses and Lightships

Telecommunication and Science